JOHN DONNE

The Elegies

AND

The Songs and Sonnets

JOHN DONNE

The Elegies

AND

The Songs and Sonnets

EDITED WITH
INTRODUCTION AND COMMENTARY
BY

HELEN GARDNER
FELLOW OF ST. HILDA'S COLLEGE, OXFORD

OXFORD
AT THE CLARENDON PRESS

Oxford University Press, Ely House, London W.1

GLASGOW NEW YORK TORONTO MELBOURNE WELLINGTON
CAPE TOWN SALISBURY IBADAN NAIROBI DAR ES SALAAM LUSAKA ADDIS ABABA
BOMBAY CALCUTTA MADRAS KARACHI LAHORE DACCA
KUALA LUMPUR SINGAPORE HONG KONG TOKYO

FIRST PUBLISHED 1965
REPRINTED LITHOGRAPHICALLY IN GREAT BRITAIN
AT THE UNIVERSITY PRESS, OXFORD
FROM CORRECTED SHEETS OF THE FIRST EDITION
BY VIVIAN RIDLER
PRINTER TO THE UNIVERSITY
1966, 1970

PREFACE

THIS edition of the Love-Poems of John Donne has developed from my edition of the *Divine Poems* in 1952. I set out with the object of carrying forward the pioneering work of Sir Herbert Grierson in four directions. I wished to re-examine the canon, to establish if not precise dates at least rather narrower limits than had so far been proposed, to provide a fuller commentary, and to revise the text.

Re-examination of the canon has led me to exclude as of doubtful authenticity five of the *Elegies*, 'Sappho to Philaenis', and two of the *Songs and Sonnets*.

I argue in the second part of the General Introduction that the fourteen *Elegies* printed together here make up Donne's 'Book of Elegies' and that they may be dated in the years between 1593 and 1596. In the third part of the General Introduction I argue that the *Songs and Sonnets* can be divided into two groups of poems and that the first group should be dated before 1600 and the second after 1602.

In accordance with these conclusions, the order in which the poems are printed here differs considerably from the established order. Since I have excluded from the twenty poems that Grierson printed as *Elegies* seven poems, and included one that appears elsewhere in his edition, my numbering of the *Elegies* would necessarily have been different from his. It seemed therefore best to print in what I think is the best order, not to renumber, and to give Grierson's number in roman numerals in the critical apparatus. The *Elegies* appear here as they appear in the Westmoreland manuscript, except that I have included as the ninth (to follow two others that like it were 'excepted' by the licenser of the first edition for impropriety) 'Love's Progress', which is not included in the set of *Elegies* in the Westmoreland manuscript. I have printed 'The Autumnal' separately, since it was written at a later date than the *Elegies* proper, and printed Grierson's tenth Elegy in stanza form among the *Songs and Sonnets*.

The *Songs and Sonnets* are divided into two sets and within each set I have arranged the poems to bring together those that seem related in theme or form, or both. Thus I have begun the first group with songs, followed by epigrams, have brought together the poems addressed to the God of Love and printed one after the other the two monologues in verse-paragraphs. The second group begins with poems that directly reflect Donne's reading in the Italian Neo-platonists, brings together the four valedictions, the celebrations of mutual love, the poems that may be called 'Problems of Love', and the two palinodes, and allows 'Twickenham Garden' and 'A Nocturnal' to be read together. I would not claim that the order corresponds with the order of composition, though I think there is probably a certain amount of correspondence and that it is likely that it brings together poems written about the same time. The order of the *Songs and Sonnets* in Grierson's edition is the order of the edition of 1635, except that he removed 'The Flea' from pride of place. In my experience as reader and teacher nobody can find a poem there, after the first three or four, without looking in the contents or first-line index, or flicking over the pages until it is found. The order, being wholly irrational, cannot be memorized. I hope it will be to the reader's convenience to find the poems sorted here in a more reasonable way, and that even those who are not convinced by my arguments as to their probable dates will be glad to find, for instance, 'Air and Angels' followed by 'Love's Growth' rather than by 'Break of Day'.

As in my edition of the *Divine Poems* I have attempted to comment as fully and exactly as possible, and tried to escape Bacon's censure on commentaries, 'wherein it is over usual to blanch the obscure places and discourse upon the plain', and Donne's sardonic characterization of a 'Critick' as one '*ingeniosus in alienis*, over-witty in other mens Writings', who 'had read an Author better, then that Author meant'. The formidable bulk of the comment on Donne's poems in the last forty years lightens an editor's task in one way, but makes it more difficult in another. It is hateful not to acknowledge debts or to appear by silence to slight or be ignorant of the work of those with whom one disagrees. But if I had given a reference at every point where a comment has been anticipated, and refuted all explanations that I think erroneous, the commentary would have been swollen out of all proportion. I have therefore confined myself to acknowledgement in places where I am conscious that without help I should have been at a loss and referred to articles only when an interested reader can find further relevant information in them. My commentary differs most from Grierson's in its stress upon literary rather than on philosophical and theological sources. Here again a choice had to be made. It would have been possible to give many more parallels from classical and Renaissance poets and to have suggested more comparisons. I have tried to steer a middle course, and to set Donne's love-poetry in a context that illuminates his debt to tradition and his originality without over-indulgence in the modern sport of hunting the *topos*. My greatest debt in commenting on Donne is to Mrs. Duncan-Jones of the University of Birmingham whose knowledge of the seventeenth century and breadth of reading are only equalled by the generosity with which she makes them available to others.

In my work on the text I have had the advantage of having more manuscripts to work from than Grierson did. In addition to the Cambridge, Luttrell, and Dobell manuscripts, which I used in the *Divine Poems*, there is the Haslewood-Kingsborough manuscript which Grosart used but which had been lost sight of when Grierson was working. The second part of this contains an important collection of the *Songs and Sonnets* which enables us to dismiss as degenerate some of the manuscripts that Grierson thought contained early readings. I have the advantage too of living in the age of the photostat and the microfilm, which permit constant checking of one's collations, whereas Grierson had in many cases to be content with seeing a manuscript only once and in some cases had to rely on the collations of others. Scrutiny will reveal that on some occasions my collations differ from Grierson's. While I would not dare to affirm that mine are without error, on the occasions where my apparatus contradicts Grierson's I have taken special care to check.

The Love-Poems are extant in many more manuscripts than are the *Divine Poems* and present more variants of significance. This has enabled me to work out more fully the relations of the manuscripts and to carry further my analysis of the text of the edition of 1633. I have come to the conclusion that the text of the first edition is highly sophisticated and that it needs' more thorough and consistent correction from the manuscripts than Grierson undertook. The arguments are set out in full in the Textual Introduction and the principles on which I have acted are given in the last section. In the Commentary, as in the *Divine Poems*, textual notes are always given first and the exegetical note follows in a new paragraph, so that the reader who is not interested in textual matters can avoid them. At the beginning of the commentary on each poem I summarize my departures from the basic text and my differences from Grierson's. I have been much helped in the textual work by my pupil Mr. Alan MacColl of Lincoln College, Oxford who was working on a thesis on 'The Circulation of Donne's Poems in Manuscript'. As well as giving me invaluable assistance in checking collations he has generously allowed me to use his full list of manuscripts in which poems by Donne are to be found. He also collated copies of the first edition for press variants.

I was fortunate in that while I was at work on the early stages of this edition Dr. John Carey of Keble College, Oxford was working at a doctoral thesis on the Ovidian Love-Elegy in England under my supervision. He read the introductory essays and much of the commentary at an earlier stage and gave me valuable help and criticism. I was fortunate also in having in my college an historian expert in the seventeenth century and a lover of its poetry and should like to thank Mrs. Menna Prestwich for her readiness to answer questions, for directing me in my historical reading, and for the stimulus of her conversation. I am much indebted to the Rev. T. Healy, S.J. who has helped me to correct proofs.

I am indebted to the trustees of the Henry W. Berg and Albert A. Berg Collection in the New York Public Library for permission to print variants from the Westmoreland manuscript; to the trustees of the George Arents Tobacco Collection in the New York Public Library for permission to print variants from the John Cave manuscript; to the Huntington Library for permission to print variants from the Bridgewater manuscript and from MS. HM 198 (the Haslewood-Kingsborough manuscript); and to the Houghton Library, Harvard University for permission to quote variants from the Carnaby, Dobell, O'Flaherty, and Stephens manuscripts. I have to thank the librarians of these institutions for supplying me with photostats or microfilms. I am similarly indebted to the Provost and Fellows of Trinity College, Dublin. I have also to thank the Librarian of the National Library of Wales for depositing the Dolau Cothi manuscript in the Bodleian for my use.

I must again thank Sir Geoffrey Keynes for allowing me to collate the Leconfield and the Luttrell manuscripts and for depositing them, along with Edward Hyde's manuscript, in the Bodleian. I must also thank Mr. James Osborn for allowing me to examine and collate his manuscript before it left this country. Mr. Esmond de Beer's generous gift of the Dowden manuscript to the Bodleian enabled Miss Margaret Crum to make a bibliographical study of the manuscripts of Group I on which I have been delighted to rely. I am grateful to the Trustees of the Marquis of Lothian for permission to include a reproduction of the Lothian portrait.

My debt to the late Sir Herbert Grierson is obvious. I had the pleasure of discussing my work with him and was touched by his abiding love for Donne's poetry and his readiness to entertain new ideas. It is a grief to me that Professor F. P. Wilson will not read this book. He gave advice at every stage and I cannot measure what I owe to his judicious and sensitive criticism. As this book was going to press the news of Evelyn Simpson's death came. This prevents me from thanking her for advice and encouragement, for constant willingness to answer questions, and for reading sections of the work and saving me from error. If this book bore a dedication it would be to her memory and to that of her husband Percy Simpson. From him I got my first glimpse of the pleasures of scholarship and from her I learned that one of its greatest rewards is the friendship of other scholars.

H. G.

St. Hilda's College
Oxford

CONTENTS

CONTENTS

CONTENTS

PLATES

REFERENCES AND
ABBREVIATIONS

QUOTATIONS from Donne's poems, other than those included in this volume and the *Divine Poems*, are from *The Poems of John Donne*, edited by H. J. C. Grierson, 2 vols. (Oxford, 1912). Quotations from the *Divine Poems* are from my edition (Oxford, 1952). These are referred to as

> Grierson
>
> Gardner, *Divine Poems*

Quotations from the *Sermons*, *Essays*, and *Devotions* are from the following modern editions: *The Sermons of John Donne*, edited by G. R. Potter and Evelyn M. Simpson, 10 vols. (University of California Press, 1953–61); *Essays in Divinity*, edited by Evelyn M. Simpson (Oxford, 1952); *Devotions upon Emergent Occasions*, edited by John Sparrow (Cambridge, 1923). For the *Paradoxes and Problems* I have used the edition by Sir Geoffrey Keynes (1923) and for *Ignatius His Conclave* the reprint of the first edition in Mr. John Hayward's edition of Donne's *Complete Poetry and Selected Prose* (1929). These are referred to as

> *Sermons*
>
> Simpson, *Essays*
>
> Sparrow, *Devotions*
>
> Keynes, *Paradoxes and Problems*
>
> Hayward

Quotations from other prose works are from the original editions and the following forms of reference are used:

Pseudo-Martyr	*Pseudo-martyr.* 1610
Biathanatos	*ΒΙΑΘΑΝΑΤΟΣ* (1646)
Letters	*Letters to Severall Persons of Honour.* 1651
Tobie Mathew Collection	*A Collection of Letters, made by Sr Tobie Mathews K^t.* 1660

Other references:

Bennett	*The Complete Poems of John Donne*, edited by Roger E. Bennett. Chicago, 1942
Chambers	*The Poems of John Donne*, edited by E. K. Chambers (The Muses' Library). 2 vols. 1896
Concordance	*A Concordance to the English Poems of John Donne*, by H. C. Combs and Z. R. Sullens. Chicago, 1940

Gosse

The Life and Letters of John Donne, by Edmund Gosse, 2 vols. 1899

Hayward

John Donne Dean of St. Paul's Complete Poetry and Selected Prose, edited by John Hayward (Nonesuch Press). 1929

Keynes

A Bibliography of Dr. John Donne, by Geoffrey Keynes, third edition. Cambridge, 1958

Burton, *Anatomy*

Robert Burton, *The Anatomy of Melancholy*, sixth edition, 1651

Castiglione

The Book of the Courtier by Count Baldassaro Castiglione, done into English by Sir Thomas Hoby, Everyman edition

Ficino

Ficino's Commentary on Plato's Symposium, edited and translated by S. R. Jayne, University of Missouri Studies, 1944

Leone Ebreo

The Philosophy of Love (Dialoghi d'Amore) by Leone Ebreo, translated by F. Friedeberg-Seeley and Jean H. Barnes, 1937

Jonson, *Works*

Ben Jonson, edited by C. H. Herford and Percy and Evelyn Simpson. 11 vols. Oxford, 1925–52

Nashe, *Works*

The Works of Thomas Nashe, edited by R. B. McKerrow, revised by F. P. Wilson. 5 vols. Oxford, 1958

Shakespeare

I have followed Professor Alexander's edition of 1951 in using the line references of Clark and Wright's Cambridge edition

Walton, *Lives*

Unless specific reference to another edition is given quotations are taken from the reprint of the edition of 1675 in the World's Classics

M.L.N.   *Modern Language Notes*

M.L.R.   *Modern Language Review*

M.P.   *Modern Philology*

N. and Q.   *Notes and Queries*

O.E.D.   *Oxford English Dictionary*

P.M.L.A.   *Publications of the Modern Language Association of America*

R.E.S.   *Review of English Literature*

T.L.S.   *Times Literary Supplement*

GENERAL INTRODUCTION

DONNE has a claim to the title of our greatest love-poet on two grounds. First, the range of mood and experience in his love-poetry is greater than can be found in the poetry of any single other non-dramatic writer. We can find almost any and every mood of man in love with woman expressed memorably and vehemently in his poetry. The qualification is necessary because there is one range of feeling that he never touches and it is a range that has given us some of the most beautiful lyric poetry in the language. He never speaks in the tone of a man overwhelmed by what he feels to be wholly undeserved good fortune. Gratitude for love bestowed, the sense of unworthiness in face of the overwhelming worth of the beloved, self-forgetting worship of her as she is: these notes Donne does not strike. But his second claim to pre-eminence is that he has given supreme expression to a theme that is rarely expressed in lyric poetry, and finds expression in drama rather than in lyric, the theme of the rapture of fulfilment and of the bliss of union in love.

> She'is all States, and all Princes, I
>   Nothing else is.
> Princes doe but play us; compar'd to this,
> All honor's mimique; all wealth alchimie . . . .

> Only our love hath no decay;
> This, no to morrow hath, nor yesterday,
> Running it never runs from us away,
> But truly keeps his first, last, everlasting day.

To match this note of passionate joy we have to turn to *Romeo and Juliet*, to *Othello*, or to *Antony and Cleopatra*.

> Let Rome in Tiber melt, and the wide arch
> Of the rang'd empire fall! Here is my space.
> Kingdoms are clay.

The poems that Donne wrote on this theme of mutual love are charged with such a tone of conviction and expressed with such a naked and natural force of language that it is commonly assumed that they must directly reflect an actual experience of such a rapturous discovery of a new heaven and a new earth in love; and many critics have taken them as celebrating his love for Ann More and their reckless marriage. But Donne himself has warned us against making any simple equation between the truth of the imagination and the truth of experience. Writing to Sir Robert Carr in 1625, in apology for the feebleness of his poem on the death of Hamilton and the reward of the blessed in heaven, he said: 'You know my uttermost when it was best, and even then I did best when I had least truth for my subjects.'

The love-poetry of Donne is, in its limited sphere, like the plays of Shakespeare in being 'of imagination all compact'. As Shakespeare was stimulated by stories he read or plays he had seen to make a play, so Donne, I believe, was stimulated by situations, some literary, some imagined, some reflecting the circumstances of his own life, by things seen on the stage or read in the study, or said by friends in casual conversation, to make poems. Whatever experiences literary or actual lie behind his poems have been transmuted in his imagination, which has worked on them to produce poems that are single and complete, as a play is single and complete. While other poets were producing sequences which, whether truly or not, at least purported to be based on their own fortunes in love, Donne produced a corpus of discrete poems. No links are suggested between them by the use of an imagined name or by connexion of circumstances.[1] The literary sources of Donne's poems can be suggested. It is a fascinating study for he transforms whatever stimulates his imagination. Some actual experiences we may see reflected; others we may guess at, if we wish. And the personality of Donne that gives unity to all we know of his life and is so apparent in his letters, sermons, and other prose works, where he speaks in *propria persona* (whether as Jack Donne, the private man, or as Doctor Donne, the public figure)[2] strongly informs his love-poems, and gives them

---

[1] Outside the *Elegies*, where literary tradition demanded the kind of verisimilitude that circumstantial detail gives, Donne's love-poems are singularly bare of reference to the circumstances of the lover or his mistress.

[2] The distinction between 'Jack Donne' and 'Doctor Donne' was made by Donne himself in a letter to Sir Robert Carr in 1619 where he described *Biathanatos* as 'a Book written by *Jack Donne*, and not by *D. Donne*' (*Letters*, p. 21). It is often used to distinguish Donne the

much of their fascination. Nobody can doubt that all Donne's works are by Donne. He is highly inimitable. None of his followers catch more than a superficial trace of his accent; as none of the post-Shakespearians catch more than a faint echo of Shakespeare's voice. In the love-poems, because he was in every sense writing *con amore*, it might be claimed that his personality found its purest expression. But their strength is a strength of the imagination, which abandons itself wholly for the space of a poem to an imagined situation or mood. Donne's love-poetry has not the brooding tone of memory or the poignant note of hope. It has the dramatic intensity of present experience.

The situations that Donne's imagination dramatizes are bewilderingly varied. He has lost his mistress's token, a gold chain, and she demands that he buy another; his mistress has sent him a cheap favour, a jet ring—as he twirls it to put it on his finger he wonders what it signifies; his perfume has given him away to the father of a young girl he was clandestinely visiting; he is about to go abroad and his mistress has pleaded to be allowed to go with him as his page; he is about to go to the wars and gives her his picture, wondering whether he will look different when he returns; he is about to go abroad and, doubting his mistress's constancy, he scratches his name on a pane of glass as a charm; a flea hops from him to his mistress while he is urging her to yield to him; he has been dreaming and just at the moment he dreams that she is his, she enters and wakes him; he is in bed watching his mistress undress and urges her to hurry; he is in bed with his mistress and the sun wakes them; he and his mistress have been walking to an fro for three hours in the morning and now as they stand still it is high noon; a friend is reproaching him for sacrificing worldly advantages for love; he is alone and unhappy in a spring garden because his mistress is too true to love him; he is alone at midnight in midwinter and more desolate than the season because his mistress is dead; it is a year since they first saw each other, but their love has

satirist and amorous poet from Donne the religious poet and preacher, 'Jack' being licentious and the 'Doctor' grave and moral. Donne himself was distinguishing between himself as a young man, writing as an individual, and himself as an older man in orders, writing with the authority and the responsibility that a profession gives and demands. In one sense all his poetry, whether amorous or religious, licentious or moral, was the work of 'Jack Donne'.

mysteriously remained unchanged in a world of change; it is spring and he loves her more than he did in winter and he wonders whether his vows in winter were therefore false; his mistress has given him a bracelet of her hair and it is a sign of the miraculous union of their souls which has been achieved without the help of their bodies; his mistress has given him a bracelet of her hair: it is a sign perhaps of her power over him, to preserve him from corruption, or perhaps of the cruelty by which she has enslaved him and condemned him to die.

Even when a poem is not strictly dramatic in that we cannot thus define the exact situation, the imagined moment, Donne assumes the role that a poem demands with dramatic zest and consistency. He can argue with a wild persistent logic that since it is the centric part that men love they should waste no time admiring women's faces, but start their voyage to the desired port from the foot; or that his friend will do far better to marry the hideous Flavia than to marry a beauty. He will declare that he can love any and every kind of woman, except a constant one; or explain the diet by which he has kept his love low; or bargain with the God of Love, offering to accept willingly later on the absurd role of an aged infatuate in return for freedom from love's servitude now. Or, if he wishes, he can play the despairing lover. In poems such as 'The Broken Heart', 'The Triple Fool', 'The Message', or 'The Legacy' he is all made of tears and sighs and groans, faithful to a mistress who denies or betrays him.

To jumble the love-poems thus together, as they appear jumbled in the great majority of manuscript collections, is to make clear the variety of moods and attitudes to which Donne gave expression and reminds us that a tone of conviction, an accent of truth, is characteristic of his love-poetry whatever mood it expresses. On aesthetic grounds we cannot say, for example, that 'A Valediction: forbidding Mourning' is more sincere than 'The Flea'. If it is argued that no woman could possibly be persuaded to lose her honour by sophistries about flea-bites, it might with equal justice be argued that no woman would be comforted by analogies drawn from compasses. 'The Flea' is persuasive because of its tone of impatient confidence sweeping aside all objections: 'A Valediction: forbidding Mourning' is persuasive because of its tone of tenderness and absolute assurance. Each expresses its mood with that lack of hesitation, or equivocation, that purity of tone, that gives sincerity to a work of art and makes it appear veracious, or imaginatively coherent. If we are to value one poem more highly than the other it must be on the non-aesthetic ground that we value its mood and sentiments more highly. Nor can we legitimately assume that poems that express idealistic sentiments must have been written at a different period from those that express a cynical view of man's love and woman's virtue. If Shakespeare's imagination could give life at the same time to a Mercutio and a Romeo, to an Iago and an Othello, why should we think it impossible for Donne to turn from the mood of 'Love's Growth' to the mood of 'Love's Alchemy'?

Donne's vividly dramatic imagination transforms what are in many cases stock themes of European love-poetry and has disguised the extent to which his inspiration is literary and the nature of his originality. He is not original in writing about a flea; but he is not content, like many Renaissance poets in all countries, to write yet another graceful but tedious variation on 'Ovid's flea', envying the flea for the liberties it takes with his mistress's person, or its good fortune in dying at such hands and on her snowy bosom. The old Petrarchan theme of the love-dream—

> Thus have I had thee as a dream may flatter,
> In sleep a king but waking no such matter—

is transformed by the brilliant stroke of bringing the lady herself into the room just as the dream reaches its climax of joy; and for the sadness of waking there is substituted disappointment in actuality and a return to the pleasures of dreaming. Ovid's narrative of how Corinna came to him one hot noon and how he lay watching her undress, an erotic memory, becomes in Donne's hands an impassioned address by the lover in which the tide of mounting passion is rendered in splendid hyperboles. In the short compass of seventeen lines 'The Apparition' modulates from what appears to be a conventional attack on a cruel mistress, through an original re-making of the classic theme that what she now refuses to enjoy

with him she will when old long for in vain,[1] to a surprising close
that seems at first sight to contradict the opening; for if he no
longer loves her why should her cruelty kill him? But the logic of
the poem's movement is a logic of the heart, humiliated pride preferring the sweets of frustration and revenge to tamer satisfactions.
When we praise Donne for his dramatic imagination we are paying
tribute to his truth of feeling. The bright light of drama, which
heightens and exaggerates, is fatal to weakness or falsity of feeling.

Puttenham said of love-poetry that it required 'a form of Poesie
variable, inconstant, affected, curious, and most witty of any others'.[2]
The versatility that makes Donne's love-poetry a kind of compen-
dium of the poetry of classical, medieval and Renaissance Europe on
the theme of love is matched by a corresponding virtuosity in the
creation and handling of metrical forms.[3] He achieves the effect of
wholly natural speech in complex stanzas with demanding rhyme
schemes. He spoke of 'Rimes vexation'; but there is no poet whose
sense appears to be so little led by the exigencies of rhyming. He
plainly strove for unobtrusive rhyme; he loves sliding rhymes, on
vowels, or on liquids or nasals, and he frequently avoids hard rhyme
by opening the following line with a vowel. But when he wishes his
rhyme is emphatic. Similarly, while keeping the accent of ordinary
speech, he is a master of placing and of repetition; as in 'The Expiration' where the placing of the repeated 'Go' and the support
given to it by assonance creates an exquisite musical effect. He is a
master of concision and economy in language, seeming effortlessly
to fill his lines, without waste of words or awkward condensation
or inversion.[4] And his use of rhetorical devices, like his handling
of literary conventions, is so individual that we are usually unaware
of the means by which he elicits our response.

[1] Cf. Horace, *Odes*, i. xxv and Wyatt's use of this threat to ungrateful beauty in 'My lute
awake'. Where Wyatt merely adopts from the classics the threat that she will lie 'withered
and old', tormented by wishes that 'dare not be told', Donne creates the brilliant vignette of
his ghost watching by the light of a flickering taper the 'feigned vestal' whose feeble lover
pretends to be asleep to escape her importunity.

[2] *The Art of English Poesie*, i. xxii.

[3] See Pierre Legouis, *Donne the Craftsman*, Paris, 1928, for an extended discussion of
Donne's stanza forms. Professor Legouis was the first, and remains one of the very few of
Donne's critics to recognize Donne's artistry.

[4] Donne's own definition of poetic form is 'such as is both curious, and requires diligence
in the making, and then when it is made, can have nothing, no syllable taken from it, nor
added to it' (*Sermons*, ii. 50).

To value Donne's love-poetry for its imaginative veracity and for its exploitation of the resources of language, and to see each poem as complete and self-explanatory is not inconsistent with valuing the poems as a whole, as expressive of a single poetic personality, and with the desire to trace in them a coherent imaginative, intellectual, and artistic development that we can relate to the course of Donne's life and to the totality of his work in verse and prose. Such a development has been obscured by uncertainty over the canon of the *Elegies* and by the problem of the dating of the *Songs and Sonnets*. Attempts to date them by biographical inferences, apart from the general unsoundness of such inferences, only concern a few of the poems and leave the mass unaccounted for. I believe that, although it is not possible to establish precise dates, and we should hardly expect this to be possible, we can, on objective grounds, distinguish groups of poems and that we can assign these to certain periods of Donne's life. Having done so we are presented with a coherent development. We can then see a true relation between the story of Donne's life, his intellectual growth and his translation of his experience of life and literature into works of art, finding it as true of Donne as of Shakespeare that 'he led a life of Allegory: his works are the comments on it'.[1]

The *Elegies*, as they are printed in this edition,[2] form a homogeneous collection of poems, unified in style and in their handling of the couplet, and inspired in the main by two literary models, the classical love-elegy, particularly the *Amores* of Ovid, and the Italian Paradox. One can also see clearly reflected in them that the young Donne was 'a great frequenter of Playes'.[3] The two strains, the Ovidian and the Paradoxical, blend very well since outrageousness and perversity mark Ovid's handling of the theme of love in the *Amores*, which are a constant offence against Roman *gravitas*. Obviously Ovidian are 'Jealousy', 'Tutelage', 'Love's War' (though it recalls two Elegies of Propertius), and 'Going to Bed'. Obviously Italianate in their paradoxical arguments are 'The Anagram' (which

---

[1] Keats, *Letters*, ed. M. Buxton Forman, 1935, p. 305.
[2] For arguments for regarding these poems as Donne's 'Book of Elegies' and excluding seven of the poems included by Grierson under the heading 'Elegies', see the second part of the Introduction, p. xxxi.
[3] Sir Richard Baker, *Chronicles of the Kings of England*, 1643, p. 156.

overgoes Tasso's 'Sopra la Bellezza') and 'Love's Progress', though this may owe something to Nashe's indecent *A Choice of Valentines*. Influenced more I think by the stage than by reading are 'The Bracelet' and 'The Perfume'; and the influence of the stage is also felt in the beautiful Elegy 'On his Mistress' which, like the other valedictory Elegy 'His Picture', transcends the world of Ovid. The *Elegies* are untouched by the idealization of women that distinguishes the courtly and Petrarchan traditions from the tradition of classical love-poetry. They are equally free of the dialectical subtleties of Neoplatonism. They show no trace of the conception of love as humble service or of the conception of love as a mystical union by which two souls become one. This is true even of the serious and impassioned valedictions. They speak of parting directly and un-philosophically without any attempt to prove that souls may remain united though bodies are parted. The brief 'Funeral Elegy', which appears linked by manuscript tradition to the Love Elegies, is in the same way content to dwell on the virtues of the dead man and the grief of his family. It makes no attempt at the elaborate panegyrical and theological conceits characteristic of the Epicedes that Donne wrote between 1609 and 1614.

It seems reasonable to regard the *Elegies* as fairly close to each other in date and from topical allusions in some they can be dated between 1593 and 1596 when Donne was a law student at Lincoln's Inn. They are thus contemporary with the first three Satires. Donne begins his poetic career by taking two Roman poets as his models: the Horace of the *Satires* and the Ovid of the *Amores*. He was no doubt attracted by the social realism of both and by the dramatic element in Roman satire and elegy. This last he develops in the *Elegies* far beyond what he found in his Roman models, following the bent of his temperament, stimulated one imagines by the flowering of the Elizabethan drama. His wit also far overgoes the wit of Ovid, drawing on medieval dialectic and legal disputations. Again for parallels we must turn to the logic-chopping of Elizabethan comedy.

The *Elegies* give an overwhelming impression of masculinity. The 'masculine persuasive force' of the language and the reckless, over-bearing argumentativeness match an arrogance that in some of the poems amounts to a brutal contempt for the partner of his pleasures, in others issues in a confident assertion of the will to enjoy her, and even in the two valedictions appears in the lover's unquestioning assumption of superiority. The *Elegies* are the product of the 'youth, strength, mirth, and wit' that Walton saw portrayed in the Marshall engraving. The young man there, with his intellectual brow, his sensual lips, his powerful nose ('the rudder of the face') and his bold gaze, plainly regards the world as his oyster. English poetry provides no precedent for the adoption of so whole-hearted a rejection of all social, moral, and religious values in the interests of youthful male desire,[1] and none of the poets who followed Donne in writing love-elegies approached his masterful vigour.

To turn from the *Elegies* to the *Songs and Sonnets* is to exchange homogeneity for extreme diversity in theme, mood, form, and style. As they are presented in this edition they are divided into two sets: poems that I believe to have been written before 1600 and poems that I believe were written after 1602;[2] and within these sets poems that have some connexion in theme, form, or style have been brought together.[3] Even so, the effect of diversity remains. Donne is a tireless experimenter in the lyric.

So much praise has been given to Donne's colloquial vigour and so much, sometimes misconceived, praise has been given to his supposed metrical irregularity[4] that it is worth stressing that although there are no sonnets in the *Songs and Sonnets* there are many

---

[1] Whether Donne himself was a rake or not he had a rake's imagination and presented himself with gusto in such a light. He plainly had such a reputation, for he had to clear himself with Sir George More in 1602 of 'that fault which was layd to me of having deceivd some gentlewomen before' as well as of 'loving a corrupt religion' (*Loseley MSS.*, ed. Kempe, 1835, p. 334). A sermon preached at Lincoln's Inn seems to reflect back on Donne's time there as a law student: 'At last he will come to that case, which *S. Augustine* . . . confesses of himself, *Ne vituperarer, vitiosior fiebam*, I was fain to sin, lest I should lose my credit, and be undervalued; *Et ubi non suberat, quo admisso, aequarer perditis*, when I had no means to doe some sins, whereby I might be equall to my fellow, *Fingebam me fecisse quod non feceram, ne viderer abjectior, quo innocentior*, I would bely myself, and say I had done that, which I never did, lest I should be undervalued for not having done it. *Audiebam eos exaltantos flagitia* . . . I saw it was thought wit to make Sonnets of their own sinnes.' (*Sermons*, ii. 107–8.)

[2] The case for thus dividing the lyrics is argued in the third part of the Introduction, p. xlvii.

[3] I am not claiming that this arrangement necessarily coincides with the order of composition, though in some cases it probably does.

[4] Apart from the *Satires*, in which a harsh style was thought decorous, and the *Verse-Letters*, in which a low style was proper, Donne's roughness has been much exaggerated, partly because the principles of elision that he worked upon have not been understood, partly because a notion that he is rough led Grierson to prefer 'less smooth' readings, and partly because of the shifting of accent in many words. I would not argue that Donne never goes too far, leaving the reader's ear puzzled; only that in lyric he does so less often than is supposed.

songs and that Donne's songs run with a delightful lilting ease. Six
of the poems in my first set are said to have been written to existing
airs and song rhythms can be heard behind many of the others, as
in the nursery-rhyme cadence of 'I can love her, and her, and you,
and you' of 'The Indifferent' and the beautiful rocking movement
of 'Break of Day', set up by continual inversion of the first foot.
Parody, in its now obsolete sense of the setting of fresh words to an
old tune, was one of the ways in which the Elizabethans liberated
themselves from the jog-trot of mid-sixteenth-century lyric verse
and learned to trust their ears rather than their fingers. Sidney,
before Donne, exercised himself in this way. If song is one root of
Donne's art as a lyric poet, the classical love-epigram is another.
Donne admired the witty brevity of Martial whom he quotes from
seven times in the *Paradoxes and Problems*.[1] The poems that I have
placed after the songs have the brevity and point of the epigrammatic
form, and the development of Donne's art might be described in
one way as his learning how to expand and enrich epigrammatic
themes without losing the point and pungency that is characteristic
of epigram.[2]

   The norm of Donne's songs is the octosyllabic line, the old staple
line of medieval verse. The norm of epigram is the decasyllabic line,
the line that catches the rhythm of speech, the line of drama. A good
many of the poems in this first set combine decasyllabics with octosyllabics, as if Donne were trying to combine the soaring of song
with the force of speech. Or we might put it that he was trying to
achieve a stanza that combined the weight of the decasyllabic with the
lightness of the octosyllabic. Equally interesting and without precedent are the two dramatic monologues in verse-paragraphs, 'Woman's
Constancy' and 'The Apparition', where matter that might have
been handled in the *Elegies* is given a form that corresponds more
closely with fluctuating feeling than regularly rhyming couplets can.

---

[1] See Evelyn Simpson, 'Donne's Reading of Martial', *A Garland for John Donne*, ed.
T. Spencer, Cambridge, Mass., 1931, pp. 44–49.
[2] Drummond said of Donne that he was 'Second to none, and far from all Second' among
the 'Anacreontick Lyricks'. But he added that 'as *Anacreon* doth not approach *Callimachus*,
tho' he excels him in his own kind, nor Horace to Virgil; no more can I be brought to think
him to excel either *Alexander's* or *Sidney's* Verses: They can hardly be compared together,
trading diverse Paths; the one flying swift but low; the other, like the Eagle, surpassing the
Clouds. I think if he would, he might easily be the best Epigrammatist we have found in
English.' (*Works*, 1711, p. 226.)

Other poems in this first set handle themes and reflect moods that remind us of the *Elegies* and of the *Satires*, or are, like them, inspired by classical models. But in others the young man about town of the *Elegies* who takes his pleasure at will is replaced by another figure: the lover who loves without reward. This is the young man of the Lothian portrait, posed 'with folded arms and melancholy hat', asking in a parody of religious language that his lady would lighten his darkness. But whether Donne is bargaining with the God of Love in 'Love's Usury', or pleading with him for mercy in 'Love's Exchange', explaining to us how he keeps his heart free so that his body may reign in 'Love's Diet', or complaining of Love's unwarranted extension of his power in 'Love's Deity', it is the same voice that speaks. The licentious young amorist and the frustrated lover are the same person, as the same eyes look out at us from the Marshall engraving and the Lothian portrait.[1] Donne infuses his own accent, his personal tone, into Ovidian licentiousness and Petrarchan frustration. He is not one to 'serve and suffer patiently' or to languish for love. He rebels against the tyranny of the God of Love, and blames and despises himself for his folly in accepting such bondage. If, as at the close of 'Love's Deity', he accepts that the lady cannot, if she is to be true, love him, it is with an ill grace and with only a grudging admission of the claims of virtue.

One song and two finely wrought love-epigrams, one employing the old conceit from the Greek Anthology that souls are breathed out in kisses, the other the conceit of the lover's image reflected in his mistress's weeping eyes, echo the two beautiful valedictory Elegies and, like them, point forward to the great theme of Donne's later love-poetry, the celebration of love as peace and not rage; but they do so without having recourse to 'mystical mathematics' and philosophic speculation and in simple metrical forms.

It is not the mark of the second set of the *Songs and Sonnets*, whose composition I place after 1602, that they all handle the theme of love as union. The set includes that bitter masterpiece 'Love's

---

[1] The sign of love-melancholy was the large-brimmed hat pulled down over the brows, as worn by 'Inamorato' on the frontispiece of *The Anatomy of Melancholy*. But obviously nobody would sit for a portrait with only the lower part of his face showing. Donne's 'melancholy hat' is therefore turned back to show his face. The expression on the face thus revealed is, like the turned back brim, at variance with the pleading motto.

Alchemy', the sombre treatment of a Petrarchan theme in 'Twicken-ham Garden', the melancholy debate on the meaning of the 'subtle wreath of hair' that his mistress gave him in 'The Funeral', and the curious speculation on what is a 'true love' in 'The Primrose'. Their distinction lies in their more subtle and complex conception of lyric form and style. Apart from the poems in quatrains and 'Image and Dream', which I put together, they are mainly in stanzas of some scope and complexity, and the creation of such stanzas enabled Donne to fuse into a single poem gifts that one would have thought incompatible: his gift for song, for pure melodic phrasing, his gift for creating the illusion of actual vehement speech, and his gift for arguing in verse. This last one would have thought as incompatible with the other two as they would seem to be incompatible with each other. This fusion of song, drama, and argument is unique in English poetry. None of Donne's followers equals him in his power to give weight and fullness to lyric stanzas without loss of pace where pace is needed and with variation of pace when feeling demands it.

But although this second group of lyrics is not confined to the theme of mutual love, it is in the poems on this theme that Donne has no model and no rival, is at his most original and at his greatest. These poems demand more than admiration for the poet's art; they express the most intimate and precious human feelings and communicate, to use words Henry James used of Browning, 'the seriousness of the great human passion'. I do not doubt that there is a connexion between Donne's love for Ann More and the appear-ance of this theme in his poetry, and that we can see reflected in these poems Donne's situation in the years that followed his marriage. But the poems themselves, even the most idealistic, are too far from the reality we know of for us to speak of them as written to Ann More, or even about her. The bond they celebrate is not the bond of marriage, a contract entered into before the eyes of the world, bringing joys and griefs but also responsibilities. The hus-band of Ann More soon became the father of their children. His wife was often sick and ailing and so was he. The lovers in these wonderful poems need fear no sublunary consequences of their ecstatic unions any more than Lancelot or Guinevere, Tristan and

Isolde, Troilus and Criseyde. The lovers of 'The Anniversary' cannot look to be buried together as married lovers may, and as Donne himself hoped to be buried with his wife:[1] instead, 'Two graves must hide mine and thy corse'. The lady in 'A Valediction: forbidding mourning' is told to hide her grief because 'the laity' must not know:

> So let us melt, and make no noise,
>   No teare-floods, nor sigh-tempests move,
> 'Twere prophanation of our joyes
>   To tell the layetie our love.

This is not an argument to use to a wife, who has no need to hide her grief at her husband's absence.[2] The superb *égoisme à deux* of these poems, their scorn for the world of everyday and the duties of daily life, their stress on secrecy and insistence on the esoteric nature of love—a religion of which Donne and his mistress are the only saints, alone fit to give 'rule and example' to other lovers and communicating their mystery only to adepts, 'loves clergie'—make these poems a quintessence of the romantic conception of passionate love as the *summum bonum*. It is a lover and his mistress, not a husband and wife, who prefer to be blest 'here upon earth' rather than to share with others the full bliss of heaven, who

> dye and rise the same, and prove
> Mysterious by this love;

and tell the sun that his duty is done by warming them and that the bed they lie in is his centre.[3]

As Donne's powerful and idiosyncratic temperament transformed the witty depravity of Ovid and the refined sentiment of Petrarch,

---

[1] See the epitaph Donne wrote for his wife's grave: '. . . maritus (miserrimum dictu) olim charae charus cineribus cineres spondet suos.' Cf. Crashaw's lines:

> To these, Whom Death again did wed,
> This Grave's the second Marriage-bed;

and Henry King's 'The Exequy'.

[2] When we consider the circumstances in which Donne left his wife in 1611, to face alone the last weary months of pregnancy and her eighth labour, it seems impossible to accept Walton's statement, first made in 1675, that 'A Valediction: forbidding Mourning' was written on this occasion.

[3] Cf. Donne's quotation from St. Jerome: '*Nihil foedius, quam uxorem amare tanquam adulteram*, There is not a more uncomely, a poorer thing, then to love a Wife like a Mistresse.' (*Sermons*, ii. 345.)

so he turned to his own uses his reading in the Neoplatonists. Their concept of love as union his imagination seized on; the philosophic system of which it is a part he ignored. The union of lovers is an end in itself in Donne's poems, needing no justification and reaching to nothing beyond itself.[1] This concept of love implies the worth of the beloved:

For, Love is so noble, so soveraign an Affection, as that it is due to very few things, and very few things worthy of it. Love is a Possessory Affection, it delivers over him that loves into the possession of that that he loves; it is a transmutatory Affection, it changes him that loves, into the very nature of that that he loves, and he is nothing else.[2]

It is true that when distinction is made, either by metaphor as in 'She is all States, and all Princes, I', or in argument as in 'Air and Angels', the superiority of the masculine is implied or conceded; but in general the 'He and She', the 'I and Thou' of Donne's earlier poetry are transformed into 'We' and 'Us'. Donne also found in the Neoplatonists many casuistical arguments to prove that bodily love was not incompatible with spiritual and that lovers united in soul should unite in body to make their union perfect. He is not original in declaring:

Loves mysteries in soules doe grow,
But yet the body is his booke.

But in poems such as 'The Good-Morrow', 'The Anniversary', 'The Canonization', or 'Love's Growth' no casuistry is needed to defend or excuse what the poems' whole tone affirms, the unity of the whole personality, of body and soul, in the union of love. To have imagined and given supreme expression to the bliss of fulfilment, and to the discovery of the safety that there is in love given and returned, is Donne's greatest glory as a love-poet.

---

[1] A partial exception is 'The Ecstasy', which at its close does attempt to relate human love to the cosmic system.

[2] *Sermons*, i. 184–5. A modern Platonist, ignorant I think of Donne's love-poetry, expresses a conception strikingly similar to his: 'Lovers or friends desire two things. The one is to love each other so much that they enter into each other and only make one being. The other is to love each other so much that, having half the globe between them, their union will not be diminished in the slightest degree.' (Simone Weil, *Waiting for God*, 1951, p. 70.)

II. THE CANON AND DATE OF THE *ELEGIES*

In Grierson's edition twenty poems, consecutively numbered, appear as Donne's *Elegies*. In the present edition only thirteen of these will be found collected together under this heading, with the addition of a fourteenth, 'a Funeral Elegy', which manuscript tradition connects with this set of poems. Of the seven poems that have been excluded, two, 'The Autumnal' (IX) and 'The Dream' (X), are unquestionably Donne's; but, for different reasons, I have taken them out from among the *Elegies* and printed them elsewhere. The five others I have printed in an appendix of doubtfully authentic poems.

'The Autumnal' could very properly appear in a collection of Elegies. It is written in couplets, and is, like 'The Anagram' and 'Love's Progress', a Verse-Paradox, defending the position that an old woman is more attractive than a young. But the tradition, which I accept, that connects it with Mrs. Herbert separates it in date from the *Elegies* proper, and it is separated from them also in manuscript tradition.

Grierson's tenth Elegy, 'The Dream', has, on the other hand, no claim to be classed as an Elegy. It is not in couplets, although it has from the first edition onwards been printed as if it were,[1] and in theme, mood, and style it has no relation to Ovidian Elegy. It is one of the poems most obviously inspired by Donne's reading in the Italian Neoplatonists. I print it, in stanzas, among the *Songs and Sonnets*, and have given it the title 'Image and Dream' to differentiate it from the other lyric called 'The Dream'.

The evidence of the manuscripts suggests that Donne's *Elegies*, like his *Satires*, circulated as a set of poems, and that there was probably a 'book of Elegies' as there was a 'book of Satires'.[2] The manuscripts of Group I collect together thirteen Elegies, made up of twelve Love Elegies and one Funeral Elegy ('Sorrow, who to this house scarce knew the way'). The Westmoreland manuscript (*W*)

---

[1] Except by Mr. Roger Bennett in 1942 and Mr. Hayward in his selection from Donne (Penguin Poets) in 1950.

[2] A 'book of Satires' exists in a manuscript in the Queen's College, Oxford, and in Harleian MS. 5110. We can infer the existence of another from Jonson's poem presenting Donne's *Satires* to Lady Bedford.

also collects thirteen Elegies, again making up its set with twelve Love Elegies and the same Funeral Elegy. The two sets have eleven Love Elegies in common and each has one that the other lacks, Group I including 'Love's Progress', missing in *W*, and lacking 'The Comparison', which *W* includes. The order of the poems in the two sets is different. The set that appears in *W* is also found in the John Cave manuscript (and its copy, the Dyce manuscript)[1] and (with the first and last Elegies missing) in a manuscript in the British Museum (*A 25*). The collection of Elegies in the Luttrell manuscript, which was copied from there in the O'Flaherty manuscript, is an expansion of the mutilated set in *A 25*.[2]

The Elegies printed together in the present edition are the eleven Love Elegies common to Group I and *W*, with the addition of 'Love's Progress' from Group I and 'The Comparison' from *W*. These are the only Love Elegies (if we deny the title to 'The Autumnal' and 'Image and Dream') that are common to all four manuscripts of Group II.[3] The collection preserved in these four manuscripts combined excellence of text with purity of canon. On the authority of Groups I and II and *W*, these thirteen Love Elegies can be accepted as unquestionably Donne's. Although most of them appear separately in manuscript miscellanies without ascription, I have never found one ascribed to any other author. I have printed with them the 'Funeral Elegy' that occurs with them in Group I, *W* and *JC*. Ovid, who was Donne's model in amorous Elegy, included in his *Amores* one Funeral Elegy (iii. 9), the tribute to his fellow-Elegist Tibullus; and Thomas Campion followed Ovid by including in his 'Liber Elegiarum', published in his *Poemata* (1595), one Funeral Elegy among his fifteen Love Elegies. The fourteen poems printed in this edition under the heading 'Elegies' compose, I believe, Donne's 'book of Elegies'.

It seems reasonable to regard the *Elegies* as having been written in quite a short space of time. There are two for which a fairly precise date can be suggested from topical references: 'The Bracelet'

[1] It may be assumed from now onwards that any statement about the contents and text of the John Cave manuscript applies also to the Dyce manuscript.

[2] See Textual Introduction, p. lxxiv.

[3] 'The Expostulation' is not in *A 18* and *TCC*. Only the close of the poem is present today in *TCD* which has lost some leaves in the centre. *N*, which is a copy of *TCD*, was made before the damage took place and has a full text.

and 'Love's War'. Both these I date 1593–4.[1] It is difficult not to connect 'His Picture' with Donne's joining the Cadiz expedition in June 1596, and I have suggested that there may be a reminiscence of the close of *A Midsummer Night's Dream* in 'The Perfume' and of *Romeo and Juliet* in 'On his Mistress', plays first staged around 1595–6. Also, the only solution I can propose to the problem of identifying the subject of the Funeral Elegy would date it in 1595.

Campion declared in his *Poemata* (1595) that he was the first British Elegist,[2] as Hall declared in his *Virgidemiarum* (1597) that he was the first English Satirist.[3] Hall's claim is contestable, since Donne's first three Satires may have been written as early as 1593; but it is possible that Campion led the way with his Latin Elegies, and their publication may certainly be taken as inaugurating the vogue of the Ovidian Elegy. All the same Donne may well have the credit of being the first to imitate Ovid's *Elegies* in English, as he was certainly the master of many poets who followed him in the genre.[4] Donne had a copy of Campion's *Poemata* in his library[5] and it is possible that the 'Liber Elegiarum' that it contained inspired him to put together his own Book of Elegies, making it up by including, among poems modelled on Ovid and rehandlings of Ovidian themes, some Verse-Paradoxes composed independently. The cumulative effect of all these suggestions and the absence of any evidence to the contrary make it safe to regard the *Elegies* as written 1593–6, in the period when Donne was at Lincoln's Inn, before he went on the Cadiz and Islands voyages and before he took service with Egerton.

But for the objections of the licenser the thirteen Elegies of Group I would have been printed in the first edition. The entry in the Stationers' Register (13 Sept. 1632) excepted the 'first, second, Tenth, Eleventh, and Thirteenth Elegies' in the '*booke of verses and*

---

[1] See Commentary, pp. 112–13 and 128–9. R. E. Bennett (*R.E.S.*, 1939, xv. 71) suggested that Hall in his *Virgidemiarum* (1597) was answering passages in 'Love's War'. This would imply that the poem had been in circulation for some time.

[2]   'Et vatem celebrent Bruti de nomine primum
               Qui molles elegos et sua furta canat.'

[3]   'I first adventure: follow me who list
              And be the second English Satyrist.'

[4] The great popularity of the Elegy from 1595 to 1640 is rather overlooked in literary histories because the work of gentlemen-writers in this genre has not been collected or anthologized as their songs and lyrics have been. Much of it is still in manuscript.

[5] See Keynes, p. 211.

Poems' that Marriott entered. As Grierson pointed out, Marriott's 'booke' must have been a manuscript of Group I, since only eight Elegies appear together in the first edition and these are the same eight, in the same order, as we should be left with if we took out from the set in Group I the first, second, tenth, eleventh, and thirteenth. But the compiler of the edition had also a manuscript of Group II to work from. This must have resembled *TCD* and *N*, since the edition includes poems found in *TCD* and *N* but not present in *TCC* and *A 18*. From this he took 'The Comparison', which occurs towards the middle of the volume in a miscellaneous section, and 'The Expostulation', which occurs towards the close in a section also containing poems of various kinds.

In the second edition of 1635, in which poems were sorted by kinds and fresh poems were added, seventeen poems are collected under the heading 'Elegies'. The first seven are the Love Elegies which had appeared together in *1633*, the Funeral Elegy having been removed and placed in the section headed 'Epicedes and Obsequies'. The next three are 'The Comparison', 'The Autumnal', and 'Image and Dream'.[1] The eleventh is a Funeral Elegy on Mrs. Bulstrode ('Language thou art too narrow') and the twelfth is 'The Bracelet', although no authority had been obtained for printing this 'excepted' poem. The next four are poems that were printed for the first time in *1635*: 'Come, Fates; I feare you not', 'His Parting from Her' (in a short version of forty-two lines), 'Julia', and 'A Tale of a Citizen and his Wife'. The seventeenth and last is 'The Expostulation'. One other of the five Elegies excepted in the entry in the Stationers' Register was included, also without authority. The beautiful Elegy that begins 'By our first strange and fatal interview' occurs, under the inept heading 'Elegie on his Mistris', among the *Epicedes and Obsequies*.[2]

No further addition was made to this collection of seventeen Elegies until 1669; but in the edition of 1650 'Variety' was printed

[1] 'The Autumnal' and 'Image and Dream' occur among the *Songs and Sonnets* in the manuscripts of Group I, the latter being written without division into stanzas. Presumably whoever prepared the copy for *1633* removed them as not being lyrics. They occur in the edition after 'The Comparison', and all three poems are headed 'Elegie'.

[2] The compiler of *1635* was misled by titles, placing the Funeral Elegy on Mrs. Bulstrode, headed simply 'Elegie' in *1633*, among the Love Elegies, and taking the title 'Elegie on his Mistris' to indicate an Epicede.

in a collection of miscellaneous items, mainly in Latin, added on some extra leaves at the end of the volume. In the edition of 1669, the last seventeenth-century edition, the full text of 'His Parting from Her' replaced the short version of 1635, and two more of the 'excepted' Elegies were printed, 'Love's Progress' and 'Going to Bed'. The fifth of the 'excepted' Elegies, 'Love's War', did not appear in print until 1802.

Of the six Elegies printed as Donne's in editions from 1633 to 1669 which I have excluded as of doubtful authenticity, 'The Expostulation' has the strongest claim to acceptance from its appearance in the first edition of 1633 which, apart from it, included only two uncanonical poems.[1] Although it was printed as Donne's from 1633 onwards it appeared as Jonson's in the posthumous *Underwoods* in 1641. Mrs. Simpson argued strongly for Donne's authorship against Jonson's, laying stress on its appearance in the first edition of Donne's poems, its inclusion in ten large manuscript collections of his works and its ascription to Donne by William Drummond. She also argued that Jonson would have protested if one of his poems had been printed as Donne's in 1633 and that, consequently, it would not have reappeared in the second edition of 1635.[2] This last argument I accept and regard the attribution to Jonson in the carelessly produced *Underwoods* as worthless. It is the argument for Donne's authorship that needs scrutiny.

The edition of 1633 was dependent on a manuscript of Group I, supplemented from a manuscript of Group II resembling *TCD* and its descendant *N*. These two manuscripts contain a certain number of poems that are not in *TCC* and its descendant *A 18*, and which have been inserted from time to time into the run of poems common to the four manuscripts of Group II. 'The Expostulation' is one of these inserted poems, and one other of these ('Whoso terms love a fire') is certainly unauthentic.[3] All we can say is that the compiler of the copy for 1633, going through his Group II manuscript to find additional poems, thought that 'The Expostulation' was Donne's;

---

[1] William Basse's 'Epitaph on Shakespeare', which was not reprinted in 1635, and a paraphrase of Psalm 137, probably by Francis Davison.
[2] See E. M. Simpson, 'Jonson and Donne', *R.E.S.*, 1939, xv. 274–82, and Jonson, *Works*, xi. 67–68.
[3] Another of the poems is not Donne's but it is correctly ascribed 'R. Cor.'

but, since he included from some other source two uncanonical poems, we cannot regard his judgement on the canon as unerring. The absence of the poem from the manuscripts of Group I, from the collection that lies behind Group II, and from *W* is, in my view, more telling than its presence in the first edition.

When it appears in manuscript it is nearly always in doubtful company. It is one of the poems common to *H 40*★ and *RP 31*; but the common source of these two manuscripts was a miscellany containing poems by a great many writers with only a few by Donne. It occurs in the Donne section of *L 74*; but it is one of a group of poems in couplet that interrupts a collection of Donne's lyrics and it follows immediately on a poem by Beaumont which the scribe has not distinguished by ascription from its neighbours which are Donne's. In *B* it occurs in a section of the manuscript in which poems by Beaumont, Sir John Roe, and others are copied with Donne's.[1] *S* has it in a set of twenty-six Elegies, made up by adding to the authentic Love Elegies some Verse-Letters and Epicedes and four poems that are certainly not Donne's, although they often appear in collections of his poems. In *Lut* and *O'F* it occurs in a heterogeneous group of poems which forms the second part of their collection of Elegies and is placed between two poems that are certainly not authentic. The scribe of *O'F* has written by the title 'Quere if Donnes or Sr Tho: Rowes'. In *Dob* and *S 96* and in *Cy, O*, and *P* its position is not suspicious, but all five manuscripts include a fair number of uncanonical pieces. The fact that 'The Expostulation' is almost invariably present in any manuscript (outside Groups I and II) that attempts to collect Donne's poems fully is, at first sight, impressive evidence in its favour; but all the manuscripts in which it appears are weak witnesses to the canon of Donne's poems.[2] The only strong external evidence for Donne's

---

[1] *B* is a patchy manuscript. Up to f. 23 it contains poems by Donne only. Ff. 23^v–39^v, the section containing 'The Expostulation', is a medley. Ff. 40–47^v contain canonical poems; f. 48 contains 'Julia' followed by a poem on the reign of Henry III of France. The remainder of the manuscript is mainly devoted to Donne's poems; but among them are to be found, in addition to 'A Tale of a Citizen and his Wife' and 'His Parting from Her', six poems that are certainly not Donne's. The scribe has throughout attempted, in a desultory fashion, to distinguish poems that are not by Donne; but he has not done this with sufficient consistency for us to argue from his failure to query 'The Expostulation' or to ascribe it to another author.

[2] The ascription to Donne in two miscellanies in which I have met the poem can be disregarded. In a manuscript at Corpus Christi College, Oxford (*CCC 327*), William Fulman ascribes the poem to Donne with a page reference and then adds 'B. Johns'. He was plainly

authorship is provided by William Drummond in the Hawthornden manuscript (*HN*), which contains 'poems belonginge to Jhon Don Transcribed by William Drummond'. The poems are by various authors and are ascribed by initials at the close. Since all the other ascriptions are correct, the ascription of 'The Expostulation' to 'J.D.' must be allowed to have weight.

When we turn to the internal evidence, one thing sets 'The Expostulation' apart from the unquestionably authentic Elegies. The reference to 'the Kinges dogges' (l. 52) dates it after 1603. In various ways it differs not only from the accepted Elegies but from Donne's love-poetry generally. As a glance at the commentary will show, it is a mosaic of borrowings from Catullus and Ovid. Donne rarely shows such close verbal indebtedness and Catullus is not a poet he normally draws upon. Again, its loose structure is unlike Donne's manner of constructing a quasi-dramatic poem. It falls into four distinct sections not logically linked. The opening lines are an attack on a false mistress (ll. 1–22). This is followed by an abject retractation (ll. 23–32). Then comes a curse on some third party (ll. 32–52). The poem ends with the proposal that the lovers should start all over again from the beginning and fall in love once more (ll. 53–70). The first section might be taken as Donne's, although it is more plaintive and less scornful than is usual with him; but the unmotivated *volte face* of the second section is unparalleled in his love-poetry. Donne is never abject before his mistress. The third section, the curse on the mischief-maker, needs to be compared with Donne's exercises on this well-established subject for ingenious poetry: the close of 'The Perfume', the close of 'The Bracelet', and his lyric 'The Curse'. The curse in 'The Expostulation' does not stand the comparison at all well. It is wholly lacking in Donne's malicious inventiveness and is content to paraphrase Catullus and Ovid. The final section of the poem is again, like the second, very uncharacteristic in temper. The speaker enjoys the prospect of love-dalliance and looks forward to wooing his mistress all over again. He is attracted by that 'art of love' that Donne always regards with impatience and scorn, and betrays none of Donne's

depending on the appearances of the poem in print. In Edward Hyde's commonplace book (*EH*) the value of the ascription to 'J.D.' is made questionable by the fact that Hyde added the same initials to Carew's 'Dearest thy tresses are not threads of gold'.

characteristic urgency, his desire to have done with the tiresome preliminaries.

'The Expostulation' is a poem of some accomplishment which handles themes that Donne handles: the abuse of an inconstant mistress and the curse. I cannot recognize in it Donne's tone. Further, it seems most unlikely that he would write a poem of this kind after 1603. Its close dependence on Latin poetry and the simplicity of its thought relate it to a kind of poetry he had by then outgrown. One has only to think of what Donne made of Ovidian themes in 'The Sun Rising' and 'The Canonization', both written after 1603, to recognize the unlikelihood of his writing 'The Expostulation' at the same time. Even when Ovid was his master he never wrote anything so tame, so lacking in masculine arrogance and stinging wit. By 1603 he had found other sources of inspiration and if he took up an Ovidian theme it was with a difference. The internal evidence against Donne's authorship is, in my view, so strong that it outweighs Drummond's ascription.[1]

Of the four Elegies that were added in *1635* Grierson rejected 'Come, Fates; I feare you not', ascribing it, correctly I believe, to Sir John Roe. He argued from manuscript ascriptions, from the regularity with which this poem appears with other poems by Roe, and from internal evidence of treatment and style.[2] Since his arguments have won general acceptance I have not considered it necessary to reprint the poem among the *Dubia* in this volume. The claims of the other three he accepted rather too easily.

'Julia' and 'A Tale of a Citizen and his Wife' were taken by the compiler of the second edition from his main source for additional poems, the O'Flaherty manuscript. In *O'F*, as in its original the Luttrell manuscript, they occur in the miscellaneous groups of poems added at the end of the Elegies proper. Otherwise, 'Julia' occurs in the Bridgewater manuscript, immediately preceding a poem on the reign of Henry III of France which, like it, is not distinguished as not by Donne, and in the first part of the Haslewood-

---

[1] Drummond was copying a book containing 'poems belonging to' Donne. Two possible explanations of his ascription can be put forward. Either, Donne, in appending initials to poems that were not his own, had omitted to ascribe this poem and Drummond finding it unascribed thought that it, like the other unascribed poems, was Donne's; or, it was initialed 'T.R.' (if we accept the suggestion in *O'F* that its author was Thomas Roe) and Drummond misread as 'I.D.'

[2] See Grierson, vol. ii, pp. cxxx–cxxxv.

Kingsborough manuscript. Here, although it occurs in the middle of a collection that is plainly intended to be a collection of Donne's poems, it immediately precedes two satires by Sir John Roe which, like it, are not distinguished by ascription from the surrounding poems by Donne. 'A Tale of a Citizen and his Wife' is also found in the Bridgewater manuscript, in a section which contains mainly poems by Donne but which includes, as well as 'His Parting from Her', six unauthentic pieces. It is also found in the Dobell manuscript and in a late miscellany, Rawlinson Poetical MS. 117 (2), where it is headed 'Dunnes tale of a Citizen and his Wife'. The value of this last ascription is weakened by the fact that the next poem in the manuscript, 'Love bred of glaunces', is headed 'Dunnes sonnett'. Both 'Julia' and 'A Tale of a Citizen and his Wife' were marked 'Not licensed nor Dr. Donns' by Giles Oldisworth in his copy of the edition of 1639.[1]

There is thus no solid external evidence for ascribing these two poems to Donne and I have no hesitation in rejecting both. 'Julia' is a generalized portrait of a bad-tempered and slanderous woman, in the 'scurrilous style of Horace's invective against Canidia, frequently imitated by Mantuan and other Humanists'.[2] It is a dull and ineffectual poem on a subject that Donne shows no interest in elsewhere. It was on other counts than scandal-mongering that he attacked women. The fact that there are as many as four classical reminiscences in its mere thirty-two lines points away from him, and its staccato rhythm is much nearer to the rhythm of Sir John Roe's verse than to his. Its heavy repetition of the same point is quite unlike Donne's fertility of invention on unpromising topics. 'A Tale of a Citizen and his Wife' must have been written in 1609 from its crop of topical references.[3] Although some students of Donne would not regard it as impossible that he should write an improper poem in 1609, at the time that he was writing *Pseudo-Martyr* and the 'Holy Sonnets', it is surely in the highest degree unlikely that he would produce a weak *pastiche* of his earlier style, echoing phrases and lines from his own fourth Satire and Elegies at a time when he had developed a new style. The anecdote the poem

[1] See Keynes, p. 162, and John Sampson, 'A Contemporary Light upon John Donne', *Essays and Studies*, vii, 1921.   [2] Grierson, vol. ii, p. cxxxvii.
[3] See Commentary, pp. 228–9.

relates is a very slight one. The wit, such as it is, lies in the double meanings in the conversation between the narrator and the citizen. It is like a parody of the conversation between Donne and the spy at court in 'Satire IV'. This parody of Donne's early style comes oddly after the jog-trot of the opening lines, which fall into a triple rhythm[1] unlike anything in Donne's poems in the couplet, and the slack narrative of lines 9 to 20. The writer is, I think, an admirer of Donne who catches at times his accent as he borrows his phrases, but who lacks his power to explode into a situation and has applied Donne's manner to a situation that would not have attracted Donne even in his youth. The characteristic situation in Donne's poetry is one in which he confronts his mistress as the dominant figure. He rarely shows any interest in the beginning of an affair. I cannot see him writing a poem of this length merely to recount the making of an assignation behind a husband's back. If the external evidence for Donne's authorship of these two poems were strong, we might have to accept that he, at some time, uncharacteristically attempted a 'Character of a She-Libeller', a poem in the manner of John Stephens's very popular attack on Mrs. Mallett, and that, as a man of forty-seven, he amused himself by translating his sardonic account of a conversation with an informer into a facetious account of a conversation with a gullible husband, introduced by twenty lines of feeble verse. But the external evidence is so weak that we need not indulge in any such suppositions.

The fourth of the Elegies added in 1635, 'His Parting from Her', is a very different matter. No critic has quoted lines from 'Julia' and 'A Tale of a Citizen and His Wife' as illustrative of Donne's genius; but many critics have praised this poem and quoted its finest passage. There are many puzzling points about it. The compiler of the edition of 1635 printed a short text although the poem is extant in full in O'F, the manuscript from which he was working. The short version that he printed is found in B and A 25.[2] The full

---

[1] To péace-teaching Láwyer, Próctor, or bráve
    Reformed or redúced Cáptaine, Knáve,
    Officer, Júgler, or Jústice of peáce
    Júror or Júdge; I touch nó fat sowes gréase.

[2] A 25 (see p. lxxviii) is in a great many hands. The poem occurs in a section (ff. 59–69) written in one hand and containing poems by various authors, including a good many by Donne. It has been intruded into this section by a different writer who has ascribed it to 'J.D.'.

version[1] is one of the poems common to H 40* and RP 31, most of which, as has been said, are not by Donne. It is also found in S 96 and S 962 (the former containing some and the latter a great many uncanonical poems), and among the miscellaneous Elegies of Lut and O'F. It occurs in O and P, but not in Cy. There is a text in a Malone manuscript (MS. 16), where it is marked as 'ex incerto authore'; and in the miscellany which forms the second part of the Trinity College, Dublin manuscript it occurs without its last ten lines and is ascribed to 'Sᵣ Fran: Wryothlesse'.

'His Parting from Her' is a poem on Donne's favourite theme, the parting of lovers, and it contains a fine opening and one beautiful passage. But critics who have quoted from it (and it is always the same passage that is quoted) have not remarked that it contains some curiously bad writing. It is easy to understand why it appears in shortened versions. Like 'The Expostulation' it falls into four clearly defined sections. It opens with an apostrophe to Night (ll. 1–12), followed by an address to Love (ll. 13–64), a defiance of Fortune (ll. 65–82), and finally (ll. 83–104) the mistress is herself addressed, presumably by letter. The poem, unlike all the accepted valedictions, is not spoken at the moment of parting but is a soliloquy by a man writing to his mistress. The situation is also the reverse of the situation in Donne's valedictions: it is the mistress who is going away (as in Amores, ii. 11) and the lover who has to remain behind. This at once makes the speaker a more plaintive and passive figure than the speakers in Donne's poems of parting. A smaller point is the use of the word 'friend', which occurs three times (ll. 30, 67, and 83), the last time in an apostrophe 'Dearest Friend',[2] and the use of 'my Dear' (l. 95). This is not Donne's idiom, even in his tenderer poems.

The most often quoted lines occur in the address to Fortune:

Rend us in sunder, thou canst not divide
Our bodies so, but still our souls are ty'd,
And we can love by letters still and gifts,
And thoughts and dreams; Love never wanteth shifts.

---

[1] The long version is the original. The text in the shorter versions has been clumsily emended to cover the joins.

[2] 'Friend', for 'Mistress', occurs in Donne's poetry only in a rather ambiguous use in that curious poem 'The Blossom'.

> I will not look upon the quickning Sun,
> But straight her beauty to my sense shall run;
> The ayre shall note her soft, the fire most pure;
> Water suggest her clear, and the earth sure.
> Time shall not lose our passages; the Spring
> Shall tell how fresh our love was in beginning;
> The Summer how it ripen'd in the eare;
> And Autumn, what our golden harvests were.
> The Winter I'll not think on to spite thee,
> But count it a lost season, so shall shee.

This is the best passage in the poem. It has not the ring of Donne. The two conceits are conventional in their application. The poet goes through the elements first and then the seasons and does not find any witty twist in the conventional comparisons. The declaration that 'we can love by letters still and gifts, and thoughts and dreams', with the weak addition to fill out the line 'Love never wanteth shifts', is a tame consolation when we compare it with Donne's other treatments of the theme of union in absence. The lines are sweet and fluent, they are not thrilling; and they come to a flat conclusion. Other passages in the poem have an obscurity and a violation of sense that is unlike Donne's obscurity. It is difficult to see what is meant by such a line as 'And then thyself into our flame didst turn' (l. 38), and the monstrous hyperbole in the address to Fortune is not Donne's kind of nonsense. It is in an amorous 'Ercles vein'.

> First let our eyes be rivited quite through
> Our turning brains, and both our lips grow to:
> Let our arms clasp like Ivy, and our fear
> Freeze us together, that we may stick here,
> Till Fortune that would rive us, with the deed
> Strain her eyes open, and it make them bleed.

I have dallied with the idea that this poem is of composite author-ship, a group of young men composing it in alternation. This would explain its extreme unevenness and the incompetence in the use of rhyme. In some passages the feebleness of the expression is obviously due to the necessity of finding a rhyme.[1] On the evidence of the

---

[1] This alone would make one doubt Donne's authorship.

manuscripts there are no strong grounds for ascribing it to Donne,
and on internal evidence there is a strong case against accepting
it as authentic.

The last of the *Elegies* that I have excluded, 'Variety', was first
printed in 1650, and as this was the first edition of his father's poems
over which the younger Donne had control it has a claim to consideration. It is also found in the John Cave manuscript, which is,
on the whole, sound in its canon. However, it does not appear there
in the collection of Elegies, which is the same set as that found in *W*.
It occurs at the end of the second section of the manuscript, containing 'Miscellanea, Poems Elegies Sonnets', under the heading
'Elegia 17ma'. It precedes 'Sappho to Philaenis', which is headed
'Elegia 18^a', and a heading 'Elegia 19th' on which no poem follows.[1]
This is rather a dubious position. It looks as if John Cave was
attempting to expand the collection from which he was copying.
Otherwise, it is known to me only in a manuscript miscellany in the
British Museum,[2] containing a few of Donne's poems, and in the two
parts of the Haslewood-Kingsborough manuscript.[3] In all three it
is unascribed. In *HK 1* it occurs before 'Julia' in a run of poems that
are mainly by Donne but its immediate neighbours are very mixed
company. In *HK 2** it occurs in an interesting small collection of
Elegies, none of them by Donne, which I have not met with elsewhere.

'Variety' is a gay and lively poem. It opens on an Ovidian theme
(*Amores*, ii. 4) which Donne used as a spring-board in 'The Indifferent'. The writer combines with Ovid's pose of the universal
lover sophisticated arguments in Donne's manner to prove the
propriety of masculine inconstancy, and reference back to the golden
age, the 'ancient time', when love was unfettered by social laws and
customs. For all his defiance he ends respectably: the time will come
when he will have to abandon love's service and finding a mistress
who combines beauty and true worth will 'love her ever and love
her alone'. The last part of the poem can be compared with Donne's

[1] The second section of *JC* has three poems headed 'Elegie' but unnumbered. John Cave
has counted on from his thirteen numbered Elegies at the beginning to arrive at 'Elegia 17ma'.
[2] British Museum Add. MS. 10309.
[3] The last thirty lines occur in a Bodleian miscellany, Don 6 9, in a text identical with
that in *HK 2**.

handling of the sobering effects of middle age in 'Love's Usury'. In 'Variety', as in some of the other Elegies discussed, we have themes treated that Donne treated; but, again, they are not treated in his way. The poem is gay and impudent where Donne is insolent and insulting, gallant where he is brutal. Metrically it has been justly singled out by Professor C. S. Lewis as a 'surprising sport',[1] anticipating the Augustan mode. It has the ring of the lighter verse of Dryden:

> How happy were our Syres in ancient time
> Who held plurality of loves no crime!
> With them it was accounted charity
> To stirre up race of all indifferently.

I cannot find any parallel in Donne's works to the easy, natural, good-tempered tone of this poem. It is altogether lighter in mood and more lilting in its cadences than even his lightest Elegies and lacks the satiric edge that he gives to even his gayest songs.

In discussing the authenticity of poems added after the first edition, Grierson rightly pointed out that the fact that many of the poems added in the second edition were by other authors meant that the authenticity of all of them must be questioned. But his conclusion that we must accept as Donne's any 'for which no more suitable candidate can be advanced'[2] cannot be accepted. In an age of amateur poets circulating their poems in manuscript, waifs and strays tend to be fathered on poets of known fame. We need positive reasons for ascribing a poem to Donne, not the merely negative reason that we cannot propose another author. To write an amorous Elegy on the model of Ovid does not require any very great powers of mind. Manuscript miscellanies of the seventeenth century are full of such Elegies, many of which never found their way into print. Almost all have good couplets, good lines, or good phrases; some are, as a whole, well turned and lively. Famous and very popular pieces, to judge by the frequency with which they were copied, are ascribed to authors who are otherwise unknown; many are never

---

[1] *English Literature in the Sixteenth Century*, 1954, p. 551.
[2] Grierson, vol. ii, p. cxxxvi.

ascribed at all. If Walton Poole could write the witty and popular 'If shaddowes be the pictures excellence', and William Baker, 'my Lord of Canterbury's follower', could write 'Not kisse? By Jove I must',[1] and both of them apparently nothing else, I see no reason to question the possibility of an unknown writer, perhaps the mysterious Sir Francis Wriothesley, having written a poem as good in parts as 'His Parting from Her', or of Sir Thomas Roe, to whom other poems are ascribed in manuscript,[2] having written 'The Expostulation'. 'Julia' and 'A Tale of a Citizen and his Wife' are so undistinguished that it is impossible to suggest an author. The gay and accomplished 'Variety' one would like to be able to ascribe. But the lack of another candidate is no argument for allowing these three poems to be Donne's. To be accepted as his, a poem that lacks external authority must show unmistakable signs of his manner, which is highly idiosyncratic. The external evidence for Donne's authorship of 'Farewell to Love' and of the 'Hymn to God my God in my Sickness' is very weak; but who can doubt that Donne and only Donne wrote these poems? Except for Drummond's ascription of 'The Expostulation' and the younger Donne's inclusion of 'Variety' in the edition of 1650, the external evidence for Donne's authorship of these six Elegies is negligible. The internal evidence seems to me to be strongly against admitting them to the canon. If I have erred by excluding them, I hope I shall be thought to have erred on the right side. It is an editor's duty to be strict in examining attributions. To print these six Elegies in an appendix of *Dubia* is not to suggest that Donne could not possibly have written them. It warns readers and critics of the danger of referring to them as Donne's and of basing any arguments about his style and its development upon them. It makes clear that if anyone wishes to claim them for Donne good arguments must be found for doing so.[3]

---

[1] Both poems were printed by Grierson in his invaluable Appendix C: see Grierson, i. 460 and 456.

[2] See MS. Lansdowne 740 (*L 74*), f. 101ᵛ.

[3] One other poem that has been claimed for Donne and has been printed among his *Elegies* by one of his modern editors I have not included even among the *Dubia*. This is a poem in quatrains, ascribed to 'Dr. D.' in the Holgate manuscript in the Pierpoint Morgan Library. See E. K. Chambers, 'An Elegy by John Donne', *R.E.S.*, 1931, vii. 69–71, and R. E. Bennett's edition of Donne's poems (Chicago, 1942) where it is printed as 'Elegy XXI'. The poem is a patchwork of phrases from two of Donne's Elegies, as E. K. Chambers noted. His suggestion that Donne 'laid it aside, and used some of the notions for other elegies inspired by the same

Although it is not an Elegy but, as Grierson labelled it, 'an Heroicall Epistle', 'Sappho to Philaenis' may be considered here. I hesitated for a long time over this poem, but I have come to the conclusion that, in spite of its appearance in the first edition of Donne's poems and its inclusion in the manuscripts of Group II, it is too uncharacteristic of Donne in theme, treatment, and style to be accepted as unquestionably his.

In addition to the manuscripts of Group II, *Lut*, *O'F*, and the Dolau Cothi manuscript contain the poem. It appears in the John Cave manuscript, following 'Variety', and is included in the Osborn and Phillipps manuscripts. All these aim at being collections of Donne's poems. It is found in *A 25*, where it is ascribed 'J.D.', in *HK 1* between 'Variety' and 'Julia', and also in a miscellany (British Museum Add. MS. 10309) that contains 'Variety'.[1]

As with 'Variety', it is on internal evidence that I question the attribution of this poem to Donne. Although two of his lyrics are spoken by a woman ('Break of Day' and 'Confined Love'), I find it difficult to imagine him wishing to assume the love-sickness of Lesbian Sappho. Like his master Ovid, who in this stands apart from the tradition of classical love-poetry, Donne appears wholly uninterested in homosexual love. He is also notoriously uninterested in the physical beauty of women and unattracted by the theme of 'pining for love'. In treatment, the poem, except for lines 35 to 50, makes little use of argument; it is repetitive and lacks Donne's habitual progressiveness. The couplets are mainly stopped, so that the poem lacks Donne's pace. Its metrical dullness is matched by the poverty of its vocabulary. The writer has a trick of using the same word or words twice or three times in a couplet, a rhetorical device effective when used occasionally but monotonous when used repeatedly. I am unable to recognize in the poem any characteristics of Donne's style.

woman, or the same theme' is a highly improbable explanation of its relation to Donne's un-doubted works. The writer has plundered 'Recusancy' and 'Tutelage' to produce a poem in a metre that Donne used for Verse-Letters, not for Elegies, which expresses sentiments quite alien to Donne's temperament. The poem is a rather smug plea by a faithful lover, pained by his mistress's suspected inconstancy. I would suggest that the author is Clement Paman, who has some parodies of Donne as patent as this in Rawlinson Poetical MS. 147.

[1] The fact that it appears three times with 'Variety' suggests that it may be by the same author.

III. THE CANON AND DATE OF THE *SONGS AND SONNETS*

In Grierson's edition fifty-five poems are printed under the heading 'Songs and Sonnets'. In the present edition fifty-four will be found. I have relegated the two last of Grierson's collection ('The Token' and 'Self-Love') to an appendix of doubtful poems, and have included the poem that Grierson printed as 'Elegy X', under the title 'Image and Dream'.

The title of the collection we owe to the editor of the second edition of 1635, who sorted the rather chaotic assemblage of poems in the first edition into their kinds. He took the headings for his sections from the O'Flaherty manuscript which, in turn, had taken them from the Luttrell manuscript. The compiler of this last had gathered the lyrics together under the title 'Sonnetts and Songes', meaning by this simply 'love lyrics', and the editor of 1635 inverted the title, making it identical with the title of the most famous of sixteenth-century collections of love-poetry, the 'Book of Songs and Sonnets' that Slender wished he had with him to help his wooing, Tottel's Miscellany.

Of the fifty-four poems printed here, fifty-two were printed in the first edition, forty-four being taken from its main source, a manuscript of Group I, and eight from a manuscript of Group II.[1] In the second edition four lyrics were added. One, 'A Lecture upon the Shadow', is found in the manuscripts of both Groups I and II. I can propose no explanation but accident for its omission from the first edition. Another, on the other hand, is rarely found in manuscript. 'A Farewell to Love' occurs only in *O'F*, the main source of the additional poems in *1635*, *S 96*, and two miscellanies *S 962* and a manuscript at Harvard (*Hd*). *O'F* and *S 96* are weak witnesses to the canon, and in the Harvard manuscript the name 'M^r An: Saintleg^r' is written against the title of the poem. But in spite of this, nobody I imagine would hesitate to ascribe this poem to Donne. It is signed as his in every line from the bitter brevity of its opening to its insulting close. The other two, 'Soules joy, now I am gone' and 'Deare Love, continue nice and chaste', I agree with Grierson in rejecting.[2] Only two more lyrics were printed as Donne's in the

---

[1] See Textual Introduction, pp. lxxxiii–lxxxiv.
[2] The first is printed as Pembroke's in the younger Donne's edition of Pembroke and

seventeenth century, apart from the addition in *1669* of an initial
stanza in a different metre to 'Break of Day'.[1] 'The Token' was first
printed in the edition of 1649, and the poem to which Chambers
gave the title 'Self-Love' was printed, like the doubtfully authentic
Elegy 'Variety', in the edition of 1650, on additional sheets inserted
into sheets taken over from the edition of 1649 or printed from the
same type. 'The Token' is a rather charming poem, a 'sonnet' of
eighteen lines, which is found in a good many manuscripts that aim
at collecting Donne's poems in full;[2] but its absence from the manuscripts of Groups I and II, and from such sound collections of lyrics
as we find in *H 40, L 74*, and *JC* is more significant than its presence
in a fair number of large indiscriminate collections. It is much more
smooth and elegant than we should expect a poem by Donne to be,
and it is in a form, the extended sonnet, that he did not use elsewhere for love-poetry. On external evidence a slightly better case
can be made for 'Self-Love', since it appears in *JC* in the middle of a
collection, which, except for 'Deare Love, continue nice and chaste',
contains only authentic pieces.[3] Although it has not Donne's accent,
it might be argued that the two lyrics ('Break of Day' and 'Confined
Love') which are, like it, written in the person of a woman are both
in a gentler manner and a more lilting rhythm than is usual with
him. But in the absence of any strong external evidence, this poem,
like 'The Token', is too unlike Donne's unquestioned lyrics to be
printed as his without qualification. The stanza 'Stay, O sweet, and
do not rise', prefixed to 'Break of Day' in *1669*, was printed followed
by a second stanza in Dowland's *A Pilgrim's Solace* in 1612.[4] In the

Ruddier's *Poems* in 1660, and is assigned to him in manuscript. Grierson rightly says of it:
'The thought is Donne's, but not the airy note, the easy style, or the tripping prosody. Donne
never writes of absence in this cheerful, confident strain. He consoles himself at times with
the doctrine of inseparable souls, but the note of pain is never absent' (vol. ii, p. cxxxvi). The
second is entirely unlike Donne in thought and style. He never takes up the plea to a mistress
to be more 'difficult'. Grierson argued from its context in manuscript and from ascription that
it should be assigned to Sir John Roe. Although none of the other poems attributed to Roe
has the charm of this song, I think Grierson's argument is sound; see vol. ii, pp. cxxix–cxxxv.
    [1] I heartily agree with Grierson in dismissing, without discussion, poems claimed for
Donne by nineteenth-century editors on such slender grounds as that they appear with his
in manuscript or are once or twice attributed to him, or echo his ideas.
    [2] It occurs in *S 96, O'F; Cy, O, P; B; S 962, HK 1*, and *Hd*.
    [3] The only other doubtful pieces in *JC*, 'Variety' and 'Sappho to Philaenis', occur at the
end of the manuscript. Apart from *JC*, 'Self-Love' is only found in *Lut, O'F*.
    [4] See Appendix B, 'Musical Settings of Donne's Poems', for the melody and for the words
of the second stanza. The poem may be inspired by Donne's poem, for the song that follows
it in *A Pilgrim's Solace* is a rewriting of Donne's 'Love's Infiniteness'.

same year it appeared by itself in Orlando Gibbons's *First Set of Madrigals*, set for five voices. No doubt this caused the stanza to become detached from its following stanza and to circulate alone. It is found as the first stanza of 'Break of Day' in *S 96* and in the margin of *A 25* it has been written against 'Break of Day' with a mark to show it should be the first stanza. From some such manuscript the corrector of the text of *1669* took it, not noticing that it is in a different metre from the metre of 'Break of Day' and is spoken by a man and not a woman. There is no reason whatever to suppose that Donne wrote this stanza which has merely become attached to his poem through likeness of theme. But since I can suggest no author I print it among the *Dubia*.

There are no early references to the *Songs and Sonnets*. Whereas Guilpin was certainly imitating the *Satires* in *Skialetheia* (1598) and Hall was very probably glancing at some of the *Elegies* in *Virgedemiarum* (1597) and Manningham quotes from 'The Storm' in 1602, no convincing parallels to the *Songs and Sonnets* have been pointed out in poems written before their appearance in print in 1633,[1] and the earliest quotation from one of them that has been noted is in a letter dated *c.* 1635.[2] As a writer of love-lyrics Donne is the master of the Carolines, not of the Jacobeans. Three of the *Songs and Sonnets* found their way into print before 1633 because they had been set to music.[3] Apart from this and Drummond's note that he had read a book of 'Jhone Done's lyriques'[4] in 1613, there is only the evidence of the numerous manuscript copies to suggest that the lyrics of the author of the much admired *Satires* were admired and valued by his contemporaries. Even here, the earliest date found on any manuscript is 1620[5] and, contrary to a common impression, the *Songs and Sonnets* do not very often appear singly in manuscript miscellanies, a good test of a poem being in general circulation. I think that Professor Milgate

---

[1] A possible exception is suggested in my note on 'The Curse', where a parallel in Marston's *The Scourge of Villainy*, 1599, is pointed out.

[2] For references here and throughout this paragraph, see Keynes, pp. 233–6, based on articles by W. Milgate in *Notes and Queries*, 1950 and 1953.

[3] See Appendix B, 'Musical Settings of Donne's Poems'.

[4] Even this may merely refer to the book containing poems by Donne and others that was lent to Drummond by Donne and copied in the Hawthornden manuscript (*HN*). Only one of the *Songs and Sonnets*, 'The Triple Fool', is found there.

[5] *S* is dated 19 July 1620 and *JC* opens with a poem by John Cave dated 3 June 1620. *P* has a note of ownership dated 1623. The only other dated manuscript is *O'F*, dated 12 October 1632.

was right to suggest that we should ascribe the lack of evidence for any general early circulation of the *Songs and Sonnets* to deliberate policy on the part of their author. They were not written for publication and Donne may well have thought that their free circulation would be unlikely to enhance his reputation as a serious person. His comment on his 'fault' in allowing even such solemn and weighty poems as the two *Anniversaries* to be printed[1] suggests that a man ambitious for a public career would wish to keep poems that so boldly flout all social values not merely from being printed but from being read by any but close friends. It is surely significant that the circulation of the *Elegies*, some of which are far more outrageous than any of the *Songs and Sonnets*, does not seem to have been similarly restricted. If I am right in placing the *Elegies* before 1597 when Donne became Egerton's secretary this is explicable. Young law-students are more anxious to gain a reputation for wit than for 'much gravitie'; but young men with a foot on the upward ladder need to be more careful. I would suggest that the *Elegies* got into circulation because at the time when he wrote them Donne had not embarked on a career, and that the lack of evidence for any wide circulation of the *Songs and Sonnets* points to their having been mainly written later when discretion had become advisable.

In spite of the fact that 1620 is the earliest date we find on any manuscript, copies must have been made and copied from long before then. The two manuscripts that are dated 1620 are, like the great majority of manuscripts, obviously at several removes from Donne's originals. Many of the best manuscripts are copies made by professional scribes who were probably copying from loose papers that had been in their owner's possession for years. This is suggested by the chaotic arrangement of many and, at the opposite extreme, the careful sorting by poetic kinds, irrespective of date of composition, that we find in others. Some manuscripts appear to represent the final stage of a process of accretion by which a 'book of Satires', a 'book of Elegies', and a 'Book' and some loose quires and loose

---

[1] Writing from Paris on 14 April 1612 to George Gerrard, Donne said: 'Of my Anniversaries, the fault that I acknowledge in my self, is to have descended to print anything in verse, which though it have excuse even in our times, by men who professe, and practise much gravitie; yet I confesse I wonder how I declined to it, and do not pardon my self.' (*Letters*, p. 238.)

sheets have been sorted and copied into a single volume. Although it seems improbable that there ever was a 'Book of Songs and Sonnets' comparable to the 'book of Satires' or 'book of Elegies', there is some evidence that sets of lyrics were copied, not as part of a general collection of Donne's poems but by themselves.[1] But, on the whole, an attempt to link poems by manuscript tradition is not possible. The evidence is inconclusive and the conclusions drawn too speculative to be employed in argument.[2] It is sounder to work from the poems themselves.

There are two objective criteria by which we can classify the *Songs and Sonnets*. We can group them on the basis of the kind of relation between a man and a woman that they assume, and we can group them by metrical form. On the first basis the poems can be clearly divided into three main groups. In the first we are in the world of the *Elegies*, the world of Latin love-poetry. By no means all the poems in this group can be called cynical, although many are. But all are untouched by the idealization of woman as the 'lady' who may command and deny as she chooses and by the sentiment of man's love as 'all made of sighs and tears'. And all, even the most tender and heartfelt, are unconcerned with the conception of love as a mystical union by which two become one. In all these poems one is aware of the dominance of the masculine partner who, if his mistress denies him what he wants, bullies or abuses her.

Twenty-three of the fifty-four *Songs and Sonnets* fall under this large general heading. We may distinguish among them various situations. In six there is no situation and we may call them cynical generalizations: 'Goe, and catche a falling starre', declaring that no woman is 'true and faire'; 'Community', arguing for male promiscuity; 'Confined Love', spoken by a woman demanding similar freedom; 'The Indifferent', although this is spoken to a particular woman; 'Love's Usury', addressed to the God of Love and claiming freedom to range while young; 'Love's Diet', boasting of how to

[1] Three extant manuscripts preserve small collections that are almost wholly collections of lyrics. *H 40* has a collection of forty-five poems of which all but five are Donne's, thirty-four being lyrics. *HK 2* contains forty poems by Donne in sequence, thirty-nine being lyrics. *L 74* contains a sequence of thirty-four poems, of which all but three are by Donne, twenty-five being lyrics.

[2] For a discussion of Grierson's attempt to connect five poems linked by manuscript tradition with Mrs. Herbert, see Appendix C, 'Lady Bedford and Mrs. Herbert'.

keep free. In all these poems it is taken for granted that women are willing but not constant; but this is no matter for grief since man is not constant either. The same attitude is embodied in the dramatic monologue 'Woman's Constancy' in which it is assumed that the woman will certainly be false, but the man does not care because most probably he will be false too. In three poems the mistress is false, but the lover reproaches her. He is her superior by virtue of his greater truth. These are 'A Jet Ring Sent', 'The Message', and 'The Legacy', the last employing the conceit familiar in sonneteers of an exchange of hearts. In one poem, 'The Apparition', the mistress has scorned him, but her refusal is not because of her chastity; she is only a 'fain'd vestall'. Four poems are persuasions to a mistress to yield or arguments against honour: 'The Prohibition', 'The Damp', 'The Flea', and 'The Dream'. The last two are fully dramatized monologues. Three other poems may be described as incidental to love affairs: 'The Bait', a cynical compliment, parodying Marlowe; 'The Curse', using the classical *Dirae* to attack that bugbear of the medieval lover, the tale-bearer; and 'The Computation', a clever reduction of the common cry 'It seems ages since I saw you' to arithmetical precision. These eighteen poems are untouched by the sentiment of courtly or chivalric love and read no lectures in 'love's philosophy'. On the same grounds I would place under this heading five poems on the parting of lovers who, it is implied, have enjoyed together the 'sweets of love': 'Break of Day', spoken by the woman; 'The Expiration'; 'Witchcraft by a Picture'; the song 'Sweetest Love, I do not goe'; and 'The Valediction of Weeping'. These five poems assume a passionate relation that is serious and whole-hearted on both sides; but, like two of the *Elegies* ('His Picture' and 'On his Mistress') they treat it passionately and unphilosophically.[1]

A second, smaller group consists of poems of unrequited love. Here the mistress refuses. She is the 'lady' who has the upper hand, while her lover is condemned to sigh and burn. She is 'too true' to love him, would indeed be 'false' if she were to do so, or she is 'cruel'; but it is not implied that she is feigning chastity and is cold

---

[1] Questions of style are, for the moment, deferred. This classification is strictly on grounds of the relation presumed.

merely to him. In this group come ten poems: 'The Paradox', 'Love's Exchange', 'Love's Deity' (where initial revolt turns to submission), 'The Broken Heart', 'The Triple Fool', 'The Will', 'Image and Dream', 'Twickenham Garden', 'The Blossom', and 'The Funeral'. For all their variety ('The Blossom' being touched by cynicism about the lady's virtue, 'The Will' by bitterness against her neglect of Love as well as of her lover, and 'Image and Dream', on the contrary being highly idealistic), they are alike in that they all treat the situation of the lover who does not 'speed'. Wholly un-Petrarchan as they are in mood, tone, and style, they handle the classic Petrarchan situation, some fully accepting the Petrarchan concept of the lady who is 'too true to be kind'.

The third group consists of poems of mutual love, in which there is no question of falseness on either side or of frustration by either lover of the other's desire. These are poems that treat of love as union, and of love as miracle, something that is outside the natural order of things. As a pendant to this group are three poems that reject such a concept explicitly and one that lightly declares that Love is an unknowable mystery. Two poems of this group are 'Platonic', in the limited colloquial sense that they deal with a love that is wholly spiritual: 'The Undertaking' and 'The Relic'. Four may be called celebrations of union: 'The Good-Morrow', 'The Anniversary', 'The Sun Rising', and 'The Canonization'. Four are analyses of love as union: 'Air and Angels', 'Love's Growth', 'Love's Infiniteness', and 'A Lecture on the Shadow'. One, 'The Ecstasy', is a narrative of a rare experience, the attainment of complete union of souls outside the body. Three are valedictions, philosophizing on the nature of the union of lovers in absence: 'A Valediction: forbidding Mourning', 'A Valediction: of my Name in the Window', 'A Valediction: of the Book'. Two, 'A Nocturnal' and 'The Dissolution', treat of the ending of such a union by death. One, 'A Fever', is on a mistress's sickness. Of the four poems that depend on this group, two ('Love's Alchemy' and 'Farewell to Love') are bitter palinodes, rejecting the idea that there is 'some Deitie in love'; the third ('The Primrose') is a curious inquiry into the nature of a 'true love' that entertains, even though it rejects, the idea of a woman being 'above all thought of sexe'; and the fourth ('Negative Love') is a light-hearted treatment of the theme that a perfect lover does not know what it is that he loves. I should have liked to call these poems 'Platonic', as I have called the last group 'Petrarchan', and with the same proviso, that they are very far from Plato as the last group are very far from Petrarch. But since in common usage 'Platonic Love' is taken to mean not the fundamental Neoplatonic conception of love as union but the more limited conception of love as a union that is purely spiritual, I will call them 'philosophic'; but with the proviso that I do not intend by this to suggest that they were written to expound a philosophy of love.

In spite of the remarkable variety of stanza forms in the *Songs and Sonnets* the poems can be roughly divided metrically on two grounds: the number of lines to a stanza and the amount of variety in length of line within the stanza. Taking first the twenty-one 'philosophic' lyrics, we find that four are in quatrains: 'The Undertaking', 'The Ecstasy', 'A Fever', and 'A Valediction: forbidding Mourning'.[1] A fifth ('Negative Love') is a song in two stanzas of nine octosyllabic lines. The remaining sixteen poems, with two exceptions, are in long stanzas ranging from nine to fourteen lines, with one poem ('The Dissolution') in a complex single stanza of twenty-four lines. The metrical norm of all these stanzas is a decasyllabic line; but they make considerable use of short lines, of as few as four syllables, and of extended lines, of twelve to fourteen. The two exceptions to this statement are 'The Good-Morrow', which is in a seven-line stanza, and 'A Valediction: of my Name in the Window', which is in a stanza of six lines. But the first extends the last line of each stanza to an alexandrine, and the second is a very long poem and its stanza, though short, has the variety in length of line characteristic of the group as a whole.[2]

To turn to the twenty-three poems that are neither 'Petrarchan' nor 'philosophic', seven are songs. Six of these have as their norm a line of seven or eight syllables,[3] the seventh ('Confined Love') is

---

[1] These are the only poems in quatrains in the *Songs and Sonnets*, with the exception of 'The Bait' whose form was dictated by the poem it parodied.

[2] Its sixty-six lines are only surpassed by the seventy-six of 'The Ecstasy' and rivalled by the sixty-three of 'A Valediction: of the Book', both poems in this group. Its syllabic pattern is 6, 10, 8, 8, 10, 8.

[3] 'Goe and catche a falling starre' (7, 7, 7, 7, 8, 8, 2, 2, 7), 'The Message' (8, 8, 7, 4, 4, 3, 3, 8), 'Sweetest Love, I do not goe' (7, 6, 7, 7, 4, 6, 6, 6), 'The Bait' (two octosyllabic couplets), 'Community' (three octosyllabic couplets), 'Break of Day' (8, 8, 8, 8, 10, 10).

very difficult to scan and runs by stress without much regard for syllable.[1] Two brief poems may be called epigrams: 'The Computation', in five decasyllabic couplets, and 'The Expiration' in two stanzas of six decasyllabic lines. Two other epigrammatic pieces are a little more adventurous metrically: 'A Jet Ring Sent' and 'Witchcraft by a Picture'.[2] 'The Prohibition' may also be classed as an epigram, particularly if we are to credit Donne with the first two stanzas only and Sir Thomas Roe with supplying a third to solve the problem posed by the first two.[3] Here an initial line of six syllables introduces seven decasyllabic lines. Two poems of this group are not in stanza form at all. The dramatic monologues 'Woman's Constancy' and 'The Apparition' are verse-paragraphs of seventeen lines rhyming irregularly and varying considerably from a decasyllabic norm. Of the nine poems that remain, six can be grouped under a common formula. They are in stanzas of moderate length (six to nine lines) which attempt to lighten the weight of a purely decasyllabic stanza, in one case by the use of two short lines, in the others by combining decasyllabics with octosyllabics.[4] They may be described as stanzas that attempt to give lightness to the natural rhythm of epigram or speech, the decasyllabic, or that attempt to give weight to the natural rhythm of song, the octosyllabic. We are left with three poems. Two, 'The Dream' (8, 8, 4, 10, 8, 10, 10, 10, 10, 10) and 'A Valediction: of Weeping' (4, 10, 10, 10, 4, 4, 10, 14) obviously belong metrically with the 'philosophic' lyrics; and we may now employ a more subjective test and say that they belong there by style and treatment as well as by stanza form. Although not concerned with the mysteries of union they bring to the persuasion against honour and the theme of the parting of lovers the subtlety that Donne brought to the theme of two becoming one and employ the same kind of elaborate conceit

---

[1] Syllabically the stanza is 10, 11 (12), 9 (10), 11, 6, 6, 7; but the rhythm is not that of a decasyllabic line.

[2] 'A Jet Ring Sent' (8, 10, 14, 10); 'Witchcraft by a Picture' (8, 10, 10, 6, 8, 10 and 8, 8, 8, 8, 10, 6, 8, 10).

[3] See Commentary, p. 162.

[4] The stanza of 'Love's Usury' is mainly decasyllabic (10, 4, 10, 10, 10, 10, 10, 4); 'Love's Diet' and 'The Curse' insert octosyllabic couplets into basically decasyllabic stanzas (10, 10, 8, 8, 10, 10 and 10, 10, 8, 8, 10, 10, 10); in 'The Damp' there are three octosyllabic lines in a mainly decasyllabic stanza (10, 8, 10, 10, 8, 8, 10, 10); in 'The Legacy' (8, 8, 8, 10, 8, 10, 10, 10) and 'The Flea' (8, 10, 8, 10, 8, 10, 8, 10, 10) the decasyllabic line only establishes itself as the dominant line at the close of the stanza.

that we find in the poems on 'love's philosophy'. The same cannot be said of 'The Indifferent'. This is a most interesting poem metrically and song rhythms plainly lie behind it.[1] In spite of the length of its two stanzas and the fact that, unlike any other poems in its group, it extends the decasyllabic, in style and treatment it stands wholly apart from the 'philosophic' poems.

The remaining ten 'Petrarchan' poems divide into types characteristic of the other two groups. 'The Funeral' and 'The Blossom' belong metrically with the 'philosophic' lyrics,[2] and the metrical monotony of 'Image and Dream', a poem in twenty-six unvaryingly decasyllabic lines, relates it to the four poems in quatrains among the 'philosophic' lyrics where, on grounds of subtlety of thought, it plainly belongs. 'The Paradox', on the other hand, is of the epigrammatic kind, twenty lines of alternating ten and six syllables, and 'Love's Deity', 'Love's Exchange', 'The Broken Heart', and 'Twickenham Garden' are in stanzas of the type that combines octosyllabics with decasyllabics.[3] Two poems resist easy classification. 'The Will' is in a nine-line stanza which extends its last line to a fourteener and has two octosyllabic lines intruded into its decasyllabic base. 'The Triple Fool' is in a long stanza with considerable variety in length of line,[4] but it does not extend any line beyond the limit of the decasyllabic, and in thought and style it has nothing in common with the poems of the 'philosophic' group.

Two things emerge from this classification of the *Songs and Sonnets*: apart from 'Negative Love', there are no 'philosophic' poems in the form of song or epigram, and there are none in the stanzas that are made up of a combination of decasyllabic with octosyllabic lines. On the other hand, there are a few poems that cannot be classed as 'philosophic' or 'Platonic' that are in the kind of stanza that Donne used for the theme of lovers' union. We have not arrived at a distinction between cynical and serious poems; but at a distinction between a simpler, and presumably earlier, and a more complex,

[1] It is in a nine-line stanza (7, 12, 12, 10, 8, 8, 10, 10, 10).
[2] The stanza of 'The Funeral' is 10, 4, 10, 10, 6, 10, 6, 14; that of 'The Blossom' is 6, 8, 10, 10, 10, 4, 10, 10.
[3] 'Love's Deity' (10, 10, 10, 10, 10 ,10, 8), 'Love's Exchange' (8, 10, 8, 10, 8, 8, 10), 'The Broken Heart' (8, 8, 8, 10, 8, 8, 10, 10), and 'Twickenham Garden' (10, 8, 8, 10, 8, 10, 8, 10, 10).
[4] The stanza of 'The Triple Fool' is 6, 8, 6, 10, 6, 10, 10, 8, 10, 10, 10.

and presumably later, conception of lyric form and style. It seems
clear that the development of this later style is connected with the
appearance of a new theme, since there are no poems that treat Neoplatonic themes in the earlier manner. On the other hand, it is
striking that some of the clearest expressions of Neoplatonic conceptions are to be found in poems written in the simplest verse-
forms: 'The Undertaking' and 'The Ecstasy' in quatrains, and 'Image
and Dream' in unvarying decasyllables. I would suggest that we
should think of the *Songs and Sonnets* as falling into two distinct sets
of poems: those written before Donne became attracted by Neoplatonic conceptions, and those which show the influence of Neo-
platonism or are written in forms that he appears to have developed
to express these subtleties. The poems that are least interesting
metrically are probably the earliest of the later set. Two of them
'Image and Dream' and 'The Ecstasy' can be shown to be closely
dependent on a Neoplatonic source, and mark, I would suggest, the
beginning of a fresh impulse to write lyrics. This led to the creation
of verse-forms of great originality in which new themes found
appropriate expression and old themes when taken up again
received a completely new expression.

The *Songs and Sonnets* thus divided find a natural place in Donne's
works. A great many of these can be dated with absolute certainty;
for others there are *termini*, and for others dates can be proposed
with a high degree of probability. There are two periods of very
considerable literary activity: the period before 1598 and the period
from 1607 to 1614. By 1598 Donne had certainly written the five
Satires, the 'Epithalamium made at Lincoln's Inn', 'The Storm', and
'The Calm', a number of short Verse-Letters and three more substantial letters to Wotton. I have argued the probability that the
Elegies belong to this period and we should also probably place there
the *Paradoxes*. There is nothing in these works to suggest any
particularly recondite reading. Donne's masters at this period were
the Roman poets, Horace, Ovid, and Martial. The poems are distinguished by their energy, wit, and realistic observation. It was
not from the poems of this period that Johnson drew examples of
far-fetched conceits. In the years between 1607 and 1614 we can
date with certainty a number of Funeral Poems (including the two

Anniversaries), two Epithalamiums, many elaborate Verse-Letters (to Lady Bedford, Sir Edward Herbert, Lady Carey and Mrs. Essex Rich, and the Countess of Salisbury), 'Annunciation and Passion' and 'Good Friday', and two prose works, *Pseudo-Martyr* and *Ignatius His Conclave*. I have argued elsewhere for dating 'La Corona' in 1607, 'A Litany' in 1608 and sixteen of the 'Holy Sonnets' in 1609,[1] and Mrs. Simpson would place *Biathanatos* in 1608. The impression made by this very considerable body of work is of the author's theological concerns. The poetry of the period from 1607 to 1614 is the poetry of a man whose mind is soaked in theological conceptions.

The empty period in Donne's literary career is from 1599 to 1607. Apart from the Verse-Letter to Wotton on his appointment to Venice in 1604, there is only one poem that can be dated with certainty in these years, 'The Progress of the Soul' whose dedication is dated August 1601. The man who wrote this poem had intellectual interests very different from those of the author of the *Satires* and the *Elegies*. He had been reading more curious authors than Horace, Ovid, and Martial. I find it hard to believe that a man whose mind was filled with these concerns and who had set himself so ambitious a task as this poem launches out on[2] was, at the same time, writing love-lyrics. I would therefore place the composition of the earlier *Songs and Sonnets* before the conception and composition of 'The Progress of the Soul', that is before 1600. At the close of 1601 Donne married, and by his marriage wrecked his career. From 1602 to 1605, when he moved to Mitcham, took a lodging in the Strand and began to devil for Morton, he was living with his wife at Pyrford, dependent on the charity of her cousin, Sir Francis Wooley. How did he employ himself in these years? He had only too much leisure for reading and writing: but there was no purpose, other than a personal one, that reading or writing could serve.

---

[1] See Gardner, *Divine Poems*.

[2] Very little work has been done on 'The Progress of the Soul', and understanding of the poem has been much confused by the suggestion that it is an attack on Queen Elizabeth, is concerned in some way with the fall of Essex, and that the soul of the apple was to end in Elizabeth's body. The dedication ends with the promise to relate all the adventures of the soul 'to this time when shee is hee whose life you shall finde in the end of this booke'. The first edition and all the manuscripts, except *O'F*, agree in reading 'shee is hee'. The reading 'shee is shee', which the second edition took from *O'F*, is a characteristic sophistication in that much 'edited' manuscript. A beginning of an attempt to study the poem in relation to its sources has been made by W. A. Murray in 'What was the Soul of the Apple', *R.E.S.*, 1959, x (N.S.), 141–55.

I would suggest that these are the years when Donne had leisure
to read widely and unprofessionally in the authors whose works
he mocked at in the satirical *Catalogus Librorum* and drew on so
extensively in the *Essays in Divinity*,[1] the Italian Cabbalists and
Neoplatonists. After 1605 he was more and more occupied with the
extensive reading that lies behind *Pseudo-Martyr* and that has as its
sometimes tiresome, but more often splendid, by-product the poems
that he wrote between 1607 and 1614. At Pyrford he had no
professional concerns. He could read as he chose and write *con amore*.
It is in these years that we should expect to find Donne reading for
no other end than to satisfy his curiosity and writing works for
which we can suggest no ulterior purpose. It is in these years that
I would place the majority of the later *Songs and Sonnets*.

A certain number of the *Songs and Sonnets* must be dated after 1600
for other reasons than their theme, style, or metrical originality.
'The Sun Rising' must, as Professor Praz pointed out many years
ago, be dated after the accession of James I from its patent reference
to that monarch's habit of rising early to follow his favourite
sport of hunting. He also argued that 'The Canonization', with its
reference to 'the Kings reall, or his stamped face', must surely have
been written when a king was on the throne. On the same ground I
would suggest, but with less conviction, that 'Farewell to Love',
where the child's gingerbread fairing is in the form of 'His highnesse
sitting in a golden Chaire' possibly refers to the image of the reigning
monarch.[2] 'The Anniversary' is so close in theme and phrase to 'The
Sun Rising' that the opening reference to 'All Kings and all their
favourites' takes on a topical colour. In all these references a tone of

---

[1] The *Catalogus Librorum* (edited by E. M. Simpson, 1930) was written after 1603, since
there is a gibe about the royal hounds in the introduction, and before 1611, when Donne in
a Latin letter to Goodyer, written on the eve of his journey to France, asks him to return
his 'epigrammata Latina, et Catalogus librorum satyricus' in order that he may revise them.
Mrs. Simpson would date the *Catalogus* in its original form in 1604–5. The date of the *Essays
in Divinity* is uncertain. Mrs. Simpson would place it just before the *Anniversaries* in 1611.
In its present form it cannot have been written much earlier since it cites books published in
1609. It is possible, however, that the *Essays* as we have them represent a working over of
earlier material, for the reading that lies behind them is quite unlike the reading that Donne
did for Morton. It is highly speculative and unorthodox: cabbalistic, neo-Pythagorean,
rabbinical, and Neoplatonic. Two authors specially singled out for praise are Pico and Franciscus Georgius, whose speculations on Genesis, embodied in the former's *Heptaplus*, and in
the latter's *Harmonia Mundi* (of which Donne possessed a copy) his Commentary on Genesis
and his *Problemata in Sacris Scripturis* (a title that Donne might have given to his *Essays*)
are a mine of unorthodox speculations, blending Greek and Jewish with Christian conceptions.

[2] See Commentary, p. 213, for a note on gingerbread fairings.

contempt can be heard. A characteristic of the poems that Donne
wrote on the union of lovers is that the old Ovidian distinction
between *negotium* and *otium* is expressed with a religious fervour.
The values of love are set over against the values of the court and
the world. The *contemptus mundi* that rings through these poems is
surely connected with Donne's situation from 1602 to 1605. Exiled
from affairs he consoles himself by scorning the world. This exalted
contempt for mere kings and princes is quite different from the
flouting of conventional moral standards that we find in the *Elegies*
and in many of the *Songs and Sonnets* that I would place earlier. It is
also quite different from the attitude towards worldly success and
the court which finds expression in 'A Litany'.[1] Two poems can be
dated by allusions: 'The Undertaking' after 1599, when Pancirolli's
Rerum Memorabilium Libri Duo was published, and 'A Valediction:
of the Book' after 1602, the date of Lipsius's *De Bibliothecis Syntagma*.[2]
If I am right in connecting 'The Ecstasy' possibly, and 'The Primrose' very probably, with Sir Edward Herbert they must be dated
well after 1600, for Edward Herbert was eleven years Donne's junior
and in 1600 was a youth of seventeen still at the University. Again,
if 'Twickenham Garden' and 'A Nocturnal' are connected with each
other and with Lady Bedford, they must have been written after
1607 when she went to live at Twickenham.[3]

    While not wishing to claim that it is possible to place every lyric
with an equal degree of confidence before or after the composition of
'The Progress of the Soul', I put forward as a workable hypothesis
the following summary account of the composition of the *Songs and
Sonnets*. At a time when he was writing the *Elegies*, Donne also wrote
a certain number of lyrics, 'songs which were made to certain ayres
which were made before' and love-epigrams inspired by one of his
favourite poets, Martial. He probably also wrote a certain number
of lyrics that are neither songs nor epigrams on themes arising out
of the *Elegies*, such as 'The Curse'.[4] Probably a little later, perhaps
at the same time as he had himself painted as 'Inamorato', with

---

[1] Cf. Stanzas XV and XVIII.
[2] See Commentary, pp. 179–80 and 192–3.
[3] See Appendix C, 'Lady Bedford and Mrs. Herbert', for discussion of these last four poems.
[4] 'The Curse' twice appears as a solitary lyric in manuscript, once with the *Satires*, 'The
Storm' and 'The Calm' (Queen's College, Oxford, MS.) and once with 'The Bracelet' (among
a miscellaneous collection of poems in *HK* 1).

'folded arms and melancholy hat', he wrote a certain number of lyrics on themes handled in the fashionable contemporary sonnet sequences. The form he mainly used was a stanza combining octo-syllabic and decasyllabic lines; all the poems that are addressed to the God of Love are in stanzas of this type. He also wrote two poems which experiment in longer and less regular stanzas ('The Triple Fool' and 'The Indifferent') and two dramatic monologues in verse-paragraphs. These last may be described as attempts to treat the kind of situation he treats in the *Elegies* with more concentration and dramatic feeling than the use of a regular form, such as couplets, allows. I would place 'The Will' at the close of this period, a very highly wrought poem, which is, with 'The Apparition' and 'The Flea', one of the masterpieces of Donne's earlier manner.[1] If Donne had died in 1600 with only the *Elegies* and these lyrics to his credit, he would still have been a remarkable love-poet. But it might have been said that he had not succeeded in uniting in a single poem his two most striking gifts: his sense of drama, as shown in some of the *Elegies*, or 'The Flea', and his power of song, as shown in 'Goe and catche a falling starre', or 'Sweetest Love, I doe not goe'.

Towards the end of the century Donne began to read cabbalistic authors, and the author of the *Satires*, now secretary to the Lord Keeper, embarked on the ambitious project of a long poem. The dedication and epistle and the fact that 'The Progress of the Soul' is extant as a single work, occupying complete manuscripts, suggest that Donne had even contemplated publication of his 'First Song', or 'Canto'. However this may be, its author's preoccupations are clear. It is a learned and obscure work, a 'sullen writ', and, except for the two *Anniversaries*, Donne's only attempt at a long poem. Four months after he wrote the dedication Donne married. In his enforced retirement he continued his remote reading and, having lost the world for love, was attracted in authors whose speculations had already fascinated him by a theory of love radically different

[1] I place 'The Will', in spite of its metrical form, with the earlier group because its con-sistently satirical tone sets it apart from the later group and relates it to Donne the satirist. Similarly, I place 'Twickenham Garden' among the later poems, and would do so even if there were no question of its connexion with Lady Bedford. Although it is in a stanza characteristic of the earlier poems, it handles it with so much more weight that the effect is quite different from the effect of such poems as 'The Broken Heart' or 'Love's Exchange'. It has also patent connexions with 'A Nocturnal'.

from the naturalistic view that had been the basis of much of his earlier love poetry and from the Petrarchan idealization of frustration. Inspired by this, and I would add by his own experience as well as by his isolation from the world and its concerns, he began to write love poems again, at first dominated by these new ideas, but developing into highly original lyrics which combine dramatic feeling and the vigour of speech with the music of song.

TEXTUAL INTRODUCTION

THE principles on which any editor of Donne's poems must proceed were established by Sir Herbert Grierson in his edition of 1912.
He made clear that the sole edition of authority was the first and
that no single manuscript provided a possible alternative to the
first edition as a base for a text. He demonstrated the dependence
of the first edition on manuscripts resembling those in two extant
groups and made clear the existence of distinct versions of certain
poems in manuscripts outside these two groups. In my edition of
the *Divine Poems* in 1952 I attempted to carry Grierson's analysis
further and to apply principles based on that analysis strictly. I
said there that, within a general theory of the transmission of
Donne's poems in manuscript, it was necessary to consider the
particular problems raised by different groups of poems. In the
discussion that follows the problems of the text of the *Elegies* and
the *Songs and Sonnets* are considered within a summary of the general
arguments set out in full in my textual introduction to the *Divine
Poems*. I have not described over again in detail manuscripts which
are dealt with fully there.

I. THE MANUSCRIPTS

Discussion of the text of Donne's poems must begin with the
manuscript copies that circulated before the appearance of the first
(posthumous) edition of 1633. The *Elegies* and *Songs and Sonnets* are
more common in manuscript collections than the *Divine Poems*; and
whereas the *Divine Poems* usually appear together as a set the number of Love Poems included varies considerably from manuscript to
manuscript. Some of the larger collections containing them appear
to be composite in origin, deriving one portion of their text from
one tradition and in the remainder following others. There are
indications of memorial corruption as well as signs of contamination.
It is possible that many fine manuscripts written by professional
scribes depend on copies made by amateurs of Donne's poetry who

wrote out poems they half knew by heart without checking as they wrote. In some of the extant manuscripts corrections and alternative readings are substituted in the text or written in the margin, the alternatives being often from another tradition than the one that the original writer was following. In others one must assume some such conflation of witnesses behind the text presented. But, in spite of these obstacles, collation can reduce the number of witnesses substantially.

No manuscript is extant containing solely the *Elegies* or solely the *Songs and Sonnets.* They are found either in manuscripts containing collections of Donne's poems, or as separate items scattered among other men's poems in commonplace books or miscellanies. For a student of Donne's reputation manuscript miscellanies are of interest. For an editor they are, in my experience, worthless. The texts they preserve are more or less corrupt examples of one or other of the traditions represented in the manuscript collections. I began with the intention of collating all extant manuscript copies; but I abandoned the enterprise as wholly unrewarding, and have contented myself with collating the text in the manuscript collections, among which three groups can be distinguished.

i

Group I contains five manuscripts: C 57 (Cambridge University Library, Add. MS. 5778), D (Dowden), H 49 (Harley 4955), *Lec* (Leconfield), SP (St. Paul's). They contain the same collection of poems in mainly the same order. This, with their common errors, establishes their descent from an exclusive common ancestor, X. The descent of the five extant manuscripts of Group I from X can fortunately be determined with certainty and expressed by the following stemma.

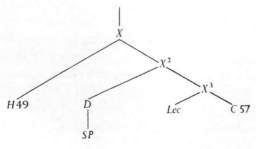

All the poems that X contained are unquestionably canonical. It included no poems that we can date after 1614 and a very limited number of Verse-Letters, a mere selection, with one exception, from those written to persons of rank. I have suggested that it might be a copy of the collection that Donne himself was putting together in 1614 when he was considering publishing his poems. However this may be, X itself was at a remove from Donne's own copies. It bequeathed a number of errors to its five extant descendants to which each added errors of its own.[1]

Of the poems included in this volume the Group I manuscripts contain thirteen of the fourteen Elegies (lacking 'The Comparison'), 'The Autumnal', which occurs among the *Songs and Sonnets*, and forty-five of the fifty-four lyrics.[2] The Elegies are collected together in the same order in all five manuscripts and include the 'Funeral Elegy'. The forty-five lyrics similarly occur together and in the same order in all five manuscripts, except that in *H 49* the final four ('The Blossom', 'The Primrose', 'The Relic', 'The Damp') are separated from the rest by three unrelated poems.

Although it cannot be classed as a manuscript of Group I, since it does not descend from X, another manuscript, *H 40* (Harley 4064), must be discussed here. There is a close textual connexion between the collection of lyrics in the manuscripts of Group I and a collection whose existence we can deduce from comparing *H 40* with another manuscript, *RP 31* (Rawlinson Poetical 31).[3] The two manuscripts have fifty poems in common which occur in the same order in both and form a miscellany of poems by Harington, Wotton, Campion, Jonson, Beaumont, and others, with seven poems by Donne and two of the doubtful Elegies. At various points in the run of poems the two manuscripts share *RP 31* has inserted twenty-three other poems, only two of which are Donne's. The additions that *H 40* makes to the common stock are far more interest-

---

[1] For full descriptions of the manuscripts of Group I and their relation to X, see Gardner, *Divine Poems*, pp. lvii–lxi. For an analysis of their make-up, see Margaret Crum, 'Notes on the Physical Characteristics of Some Manuscripts of the Poems of Donne and of Henry King', *The Library*, June 1961.
[2] *C 57* and *Lec* omit 'The Prohibition', present in the other three, and so have only forty-four. The nine lyrics missing in all five are 'A Nocturnal', 'The Dissolution', and 'Farewell to Love', and six love-epigrams: 'Witchcraft by a Picture', 'A Jet Ring Sent', 'Negative Love', 'The Expiration', 'The Computation', and The Paradox'.
[3] The connexion was noted by Grierson (vol. ii, pp. ciii–civ).

ing.[1] Forty-four poems have been added at various points, a few singly but mostly in batches; all but five are by Donne, and of these thirty-four are lyrics.[2]

The manner in which these thirty-four lyrics occur suggests that the copyist was working from a collection on quires and loose sheets that had been slipped between the pages of a volume containing the miscellany that *H 40*★ shares with *RP 31*. Comparison between *H 40* and the manuscripts of Group I suggests strongly that the copyist of *X* was working from the same collection.[3] All the thirty-four lyrics of *H 40* are found in the manuscripts of Group I.[4] *H 40* lacks the first poem in Group I ('The Message') and the last five ('The Funeral', 'The Blossom', 'The Primrose', 'The Relic', 'The Damp'). The five preceding these in Group I occur, in the same order, as the last batch in *H 40*, and three of the other four missing poems ('The Sun-Rising', 'Love's Growth', 'Confined Love', 'The Dream') occur in close proximity in Group I.[5] It would seem that the copyist of *X* had some extra quires and a loose sheet or two to work from. In the text they preserve the two collections agree closely. With the exception of one poem, 'The Flea', in which the manuscripts of Group I preserve a distinct text, *H 40* reads consistently with Group I. Only eleven of the poems in *H 40* have titles and these agree with the titles of these poems in Group I. Twenty of the remaining twenty-three poems they have in common are without titles in both collections. Except for a *lacuna* in 'Twickenham Garden', *H 40* is free of the distinctive Group I errors and cannot therefore descend from *X*. It presents an excellent text, remarkably free from individual errors, though it has enough of these for us to be unable to place it above *X* in the line of descent.

H 40 is thus an important manuscript since it provides a check

---

[1] As the manuscript is clearly composite, I distinguish in my list of *Sigla* between *H 40*, the Donne collection, and *H 40*★, the miscellany that is found also in *RP 31*.

[2] The five non-lyrical poems by Donne are 'The Autumnal', which occurs among the lyrics in the Group I manuscripts, and two Verse-Letters and two Epicedes which are present in the Group I manuscripts.

[3] Miss Crum deduced from her study of the manuscripts of Group I that the copyist of *X* was working from poems on quires and loose sheets, presumably the author's papers.

[4] Of the eleven poems present in Group I but missing in the collection in *H 40*, one ('The Prohibition') is one of the three lyrics common to *H 40*★ and *RP 31*. We cannot therefore judge whether it was or was not among the extra poems available to the copyist of *H 40*.

[5] The Group I manuscripts have in a run 'Love's Growth', 'Love's Exchange', 'Confined Love', and 'The Dream'.

on the Group I tradition in thirty-four of the *Songs and Sonnets*. When *H 40* does not support Group I against the other manuscripts we must normally presume that Group I is following an error in *X*. Since, as Grierson first pointed out, the greater part of the edition of 1633 was based on a manuscript of Group I a check on this tradition is of great value.

ii

Group II contains four manuscripts: *A 18* (British Museum Add. MS. 18467), *N* (Norton), *TCC* (Trinity College, Cambridge), and *TCD* (Trinity College, Dublin). *A 18* is a copy of *TCC* and *N* is a copy of *TCD*. *TCD* is a slightly expanded and at times better arranged version of the collection found in *TCC*. Since it has a rather better text it cannot descend from *TCC*, but must be an expansion of a large collection of Donne's works on which they both depend. This collection I call *Υ*.[1]

Υ must have been put together in its final form after 1625, since it contained the Hamilton Elegy. Unlike *X*, the collection in Group I, it included, as well as poems written after 1614, a great many Verse-Letters and the prose *Paradoxes and Problems*. But, like *X*, it was made by someone who knew well how to distinguish Donne's poems from those by other wits. Apart from the sixth Satire ('Sleep, next Society'), which is initialed 'J.R.', and 'Sappho to Philaenis', whose authenticity I doubt, only one poem in the collection common to both manuscripts (a short lyric, 'Whoso terms love a fire') is not accepted as canonical. The compiler made little attempt to group poems by kinds and the *Elegies* and *Songs and Sonnets* appear in groups or singly among a medley of Verse-Letters and Epicedes.[2]

Of the poems printed in this volume, *Υ* contained thirteen of the *Elegies*, 'The Autumnal', and fifty-one of the *Songs and Sonnets*. Like *X* it included none of the Elegies that I print here as of doubtful authenticity, but, unlike *X*, it included 'Sappho to Philaenis'.[3]

---

[1] *TCC* and its copy *A 18* lack the opening poems of *TCD*, *N*. Comparison with *L 74* supports the view that they stood in *Υ* and that *TCC* has lost some opening leaves.
[2] For fuller description of the manuscripts of Group II, see Gardner, *Divine Poems*, pp. lxvi–lxviii.
[3] The missing Elegy is the 'Funeral Elegy', the missing lyrics are 'Farewell to Love', 'Love's Usury', and 'Love's Infiniteness'. 'The Expostulation' occurs in *TCD* but is not in *TCC*, so cannot have been in *Υ*.

Comparison of *TCC* and *TCD* with another manuscript, *L 74* (Lansdowne 740)[1] suggests that the large collection in *Y* grew by accretion from a smaller one preserved in *L 74*. *L 74* is a composite manuscript of separate items bound together, one of which (ff. 58–136) is a collection of poems. Except for ff. 70–72, which are manifestly in a different hand, the whole section is the work of one writer; but he has left blanks between batches of poems, and the different inks and pens used, as well as differences in his writing, suggest that he copied the poems at different times.[2] The collection begins with four of the *Satires*, 'The Bracelet' and 'Satire 6', all unascribed. Another writer has then supplied the missing Satire (ff. 70–72). After blanks come Overbury's 'The Wife', five of Donne's Elegies (unascribed), 'The Autumnal' (with a marginal note 'Widow Her: J.D.') and a long poem in octosyllabics. After more blanks come three short scurrilous pieces, and then 'The Storm', 'The Calm', 'The Anagram', 'To Mr. Rowland Woodward', 'To Sir Henry Wotton' ('Here's no more newes'), 'Dear Love, continue nice and chaste', which ends 'Finis Sir John Roe',[3] and 'Confined Love'.[4] After a blank come two anonymous pieces, two ascribed to Sir Thomas Roe, Sir John Roe's two epistles to Ben Jonson (unascribed), and four Elegies by Sir John Roe, the first ascribed to him. Then comes 'The Legacy', ascribed 'J.D.', the first of a sequence of thirty-four poems of which all but three are by Donne, twenty-five being lyrics. If we take out from the first part of *L 74* the poems that are by Donne we find that, with the exception of three Elegies, for which two other Elegies are substituted, we have the opening poems of *TCD*.[5] Immediately after these the Group II manuscripts have twenty-seven

---

[1] See Grierson, vol. ii, pp. civ–cv.

[2] I have to thank Mr. T. C. Skeat for examining the manuscript for me.

[3] The last three poems were originally ascribed to Sir John Roe, but the writer has corrected the ascription of the first to 'J. Donne'.

[4] Ascribed 'J.D.' by a later hand which has also claimed for Donne two of the poems ascribed to Sir Thomas Roe.

[5] Omitting poems that are not by Donne we have the following sequence in *L 74*: *Satires* (3, 4, 5, 2), 'The Bracelet', 'Satire 6', 'Satire 1', 'The Comparison', 'The Perfume', 'Recusancy', 'Love's War', 'Going to Bed', 'The Autumnal', 'The Storm', 'The Calm', 'The Anagram', Letters to Woodward and Wotton. The sequence in Group II is: *Satires* (1, 3, 4, 5, 6, 2), 'The Bracelet', 'The Storm', 'The Calm', 'The Anagram' (*TCC* opens here), Letters to Woodward and Wotton, 'The Comparison', 'The Perfume', 'Change', 'Tutelage', 'The Autumnal'. Comparison with *L 74* makes it certain that the opening poems of *TCD* stood in *Y* and have been lost from *TCC*, since *TCC* opens in the middle of a run of poems common to *TCD* and *L 74*.

of the thirty-one poems by Donne that appear later on in *L 74*, with considerable correspondence in their order. In the text they preserve *L 74* and the Group II manuscripts agree very closely, but *L 74* is free from the distinctive Group II errors. Its text is very good.

The writer of *L 74* obviously intended an ascription to cover all the poems that followed until a fresh ascription was made. The thirty-four poems that begin with 'The Legacy' are presented as a 'Donne collection', and it is mainly a collection of lyrics.[1] Along with the mainly lyrical collection in *H 40*, this collection is evidence that Donne's lyrics were copied as a set of poems. The two collections have twenty-one poems in common.[2] When they are compared the most striking difference is that *L 74* lacks almost all the 'philosophic' lyrics. *L 74* agrees with *H 40* in its paucity of titles. Only four of its twenty-five lyrics are given titles,[3] three are titles found in *H 40*, the other ('Love's Will' for 'The Will') is a title that is not found elsewhere. A feature of the Group II manuscripts is that almost all the lyrics are given titles, and, as Grierson noted, the edition of *1633* adopted many of its titles from its Group II manuscript. Comparison with *L 74* suggests that we owe most of the titles of the edition to the compiler of *Y* rather than to the author of the poems.

As *H 40* provides a check on a portion of the tradition in the manuscripts of Group I, so *L 74* provides a check on a portion of the tradition in the manuscripts of Group II. The close connexion between *L 74* and the first part of *TCC*, *TCD* means that in discussing a 'Group II reading' we should distinguish between readings occurring in poems that *Y* shared with *L 74* and those occurring in poems that *Y* derived from some other source. *L 74* frequently reads against *H 40* and when it does we usually find Group II reading against Group I. When a poem is not present in *L 74* Groups I and

---

[1] The three unauthentic poems are Hoskyns's 'Absence, hear thou my protestation', Beaumont's verses to the Countess of Rutland, and the doubtful Elegy 'The Expostulation'. The non-lyrical poems are five poems connected with Lady Bedford (Epicedes on Lady Markham and Mrs. Bulstrode and Verse-Letters) and one Elegy, 'Recusancy'. These occur together, breaking the run of lyrics.

[2] Of the nine poems missing in both Group I and *H 40*, *L 74* has only one, 'The Paradox'. Of the eleven present in Group I but missing in *H 40*, *L 74* has three: 'The Funeral', 'The Sun Rising', and 'The Dream'.

[3] Titles from the edition of *1633* have been supplied by a later hand. Grierson's textual apparatus is misleading here since he cites titles from *L 74* as if they were original.

II normally read together. If we are considering the possibility of 'earlier or later versions' of poems, it is possible that Group II preserves 'earlier versions' in poems that it has in common with *L 74*, and 'later versions' in the poems that the compiler of *Y* added to make up his very full collection.

The relations of Groups I and II, *H 40* and *L 74* can be expressed by the following stemma.

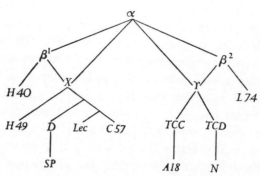

A manuscript unknown to me when I edited the *Divine Poems* has to be considered here, the Dolau Cothi manuscript (*DC*) in the National Library of Wales.[1] This contains a very full collection of Donne's poems, with no unauthentic pieces (except the doubtful 'Sappho to Philaenis') included, transcribed in one hand. There are no indications of the date at which it was written. It opens with '*La Corona*' and the first eight of the twelve 'Holy Sonnets' of 1633, followed by the letters to the Countess of Salisbury and to Lady Carey, 'Sappho to Philaenis', 'Image and Dream', and 'The Autumnal'. Then come ten Elegies ('The Comparison', 'Love's Progress', and 'Going to Bed' are missing), 'The Storm', 'The Calm', and the Epigrams. Fifty-one of the *Songs and Sonnets* appear next ('The Paradox' and 'Farewell to Love' are missing and 'Image and Dream' appears earlier). The Lincoln's Inn Epithalamium begins on page 106, but only four verses are extant. The manuscript has lost pages 109 to 124 which no doubt contained the other two Epithalamiums. The text begins again in the middle of the Elegy on Lady Markham which is followed by 'Death I recant' and the Elegy on Prince Henry.

[1] Reported to me by Mr. A. E. MacColl.

The end of this and the beginning of the Harington Elegy have again been lost. After these funeral poems come 'Good Friday', 'Annunciation and Passion', 'Resurrection', 'The Cross', and a long series of Verse-Letters. The collection ends with the 'Lamentations of Jeremy' and 'A Litany'. Apart from the rather strange absence of the *Satires* this is a remarkably complete collection.

In the order in which the poems are transcribed there is no contact with Group II until we reach the collection of Verse-Letters. This, with some small and mainly explicable differences, is identical with the collection of Verse-Letters in *TCD* and *N*.[1] There are other obvious connexions between *DC* and Group II, apart from the fact that it contains poems only otherwise found in Group II, *Lut* and *O'F*. The *Songs and Sonnets* have, with two exceptions, the Group II titles, and an interesting heading otherwise found only in Group II appears in *DC*. In the Group II manuscripts three of the *Songs and Sonnets* appear under the heading 'Songs which were made to certaine Aires which were made before', and *DC* has the same three songs, with three more in addition, under the same heading. In spite of these striking connexions it is not possible to explain *DC* as descended from a rearrangement of the rather chaotic collection in *T*. Its text varies greatly. In some poems, notably the Harington Elegy, its readings suggest that the copyist hardly understood English; in others it is good: but it is not consistently a Group II text. It shows very curious affinities with the text of the first edition of 1633 and must be discussed in considering the relation of the edition to the manuscripts.

iii

In my edition of the *Divine Poems* only six more manuscripts needed consideration: *B* (Bridgewater), *Dob* (Dobell), *Lut* (Luttrell), *O'F* (O'Flaherty), *S96* (Stowe 961) and *W* (Westmoreland). These, although not a group in the sense that they could be shown to depend on a common ancestor, formed a group in the sense that they agreed in preserving a tradition distinct from the tradition

---

[1] *TCD* and *N* expand the collection of Verse-Letters they share with *TCC* and *A18*. The differences between the collections in *TCD* and *DC* are that *TCD* includes the letter to the Countess of Salisbury that appears earlier in *DC* and *DC* includes two letters that appear earlier in *TCD*. In addition, *DC* includes the sonnet to 'E. of D.' which is not present in *TCD*.

preserved in Groups I and II.[1] An editor of Donne's love-poetry has
more manuscripts to deal with and they are more difficult to classify.
It is convenient to begin with *W* which stands apart from the others.

W is in the hand of Donne's friend Rowland Woodward.[2] But in
spite of being in one hand throughout, it falls clearly into three
parts. The first part is a collection of Donne's early poems: *Satires*,
Elegies, Verse-Letters addressed to men, and the 'Lincoln's Inn
Epithalamium'. It contains, with one explicable exception, no poem
we should date after 1598.[3] The second part contains '*La Corona*' and
all nineteen of the 'Holy Sonnets', both composed much later. The
third part contains the *Paradoxes and Problems*, the *Epigrams* and a
single lyric, 'A Jet Ring Sent'. *W* appears to be a fair copy of works
by Donne in the writer's possession. Like Group I, *W* has thirteen
of the fourteen *Elegies* I print together, including the 'Funeral Elegy'.
The order of the poems varies in the two sets and each set has one
that the other lacks. *W* includes 'The Comparison', missing in Group I,
but lacks 'Love's Progress'.[4] The text in *W* agrees substantially with
the text in Groups I and II. In almost all cases where these three
witnesses disagree the difference is trivial or one reading is plainly
erroneous. The fact that Groups I and II and *W* witness, with minor
individual aberrations, to the same text of the *Elegies* rules out, in my
opinion, the possibility that some of the variants in other manuscripts
represent Donne's earlier versions. Everything points to the first
section of *W* being an early collection. Here, if anywhere, we should
expect to find the text that circulated in the 1590's. Everything also
points to the copies in *W* being very close to Donne's own papers. *W*
contains familiar letters not found elsewhere; its text is very good,
and its extrinsic authority high.

I wish now to restrict the title of Group III to four manuscripts:[5]

---

[1] The fact that a distinct 'Group III text' appeared only in some poems, as well as the
nature of the variants, suggested that many of the different readings had arisen from alterations
made by the author rather than from scribal error. I agreed with Sir Herbert Grierson and
Mrs. Simpson in arguing that in the *Divine Poems* the manuscripts of Group III preserved
earlier authentic readings.

[2] Mr. MacColl, who has examined letters of Woodward, has convinced me of this.

[3] For a full description of *W*, see Gardner, *Divine Poems*, pp. lxxviii–lxxxi.

[4] The set of Elegies in *W*, in the order in which they appear there, is found also in *A 25*
and *JC*. The first poem of the set must have been missing in the exemplar of *A 25* as the set
begins with the second headed 'Elegya 2', and the last, the 'Funeral Elegy', is also missing.

[5] In editing the *Divine Poems* I included *B* and *S* in Group III. They read with Group III
in the *Divine Poems*, but read erratically elsewhere.

Dob (Dobell), *Lut* (Luttrell), *O'F* (O'Flaherty), *S 96* (Stowe 961).[1]
These are all large collections and they all include a certain number
of uncanonical poems. *Dob*, a beautiful and carefully written manuscript, is unique among collections of Donne's poetry in containing
not only the prose *Paradoxes and Problems* but also some of the *Sermons. S 96*, also elegantly written, contains only poetry. Both
manuscripts show some attempt to arrange poems by kinds. Both
are distinguished by containing poems rarely found elsewhere.[2]
There is little evidence of a common origin in the order in which
poems appear, but clear evidence in the text. *S 96* and, to an even
greater extent, *Dob* hardly ever present nonsense. Each has some
readings not found in any other manuscript that, if supported,
would be regarded as significant variants. But apart from these, and
the inevitable amount of minor variation, they show striking agreement. They preserve in many poems, along with what must be
regarded as individual sophistications, a distinct tradition, offering
readings that an editor is bound to consider against the readings of
Groups I and II. Of the fourteen *Elegies, Dob* lacks three and *S 96*
one; of the fifty-four *Songs and Sonnets, Dob* lacks seven and *S 96*
ten.

Lut, a well-written manuscript but less elegant than *Dob* and
S 96, was written after Donne's death, since it refers to his burial in
St. Paul's instead of in his wife's grave, and before its copy *O'F*, which
is dated 12 October 1632. The compiler of *Lut* was working from a
manuscript with a text resembling that in *Dob* and *S 96*; but he also
had access to a manuscript of Group II since *Lut* (and its copy *O'F*)
contain poems only found elsewhere in the manuscripts of Group II.
The writer of *Lut* was aware of textual difficulties. From time to
time he sets an alternative reading in the margin and at times he
has corrected his text. I suspect that at other times he has adopted
a reading from his second manuscript and that at other times he
has silently made 'improvements' of his own. The text of *Lut* is in
the main the text of *Dob* and *S 96*, but it is contaminated with the
text of Group II and on some occasions with the text in some other

---

[1] For fuller descriptions of these manuscripts, see Gardner, *Divine Poems*, pp. lxix–lxxiv.
[2] *Dob* contains 'To Mr. Tilman' and *S 96* contains 'Farewell to Love'. The only other
collection to contain either is *O'F. S 96* is the only collection to contain the 'Hymn to God
my God, in my sickness'.

manuscripts. The compiler of *Lut* arranged his poems fairly consistently under headings. The compiler of *O'F*, who was working
from *Lut*, carried out the arrangement of poems, under the same
headings, with complete consistency, added a few more poems and
the *Paradoxes and Problems*, and produced the fullest and best arranged
extant manuscript of Donne's works. If, as seems highly probable,
he was attempting to prepare copy for the press, he was anticipated
by the appearance of the edition of 1633. Two persons, one possibly
the original writer, went through *O'F* correcting many, but by no
means all, of its distinctive Group III readings to the readings of
1633.[1] But even before this was done *O'F*, like its parent *Lut*, was
an 'edited' manuscript.[2] In spite of their differences, however, *Dob*,
S 96, *Lut*, and *O'F* give joint witness to a third manuscript tradition.

Twenty-four poems and two six-line epigrams are collected
together in *Lut* under the heading 'Elegies'. They begin with 'The
Perfume' headed 'Elegye 2', after three pages left blank (presumably
for the missing 'Elegy 1'. 'The Perfume' is the third Elegy of the
set in *W*, and the first ten Elegies in *Lut* are the third to the twelfth
of *W*. *Lut* then proceeds with 'The Autumnal' and 'Love's Progress'.
These are followed by a medley of poems including (among six that
Grierson did not even think worthy to appear in an appendix) four
of the Elegies I print as of doubtful authenticity. At the close comes
'The Bracelet', the opening poem in the set of Elegies in *W*. Exactly
the same poems in the same order, but with 'The Comparison'
supplied as the missing 'Elegy 1', appear in *O'F*. The lyrics under
the heading 'Sonnetts and Songs' are collected together in *Lut* at
the end of the manuscript. Fifty-three are included, the missing
one being 'Farewell to Love'. Six brief lyrics that are not Donne's
are included. *O'F* has the same collection, but adds three more
uncanonical pieces and 'Farewell to Love'. It is important to establish the relations of *O'F* to other manuscripts since it was the main
source of the additional poems in the second edition of 1635 and

[1] The corrector was working from the edition and not from a manuscript of Group I,
since, on occasion he corrects to a reading only found in the edition. Thus, he corrects 'extract',
the reading of all extant manuscripts, to 'contract', the reading of *1633* in 'The Canonization'
(l. 40).

[2] The same is true, though to a less extent, of *Dob* and *S 96*. Both show occasional corrections, in the margin and in the text, that point to recourse to another manuscript.

of the corrections that the second edition makes in the poems it reprints from the first. O'F also provided the headings under which the poems were rearranged in the second edition.

iv

The next group that can be distinguished contains *Cy* (Carnaby), *O* (Osborn), and *P* (Phillipps).[1] *O* and *P*, unlike the manuscripts so far described, are pocket-size. *O* is very neatly written; *P*, which has the owner's name, 'Henry Champernowne' and the date '1623' on its first page, is not so neat. The two manuscripts contain, with trifling differences, the same large collection of poems with the *Paradoxes and Problems*. These last, like the *Satires* and some sequences of poems, are differently placed in the two manuscripts.[2] *O* and *P* share with extraordinary closeness a poor text and often read nonsense in unison. But they also agree in a good many superficially plausible readings against Groups I, II, and III. They include all fourteen *Elegies*; *O* has forty-four of the *Songs and Sonnets* and *P* forty-five. Many of the readings of *O* and *P*, including some patent errors, are found in *Cy*. This is a smaller collection, including only poems; but since the scribe broke off in the middle of a poem we cannot judge how large the collection that he was copying may have been. *Cy* lacks one of the *Elegies* and has only twenty-five of the lyrics. Its text is much less bad than that in *O* and *P*, and in the *Elegies* I suspect the writer was either correcting his text from a better manuscript or was copying a text that had been so corrected. But *Cy* reads far too often exclusively with *O* and *P* for their close relationship to be in doubt.

An editor has to decide whether, in spite of their manifest corruption, *Cy*, *O*, and *P* preserve readings worth consideration, either as witnessing to a fourth tradition to be weighed against the other three, or as preserving an alternative version. In the case of the *Songs and Sonnets* this question can be answered with some certainty. All three manuscripts can be shown to depend on a collection of the

[1] *Cy* and *P* were used by Grierson (see vol. ii, pp. c–ci) who noted the connexion between them. *O* was sold at Hodgson's, from the library of Major J. B. Whitmore, 21 November 1958. Its buyer, Mr. James Osborn, kindly deposited it in the Bodleian for me to collate.

[2] It looks as if they both descend directly from the same collection copied on 'books' or on loose quires and that each has sorted these differently.

Songs and Sonnets found in the second part of the Haslewood-Kingsborough manuscript (*HK 2*), and this in turn appears to derive partly from the collection already discussed in *L 74*.

The Haslewood-Kingsborough manuscript was used by Grosart. Grierson did not know of its whereabouts and, judging from the description in Thorpe's *Catalogue* of 1831, dismissed it as a miscellaneous anthology.[1] He cited a few readings from it in his apparatus from Grosart's edition. It is actually two entirely distinct manuscripts bound together (*HK 1* and *HK 2*), and the second of these is in itself composite. Although both *HK 1* and *HK 2* are miscellanies, each contains solid blocks of poems by Donne and so is, strictly speaking, a miscellany containing a Donne collection.[2] The second manuscript, *HK 2*, which from its hands and from its contents appears considerably earlier than the first, contains (ff. 1–5) five of the *Elegies*, a Verse-Letter to Wotton, 'Image and Dream', 'The Autumnal', and Sir John Roe's two epistles to Ben Jonson. Then, after some miscellaneous poems, come (ff. 12–33ᵛ) 'The Storm', 'The Calm', and 'A Litany', followed by thirty-nine of the *Songs and Sonnets*. These occur in an uninterrupted sequence, except that Donne's letter to Herbert ('Man is a lumpe') separates the last two. This collection of lyrics has to be compared with the collection of thirty-four found in *H 40* and the collection of twenty-five found in *L 74*. Thirty-one poems are common to *H 40* and *HK 2*. Like *H 40*, *HK 2* lacks 'The Funeral', 'The Blossom', 'The Primrose', 'The Relic', 'The Damp'; and it ends its collection with the same five poems as end the collection in *H 40*. Of the eight poems that *HK 2* adds to the poems that it shares with *H 40*, seven appear in close proximity, as they would if they had been added to an existing collection. But, in spite of these connexions in content and order with *H 40*, *HK 2* reads habitually with *L 74* and Group II against *H 40* and Group I, or else reads independently of both. In poems that do not occur in *L 74* it shows no connexion with Group II, and often reads independently against Groups I, II, and III. In the

---

[1] See Grierson, vol. ii, p. cx. For a history of the manuscript, now in the Huntington Library, see Josephine Waters Bennett, 'Early Texts of Two of Ralegh's Poems', *H.L.Q.*, July 1941.

[2] I have treated *HK 2* in the same way as *H 40*, using *HK 2* for the Donne collection and *HK 2** for the miscellany in which it is embedded.

twenty-three lyrics common to *HK 2* and *L 74*, it is plain that *HK 2* contains an inferior version of the text in *L 74*. It shares its rare errors and adds to them errors and distinctive readings of its own. Its weakness here disinclines me to regard seriously the readings that it presents in the remaining twenty-six lyrics that it took from some other source than *L 74*. It can be called here a fourth tradition; but I believe we can safely regard it as a degenerate one.

In any of the *Songs and Sonnets* where there are a sufficient number of significant variants to allow the construction of a stemma, *Cy*, *O*, *P* will always be found below *HK 2*, and in the remainder it is nearly always clear that their text is a corruption of the text of *HK 2*. Their readings are, therefore, valueless in any attempt to construct the original text. Their interest lies in their relation to manuscripts which cannot be grouped, such as *B*, *A 25*, and *JC*, and in the fact that the sophisticated *Lut* and *O'F* show occasional contamination with their tradition. In the *Elegies*, *Cy* and *O*, *P* diverge frequently. The better text in *Cy* we must, I think, ascribe partially to contamination with a sounder tradition, since *Cy* shows sufficiently striking agreement with *O*, *P* for us to retain belief in a common origin here as well as in the *Songs and Sonnets*.

Since the remaining manuscript collections resist classification, it is convenient to sum up the relation of the four traditions established so far. In the *Elegies* the nature of the vast majority of the variants prevents the construction of a stemma.[1] They are usually either wholly insignificant, or easily reversible, or have arisen from such an obvious cause that they might well have occurred independently in unconnected manuscripts. In the *Songs and Sonnets*, although many of the poems show no significant variants, the position as a whole is different. In the stemma that follows, the number of lyrics included in a manuscript is given in brackets, a dotted line indicates the contact of a manuscript with a different tradition from the one that it generally follows, and a hatched line that the descent is probably through several intermediaries. To simplify, I have not repeated the stemma showing the descent of the Group I manuscripts from *X*.

---

[1] In the whole of the *Elegies* there is only one difference of reading that represents an important difference in the sense: 'Going to Bed', l. 46 (see Commentary, p. 133).

Manuscripts of the *Songs and Sonnets*

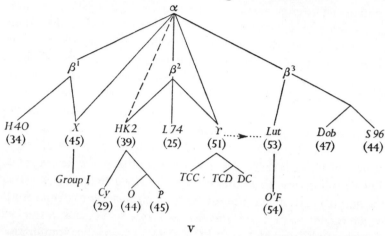

v

The other manuscript collections must be discussed individually. *A 25* (British Museum Add. MS. 25707) is in a great many hands. The original writers left blanks and spaces which have been filled with a collection of poems, many by Henry King, in a hand that is possibly Philip King's.[1] Without this additional material, *A 25* contains (ff. 8–23ᵛ) eleven of the thirteen Elegies in *W*, numbered 2 to 12, followed by nineteen poems initialed 'J.D.',[2] including thirteen of the *Songs and Sonnets* and 'The Autumnal'. The missing 'Elegy 1' ('The Bracelet') has been supplied by another hand (ff. 5–6ᵛ) which has also added the Harington Elegy and 'Love's Progress' on ff. 24–28. On f. 28ᵛ the first writer has added 'The Curse'. A miscellaneous collection of poems in a third hand occupies ff. 29–56ᵛ; it contains some poems by Donne including eight of the *Songs and Sonnets*. The writer adds initials to most of the poems which are, in the main, correct. Another miscellaneous collection, in yet a fourth hand, occupies ff. 59–69.[3] Two songs 'Goe and catche a falling starre' and 'The Message' occur here. Between these two miscellanies the hand that has added poems in the blank spaces has written 'Sappho to Philaenis' and 'The Ecstasy'. The symbol *A 25* in a critical apparatus can thus represent different things. In the *Elegies*, *A 25* reads generally

[1] See Margaret Crum, *The Library*, June 1961.
[2] Some of these are in a fainter ink than the others, as if copied at a different time.
[3] After f. 69 the manuscript is in a medley of hands and there are no more Donne items.

with *W* and *JC*. In the twenty-five *Songs and Sonnets* that it contains
its witness is, as one would suppose from the appearance of the poems
in the manuscript, divided; but in general it tends to agree, sometimes
strikingly, with *HK2* and at other times to degenerate from it.

JC, one of the most attractive, physically, of the Donne manuscripts,[1] is written in a single hand, but is in two parts. It opens with
a poem on Donne's *Satires* with 'Jo. Ca. June 3 1620' at the foot.
Since its copy (*D 17*) is dated 1625, *JC* must have been written
between these dates. It opens with the five *Satires*, 'A Litany', 'The
Storm', and 'The Calm'. The second part is headed 'Elegies and
Epigrams by Mr. John Donne' and introduced by a quotation from
Persius. It begins with the thirteen Elegies of *W*. A subsection
headed 'Miscellanea. Poems. Elegies. Sonnetts by the same Author'
follows, containing fifty-two items.[2] These include thirty-two lyrics
as well as the fourteenth Elegy ('Love's Progress'), 'The Autumnal',
'Sappho to Philaenis', and 'Variety'. In the *Elegies JC* reads with
W, diverging from it sometimes in company with *A 25*, sometimes
independently. In the *Songs and Sonnets* its position is less easy to
define. It is plainly at the end of any line of transmission since it
has a good many readings not found elsewhere, often plainly
erroneous. In the poems that they share *JC* tends to read with *A 25*,
and so with *HK 2*; but otherwise it tends to agree with *H 40* and
Group I. It has, along with what are obviously individual aberrations,
a few readings that would, if the text were generally more reliable,
be regarded with respect. But, in spite of the evident admiration
for Donne evinced by his poem, I cannot regard John Cave's manuscript as having any very close contact with Donne's originals.

HK 1 appears to be a much later manuscript than *HK 2*, in italic
where the other is in secretary. It is paged, not foliated. Pp. 1–63
contain a miscellany, including a good deal of Herrick. The only
poems by Donne are 'The Curse' and 'The Bracelet', occurring
together, and 'Going to Bed'. Pp. 64–105 contain a collection of
poems distinguished by the fact that they all have the letters 'L.C.'
placed against them in the margin. Many of these are very neatly
written in double columns with a rule separating one poem so

---

[1] For *JC* and *D 17* see Gardner, *Divine Poems*, p. lxxv, n. 4.
[2] In numbering the writer has omitted 'xxviii', so the last poem is numbered 'liii'.

transcribed from the next. A great many, but by no means all, of these poems are Donne's. There follows a miscellaneous collection of poems by Corbett, Carew, Randolph, Pembroke, Ruddier, and Strode and then (pp. 165–75) a further collection of poems initialed 'L.C.' and again mainly written in double columns. The great majority of these are Donne's. The manuscript concludes with further miscellaneous poems, including as late a poem as Suckling's 'Sessions of the Wits'. *HK 1* is essentially a late Caroline miscellany; it can hardly have been copied much earlier than 1640. But the poems mysteriously marked 'L.C.' probably formed a distinct collection, and the manner in which they are copied suggests that the scribe was entering poems from a much smaller manuscript whose pages he is reproducing by his double columns and rules. It is difficult to see any other reason for his suddenly adopting this method of writing out his poems. The 'L.C.' collections contain a good many poems not by Donne, many of which often appear with his. Of poems printed as indisputably his in this volume they contain three Elegies and twenty-four of the *Songs and Sonnets*. They present a respectable text, free of gross errors, reading on the whole with *H 40* and Group I but showing occasional connexions with *JC* and *S*.

　　B (Bridgewater),[1] a large collection that makes little attempt to arrange the poems and has a good many spurious pieces, has a poor text. It contains all fourteen *Elegies* and forty-seven of the *Songs and Sonnets*. In the *Divine Poems B* reads with Group III. In the *Elegies* it shows some contact with Group III, but it often reads closely with *Cy, O, P* and with *O, P* when they diverge from *Cy*. In the *Songs and Sonnets*, on the other hand, *B* never reads significantly with Group III. It reads rather more often with *L 74*, Group II, *HK 2* than with *H 40*, Group I; but it shows contact here also with *Cy, O, P*.

　　S (Stephens), dated 19 July 1620, like *B* an ambitious collection and like *B* containing many spurious poems, has an even worse text. It contains all fourteen *Elegies* and forty-six of the *Songs and Sonnets*. In the *Divine Poems S*, like *B*, reads with Group III. In the *Elegies* and *Songs and Sonnets* its textual relations vary from poem to

---

[1] For further information on *B, S, S 962, K* see Gardner, *Divine Poems*, pp. lxxii and lxxiv–lxxvi.

poem. At times it agrees very closely with Group III, at others with
Cy, O, P, at others it follows Group I or Group II, but always with a
crop of errors of its own. My belief is that S is very far from Donne's
papers shown to his friends, and that the writer has copied poems
picked up at various times which he has roughly sorted and brought
together.

The same appears to be true of *S 962* (Stowe 962), a very large
miscellany containing a great many of Donne's poems not collected
together. As it contains a poem dated 1637 *S 962* must have been
written after the appearance of Donne's poems in print. The excellence of some of its texts suggests that they were copied from
an edition rather than from manuscript.[1] It contains eleven of the
Elegies and forty-nine of the *Songs and Sonnets*. *S 962* often reads
with Group III; but in a good many poems it reads either with
Group I or with Group II. In many cases this means that it is
reading with the editions of 1633 and 1635 and I suspect that it
was either following copy that had been corrected from print or
else taking extra poems from one of the editions.

K (King), an extremely pretty little manuscript, containing
twelve of the *Elegies* and twenty-six of the *Songs and Sonnets*, has the
worst text that I have seen and I have not attempted to establish
what traditions it is garbling.

vi

Collation of these twenty-eight manuscripts (nine of which were
not available to Grierson) has convinced me that in the construction
of a text only Group I (supported in some poems by *H 40*), Group II
(supported in some poems by *L 74*), Group III, and, in the *Elegies*,
W are of value; and that the manuscripts in the groups must be
treated as members of a group.[2] The further work that I have done
since editing the *Divine Poems* has made me alter the view suggested
there that Donne was accustomed to handing odd poems to friends
to take copies, or made copies of single poems for his friends

---

[1] Recourse to the edition of 1635 would explain the inclusion of 'Farewell to Love',
otherwise only found in *O'F* and *Hd*.

[2] Thus, no editor should cite as valuable the readings of a single manuscript, such as *O'F*,
without taking into account whether it is reading with its group. Failure to respect this
principle vitiates the textual revision in two modern editions, R. E. Bennett's *Complete Poems*,
1942, and Theodore Redpath's *Songs and Sonets*, 1956.

himself, and that the 'remote origin' of some large collections lies in such early single copies which have been gathered together.[1] What evidence there is points to the *Elegies* having circulated as a set of poems and to the *Songs and Sonnets* having been copied and got into circulation as a substantial body of poems.[2] Analysis of the manuscript relations does not support the notion that manuscripts such as *Cy*, *O*, *P*, or *B*, *S*, or *JC* are likely to contain genuine readings: either the poet's first thoughts, or second thoughts that occurred to him when writing out a particular copy.

I see no evidence for any revision in the text of the *Elegies* and in the great majority of the *Songs and Sonnets*. There is no particular reason why Donne should have wished to revise them. The *Satires* and the *Divine Poems* are a different matter. The *Satires* were the poems on which his reputation appears largely to have rested. He thought well enough of them to have them presented by Jonson to Lady Bedford and he could hardly have excluded them from the projected edition of 1614. There is every reason why he should wish to revise poems written between 1593 and 1598 for a presentation copy in 1608 and for publication in 1614. The same holds for the *Divine Poems*. A man on the verge of ordination might well wish to make alterations in poems written some years before when he was a layman.[3] There is no evidence that Donne regarded the *Elegies* and *Songs and Sonnets* as poems likely to advance his career, and there is some evidence that he kept the latter especially for the eyes of friends. In one of them, 'The Curse', which from its appearances in manuscript would seem to have circulated alone and to be an early poem, there are unquestionably two authentic versions of the last three lines of one stanza. In 'The Will' it is possible either that a stanza was deliberately omitted, or that a new stanza was added by the author, or that there are alternative versions of the second stanza. In 'The Good-Morrow' it is possible that two versions of the concluding lines may represent the author's first draft and an improvement; they may as possibly be the poet's

---

[1] See Gardner, *Divine Poems*, p. lxxvii.

[2] This view has been confirmed by the exhaustive study that Mr. MacColl has made of manuscripts containing Donne's poems.

[3] The poems where I believe there to be two texts are 'La Corona', 'Holy Sonnets', and 'Annunciation and Passion', written between 1607 and 1609. In 'Good Friday', written just before Donne's ordination, there are no significant variants.

own words and a corruption. In 'The Flea' and 'The Relic' there are sufficient variants for us to speak of the 'Group I text' of 'The Flea' and the 'Group II text' of 'The Relic'. In neither case are the variants of a kind to compel the hypothesis of authorial revision. In the great majority of the *Songs and Sonnets* the possibility of two versions does not even arise. In the few where it does (apart from the poems mentioned), either the manuscripts preserving alternative readings are untrustworthy, or the differences are so uninteresting that it is difficult to see why a poet should have troubled to make them.

II. THE EDITIONS

Editions of Donne's poems appeared in 1633, 1635, 1639, 1649, 1650, 1654, and 1669. The copy for the first edition was entered to John Marriott on 13 September 1632 and printed for him by M. F. (Miles Fletcher). The entry excepted five Elegies and the *Satires*; but a subsequent entry allowed the *Satires*. The second edition (1635) was printed by the same printer for the same publisher, as were the third and fourth. The fifth edition (1650), the first over which the younger John Donne had control, was also printed for Marriott but the printer's name is not given; the sixth (1654), a reissue of the fifth with a cancel title-page, was 'printed by J. Flesher' but mentions no publisher. The seventh and last of the seventeenth-century editions (1669) was 'printed by T. N. (Thomas Newcomb) for Henry Herringman'.[1]

i

As Grierson pointed out, the order in which the poems appear in the first edition can be explained by reference to their appearance in the manuscripts of Group I and Group II. The main source was a manuscript of Group I which was supplemented by the addition of poems from a manuscript of Group II and by the reprinting of the 'Elegy on Prince Henry' and the two *Anniversaries*. Eight poems headed 'Elegy' (numbered I to VIII) occur together. These eight are what we would have left if we took out from the set of thirteen

---

[1] See Keynes, pp. 152–66. The account of the editions of 1633 and 1635 that follows is summarized from a fuller discussion in my *Divine Poems*, pp. lxxxii–xc.

in the manuscripts of Group I the 'first, second, Tenth, Eleventh, and Thirteenth Elegies', in conformity with the 'exception' made in the Stationers' Register. A ninth Elegy, 'The Comparison' (not found in the Group I manuscripts but present in those of Group II), occurs much later in the volume, followed by 'The Autumnal' and 'Image and Dream' (both found among the *Songs and Sonnets* in the Group I manuscripts). All three are headed 'Elegie' and the last is printed as if it were in couplets. The *Songs and Sonnets* occur together, interrupted by the reprint of the two *Anniversaries*. With the addition of two at the beginning and six at the close, and the removal of 'The Autumnal' and 'Image and Dream', the collection is the same as the collection in two of the Group I manuscripts, *C 57* and *Lec*,[1] with the exception of one inexplicable omission ('A Lecture upon the Shadow') and one poem, 'The Undertaking', appearing earlier in the edition than in the manuscripts.[2]

The conclusion to be drawn from the order in which the poems appear is made certain by collation. There can be no doubt that Marriott's main source was a manuscript of Group I. On a number of occasions, as can be seen from the critical apparatus to the *Divine Poems* and to the poems in this volume, the edition reads with *C 57* (and *Lec*) against the other Group I manuscripts.[3] Taken with agreement in contents, the number of occasions when the edition follows individual readings in *C 57* makes it certain that the manuscript used must have been very close to *C 57*. There can also be no doubt that the edition makes use of a manuscript of Group II. In the poems that it adds to those present in the Group I manuscripts it follows the text of Group II; it gives titles that are only found in the manuscripts of Group II to poems untitled in the manuscripts of Group I; it also adopts readings from Group II into the text of some of the poems taken from its Group I manuscript.

[1] 'The Prohibition' and 'Epitaph: On Himself' are included among the *Songs and Sonnets* in *D, H 49, SP*, but are missing in *C 57, Lec*. In *1633* 'The Prohibition' occurs among the six poems added at the close of the collection from the Group II manuscript and 'Epitaph: On Himself' is not included in the volume.

[2] In *1633* 'The Undertaking' appears where 'Image and Dream' occurs in the Group I manuscripts. It was possibly moved from its place in the manuscript to fill a gap left by the removal of 'Image and Dream'.

[3] *Lec* has fewer poems than *C 57*. *C 57* agrees with *1633* on fifty-five occasions. Five of these are bad misreadings and one an omission of a word. The number of agreements in trivial variation, not calling for correction by an intelligent copyist, is even more significant than agreement in manifest error.

But there are certain facts that cannot be explained by the hypothesis that the only source of the copy for *1633* was a manuscript resembling *C 57*, supplemented and corrected by a manuscript resembling *TCD*. In 'The Prohibition' (missing in *C 57*) the edition prints the third stanza which is not present in the Group II manuscripts; in 'The Will' it prints a stanza which is not found in the manuscripts of either Group I or Group II; and in 'The Computation' (not in Group I), where it follows the text of Group II against Group III, it supplies a line that is missing in all the Group II manuscripts. Also the text in the edition, in its freedom from obvious error, is superior to the text in any extant manuscript. An editor's problem is, while recognizing its dependence upon certain manuscripts, to account for its superiority to its sources.

There are two possible explanations. One is that the Group I manuscript used was very carefully corrected, largely by comparison with the Group II manuscript, but also by reference to some other source, and that whoever prepared the copy for *1633* must have the honour of being Donne's first editor. The other, which I argued for in my edition of the *Divine Poems*, is that Marriott's Group I manuscript had been authoritatively corrected before it came into his hands. I accepted Grierson's suggestion that the owner of the manuscript might well have been Goodyer, since the edition of 1633 includes some of Donne's letters to him, and I thought it possible that Goodyer, being a close friend of Donne's, might well have corrected a copy made for him by a professional scribe by reference to Donne's own copies. I was led to prefer this explanation by the fact that, to judge by the test of the poems taken from it, the Group II manuscript was a poor one and that the hypothetical editor had done little to improve it. I was also more impressed by the excellence of the first edition than I am now, and I had not realized how much sporadic 'editorial conflation' exists in the manuscripts.[1] Further, I was, outside the *Divine Poems*, relying on Grierson's collations, and these, particularly in the *Songs and Sonnets*, are

---

[1] The erratic manner in which *Dob* and, even more, *Lut* and *O'F* adopt readings from other traditions, and the inconsistency with which *O'F* corrects to the readings of *1633* and *1635* adopts readings from *O'F*, are parallels to the manner in which *1633* at times keeps to the text in Group I, at times adopts single readings from Group II, at times follows the Group II text in a whole poem, and again at times leaves obvious errors uncorrected.

seriously incomplete and sometimes incorrect.[1] I have now come to the conclusion that the text in *1633* is a highly sophisticated text.

I have come to this conclusion from an examination of those readings in the edition for which there is no support, or only random support, in the manuscripts. Some of these are clearly corrections made by someone who has misunderstood the sense. A simple example is the alteration of 'that thou falls', the reading of both Groups I and II, to 'that thou falst', in 'A Valediction: of Weeping' (l. 8).[2] A more striking example occurs in 'The Anniversary' (ll. 21–22), where all the manuscripts read

> And then wee shall be throughly blest,
> But wee no more, then all the rest.
> Here upon earth, we'are Kings . . .

The edition reads 'But now no more', presumably because the corrector thought the repetition of 'wee' an error and, not going on to see the sense of the next lines, took it that a contrast to 'then' was needed. But, as the next lines show, the contrast intended is between the bliss of the lovers in heaven which, although full bliss, will not be greater than the bliss of others, and their bliss on earth which is without parallel. The corrector has produced a line that says exactly the opposite of what the stanza as a whole intends. A similar error occurs in 'The Canonization' (l. 40), where for 'extract', the reading of all the manuscripts, the edition reads 'contract'. The alteration seems influenced by the neighbourhood of the adjective 'whole'. The alchemical metaphor in 'Who did the whole worlds soule extract' is reduced to the apparently more obvious notion of 'contracting' the soul of the 'whole world' into the small space of the lovers' eyes. But, on reflection, it can be seen that it is absurd to apply spatial notions to the soul, and that this idea of much in little weakly anticipates the next thought: that the eyes, by this infusion of the *anima mundi*, are made mirrors and spies to epitomize all. Another example of misunderstanding of sense occurs in 'A Valediction: of the Book' (l. 53) where, for the

---

[1] Grierson worked before the days of photostat and microfilm and many of the manuscripts that he consulted were at the time in private hands and could not be consulted more than once.

[2] The manuscripts of Group III and some others make the same error, misled by the wish to correct a seemingly false concord.

difficult reading 'their nothing', the edition reads 'there something'. Here we have not only a weak anticipation of the following lines, but also a redundant 'there'. In this case the edition has the support of two degenerate manuscripts, *O* and *P*, agreeing accidentally with one of their characteristic corruptions.[1]

A marked feature of the text in *1633* is the care with which elisions are marked.[2] Whoever prepared the copy was plainly interested in metre. This interest has led him to 'improve' various lines. He plainly disliked the omission of a weak initial syllable, a license that is common in song and gives no difficulty to any reader who does not scan by the thumb. In 'The Undertaking' the manuscripts give us an opening stanza in which the first and third lines lack an initial syllable:

> I have done one braver thing
> Then all the *Worthies* did,
> Yet a braver thence doth spring
> Which is, to keepe that hid.

This pattern is repeated in the final stanza:

> Then you'have done a braver thing
> Then all the *Worthies* did,
> And a braver thence will spring
> Which is to keepe that hid.

The edition supplies an initial syllable to the third line of the first stanza, reading 'And yet a braver thence doth spring', and also fails to mark the elision 'you'have' in the first line of the last.[3] A similar unnecessary 'and' is obtruded in 'Love's Infiniteness' (l. 5), where the strong manuscript reading 'All my treasure, which should purchase thee' is emended to 'And all my treasure . . . ,' and in 'The Primrose' (l. 17). Here the elision in 'study'her' is not marked and the unnecessary 'and', put in to regularize the line, has produced a line that is a foot too long: 'My heart to study her and not to love.' Further examples of editorial sophistication will be found in the

---

[1] In all four cases I adopt the manuscript reading. Grierson did so in two, and in two retained the reading of *1633*.

[2] This is done with a consistency that reminds us of some dramatic texts.

[3] Like many amateurs, the improver did not improve consistently. Here, in the first stanza he has regularized the third and left alone the first line; and in the last stanza he has regularized the first, by omitting to mark an elision, and left the third.

textual notes.[1] On those given it seems to me impossible to regard
the first edition as deriving its unique readings from an authoritative
source.

The question whether it was this same 'corrector' who conflated
the text in the Group I manuscript with the text in the manuscript
of Group II is complicated by the anomalous Dolau Cothi manuscript.[2] *DC* is fundamentally a Group II manuscript, but it has some
striking affinities with the text in *1633*. Whereas it generally has
the titles that *1633* adopted from Group II in the form in which
they are found in manuscript, on three occasions it has titles only
found in the edition.[3] It omits, with *1633*, ll. 53–54 of 'The Anagram',
present in all other manuscripts, and ll. 7–8 of 'The Perfume' which
1633, following Group I in error, also omits. Where there is a choice
between a Group I and a Group II version of a poem, *DC* makes the
same choice as *1633*.[4] On the other hand, *DC* never reads with *1633*
against both Groups I and II; that is, it has none of the unsupported
readings of the edition. It also lacks the third stanza of 'The Prohibition' and the third stanza of 'The Will', agreeing here with
Group II against the edition. This makes it impossible to suggest
that *DC* derives from a Group II manuscript that had been corrected
from the edition. Its connexions must be with the manuscript that
provided the copy for *1633* at a stage before the 'editor' had made
his final corrections and improvements. Whether these final sophistications were made by the same person who conflated the manuscript of Group II with the manuscript of Group I is impossible
to tell. But however many persons were concerned, their efforts
produced copy for the first edition that was as sophisticated as the
work of the rival 'editor' of Donne's poems whose labours can be
analysed in the O'Flaherty manuscript.[5]

---

[1] The editor was not always wrong in correcting his manuscript. He made an essential
correction in 'The Dream' (l. 20). I read with him here, not because I think the first edition has
weight against a consensus of the manuscripts, but because the unmetrical reading of Groups
I, II, and III must be corrected.

[2] See pp. lxx–lxxi.

[3] *DC* has 'Love's Alchemy' for the invariable manuscript title 'Mummy', and 'The Broken
Heart' and 'Love's Usury' for poems that are without title in all manuscripts.

[4] *DC* reads with *1633* and Group I in 'The Flea', 'The Good-Morrow', and 'The Curse'
(ll. 14–16). It also reads with Group I against Group II in 'A Lecture upon the Shadow'
(not printed in *1633*). On the other hand, in 'The Relic', where *1633* reads with Group II
against Group I in all but one reading, *DC* reads with Group II without exception.

[5] See pp. lxxiii–lxxiv.

ii

In the second edition in 1635 new poems were added, the contents were rearranged, and a considerable number of alterations
were made in poems reprinted from the first edition. A number of
titles were also supplied. Of the twenty-eight poems added, twenty-
three are to be found in *O'F*, more than any other single extant
manuscript can provide,[1] the rearrangement of the poems is made
under headings that *O'F* took from *Lut*, and the alterations in the
text, although in most cases to readings that *O'F* shares with other
Group III manuscripts, are occasionally to a reading that is only
found in *Lut*, *O'F* or in *O'F* alone.[2] The second edition is therefore
in the main not substantive, being a reprint of the first with
additions and alterations from *O'F*. But in a few of the poems
added it was drawing on another source and the titles that it
supplied were not drawn from any extant manuscript.

Two of the 'excepted' Elegies were printed in 1635 although no
authority to print them had been obtained. These are 'The Bracelet' and 'On his Mistress'.[3] Although the first is extant in *O'F*, the
text was not taken from there but from what must have been
a poorer manuscript, resembling *Cy*, *O*, *P*.[4] The text of 'On his
Mistress', on the other hand, follows the text in *Lut*, *O'F* strikingly
against all other manuscripts. The *Songs and Sonnets* were brought
together under this heading; and 'A Lecture upon the Shadow' and
'Farewell to Love' were added. The first, which appears to have
been accidentally omitted from the first edition, was printed from
a Group II manuscript, the second was taken from *O'F*.

The second edition also included some poems of doubtful authorship, including three Elegies printed in this volume. 'Julia' and 'A
Tale of a Citizen and his Wife' were taken from *O'F*; but 'His

---

[1] One 'Upon the Translation of the Psalms', is only extant in *O'F*.
[2] A striking example in the *Songs and Sonnets* is the alteration of the close of the first stanza
of 'Sweetest Love, I do not goe' to a version only found in *Lut*, *O'F*.
[3] In *1635* the Funeral Elegy has been removed from among the eight 'Elegies' of *1633*
and placed among the Epicedes. 'The Comparison', 'The Autumnal', 'Image and Dream',
and 'Language thou art too narrow, and too weak' are printed as Elegies VIII to XI, and 'The
Bracelet' as Elegy XII. 'On his Mistress' appears not with the Elegies but, absurdly, among
the Epicedes.
[4] In the exemplar of *Lut* 'The Bracelet', the first poem of the set of Elegies in *W*, *A 25*,
JC, had apparently been lost. It does not occur until the end of the heterogeneous collection
of 'Elegies' in *Lut*, *O'F* and its presence might easily be overlooked.

Parting from Her' was printed in a short version from another source.

iii

The only subsequent edition that need concern us is Herringman's edition of 1669.[1] Two more of the 'excepted' Elegies, 'Love's Progress' and 'Going to Bed', were printed here and a full text of 'His Parting from Her' was substituted for the short text of 1635. The text in this last seventeenth-century edition was considerably revised, sometimes by a return to the readings of the first edition, sometimes by reference to manuscript, at other times, it appears, by editorial conjecture. Either the manuscripts used for the three additional poems[2] were very poor ones, or the editor exercised a good deal of licence in printing from them, since many of the readings of *1669* have no manuscript support at all. The sources he was drawing on in his endeavour to present a better text would seem similarly to have been late representatives of a bad tradition. This edition, appearing nearly forty years after Donne's death, cannot be regarded as having any authority.

III. CONCLUSIONS

The edition of 1633 remains the only possible base for a critical edition. It was very carefully printed and its accidentals are consistent with the best seventeenth-century usage. No manuscript can replace it. But it must be emended from the manuscripts. It must be corrected when it misprints, misreads, or follows its Group I manuscript in errors peculiar to it. (That is, all readings that have the support of only *C 57*, *Lec* must be rejected.) It should also on many, but not necessarily all, occasions be corrected when it has the support of Group I only.[3] When the edition has no manuscript support, or only random support, the reading of the manuscripts (if they agree against the edition) should be adopted. Since so many

[1] Editions between those of 1635 and 1669 add only three doubtfully authentic poems: 'The Token' (1649) and 'Variety' and 'Self-Love' (1650).

[2] The edition of 1669 also adds the stanza 'Stay oh sweet and do not rise' as the first stanza of 'Break of Day'.

[3] The relations of Group III to Groups I and II are not sufficiently clear and stable for us to be certain that we are always dealing with three distinct traditions. We cannot, therefore, allow a simple majority rule of two against one to determine the choice of reading.

of the unsupported readings of *1633* can be shown to be sophistications, it can be given no weight against a consensus of the
manuscripts.[1]

Since the first edition was based on the manuscripts of Groups I
and II, since in many cases it is impossible on grounds of intrinsic
merit to make any choice between the readings when Group III
reads against Groups I and II,[2] and since the preceding discussion
suggests that the Group III manuscripts are further from Donne's
papers than the manuscripts of Groups I and II, I have retained the
reading of the edition when it has the support of Groups I and II
and been content to record the reading of Group III as a variant.
A more difficult decision is required when Groups I and II diverge.
A modern editor has two courses open to him. Either he may decide
that he will accept the judgement of his remote predecessor, the
editor of *1633*, on the ground that he was a contemporary of the
poet and, therefore, more likely to make a right choice than an
editor working over 300 years later. Or he may decide that, since
many of the unsupported readings of the edition show misunderstanding of Donne's sense or weakening of his idiom, he is free
to disregard his predecessor's choice and choose what seem to him
the most lively and idiomatic readings. I was tempted to follow the
first, as the safer, course; but I have come to think this would be
cowardly. Donne is a great writer and a daring one, and I cannot
think his editor should be timid. I have, therefore, felt at liberty
to exercise my own judgement between the readings of Groups I
and II and have not automatically accepted the choice made in the
edition of *1633*.[3] Again, in poems that are not found in the manuscripts of Group I and that the edition of *1633* took from a Group II
manuscript, I have at times preferred the reading of Group III.

There is a problem peculiar to the *Elegies*. Of the fourteen that I
print together, one was not printed until the nineteenth century;
two appeared in *1635*, one printed from the highly idiosyncratic

---

[1] On this point I have changed my mind since I edited the *Divine Poems*. There was no
example in them of a significant reading in *1633* for which there was no manuscript support.
[2] For instance, in 'Love's Growth' Group III reads 'vexing' for 'paining' and 'active' for
'working'. There are no grounds for arguing that the Group III readings are either superior
or inferior.
[3] Thus, I have not followed *1633* in adopting the Group I text of 'The Flea'; but have
preferred the livelier readings of *H 40* and all other manuscripts.

O'F, and the other from a poor manuscript; and two were first printed in 1669, also from poor manuscripts. The text of these five poems has to be reconstructed from reliable manuscript tradition.

ii

With the exception of the five Elegies not included in *1633*, the text that follows is based on the first edition. I have preserved its spelling and punctuation, but not its typography.[1] Emendations of punctuation are made sparingly and on my own judgement, although in most cases they agree with the second edition or with good manuscripts. In a few cases, where the pointing is in serious question, I have given fuller information in a textual note; but in the apparatus I have been content to record departures from the punctuation of the edition, since I have rarely been swayed in making such a departure by anything but my own sense of its necessity. On the whole I concur with Grierson in strengthening stops.

The text of the five Elegies not included in *1633* is taken from the manuscript nearest to the edition, *C 57*. I have normalized its spelling to that of the first edition and silently supplemented its punctuation, again in accordance with the usage of *1633*. This appears to be the best solution to a problem created by the accidents of publication. One of the five must, in any case, be printed from manuscript. The text of the other four requires a great deal of correction and in 'The Bracelet', and even more in the two poems published in 1669, the accidents of the text are very unsatisfactory. To print from a good manuscript, recording all the readings of the first edition but ignoring its accidents, results in a much smaller critical apparatus in which points of interest are not buried in a mass of insignificant detail. But to print five out of fourteen Elegies *literatim* from manuscript would give an improper impression of disunity in a set of poems written at the same time. Manuscript spelling and punctuation is far more archaic and arbitrary than that of the edition, and since it is not the poet's own there seems no good

---

[1] I have not preserved long *ſ* or the ligatured *&*, and have expanded printers' contractions. The typography of the titles is also standardized.

reason for preserving it. I have therefore altered any spelling not found in *1633* to the spelling of the edition.

Although I do not believe that more than a few of the titles are Donne's own, titles are such a convenience that I have kept them wherever the editions have supplied them. I have completed the work of the editor of the second edition by giving titles of my own to the two Elegies he left untitled and, to avoid confusion, have distinguished the two poems called 'The Dream' in *1635* by re-titling one of them 'Image and Dream'.[1]

To avoid the repetition of a long list of manuscripts at the beginning of the commentary on each poem, a list of the collections in which the *Elegies* appear is given at the beginning of the commentary on the *Elegies*, and a similar list is given at the beginning of the commentary on the *Songs and Sonnets*. If a particular poem is not found in any one of these the fact is noted at the head of the commentary on that poem. I give there also a list of miscellanies in which the poem is found.[2] Miscellanies for which sigla have been provided are listed first, followed by those whose interest and importance are not sufficient to demand a special designation.

In the critical apparatus, in the same way, a list of manuscripts from which readings are given will be found at the beginning of the *Elegies* and another, slightly different, list at the beginning of the *Songs and Sonnets*. And, again, if a poem is missing in any of these this is noted in the apparatus to that poem. In both the commentary and the apparatus I have changed my formula on those occasions in the *Songs and Sonnets* when a poem is extant in only a few manuscripts. In general, it seemed to me that it would be more helpful to readers of the apparatus to have the formula '*A 25, JC omit*' rather than a list of manuscripts in which a poem occurs which they would have to scan to discover in which manuscripts it was missing. But, conversely, with a poem such as 'Negative Love', the formula '*In TC, O'F, A 25: Σ omit*' seemed more helpful than a list of manuscripts in which the poem is not found which the

---

[1] I have given the title 'Recusancy' to the Elegy beginning 'Oh let me not serve so', and the title 'Tutelage' to the Elegy beginning 'Nature's lay Idiot'.

[2] Mr. A. E. MacColl has very kindly allowed me to print his lists. The lists of miscellanies in this volume are therefore as full as intelligence and industry can make them. The lists in the *Divine Poems* were only of miscellanies I had actually seen.

reader would have to scan in order to discover where it did
occur.

The manuscripts from which readings are given have been
selected to represent the groups and their readings are recorded
by groups and not alphabetically. *C 57* and *H 49* represent Group I.
In the *Songs and Sonnets* they are joined by *H 40* whose readings are
given first since it has the best version of the 'Group I text'. *TCD*
represents Group II, and I have adopted from Grierson the use of
the symbol *TC* to indicate that the reading cited from *TCD* has the
support of *TCC*. When they diverge, the readings of both are given.
In the *Songs and Sonnets* they are joined by *L 74* whose readings are
given first since, in the poems it shares with *TC*, it presents the
best 'Group II text'. *Dob*, *O'F* and *S 96* represent Group III. Since
the Group III tradition is not consistent, it is necessary to add the
readings of *S 96* to those of *Dob* and *O'F* to establish which is the
'Group III reading' when they disagree. When the reading of *O'F*
has been corrected, it is cited as having its original reading, but
'(*b.c.*)', that is '(before correction)', has been added to indicate
that the reading has been corrected to the reading of *1633*. In the
Elegies the readings of *W* are added, followed by those of the less
reliable manuscripts: *A 25* and *JC*; *Cy* and *P*; *B*; *S*. In the *Songs and
Sonnets* I give, after the readings of *Dob*, *O'F*, *S 96*, those of *HK 2*;
Cy and *P*; *A 25*, *B*, *JC*, *S*.

The apparatus is strictly selective. Its first purpose is to record
all departures from the basic text. Its second is to preserve all
readings that an editor should consider: that is, all readings that
are not plainly erroneous in Groups I, II, and III, and (in the *Elegies*)
W. Its third is to record the witness of the less reliable manuscripts.
I have recorded readings from these sparingly and have not normally
cited them for their own sake. That is, I have, in the main, recorded
their witness only in support of, or in opposition to, readings cited
from the main groups, and have ignored their manifold errors and
trivial aberrations. But I have on a few occasions given interesting
readings from them, although I believe them to have no authority,
and have at times referred to others in the textual notes.[1]

[1] Grierson's apparatus is, of course, highly selective. Readings in newly discovered manuscripts are sometimes claimed to be of interest on the ground that they 'are not recorded by
Grierson'. These are usually readings common in the worse manuscripts that Grierson rightly

Readings from editions subsequent to the first are not recorded; but the titles added in *1635* are given in the apparatus and I have listed the verbal alterations made in *1635* in poems it reprinted from *1633* in Appendix A. The readings of Grierson's edition of 1912 are recorded when they differ from mine, and, occasionally, the readings of Mr. Hayward's edition of 1929 when they differ from Grierson's.

Any titles given in manuscript are recorded. If a manuscript is not cited as having a title it should be assumed that the poem occurs either without title or with some such heading as 'Elegy', 'Song', or 'Sonnet'.

Note. I have to thank Mr. MacColl for collating thirteen copies of *1633*[1] for press variants on the collating machine at the British Museum and the librarians of the Oxford colleges concerned for making this possible by lending their copies. Professor G. Blakemore Evans kindly collated the two copies in the library of the University of Illinois at Urbana. The variants discovered are not of much interest. They are noted in the apparatus. On one occasion my punctuation restores the punctuation of the uncorrected state; see note to 'A Valediction: of my Name in the Window', ll. 31–32. Otherwise I print from the corrected state.

thought unworthy of record. See, for instance, C. F. Main, 'New Texts of John Donne', *Studies in Bibliography*, vol. ix, 1957, which lists readings from a Harvard manuscript copy of 'Going to Bed'. The text is merely a poor relation of the text in *Cy, O, P.*

[1] Bodleian Library (2), British Museum (2), All Souls, Balliol, Brasenose, Christ Church, Corpus Christi, Queen's, St. John's, Wadham, and Worcester Colleges.

LIST OF SIGLA

Classified List of Manuscripts of the Elegies *and* Songs and Sonnets

(i) MSS. containing collections of Donne's poems

GROUP I

C 57	Cambridge University Library, Add. MS. 5778.
D	Dowden MS. Bodleian Library, MS. Eng. Poet. e 99 (formerly in the library of Mr. Wilfred Merton).
H 49	British Museum, Harleian MS. 4955.
Lec	Leconfield MS. In the library of Sir Geoffrey Keynes.
SP	St. Paul's Cathedral Library, MS. 49 B 43.
H 40	British Museum, Harleian MS. 4064.

GROUP II

A 18	British Museum, Add. MS. 18647.
N	Norton MS. Harvard College Library, MS. Eng. 966/3 (formerly MS. Nor. 4503).
TCC	Trinity College, Cambridge, MS. R 3 12.
TCD[1]	Trinity College, Dublin, MS. G 2 21.
L 74	British Museum, Lansdowne MS. 740.
DC	National Library of Wales, Dolau Cothi MS.

GROUP III

Dob	Dobell MS. Harvard College Library, MS. Eng. 966/4 (formerly MS. Nor. 4506).
Lut	Luttrell MS. In the library of Sir Geoffrey Keynes.
O'F[2]	O'Flaherty MS. Harvard College Library, MS. Eng. 966/5 (formerly MS. Nor. 4504).
S 96	British Museum, Stowe MS. 961.

IV

W	Westmoreland MS. Berg Collection, New York Public Library.

[1] *TC* is used for *TCD* reading with *TCC*.
[2] *O'F (b.c.)*: O'Flaherty, before correction. This indicates that the reading cited has been corrected to the reading of *1633*.

V

HK 2	Haslewood-Kingsborough MS., second part, Huntington Library MS. HM 198.

(*a*)

Cy	Carnaby MS. Harvard College Library, MS. Eng. 966/1 (formerly MS. Nor. 4502).
O	Osborn MS. In the library of Mr. James Osborn, Yale University. (Sold at Hodgson's, 21 November 1958, from the library of Major J. B. Whitmore.)
P	Phillipps MS. Bodleian Library, MS. Eng. Poet. f 9.

(*b*)

A 25	British Museum, Add. MS. 25707.
D 17	Victoria and Albert Museum, Dyce Collection, MS. D 25 F 17.
JC	John Cave MS. George Arents Tobacco Collection, New York Public Library. (Formerly in the library of Mr. Richard Jennings.)

(*c*)

B	Bridgewater MS. Huntington Library, MS. EL 6893.
K	King MS. In the library of Mr. James Osborn, Yale University. (Raphael King, Catalogue 51, Item 73.)
S	Stephens MS. Harvard College Library, MS. Eng. 966/6 (formerly MS. Nor. 4500).

(ii) Manuscripts containing Donne's poems with those of other authors[1]

CCC	Corpus Christi College, Oxford, MS. 327.
EH	Edward Hyde MS. In the library of Sir Geoffrey Keynes.
Grey	S. African Public Library, Cape Town, MS. Grey 2 a 11.
H 40[2]	British Museum, Harleian MS. 4064.
Hd	Harvard College Library, MS. Eng. 966/17.
HK 1	Haslewood-Kingsborough MS., first part. Huntington Library, MS. HM 198.
HK 2[3]	Haslewood-Kingsborough MS., second part. Huntington Library, MS. HM 198.

[1] This is a select list, containing only those miscellanies that have a substantial number of poems by Donne and a few that are of special interest.

[2] *H 40* is a miscellany to which has been added a small collection of Donne's poems. It appears therefore both among MSS. and among Miscellanies. I distinguish its parts by using *H 40** for the miscellany it largely shares with *RP 31*.

[3] *HK 2*, like *H 40*, is a miscellany containing a Donne collection and I use *HK** for the miscellany.

HN	Hawthornden MS. National Library of Scotland, MS. 2067.
Hol	Holgate MS. Pierpoint Morgan Library, New York, MS. 1058.
La	Edinburgh University Library, Laing MS. iii. 493.
RP 31	Bodleian Library, Rawlinson Poetical MS. 31.
RP 117 (2)	Bodleian Library, Rawlinson Poetical MS. 117, second part.
Sp	Sparrow MS. In the library of Mr. John Sparrow.
S 962	British Museum, Stowe MS. 962.
TCD (2)	Trinity College, Dublin, MS. G 2 21, second part.
Wel	Welbeck MS. In the library of the Duke of Portland, deposited in the library of the University of Nottingham.

The editions of Donne's poems from 1633 to 1699 are cited under their dates, as *1633*, *1635*, &c.

The Poems of John Donne, ed. H. J. C. Grierson, 2 vols. (Oxford, 1912), is cited as *Gr*.

The symbol Σ is used in the apparatus and commentary when the great majority of manuscripts agree in a reading or in the inclusion or omission of a poem. It denotes all manuscripts except those specifically excepted.

ANNO DÑI. 1591.
ÆTATIS SVÆ·18·

This was for youth, Strength, Mirth, and wit that Time
Most count their golden Age; but t'was not thine.
Thine was thy later yeares, so much refind
From youths Droße, Mirth, & wit; as thy pure mind
Thought (like the Angels) nothing but the Praiße
Of thy Creator, in thoße last, best Dayes.
* Witnes this Booke, (thy Embleme) which begins*
* With Love; but endes, with Sighes, & Teares for sins.*

Will:Marshall .ſculpſit .   IZ:WA:

JOHN DONNE
From the 1635 edition of the *Poems*

ELEGIES

The Bracelet

UPON THE LOSSE OF HIS MISTRESSES CHAINE, FOR WHICH HE MADE SATISFACTION

NOT that in colour it was like thy haire,
For Armelets of that thou maist let me weare;
Nor that thy hand it oft embrac'd and kist,
For so it had that good which oft I mist;
Nor for that seely old moralitie,   5
That as those links are tyed our love should be;
Mourne I that I thy seavenfold chaine have lost,
Nor for the luck sake; but the bitter cost.
  Oh shall twelve righteous Angels, which as yet
No leaven of vile soder did admit,   10
Nor yet by any fault have stray'd or gone
From the first state of their creation,
Angels, which heaven commanded to provide
All things to me, and be my faithfull guide,
To gaine new friends, t'appease great enemies,   15
To comfort my soule, when I lye or rise;
Shall these twelve innocents, by thy severe
Sentence (dread Judge) my sins great burden beare?
Shall they be damn'd, and in the furnace throwne,
And punisht for offences not their owne?   20

ELEGIES. *Text from 1633 unless otherwise stated. Readings are given from the following representative MSS.: C 57, H 49; TC (TCD with TCC); Dob, O'F, S 96; W, A 25, JC; Cy, P; B, S. When a poem is not found in one of these the omission is noted.*

  The Bracelet, &c. (*Elegy XI Gr*). *TCC omits. First printed in 1635. Text from C 57 with spelling regularized to that of 1633, punctuation supplemented and paragraphing supplied. Title from 1635*: Armilla. To a Lady whose chaine was lost *Dob*, (The Bracelett: To . . .) *S 96*: To a Lady whose chayne was lost. The Bracelet. Armilla *O'F*: Mr. John Donne to a Ladie whose Chaine he had lost *Cy*: The Bracelet *JC, B*; The Chaine *P*   3 thy *Σ*: this *C 57, TCD* 6 those] these *1635, Gr*   are tyed] are knitt *Cy*: were ty'ed *B*: were knit *1635, Gr* love] loves *Dob, A 25, JC, B*: hearts *O'F, S 96*   7 thy *Σ*: this *C 57*   8 luck] luckes *Dob, O'F, W*   11 fault] taint *Dob, O'F, S 96, W, JC*: taynts *B*: way *1635, Gr* or *Σ*: and *C 57, TCD*

They save not me, they doe not ease my paines
When in that hell they are burnt and tyed in chaines.
   Were they but Crownes of France, I cared not,
For most of them their naturall country rot
I thinke possesseth; they come here to us   25
So leane, so pale, so lame, so ruinous.
And howso'er French Kings most Christian be,
Their Crownes are circumcis'd most Jewishly.
Or were they Spanish Stamps, still travailing,
That are become as Catholique as their King,   30
Those unlick'd beare-whelps, unfil'd Pistolets,
That, more then cannon-shot, availes or lets,
Which, negligently left unrounded, looke
Like many-angled figures in the booke
Of some greate Conjurer, which would enforce   35
Nature, as these do Justice, from her course;
Which, as the soule quickens head, feet, and heart,
As streames, like veines, run through th'earths every part,
Visit all countries, and have slily made
Gorgeous *France* ruin'd, ragged, and decay'd,   40
Scotland, which knew no state, proud in one day,
And mangled seventeen-headed *Belgia.*
Or were it such gold as that wherewithall
Almighty Chymicks from each minerall
Having by subtile fire a soule out-pull'd   45
Are durtily and desperately gull'd;
I would not spit to quench the fire they'were in,
For they are guilty of much heinous sin.
But shall my harmless Angels perish? Shall
I lose my guard, my ease, my food, my all?   50
Much hope, which they should nourish, will be dead,
Much of my able youth, and lustyhead

---

23 cared Σ: car'd *C 57, H 49, TCD*   24 them] those *A 25*: these *Cy, P, 1635, Gr*
naturall country] ... countrys *O'F, Cy, Gr*: countryes naturall *P, 1635*   26 leane ...
pale ... lame] ... lame ... pale *TCD*: pale ... lame ... leane *A 25, Cy, P, 1635, Gr*: lame
... leane ... pale *B*   35 which] that *A 25, Cy, P, 1635, Gr*: and so in 60, 87, 106
38 run Σ: runs *C 57, H 49*   40 ruin'd, ragged] ragged, ruind *Dob, O'F, S 96, W,
A 25, JC, B, S*   47 they'were in] ... are ... *Dob, S, 1635, Gr*: therein *A 25,
Cy, P*

Will vanish; if thou love, let them alone
For thou wilt love me lesse when they are gone.
   Oh be content, that some loud-squeaking Cryer,   55
Well-pleas'd with one leane thred-bare groate for hire,
May like a devill rore through every street,
And gall the finders conscience if they meet.
Or let me creepe to some dread Conjurer,
Which with fantastique schemes fullfills much paper,   60
Which hath divided Heaven in tenements,
And with whores, theeves and murtherers stuft his rents
So full, that though he passe them all in sin,
He leaves himself no room to enter in.
And if, when all his art and time is spent,   65
He say 'twill ne'r be found; Oh be content.
Receive from him the doome ungrudgingly
Because he is the mouth of Destiny.
   Thou say'st (alas) the gold doth still remaine
Though it be chang'd, and put into a chaine.   .   70
So, in the first, fall'n Angels resteth still
Wisdom and knowledge, but 'tis turn'd to ill;
As these should do good workes, and should provide
Necessities, but now must nurse thy pride.
And they are still bad Angels, mine are none,   75
For forme gives being, and their forme is gone.
Pity these Angels yet; their dignities
Passe Vertues, Powers, and Principalities.
   But thou art resolute; Thy will be done.
Yet with such anguish as her only sonne   80
The mother in the hungry grave doth lay,
Unto the fire these Martyrs I betray.
Good soules, for you give life to every thing,
Good Angels, for good messages you bring,

54 me Σ: *omit C 57, H 49*   55 Oh] And *P, 1635, Gr*   58 they] he *JC, P, 1635*
60 schemes] scenes *TCD, P, 1635* : sheaves *S*   fullfills] fills *S 96* : fills vp *P* : fills so *B* : fils ful
S, 1635, Gr   60 Which] That *A 25, Cy, P, 1635, Gr*   62 his] her *H 49, TCD,
Dob, O'F, S 96* : their *B*   65 And] But *P, 1635, Gr*   66 Oh] yet *Cy, P, 1635, Gr*
67 from him the doome] . . . that doome *P, 1635, Gr* : the doome from him *Dob, O'F, S 96,
W, JC, B, S*   71 the] those *Dob, O'F, S 96, W, JC, B*   77 Angels yet; *B,
1635* : . . . yet, *TCD, O'F, S 96, W, A 25, JC* : Angels, yet *C 57, H 49, Dob, Cy, P, S* : Angels;
yet *Gr; see note*

Destin'd you might have been to such a one 85
As would have lov'd and worship'd you alone,
One which would suffer hunger, nakednesse,
Yea death, ere he would make your number lesse;
But I am guilty of your sad decay,
May your few fellowes longer with me stay. 90
    But oh, Thou wretched Finder, whom I hate
So much that I'almost pity thy estate;
Gold being the heaviest metall amongst all,
May my most heavy curse upon thee fall.
Here fetter'd, manacl'd, and hang'd in chaines 95
First mayst thou be, then chain'd to hellish paines;
Or be with forraigne gold brib'd to betray
Thy country,'and faile both of that and thy pay.
May the next thinge thou stoop'st to reach containe
Poyson, whose nimble fume rot thy moist braine, 100
Or libells, or some interdicted thinge,
Which negligently kept thy ruine bringe.
Lust-bred diseases rot thee'and dwell with thee
Itchy desire and no abilitie.
May all the hurt which ever Gold hath wrought, 105
All mischiefes which all devills ever thought,
Want after plenty, poore and gouty age,
The plagues of travellers, love and marriage
Afflict thee; and at thy lifes latest moment
May thy swolne sins themselves to thee present. 110
    But I forgive. Repent thou honest man.
Gold is restorative; restore it then.
Or if with it thou beest loath to depart
Because 'tis cordiall, would 'twere at thy heart.

---

85 a] an *S 96, S, 1635, Gr*   92 So much that] ... much as *Dob, S 96, W, JC*: So as *O'F*: So that *Cy, P, 1635, Gr*: So much *B*   almost *Σ*: shall most *S 96*: omit *C 57, H 49*   estate *Σ*: state *C 57, H 49, Dob, S 96, W, A 25, JC*; *see note*   95–110 *Omit O'F*   96 to *Σ*: in *C 57, H 49, Dob, S 96, Cy*   104 Itchy] Itching *P, 1635, Gr*   105 hurt which ever Gold hath] ill ... *A 25*: evills that gold ever *P, 1635, Gr*   106 mischiefes] mischiefe *1635*   108 love and marriage] love, Marriage *Cy, P, 1635*: love; marriage *Gr*   109 latest] last *Dob, A 25, Cy, B, 1635, Gr*   111 thou] then *H 49, Dob, S 96, W, JC, B*: thee *Cy, P, 1635, Gr*   113 Or] But *A 25, Cy, P, B, S, 1635, Gr*   with] from *A 25, Cy, P, S, 1635, Gr.*

The Comparison

As the sweet sweat of Roses in a Still,
   As that which from chaf'd muskats pores doth trill,
As the Almighty Balme of th'early East,
Such are the sweat drops on my Mistris breast,
And on her necke her skin such lustre sets,   5
They seeme no sweat drops, but pearle carcanets.
Ranke sweaty froth thy Mistresse brow defiles,
Like spermatique issue of ripe menstruous boiles,
Or like that skumme, which, by needs lawlesse law
Enforc'd, Sanserra's starved men did draw   10
From parboild shooes, and bootes, and all the rest
Which were with any soveraigne fatnes blest,
And like vile lying stones in saffrond tinne,
Or warts, or wheales, they hang upon her skinne.
Round as the world's her head, on every side,   15
Like to that fatall Ball which fell on Ide,
Or that whereof God had such jealousie,
As, for the ravishing thereof we die.
Thy head is like a rough-hewne statue'of jeat,
Where marks for eyes, nose, mouth, are yet scarce set;   20
Like the first Chaos, or flat seeming face
Of Cynthia, when th'earths shadowes her embrace.
Like Proserpines white beauty-keeping chest,
Or Joves best fortunes urne, is her faire brest.
Thine's like worme eaten trunkes, cloth'd in seals skin,   25
Or grave, that's durt without, and stinke within.
And like that slender stalke, at whose end stands
The wood-bine quivering, are her armes and hands.

The Comparison (Elegy VIII Gr). C 57, H 49 omit. Title from 1635.   4 on TC, W,
A 25, JC, S: of 1633, Dob, O'F, S 96, Cy, P, B, Gr   breast,] breast. 1633   5 necke]
⟨brow⟩ Gr   6 carcanets W, A 25, JC, S: coronets 1633, TC, Dob, O'F, S 96, Cy, B,
Gr: Carolettes P   7 Mistresse MSS.: Mistresse's 1633, Gr   8 boiles,] boiles. 1633
9 that Dob, S 96, W, A 25, JC, S: the 1633, TC, O'F, Cy, P, B, Gr   13 lying stones
MSS.: stones lying 1633; see note   14 they hang Σ: that ... Cy: wᶜʰ ... P: it hangs
1633   16 that Σ: the 1633, TC, P, Gr   19 head] head 1633   statue'of]
statue of 1633   26–29 Omit Dob, S 96, B   26 durt Σ: dust 1633, Cy, Gr
28 hands.] hands, 1633

Like rough bark'd elmboughes, or the russet skin
Of men late scurg'd for madnes, or for sinne,   30
Like Sun-parch'd quarters on the citie gate,
Such is thy tann'd skins lamentable state.
And like a bunch of ragged carrets stand
The short swolne fingers of thy gouty hand.
Then like the Chymicks masculine equall fire,   35
Which in the Lymbecks warme wombe doth inspire
Into th'earths worthlesse durt a soule of gold,
Such cherishing heat her best lov'd part doth hold.
Thine's like the dread mouth of a fired gunne,
Or like hot liquid metalls newly runne   40
Into clay moulds, or like to that Ætna
Where round about the grasse is burnt away.
Are not your kisses then as filthy,'and more,
As a worme sucking an invenom'd sore?
Doth not thy fearefull hand in feeling quake,   45
As one which gath'ring flowers, still fear'd a snake?
Is not your last act harsh, and violent,
As when a Plough a stony ground doth rent?
So kisse good Turtles, so devoutly nice
Are Priests in handling reverent sacrifice,   50
And such in searching wounds the Surgeon is
As wee, when wee embrace, or touch, or kisse.
Leave her, and I will leave comparing thus,
She, and comparisons are odious.

34 thy Σ: her 1633, JC, S   hand.] hand; 1633   37 durt Σ: dust A 25: part 1633,
TC, Cy   41 to that] that TC, W, A 25, Cy, P, S: that flaming JC; see note
43 filthy,'and] filthy, and 1633   46 fear'd TC, Dob, O'F, S 96, W, A 25, JC: feares
1633, Cy, P, B, S, Gr   48 when MSS.: where 1633   51 such MSS.: nice 1633

The Perfume

ONCE, and but once found in thy company,
  All thy suppos'd escapes are laid on mee;
And as a thiefe at barre, is question'd there
By all the men, that have beene rob'd that yeare,
So am I, (by this traiterous meanes surpriz'd)   5
By thy Hydroptique father catechiz'd.
Though he had wont to search with glazed eyes,
As though he came to kill a Cockatrice,
Though hee have oft sworne, that hee would remove
Thy beauties beautie, and food of our love,   10
Hope of his goods, if I with thee were seene,
Yet close and secret, as our soules, we'have beene.
Though thy immortall mother which doth lye
Still buried in her bed, yet will not dye,
Take this advantage to sleepe out day-light,   15
And watch thy entries, and returnes all night,
And, when she takes thy hand, and would seeme kind,
Doth search what rings, and armelets she can finde,
And kissing notes the colour of thy face,
And fearing least thou'art swolne, doth thee embrace;   20
And to trie if thou long, doth name strange meates,
And notes thy palenesse, blushings, sighs, and sweats;
And politiquely will to thee confesse
The sinnes of her owne youths ranke lustinesse;
Yet love these Sorceries did remove, and move   25
Thee to gull thine owne mother for my love.
Thy little brethren, which like Faiery Sprights
Oft skipt into our chamber, those sweet nights,

And, kist and ingled on thy fathers knee,
Were brib'd next day, to tell what they did see: 30
The grim eight-foot-high iron-bound serving-man,
That oft names God in oathes, and onely than,
He that to barre the first gate, doth as wide
As the great Rhodian Colossus stride,
Which, if in hell no other paines there were,   35
Makes mee feare hell, because he must be there:
Though by thy father he were hir'd for this,
Could never witnesse any touch or kisse.
But Oh, too common ill, I brought with mee
That, which betray'd mee to mine enemie: 40
A loud perfume, which at my entrance cryed
Even at thy fathers nose, so wee were spied.
When, like a tyran King, that in his bed
Smelt gunpowder, the pale wretch shivered.
Had it beene some bad smell, he would have thought   45
That his owne feet, or breath, that smell had wrought.
But as wee in our Ile emprisoned,
Where cattell onely,'and diverse dogs are bred,
The pretious Unicornes, strange monsters, call,
So thought he good, strange, that had none at all.   50
I taught my silkes, their whistling to forbeare,
Even my opprest shoes, dumbe and speechlesse were,
Onely, thou bitter sweet, whom I had laid
Next mee, mee traiterously hast betraid,
And unsuspected hast invisibly   55
At once fled unto him, and staid with mee.
Base excrement of earth, which dost confound
Sense, from distinguishing the sicke from sound;
By thee the seely Amorous sucks his death
By drawing in a leprous harlots breath;   60

29 And, kist] And kist, *1633*   ingled] nigled *H 49, TC, Cy*: iuggled *B*: dandled *Dob,
O'F, S 96; see note*   30 see:] see. *1633*   31 grim eight . . . high iron] grim-eight . . .
high-iron *1633*   37 for *Σ*: to *1633, S, Gr*   38 kisse.] kisse; *1633*   40 mine *Σ*:
my *1633, C 57, H 49, Cy, Gr*   42 wee were *Σ*: were wee *1633, C 57, O'F, Cy, Gr*
43 When] Then *Dob, O'F, S 96*   44 shivered.] shivered; *1633*   60 breath;]
breath, *1633*

By thee, the greatest staine to mans estate
Falls on us, to be call'd effeminate;
Though you be much lov'd in the Princes hall,
There, things that seeme, exceed substantiall;
Gods, when yee fum'd on altars, were pleas'd well,   65
Because you'were burnt, not that they lik'd your smell;
You'are loathsome all, being taken simply'alone:
Shall wee love ill things joyn'd, and hate each one?
If you were good, your good doth soone decay;
And you are rare, that takes the good away.   70
All my perfumes, I give most willingly
To'embalme thy fathers corse; What? will hee die?

Jealosie

FOND woman, which would'st have thy husband die,
And yet complain'st of his great jealousie;
If swolne with poyson, hee lay in'his last bed,
His body with a sere-barke covered,
Drawing his breath, as thick and short, as can   5
The nimblest crocheting Musitian,
Ready with loathsome vomiting to spue
His Soule out of one hell, into a new,
Made deafe with his poore kindreds howling cries,
Begging with few feign'd teares, great legacies,   10
Thou would'st not weepe, but jolly,'and frolicke bee,
As a slave, which to morrow should be free;
Yet weep'st thou, when thou seest him hungerly
Swallow his owne death, hearts-bane jealousie.
O give him many thanks, he'is courteous,   15
That in suspecting kindly warneth us.
Wee must not, as wee us'd, flout openly,
In scoffing ridles, his deformitie;

64 substantiall;] substantiall. *1633*   66 smell;] smell, *1633*   67 simply'alone :]
simply alone, *1633*

Jealosie (Elegy I *Gr*). *Title from 1635*   1 woman,] woman *1633*   9 poore]
pure *C 57, H 49, W*   12 free;] free *1633*

Nor at his boord together being satt,
With words, nor touch, scarce lookes adulterate.   20
Nor when he swolne, and pamper'd with great fare,
Sits downe, and snorts, cag'd in his basket chaire,
Must wee usurpe his owne bed any more,
Nor kisse and play in his house, as before.
Now I see many dangers; for that is   25
His realme, his castle, and his diocesse.
But if, as envious men, which would revile
Their Prince, or coyne his gold, themselves exile
Into another countrie,'and doe it there,
Wee play'in another house, what should we feare?   30
There we will scorne his houshold policies,
His seely plots, and pensionary spies,
As the inhabitants of Thames right side
Do Londons Mayor; or Germans, the Popes pride.

[Recusancy]

OH, let mee not serve so, as those men serve
Whom honours smoakes at once fatten and sterve;
Poorely enrich't with great mens words or lookes;
Nor so write my name in thy loving bookes
As those Idolatrous flatterers, which still   5
Their Princes stiles, with many Realmes fulfill
Whence they no tribute have, and where no sway.
Such services I offer as shall pay
Themselves, I hate dead names: Oh then let mee
Favorite in Ordinary, or no favorite bee.   10
When my Soule was in her owne body sheath'd,
Nor yet by oathes betroth'd, nor kisses breath'd

21 great] high *Dob, O'F, S 96, P, B*: his *Cy*   fare,] fare *1633*   25 that *MSS.*:
it *1633*   30 We into some third place retyred were *Dob, O'F, S 96, Cy, P, B*
34 Mayor; *MSS.*: Major, *1633, Gr*

[Recusancy] (Elegy VI *Gr*). *Title supplied; see note*   2 fatten] flatter *TC, S 96, Cy, P*
6 with *MSS.*: which *1633*

Into my Purgatory, faithlesse thee,
Thy heart seem'd waxe, and steele thy constancie.
So, carelesse flowers strow'd on the waters face,   15
The curled whirlepooles suck, smack, and embrace,
Yet drowne them; so, the tapers beamie eye
Amorously twinkling, beckens the giddie flie,
Yet burnes his wings; and such the devill is,
Scarce visiting them, who are intirely his.   20
When I behold a streame, which, from the spring,
Doth with doubtfull melodious murmuring,
Or in a speechlesse slumber, calmely ride
Her wedded channels bosome, and then chide
And bend her browes, and swell if any bough   25
Do but stoop downe, to kisse her upmost brow:
Yet, if her often gnawing kisses winne
The traiterous banke to gape, and let her in,
She rusheth violently, and doth divorce
Her from her native, and her long-kept course,   30
And rores, and braves it, and in gallant scorne,
In flattering eddies promising retorne,
She flouts the channell, who thenceforth is drie;
Then say I; that is shee, and this am I.
Yet let not thy deepe bitternesse beget   35
Carelesse despaire in mee, for that will whet
My minde to scorne; and Oh, love dull'd with paine
Was ne'r so wise, nor well arm'd as disdaine.
Then with new eyes I shall survay thee,'and spie
Death in thy cheekes, and darknesse in thine eye.   40
Though hope bred faith and love; thus taught, I shall
As nations do from Rome, from thy love fall.
My hate shall outgrow thine, and utterly
I will renounce thy dalliance: and when I
Am the Recusant, in that resolute state,   45
What hurts it mee to be'excommunicate?

---

24 then] there *TC, O'F, A 25, JC, Cy, P*   26 to *Σ*: or *1633, C 57, Gr*
28 banke *TC, Dob, S 96, W, A 25, JC, B, S*: banks *1633, C 57, H 49, Cy, P*   33 the]
her *TC, O'F, Cy, P*   40 eye.] eye; *1633*   41 bred *1633, W, A 25*: breede *Σ; see note*

[Tutelage]

NATURES lay Ideot, I taught thee to love,
   And in that sophistrie, Oh, thou dost prove
Too subtile: Foole, thou didst not understand
The mystique language of the eye nor hand:
Nor couldst thou judge the difference of the aire   5
Of sighes, and say, this lies, this sounds despaire:
Nor by the'eyes water call a maladie
Desperately hot, or changing feaverously.
I had not taught thee then, the Alphabet
Of flowers, how they devisefully being set   10
And bound up, might with speechlesse secrecie
Deliver arrands mutely,'and mutually.
Remember since all thy words us'd to bee
To every suitor; I,'if my friends agree;
Since, household charmes, thy husbands name to teach,   15.
Were all the love trickes, that thy wit could reach;
And since, an houres discourse could scarce have made
One answer in thee, and that ill arraid
In broken proverbs, and torne sentences.
Thou art not by so many duties his,   20
That from the worlds Common having sever'd thee,
Inlaid thee, neither to be seene, nor see,
As mine: which have with amorous delicacies
Refin'd thee'into a blis-full paradise.
Thy graces and good words my creatures bee;   25
I planted knowledge and lifes tree in thee,
Which Oh, shall strangers taste? Must I alas
Frame and enamell Plate, and drinke in Glasse?
Chafe waxe for others seales? breake a colts force
And leave him then, beeing made a ready horse?   30

[Tutelage] (Elegy VII *Gr*). *S 96 omits. Title supplied; see note*   6 despaire:] despaire.
1633   7 call] know *Dob, O'F* (*b.c.*): cast *S*   12 mutely,'and] mutely,and *1633*
14 I,'if] I, if *1633*   agree;] agree. *1633*   23 which *Σ*: who *1633, C 57, Cy, P, S, Gr*
25 words] workes *C 57, H 49, TCC, Dob*   bee;] bee, *1633*   28 Glasse?] glasse. *1633*

Loves Warre

TILL I have peace with thee, warre other men,
      And when I have peace, can I leave thee then?
All other warres are scrupulous; only thou,
O faire, free City, mayst thy selfe allow
To any one: In Flanders who can tell   5
Whether the master presse, or men rebell?
Only wee knowe, that which all Ideots say,
They beare most blowes which come to part the fraye.
France in her lunatique giddiness did hate
Ever our men, yea and our God of late,   10
Yet she relies upon our Angels well,
Which ne'r retourne; no more then they which fell.
Sick Ireland is with a strange warre possest,
Like to'an Ague, now rageinge, now at rest,
Which time will cure; yet it must do her good   15
If she were purg'd, and her heade-veine let blood.
And Midas joyes our Spanish journeys give,
Wee touch all gold, but find no foode to live;
And I should be in that hot parching clime
To dust and ashes turn'd before my time.   20
To mewe me in a ship is to enthrall
Mee in a prison that were like to fall;
Or in a cloyster, save that there men dwell
In a calme heaven, here in a swaggering hell.
Long voyages are longe consumptions,   25
And ships are carts for executions,
Yea they are deaths; Is't not all one to fly
Into another world as 'tis to dye?
Here let mee warre; in these armes let mee lye;
Here let mee parlee, batter, bleede, and dye.   30

Loves Warre (Elegy XX Gr). *First printed in F. G. Waldron,* A Collection of Miscellaneous Poetry, *1802, from MS. D 17. Text from C 57 with spelling regularized to that of 1633 and punctuation supplemented. Title from Gr:* Making of Men *B; see note*   19 should *Σ*: shall C 57, H 49   that *O'F, W, A 25, JC, B:* the *C 57, H 49, TC, Dob, S 96, Cy, P, S, Gr* 30–31 *Omit P*

Thine armes emprison mee, and mine armes thee;
Thy hart thy ransome is, take mine for mee.
Other men warre that they their rest may gaine,
But we will rest that wee may fight againe.
Those warres the ignorant, these th'experienc'd love;   35
There wee are alwayes under, here above.
There engines far off breede a just true feare,
Neare thrusts, pikes, stabs, yea bullets hurt not here.
There lyes are wrongs, here safe uprightly lye;
There men kill men, we'will make one by and by.   40
Thou nothing; I not halfe so much shall do
In these warres as they may which from us two
Shall spring. Thousands we see which travaile not
To warres, but stay, swords, armes and shot
To make at home: And shall not I do then   45
More glorious service, staying to make men?

To his Mistris Going to Bed

COME, Madame, come, all rest my powers defie,
   Until I labour, I in labour lye.
The foe oft-times, having the foe in sight,
Is tir'd with standing, though they never fight.
Off with that girdle, like heavens zone glistering   5
But a farre fairer world encompassing.
Unpin that spangled brest-plate, which you weare
That th'eyes of busy fooles may be stopt there:
Unlace your selfe, for that harmonious chime
Tells me from you that now 'tis your bed time.   10

31 Thine *TC, Dob, O'F, S 96, A 25, Cy, B, S*: thy *C 57, H 49, W, JC.*   38 Neare *Σ*: Ne're *C 57*

To his Mistris Going to Bed (Elegy **XIX** *Gr*). *First printed in 1669. Text from C 57 with spelling regularized to that of 1633, punctuation supplemented and paragraphing supplied. Title from 1669*: Going to Bed *B, Gr*   4 they] he *Dob, S 96, A 25, Cy, P, B, S, 1669, Gr*   5 zone] zones *TC, Dob, W*   glistering] glittering *Dob, 1669, Gr*   8 that I may see my shrine that shines so faire *Cy, P*   10 'tis your] is . . . *Dob, O'F*: 'tis full *A 25*: it is *1669, Gr*

Off with that happy buske, whom I envye
That still can be, and still can stand so nigh.
Your gownes going off such beauteous state reveales
As when from flowery meades th'hills shadow steales.
Off with your wyrie coronet and showe   15
The hairy dyadem which on you doth growe.
Off with those shoes: and then safely tread
In this loves hallow'd temple, this soft bed.
In such white robes heavens Angels us'd to bee
Receiv'd by men; Thou Angel bring'st with thee   20
A heaven like Mahomets Paradise; and though
Ill spirits walk in white, we easily know
By this these Angels from an evill sprite:
They set our haires, but these the flesh upright.
    Licence my roving hands, and let them goe   25
Behind, before, above, between, below.
Oh my America, my new found lande,
My kingdome, safeliest when with one man man'd,
My myne of precious stones, my Empiree,
How blest am I in this discovering thee.   30
To enter in these bonds is to be free,
Then where my hand is set my seal shall be.
    Full nakedness, all joyes are due to thee.
As soules unbodied, bodies uncloth'd must bee
To taste whole joyes. Gems which you women use   35
Are as Atlanta's balls, cast in mens viewes,
That when a fooles eye lighteth on a gem
His earthly soule may covet theirs not them.

11 whom] which *O'F, S 96, A 25, JC, Cy, P, 1669, Gr*: yᵗ *B*   13 gownes] gown *O'F, A 25, Cy, P, 1669, Gr*   14 from] through *1669*   shadow] shadows *P, 1669*   15 your] that *Dob, Cy, P, B, 1669, Gr*   16 on you] on your head *1669*   17 Off with those shoes: and then *H 49, TC*: ... these ... *C 57*: ... shoes you weare and *Dob, O'F, S 96*: Off with yᵒʳ hose and shoes, then *S*: Now off with those shoes and then *W, A 25, JC, Cy, P, B, 1669, Gr; see note*   `safely *TC, Dob, O'F, S 96, W, A 25, B, S*: softly *C 57, H 49, JC, Cy, P, 1669*   20 Receiv'd by] Revealed to *1669*   22 Ill] All *O'F, Cy, P, B, 1669*   24 They] Those *O'F, 1669, Gr*   the] our *Dob, O'F, S 96, A 25, JC, Cy, P, B, S, 1669, Gr*   26 Before, behinde, betweene, above *B, 1669, Gr*: Above, behinde, before, beneath *S 96*   28 kingdome, safeliest] ... safest *S 96, A 25, B, S*: kingdom's safest *O'F, Cy, P, 1669*   30 How am I blest in thus *1669*   31 in *Dob, W, A 25, JC, B, S*: into *C 57, H 49, TC, O'F, S 96, Cy, P*   these *Σ*: those *C 57, A 25*   bonds *Σ*: Bands *C 57*   32 Then *Σ*: There *C 57, JC, P*: That *S*   36 as] like *Dob, S 96, JC, 1669, Gr*   balls] ball *1669*   38 covet] courte *P, 1669*   theirs] those *S*: yᵗ *O'F, B, 1669*

Like pictures, or like bookes gay coverings made
For laymen, are all women thus arraid;   40
Themselves are mystique bookes, which only wee
Whom their imputed grace will dignify
Must see reveal'd. Then since I may knowe,
As liberally as to a midwife showe
Thy selfe; cast all, yea this white linnen hence.   45
Here is no pennance, much lesse innocence.
   To teach thee, I am naked first: Why than
What need'st thou have more covering than a man.

Loves Progress

WHO ever loves, if hee doe not propose
   The right true end of love, hee's one which goes
To sea for nothing but to make him sicke.
And love's a beare-whelpe borne; if wee'overlicke
Our love, and force it new strange shapes to take   5
We erre, and of a lumpe a monster make.
Were not a Calf a monster that were growne
Fac'd like a man, though better than his owne?
Perfection is in unitie; Preferre
One woman first, and then one thing in her.   10
I, when I value gold, may thinke upon
The ductillness, the application,
The wholesomeness, the ingenuity,
From rust, from soyle, from fyre ever free,

41 Themselves are only mysticke bookes, which we B, 1669: ... musique bookes ... P
43 see Σ: be C 57, H 49, TCD   since] since that O'F, JC, 1669, Gr: sweet that Cy, P:
(sweet) since B; see note   44 a] thy JC, 1669   46 Here ... much lesse Dob, S 96,
A 25: There ... much lesse C 57, H 49, TC, W: There ... due to O'F, JC, Cy, P, B, S,
1669, Gr; see note

   Loves Progress (Elegy XVIII Gr). Dob, W omit. First printed in Wit and Drollery, 1661.
Printed in 1669. Text from C 57 with spelling regularized to that of 1633, punctuation supplemented and paragraphing supplied. Title from H 49, O'F, A 25, JC, B, S   2 which]
that O'F, S 96, Cy, P, S, 1669, Gr   4 And love's] Love is JC, S, 1669, Gr.
wee'overlicke] wee o're licke S 96, JC, S, 1669, Gr   5 strange] strong 1669
14 ever] for ever O'F, S 96, Cy, S

But if I love it, 'tis because 'tis made   15
By our new Nature, use, the soule of trade.
   All these in women wee might thinke upon
(If women had them) but yet love but one.
Can men more injure women than to say
They love'them for that by which they are not they?   20
Makes virtue woman? Must I cool my blood
Till I both bee, and find one, wise and good?
May barren Angels love so: But if wee
Make love to woman, Vertue is not shee,
As Beauty's not, nor Wealth. Hee that strayes thus,   25
From her to hers, is more adulterous
Than if hee tooke her mayde. Search every spheare
And firmament, our Cupid is not there.
He's an infernall God, and under ground
With Pluto dwells, where gold and fyre abound.   30
Men to such Gods their sacrificing coales
Did not in Altars lay, but pits and holes.
Although wee see celestiall bodies move
Above the earth, the earth we till and love:
So we her ayres contemplate, words and hart   35
And vertues; But we love the Centrique part.
   Nor is the soule more worthy, or more fit
For love than this, as infinite as it.
But in attaining this desired place
How much they stray that set out at the face.   40
The hair a forrest is of ambushes,
Of springes, snares, fetters and manacles.
The brow becalms us, when 'tis smooth and plaine,
And when 'tis wrinkled, shipwracks us againe;
Smooth 'tis a Paradise where we would have   45
Immortall stay, and wrinkled 'tis our grave.

---

18 but] and *S 96*, *S*, *1669*, *Gr*   20 they are] they're *1669*, *Gr*   25 Beauty's
not] Beauties no *1669*   27 if hee tooke] hee that tooke *O'F*, *Cy*, *P*, (takes) *B*, *S*
32 in] on *O'F*, *S 96*, *Cy*, *JC*, *S*, *1669*   34 till *Σ*: fill *C 57*   38 it *Σ*: yett *C 57*
40 stray] err *S 96*, *S*, *1669*, *Gr*   42 springes *O'F*, *A 25*, *JC*, *Cy*, *P*, *B*, *S*: springs *C 57*,
H 49, *TC*, *1669*   46 and] but *1669*   our] a *S 96*, *1669*

The nose like to the first Meridian runs
Not 'twixt an East and West, but 'twixt two suns.
It leaves a cheeke, a rosy hemispheare,
On either side, and then directs us where   50
Upon the Ilands Fortunate wee fall
(Not faint Canarye but Ambrosiall),
Her swelling lips: to which when we are come
Wee anchor there, and think our selves at home,
For they seem all: there Syrens songs, and there   55
Wise Delphique Oracles doe fill the eare;
There in a creeke where chosen pearles doe swell
The Remora, her cleavinge tongue doth dwell.
These, and the glorious promontorye, her chinne,
O'rpast; and the straight Hellespont between   60
The Sestos and Abydos of her brests,
Not of two Lovers, but two Loves, the nests,
Succeeds a boundless sea, but that thine eye
Some Iland moles may scatter'd there descrye;
And sailing towards her India, in that way   65
Shall at her faire Atlantique navell stay;
Though thence the currant be thy pilot made,
Yet ere thou bee where thou wouldst bee embay'd,
Thou shalt upon another forrest set
Where some doe shipwracke, and no farther gett.   70
When thou art there, consider what this chace
Mispent, by thy beginning at the face.
    Rather set out below; practise my art.
Some symetrie the foote hath with that part
Which thou dost seeke, and is thy map for that,   75
Lovely enough to stop, but not stay at;
Least subject to disguise and change it is,
Men say, the devill never can change his.

47 first] sweet *1669*   52 Canarye] Canaries *TC, O'F, S 96, S, 1669, Gr*   53 Unto
her swelling lips when we are come *1669*   57 There] Here *H 49* : Then *Cy, P, B, 1669*
where *Σ*: when *C 57, H 49* : *omit P*   60 Being past the Straits of Hellespont between
1669   63 that] yet *1669, Gr*   66 faire *Σ*: *omit C 57*   67 thence] hence *P* :
there *1669*   thy] the *1669*   68 wouldst] shouldst *1669*   70 some doe] many
O'F, S, 1669, Gr

It is the embleme that hath figured
Firmness; 'tis the first part that comes to bed.   80
Civility, wee see, refin'd the kisse
Which, at the face begun, transplanted is
Since to the hand, since to th'Imperiall knee,
Now at the Papall foote delights to bee.
If Kings thinke that the nearer way and doe   85
Rise from the foote, lovers may doe so too.
For as free spheares move faster far than can
Birds, whome the ayre resists, so may that man
Which goes this empty and etheriall way
Than if at beauties elements hee stay.   90
Rich Nature hath in woman wisely made
Two purses, and their mouthes aversely laid;
They then which to the lower tribute owe
That way which that exchequer lookes must goe.
Hee which doth not, his error is as greate   95
As who by Clyster gave the stomach meate.

Change

ALTHOUGH thy hand and faith, and good workes too,
Have seal'd thy love which nothing should undoe,
Yea though thou fall backe, that apostasie
Confirme thy love; yet much, much I feare thee.
Women are like the Arts, forc'd unto none,   5
Open to'all searchers, unpriz'd, if unknowne.
If I have caught a bird, and let him flie,
Another fouler using these meanes, as I,
May catch the same bird; and, as these things bee,
Women are made for men, not him, nor mee.   10

79 that Σ: which C 57, H 49, A 25, JC   82 begun] began O'F, S 96, Cy, P, 1669,
Gr; see note   94 lookes Σ: bookes C 57: opes JC   96 Clyster Σ: Glysters C 57,
H 49: glister P, B, S, 1669   gave] gives TCD, O'F, Cy, P, B, S, 1669

Change (Elegy III Gr). Title from 1635   5 Women] Women, 1633   8 these]
those TC, W, A 25, JC, Cy, P, B: the O'F, S 96

Foxes and goats; all beasts change when they please,
Shall women, more hot, wily, wild then these,
Be bound to one man, and did Nature then
Idly make them apter to'endure then men?
They'are our clogges, and their owne; if a man bee   15
Chain'd to a galley, yet the galley'is free;
Who hath a plow-land, casts all his seed corne there,
And yet allowes his ground more corne should beare;
Though Danuby into the sea must flow,
The sea receives the Rhene, Volga, and Po.   20
By nature, which gave it, this liberty
Thou lov'st, but Oh! canst thou love it and mee?
Likenesse glues love: Then if soe thou doe,
To make us like and love, must I change too?
More then thy hate, I hate'it, rather let mee   25
Allow her change, then change as oft as shee,
And soe not teach, but force my'opinion
To love not any one, nor every one.
To live in one land, is captivitie,
To runne all countries, a wild roguery;   30
Waters stincke soone, if in one place they bide,
And in the vast sea are worse putrifi'd:
But when they kisse one banke, and leaving this
Never looke backe, but the next banke doe kisse,
Then are they purest; Change'is the nursery   35
Of musicke, joy, life, and eternity.

---

15 and Σ: not *1633*, *TC*, *O'F*, *Gr*; *see note*   23 Then if so thou do Σ: And then . . .
O'F, *S 96*, *S*: and if that thou so doe *1633*, *Gr*; *see note*   32 worse Σ: worst *JC*, *B*:
more *1633*, *Gr*

The Anagram

MARRY, and love thy *Flavia*, for, shee
   Hath all things, whereby others beautious bee,
For, though her eyes be small, her mouth is great,
Though they be Ivory, yet her teeth are jeat,
Though they be dimme, yet she is light enough,   5
And though her harsh haire fall, her skinne is rough;
What though her cheeks be yellow,'her haire is red,
Give her thine, and she hath a maydenhead.
These things are beauties elements, where these
Meet in one, that one must, as perfect, please.   10
If red and white and each good quality
Be in thy wench, ne'r aske where it doth lye.
In buying things perfum'd, we aske; if there
Be muske and amber in it, but not where.
Though all her parts be not in th'usuall place,   15
She'hath yet an Anagram of a good face.
If we might put the letters but one way,
In the leane dearth of words, what could wee say?
When by the Gamut some Musitions make
A perfect song, others will undertake,   20
By the same Gamut chang'd, to equall it.
Things simply good, can never be unfit.
She's faire as any, if all be like her,
And if none bee, then she is singular.
All love is wonder; if wee justly doe   25
Account her wonderfull, why not lovely too?
Love built on beauty, soone as beauty, dies,
Chuse this face, chang'd by no deformities.
Women are all like Angels; the faire be
Like those which fell to worse; but such as shee,   30

The Anagram (Elegy II *Gr*). *Title from 1635*   4 are *Σ*: be *1633, C 57*, H *49, ℐC, Gr*
6 rough] tough *Dob, O'F, S 96*   7 yellow, 'her] yellow, her *1633*   haire is *Σ*:
haire's *1633, O'F, Gr; see note*   18 the] that *TC, Dob, W, A 25, ℐC, B, S*   22 unfit.]
unfit; *1633*   28 deformities.] deformities; *1633*   29–31 *Omit A 25*

Like to good Angels, nothing can impaire:
'Tis lesse griefe to be foule, then to'have beene faire.
For one nights revels, silke and gold we chuse,
But, in long journeyes, cloth, and leather use.
Beauty is barren oft; best husbands say   35
There is best land, where there is foulest way.
Oh what a soveraigne Plaister will shee bee,
If thy past sinnes have taught thee jealousie!
Here needs no spies, nor eunuches; her commit
Safe to thy foes; yea, to a Marmosit.   40
When Belgiaes citties, the round countries drowne,
That durty foulenesse guards, and armes the towne:
So doth her face guard her; and so, for thee,
Which, forc'd by business, absent oft must bee,
Shee, whose face, like clouds, turnes the day to night,   45
Who, mightier then the sea, makes Moores seem white,
Who, though seaven yeares, she in the Stews had laid,
A Nunnery durst receive, and thinke a maid,
And though in childbirths labour she did lie,
Midwifes would sweare, 'twere but a tympanie,   50
Whom, if shee'accuse her selfe, I credit lesse
Then witches, which impossibles confesse,
Whom Dildoes, Bedstaves, and her Velvet Glasse
Would be as loath to touch as Joseph was:
One like none, and lik'd of none, fittest were,   55
For, things in fashion every man will weare.

---

37 bee,] bee *1633*   49 childbirths *H 49, TC, Dob, W, S*: childbirthe *S 96, A 25, JC,
Cy, P, B*: childbeds *1633, C 57, O'F (b.c), Gr*   51 shee'accuse] shee accuse *1633*
52 confesse,] confesse. *1633*   53–54 *From MSS.: omit 1633*

On his Mistris

Y our first strange and fatall interview,
B   By all desires which thereof did ensue,
By our long sterving hopes, by that remorse
Which my words masculine perswasive force
Begot in thee, and by the memory   5
Of hurts which spies and rivalls threatned mee,
I calmely beg; but by thy parents wrath,
By all paines which want and divorcement hath,
I conjure thee; and all those oathes which I
And thou have sworne, to seal joint constancie,   10
Here I unsweare, and over-sweare them thus:
Thou shalt not love by meanes so dangerous.
Temper, oh faire Love, loves impetuous rage,
Be my true mistris still, not my feign'd page.
I'll goe, and, by thy kind leave, leave behinde   15
Thee, onely worthy to nurse in my minde
Thirst to come back; oh, if thou dye before,
From other lands my soule towards thee shall soare.
Thy (else Almighty) Beauty cannot move
Rage from the seas, nor thy love teach them love,   20
Nor tame wilde Boreas harshness; Thou hast read
How roughly hee in peices shivered
Faire Orithea, whome he swore hee lov'd.
Fall ill or good, 'tis madness to have prov'd
Dangers unurg'd; Feede on this flatterye,   25
That absent lovers one in th'other bee.
Dissemble nothing, not a boy, nor change
Thy bodies habit, nor mindes; bee not strange

On his Mistris (Elegy XVI Gr). Cy omits. First printed in 1635. Text from C 57 with spelling
regularized to that of 1633 and punctuation supplemented. Title from 1635: On his Mistress
desire to be disguised and to goe like a Page with him Dob, (. . . desiring . . .) O'F, S 96 : His
wife would have gone as his Page B   7 parents] fathers O'F, 1635, Gr   9 those]
these H 49: the Dob, O'F, S 96, P, B, 1635, Gr   12 meanes] wayes O'F, S, 1635, Gr
18 My soule from other lands to thee O'F, 1635, Gr   24 Fall Σ: Full C 57
28 mindes TC, W, A 25, JC, B: Mynde C 57, H 49, Dob, O'F, S 96, P, S, 1635

To thy selfe onely; All will spye in thy face
A blushing womanly discovering grace.   30
Richly cloth'd Apes are call'd Apes, and as soone
Ecclips'd as bright, wee call the moone, the moone.
Men of France, changeable Camelions,
Spittles of diseases, shops of fashions,
Loves fuellers, and the rightest companie   35
Of Players which uppon the worlds stage bee,
Will quickly knowe thee,'and knowe thee; and alas
Th'indifferent Italian, as wee passe
His warme land, well content to thinke thee page,
Will haunt thee, with such lust and hideous rage   40
As Lots faire guests were vext: But none of these,
Nor spungie hydroptique Dutch, shall thee displease,
If thou stay here. Oh stay here, for, for thee
England is only'a worthy gallerie,
To walk in expectation, till from thence   45
Our greate King call thee into his presence.
When I am gone, dreame mee some happinesse,
Nor let thy lookes our long hid love confesse,
Nor praise, nor dispraise mee, blesse, nor curse
Openly loves force; nor in bed fright thy nurse   50
With midnights startings, crying out, oh, oh,
Nurse, oh my love is slaine; I saw him goe
Ore the white Alpes, alone; I saw him, I,
Assayld, fight, taken, stabb'd, bleede, fall, and dye.
Augure mee better chance, except dreade Jove   55
Think it enough for mee, to'have had thy love.

---

35 Loves *TC, O'F, A 25, S, 1635*: Lives *C 57, H 49, Dob, S 96, W, JC, P, B; see note*
37 knowe thee, and knowe thee; and alas *TC, W,* (... and thee ...) *A 25,* (... thee alas) *S:*
knowe thee and alas *C 57, H 49, Dob, S 96, JC, P, B:* knowe thee, and no lesse, alas *O'F,*
1635, Gr; see note   39 well *Σ:* will *C 57*   40 haunt] hunt *Dob, O'F, S 96,*
1635, Gr   46 greate ... call ... into *W, A 25, JC:* ... to *C 57, H 49:* ... doe call
... to *TC:* greatest ... call ... to *Dob, O'F, S 96, P, B, 1635, Gr; see note*   49 blesse] nor
blesse *Dob, O'F, S 96, P, B, S, 1635, Gr*   51 midnights *H 49, TC, O'F, W, A 25, 1635:*
midnight *C 57, Dob, S 96, JC, P, B, S*

His Picture

HERE take my Picture, though I bid farewell;
    Thine, in my heart, where my soule dwels, shall dwell.
'Tis like me now, but I dead, 'twill be more
When wee are shadowes both, then 'twas before.
When weather-beaten I come backe; my hand,   5
Perchance with rude oares torne, or Sun beams tann'd,
My face and brest of hairecloth, and my head
With cares rash sodaine hoarinesse o'rspread,
My body'a sack of bones, broken within,
And powders blew staines scatter'd on my skinne;   10
If rivall fooles taxe thee to'have lov'd a man,
So foule, and course, as, Oh, I may seeme than,
This shall say what I was: and thou shalt say,
Doe his hurts reach mee? doth my worth decay?
Or doe they reach his judging minde, that hee   15
Should like'and love lesse, what hee did love to see?
That which in him was faire and delicate,
Was but the milke, which in loves childish state
Did nurse it: who now is growne strong enough
To feed on that, which to'disus'd tasts seemes tough.   20

His Picture (Elegy V Gr). Dob omits. Title from 1635 : The Picture P : Travelling he leaves
his Picture with his mystris B   6 Perchance W, A 25, JC : Perhaps 1633, Σ, Gr; see
note   8 rash] harsh O'F : as S   sodaine hoarinesse o'rspread O'F, W, JC : ...
woarinesse ... A 25 : sodaine stormes, being o'rspread 1633, TC, Gr : sodaine stormes ore
sprede C 57, H 49, S 96, Cy : cruell sudeine stormes orespread P : sudden cruel stormes oreprest
B : suddaine stormes orepressed S; see note   16 like'and] like and Σ : now 1633, TC,
Gr; see note   19 nurse] nourish TC, P, S   20 to'disus'd] to disus'd 1633 : to
disused Gr; see note

A Funeral Elegy

TO L.C.

SORROW, who to this house scarce knew the way,
Is, Oh, heire of it, our All is his prey.
This strange chance claimes strange wonder, and to us
Nothing can be so strange, as to weepe thus.
'Tis well his lifes loud speaking workes deserve,   5
And give praise too, our cold tongues could not serve:
'Tis well, hee kept teares from our eyes before,
That to fit this deepe ill, we might have store.
Oh, if a sweet briar, climbe up by a tree,
If to a paradise that transplanted bee,   10
Or fell'd, and burnt for holy sacrifice,
Yet, that must wither, which by it did rise,
As we for him dead: though no familie
Ere rigg'd a soule for heavens discoverie
With whom more Venturers more boldly dare   15
Venture their states, with him in joy to share,
Wee lose what all friends lov'd, him; he gaines now
But life by death, which worst foes would allow,
If hee could have foes, in whose practise grew
All vertues, whose names subtile Schoolmen knew.   20
What ease can hope that wee shall see'him, beget,
When wee must die first, and cannot dye yet?
His children are his pictures, Oh they bee
Pictures of him dead, senselesse, cold as he.
Here needs no marble Tombe, since hee is gone,   25
He, and about him, his, are turn'd to stone.

A Funeral Elegy To L.C. *TC, A 25 omit. Title supplied*: Elegie on the L.C. *1635; see note.
Printed as the sixth of the Elegies in 1633 and among the Epicedes and Obsequies in 1635, Gr*
1 way,] way: *1633*   4 thus.] thus; *1633*   9 by a] by'a *1633*   16 share,]
share *1633*   17 him;] him, *1633*   20 knew.] knew; *1633*   21 ease] ease,
1633   24 he.] he, *1633*

The Autumnall

No *Spring*, nor *Summer* Beauty hath such grace,
As I have seen in one *Autumnall* face.
Yong Beauties force your love, and that's a Rape,
This doth but counsaile, yet you cannot scape.
If 'twere a shame to love, here 'twere no shame,   5
Affection here takes Reverences name.
Were her first yeares the Golden Age; That's true,
But now shee's gold oft tried, and ever new.
That was her torrid and inflaming time,
This is her tolerable Tropique clyme.   10
Faire eyes, who askes more heate then comes from hence,
He in a fever wishes pestilence.
Call not these wrinkles, graves; If graves they were,
They were Loves graves; for else he is no where.
Yet lies not Love dead here, but here doth sit   15
Vow'd to this trench, like an Anachorit.
And here, till hers, which must be his death, come,
He doth not digge a Grave, but build a Tombe.
Here dwells he, though he sojourne ev'ry where,
In Progresse, yet his standing house is here.   20
Here, where still Evening is; not noone, nor night;
Where no voluptuousnesse, yet all delight.
In all her words, unto all hearers fit,
You may at Revels, you at Counsaile, sit.
This is loves timber, youth his under-wood;   25
There he, as wine in June, enrages blood,

The Autumnall (Elegy IX Gr). *Text from 1633. MSS.*: H 40, C 57, H 49; L 74, TC; Dob,
O'F. *Title from 1633 which has* Elegie./The Autumnall: Elegie Autumnall H 40, C 57, H 49,
Dob: Widdow Her L 74: Elegie. 12. On the Lady Herbert afterwards Danvers O'F: Elegie
TC; *for other titles in MSS. see note. The text in 1633 is indented and heavily italicized*
2 face.] face, 1633   3 your H 40, L 74, TC, Dob, O'F: our 1633, C 57, H 49, Gr
5 'twere] t'were 1633 bis   6 Affection ... takes H 49, L 74, TC, Dob: ... take H 40:
Affliction ... C 57: Affections ... take 1633, O'F   8 shee's MSS.: they'are 1633
10 tolerable] habitable L 74, TC, O'F   11 heate] heate, 1633 uncorrected   15 Love]
love 1633   16 an Anachorit] an Anchorite L 74, TC: to an Anchorit O'F   19 where,]
where; 1633 uncorrected   24 Counsaile] counsaile 1633   26 enrages] breeds
C 57: bringes H 49

Which then comes seasonabliest, when our tast
And appetite to other things, is past.
Xerxes strange Lydian love, the Platane tree,
Was lov'd for age, none being so large as shee,   30
Or else because, being yong, nature did blesse
Her youth with ages glory, Barrennesse.
If we love things long sought, Age is a thing
Which we are fifty yeares in compassing.
If transitory things, which soone decay,   35
Age must be lovelyest at the latest day.
But name not Winter-faces, whose skin's slacke;
Lanke, as an unthrifts purse; but a soules sacke;
Whose Eyes seeke light within, for all here's shade;
Whose mouthes are holes, rather worne out, then made;   40
Whose every tooth to a'severall place is gone,
To vexe their soules at Resurrection;
Name not these living Deaths-heads unto mee,
For these, not Ancient, but Antiques be.
I hate extreames; yet I had rather stay   45
With Tombs, then Cradles, to weare out a day.
Since such loves naturall lation is, may still
My love descend, and journey downe the hill,
Not panting after growing beauties, so,
I shall ebbe on with them, who home-ward goe.   50

27 seasonabliest] seasonablest *L 74, TC, Dob, O'F*   28 past.] past; *1633*
40 made;] made *1633*   41 to'a] to a *1633*   44 Ancient] Ancients *O'F*   Antiques
L 74, TC, Dob, O'F: Antiquityes *H 40*: Antique *1633, C 57, H 49, Gr*   47 naturall
lation *H 40, H 49, L 74, TC*: natural statyon *C 57, Dob, O'F*: motion natural *1633*
50 on *MSS.*: out *1633, Gr*   home-ward] home-wards *H 40, C 57, H 49, Dob, O'F*

JOHN DONNE
The Lothian Portrait

SONGS AND SONNETS

(I)

Song

GOE, and catche a falling starre,
Get with child a mandrake roote,
Tell me, where all past yeares are,
  Or who cleft the Divels foot,
Teach me to heare Mermaides singing,   5
Or to keep off envies stinging,
      And finde
      What winde
Serves to'advance an honest minde.

If thou beest borne to strange sights,   10
  Things invisible to see,
Ride ten thousand daies and nights,
  Till age snow white haires on thee,
Thou, when thou retorn'st, wilt tell mee
All strange wonders that befell thee,   15
      And sweare
      No where
Lives a woman true, and faire.

If thou findst one, let mee know,
  Such a Pilgrimage were sweet,   20
Yet doe not, I would not goe,
  Though at next doore wee might meet,

SONGS AND SONNETS. *Text from 1633 unless otherwise stated. Readings are given from the following representative MSS.: H 40, C 57, H 49; L 74; TC (TCD with TCC); Dob, O'F, S 96; HK 2, Cy, P; A 25, B, JC, S. When a poem is not found in one of these the omission is noted. When a poem is extant in only a few manuscripts, the complete list of MSS. in which it occurs is given.*

Song. *Title from 1633. This and the following five poems occur in DC under the heading* 'Songs which were made to certaine Aires that were made before'.   9 to'advance] to advance 1633   11 to see] see H 40, C 57, H 49, L 74, TC, B (b.c.): goe see Dob, S 96, S; *see note* 14 when thou retorn'st] at thy returne Dob, O'F, S 96   21 not, I] not, for I Dob, O'F, S 96, S

Though shee were true, when you met her,
And last, till you write your letter,
    Yet shee   25
    Will bee
False, ere I come, to two, or three.

The Message

SEND home my long strayd eyes to mee,
  Which (Oh) too long have dwelt on thee,
Yet since there they'have learn'd such ill,
    Such forc'd fashions,
      And false passions,
        That they be   5
        Made by thee
Fit for no good sight, keep them still.

Send home my harmlesse heart againe,
Which no unworthy thought could staine,   10
Which if it be taught by thine
    To make jestings
    Of protestings,
        And crosse both
        Word and oath,   15
Keepe it, for then 'tis none of mine.

Yet send me back my heart and eyes,
That I may know, and see thy lyes,
And may laugh and joy, when thou
    Art in anguish   20
    And dost languish

24 last] *omit* TCC: last so *O'F, S 96, A 25, JC*: lasts so *Dob, S*
    The Message. *H 40, L 74 omit. Title from 1635. This and the following two poems occur in* TC
under the heading 'Songs wch were made to certaine Aires wch were made before'.   3
they'have] they have *1633*   11 Which if it be taught] But if ... *O'F, Gr*: Yet since
there 'tis taught *HK 2, A 25*: Yet since it hath learn't *P, B, JC; see note*   14 crosse
MSS.: breake *1633*   19 laugh and joy, when thou] ioy and laugh ... *O'F, A 25*: lie
and laugh ... *HK 2*: laugh when that thou *C 57, H 49, Dob, S 96, Cy, S*

For some one
That will none,
Or prove as false as thou art now.

Song

SWEETEST love, I do not goe,
For wearinesse of thee,
Nor in hope the world can show
    A fitter Love for mee;
      But since that I   5
Must dye at last, 'tis best,
To use my selfe in jest
    Thus by fain'd deaths to dye.

Yesternight the Sunne went hence,
    And yet is here to day,   10
He hath no desire nor sense,
    Nor halfe so short a way:
      Then feare not mee,
But beleeve that I shall make
Speedier journeyes, since I take   15
    More wings and spurres then hee.

O how feeble is mans power,
    That if good fortune fall,
Cannot adde another houre,
    Nor a lost houre recall!   20
      But come bad chance,
And wee joyne to it our strength,
And wee teach it art and length,
    It selfe o'r us to'advance.

Song. L 74, Cy omit. Title from 1633. The first four lines of each stanza appear as two long lines in H 40, C 57, H 49, TC, A 25, B, JC; the sixth and seventh also appear as one long line in H 40, C 57, H 49, TC, B   4 mee;] mee, 1633   6–8 At the last must part tis best/Thus to vse my selfe in iest/ By fayned deaths to dye O'F   8 deaths] death H 40, S 96, HK 2, P, JC, S   dye.] dye; 1633   15 journeyes, since I] returne, since I do Dob, S 96 : journeys and do JC   20 recall !] recall? 1633   22 joyne] add O'F, HK 2, A 25, JC   to it] to'it 1633

When thou sigh'st, thou sigh'st not winde,   25
   But sigh'st my soule away,
When thou weep'st, unkindly kinde,
   My lifes blood doth decay.
     It cannot bee
That thou lov'st mee, as thou say'st,   30
If in thine my life thou waste,
   Thou art the best of mee.

Let not thy divining heart
   Forethinke me any ill,
Destiny may take thy part,   35
   And may thy feares fulfill;
     But thinke that wee
Are but turn'd aside to sleepe;
They who one another keepe
   Alive, ne'r parted bee.   40

The Baite

COME live with mee, and bee my love,
   And we will some new pleasures prove
Of golden sands, and christall brookes,
With silken lines, and silver hookes.

There will the river whispering runne   5
Warm'd by thine eyes, more then the Sunne.
And there the'inamor'd fish will stay,
Begging themselves they may betray.

When thou wilt swimme in that live bath,
Each fish, which every channell hath,   10
Will amorously to thee swimme,
Gladder to catch thee, then thou him.

25-32 *Omit TCD*   32 Thou] That *Dob, O'F, B*   36 fulfill]; fulfill, *1633*
    The Baite. *L 74, Dob, A 25, B, S omit. First printed in William Corkine's Second Book of Ayres, 1612. Title from 1635.*   3 brookes,] brookes: *1633*   6 thine *TCD, O'F, HK 2*: thy *1633, Σ, Gr*   11 to] unto *O'F, HK 2, Cy, P, JC*

If thou, to be so seene, beest loath,
By Sunne, or Moone, thou darknest both,
And if my selfe have leave to see,   15
I need not their light, having thee.

Let others freeze with angling reeds,
And cut their legges, with shells and weeds,
Or treacherously poore fish beset,
With strangling snare, or windowie net: 20

Let coarse bold hands, from slimy nest
The bedded fish in banks out-wrest,
Or curious traitors, sleave-silke flies
Bewitch poore fishes wandring eyes.

For thee, thou needst no such deceit,   25
For thou thy selfe art thine owne bait,
That fish, that is not catch'd thereby,
Alas, is wiser farre then I.

Communitie

GOOD wee must love, and must hate ill,
For ill is ill, and good good still,
But there are things indifferent,
Which wee may neither hate, nor love,
But one, and then another prove,   5
As wee shall finde our fancy bent.

If then at first wise Nature had
Made women either good or bad,

---

15 selfe] heart TC   18 with MSS.: which 1633   21–24 Omit S 96
23 sleave-silke Σ: with silke Cy, P: sleavesicke 1633   25 thou needst] there needs H 40,
C 57, H 49, S 96, HK 2, JC   27 catch'd] caught TC, S 96, HK 2, Cy, P
Communitie. A 25 omits. Title from 1635.   3 there Σ: these 1633, C 57, Cy (b.c.)
7 had] had, 1633

Then some wee might hate, and some chuse,
But since shee did them so create,   10
That we may neither love, nor hate,
    Onely this rests, All, all may use.

If they were good it would be seene,
Good is as visible as greene,
    And to all eyes it selfe betrayes: 15
If they were bad, they could not last,
Bad doth it selfe, and others wast,
    So, they deserve nor blame, nor praise.

But they are ours as fruits are ours,
He that but tasts, he that devours,   20
    And he which leaves all, doth as well:
Chang'd loves are but chang'd sorts of meat,
And when hee hath the kernell eate,
    Who doth not fling away the shell?

Confined Love

SOME man unworthy to be possessor
Of old or new love, himselfe being false or weake,
    Thought his paine and shame would be lesser,
If on womankind he might his anger wreake,
        And thence a law did grow,   5
        One should but one man know;
        But are other creatures so?

    Are Sunne, Moone, or Starres by law forbidden,
To smile where they list, or lend away their light?
    Are birds divorc'd, or are they chidden   10
If they leave their mate, or lie abroad a night?

---

15 betrayes :] betrayes, *1633*   21 which *Σ*: that *1633*, *TCC*, *O'F*, *B*, *Gr*

Confined Love. *H 40, S 96, A 25 omit. Title from 1635*: To yᵉ worthiest of all my Lovers *Cy*: To the worthiest of all my lov my virtuous Mʳˢ P.   3 lesser] the lesser *Dob, HK 2, Cy, P, JC*   6 should *MSS.*: might *1633, Gr*

Beasts doe no joyntures lose
Though they new lovers choose,
But we are made worse then those.

Who e'r rigg'd faire ship to lie in harbors,   15
And not to seeke new lands, or not to deale withall?
Or built fair houses, set trees, and arbours,
Only to lock up, or else to let them fall?
Good is not good, unlesse
A thousand it possesse,   20
But doth wast with greedinesse.

Breake of Day

'TIS true, 'tis day, what though it be?
  O wilt thou therefore rise from me?
Why should we rise, because 'tis light?
Did we lie downe, because 'twas night?
Love which in spight of darknesse brought us hether,   5
Should in despight of light keepe us together.

Light hath no tongue, but is all eye;
If it could speake as well as spie,
This were the worst, that it could say,
That being well, I faine would stay,   10
And that I lov'd my heart and honor so,
That I would not from him, that had them, goe.

Must businesse thee from hence remove?
Oh, that's the worst disease of love,

12 doe] did C 57, H 49, TC, Dob, HK 2, Cy, P, S   13 choose] chose TCD, Dob, P, B
17 built] build C 57, H 49, TC

Breake of Day. Cy omits. First printed in William Corkine's Second Book of Ayres, 1612.
Title from 1633, TC.   2 O wilt thou] Wilt thou L 74, TC, S 96, HK 2: And will you
O'F, B: Will you JC   therefore] Omit H 40, C 57, H 49, S   4 'twas] t'was 1633
uncorrected   5 spight] despight H 40, C 57, H 49, L 74, TC, S   6 keepe] hould L 74,
TC, S 96, HK 2   9 were] is L 74, TC, Dob, O'F, S 96, HK 2, P,S   11 lov'd] love
L 74, TC, O'F, B, JC   11 so,] so 1633 uncorrected   12 had] hath L 74, TC,
Dob, O'F, S 96, HK 2, P, A 25, B, JC

The poore, the foule, the false, love can 15
Admit, but not the busied man.
He which hath businesse, and makes love, doth doe
Such wrong, as when a maryed man doth wooe.

The Computation

FOR the first twenty yeares, since yesterday,
I scarce beleev'd, thou could'st be gone away,
For forty more, I fed on favours past,
And forty'on hopes, that thou would'st, they might last.
Teares drown'd one hundred, and sighes blew out two, 5
A thousand, I did neither thinke, nor doe,
Or not divide, all being one thought of you;
Or in a thousand more, forgot that too.
Yet call not this long life; But thinke that I
Am, by being dead, Immortall; Can ghosts die? 10

The Expiration

SO, so, breake off this last lamenting kisse,
Which sucks two soules, and vapors both away,
Turne thou ghost that way, and let mee turne this,
And let our selves benight our happiest day,

17 which] that *L 74, TC, O'F, HK 2, P, A 25, B, JC*   18 when ... doth] if ...
should *L 74, TC, O'F, HK 2, B, JC*

The Computation. *In TC, Dob, O'F, HK 2, P, B, S:* omit *H 40, C 57, H 49, L 74, S 96,
Cy, A 25, JC. Title from 1633, TC*   1 the] my *Dob, O'F, HK 2, P, B, S*   twenty]
B uses numerals throughout   2 thou could'st] ... would'st *TCC*: you could *Dob, O'F, HK 2,
B, S*: you would *P*   3 For] And *Dob, O'F, HK 2, P, B, S*   4 thou would'st,
they might] you with they might *HK 2, P,* (... maye) *Dob, B*: you wish they ... *O'F*: your
wish may ever *S*   5 Teares have one hundred drown'd, sighes blown out two *Dob, O'F,
HK 2, P (which omits* sighes ... two), *B, S*   6 A] One *Dob, O'F, HK 2, P, B, S*
neither] nothing *Dob, O'F, HK 2, P, B, S*   doe,] doe. *1633*   7 *Omit TC*   8 a]
one *Dob, O'F, HK 2, P, B, S*   9 call] think *Dob, O'F, HK 2, P, B, S*

The Expiration. *H 40, C 57, H 49, L 74, Cy omit. First printed in Alphonso Ferrabosco's Ayres,
1609. Title from 1633, TC:* Valediction *Dob, O'F, B:* Valedictio *S 96:* Valedice *HK 2:*
Valedico *P:* Valedictio Amoris *S.*   1 breake] leave *Dob, O'F, S 96, HK 2, P, A 25,
B, S*   2 both] Both *1633*   4 selves] sowles *Dob, O'F, S 96, P, B, JC, S*
happiest] happy *Dob, O'F, S 96, HK 2, P, A 25, B, JC, S*

We ask'd none leave to love; nor will we owe   5
Any, so cheape a death, as saying, Goe;

Goe; and if that word have not quite kil'd thee,
  Ease mee with death, by bidding mee goe too.
Oh, if it have, let my word worke on mee,
  And a just office on a murderer doe.   10
Except it bee too late, to kill me so,
Being double dead, going, and bidding, goe.

Witchcraft by a Picture

I FIXE mine eye on thine, and there
  Pitty my picture burning in thine eye,
My picture drown'd in a transparent teare,
    When I looke lower I espie;
      Hadst thou the wicked skill   5
By pictures made and mard, to kill,
How many wayes mightst thou performe thy will?

But now I'have drunke thy sweet salt teares,
  And though thou poure more I'll depart;
My picture vanish'd, vanish feares,   10
    That I can be endamag'd by that art;
      Though thou retaine of mee
One picture more, yet that will bee,
Being in thine owne heart, from all malice free.

5 ask'd Σ: aske 1633, HK 2, P, S   9 Oh] Or Dob, O'F, S 96, HK 2, P, B, S
word] words TCD, ʒC

Witchcraft by a Picture. H 40, C 57, H 49, L 74, A 25, S omit. Title from 1633, TC:
Picture Dob, O'F, S 96, HK 2, ʒC: The Picture Cy, P.   4 espie;] espie, 1633
6 kill,] kill? 1633   8 I'have] I have 1633   sweet salt] sweetest Dob, O'F, S 96, HK 2,
Cy, P, ʒC   9 thou . . . I'll] thou therefore . . . will H 40, B   11 that] thy
Dob (b.c.), O'F, S 96: thine ʒC   14 from all] from Dob, O'F, S 96: from thy H 40, B

A Jeat Ring Sent

THOU art not so black, as my heart,
    Nor halfe so brittle, as her heart, thou art;
What would'st thou say? shall both our properties by thee
      bee spoke,
Nothing more endlesse, nothing sooner broke?

    Marriage rings are not of this stuffe;   5
  Oh, why should ought lesse precious, or lesse tough
Figure our loves? Except in thy name thou have bid it say,
  I'am cheap, and nought but fashion, fling me'away.

    Yet stay with mee since thou art come,
  Circle this fingers top, which did'st her thombe.   10
Be justly proud, and gladly safe, that thou dost dwell with
      me,
  She that, Oh, broke her faith, would soon breake thee.

The Paradox

NO Lover saith, I love, nor any other
    Can judge a perfect Lover;
Hee thinkes that else none can nor will agree,
    That any loves but hee:
I cannot say I lov'd, for who can say   5
    Hee was kill'd yesterday?
Love with excesse of heat, more yong then old,
    Death kills with too much cold;
Wee dye but once, and who lov'd last did die,
    Hee that saith twice, doth lye: 10

A Jeat Ring Sent. *In TC, O'F: omit Σ. Title from 1633, MSS.*   7 loves] love
O'F   say,] say *1633*

The Paradox. *In L 74, TC, O'F, S 96, S: omit Σ. Title from 1635.*   3 nor *MSS.:*
or *1633*   6 yesterday?] yesterday. *1633*   8 cold;] cold *1633 uncorrected*   10 twice,]
twice *1633 uncorrected*

For though hee seeme to move, and stirre a while,
    It doth the sense beguile.
Such life is like the light which bideth yet
    When the lights life is set,
Or like the heat, which fire in solid matter   15
    Leaves behinde, two houres after.
Once I lov'd and dyed; and am now become
    Mine Epitaph and Tombe.
Here dead men speake their last, and so do I;
    Love-slaine, loe, here I lye.   20

The Prohibition

TAKE heed of loving mee,
    At least remember, I forbade it thee;
    Not that I shall repaire my'unthrifty wast
Of Breath and Blood, upon thy sighes, and teares,
    By being to thee then what to me thou wast;   5
But, so great Joy, our life at once outweares,
    Then, least thy love, by my death, frustrate bee,
    If thou love mee, take heed of loving mee.

    Take heed of hating mee,
Or too much triumph in the Victorie.   10
    Not that I shall be mine owne officer,
And hate with hate againe retaliate;
    But thou wilt lose the stile of conquerour,
If I, thy conquest, perish by thy hate.
    Then, least my being nothing lessen thee,   15
    If thou hate mee, take heed of hating mee.

14 lights life *L 74, S*: lifes light *1633, TC, O'F, S 96*   15 which] which, *1663*
16 behinde,] behinde *1633 uncorrected*   17 lov'd *MSS.*: love *1633*   20 Love-slaine]
Love slaine *1633 uncorrected*   lye *O'F, S 96*: dye *1633, L 74, TC, S*

The Prohibition. *H 40, C 57, L 74, A 25, S omit. TC, Dob, S 96 omit stanza 3: B gives the
first two stanzas under the heading* J.D. *and the third under* T.R. *Title from 1633, TC.*
2 forbade] forbidd *Dob, O'F, S 96, HK 2, Cy, P*   4 teares,] teares: *1633 uncorrected*
5 By . . . wast *S 96, Cy, JC*: By being to me . . . *Dob, O'F (b.c.), HK 2, P, B: omit H 49,
TC*: By being to mee then that which thou wast *1633*

Yet, love and hate mee too,
So, these extreames shall neythers office doe;
Love mee, that I may die the gentler way;
Hate mee, because thy love's too great for mee;   20
Or let these two, themselves, not me decay;
So shall I live, thy Stage, not Triumph bee;
Then, least thy love, hate and mee thou undoe,
Oh let mee live, yet love and hate mee too.

The Curse

WHO ever guesses, thinks, or dreames he knowes
Who is my mistris, wither by this curse;
His only,'and only'his purse
May some dull heart to love dispose,
And shee yeeld then to all that are his foes;   5
May he be scorn'd by one, whom all else scorne,
Forsweare to others, what to her he'hath sworne,
With feare of missing, shame of getting, torne:

Madnesse his sorrow, gout his cramps, may hee
Make, by but thinking, who hath made him such: 10
And may he feele no touch
Of conscience, but of fame, and bee
Anguish'd, not that 'twas sinne, but that 'twas shee:
In early and long scarcenesse may he rot,
For land which had been his, if he had not   15
Himselfe incestuously an heire begot:

---

18 neythers *H 49, JC*: neyther *O'F*: neyther their *Cy*: ne'r their *1633, HK 2, P, B*
20 thy] my *1633 uncorrected*   love's] love is *1633*   22 I live,] I live *1633*: I, live, *Gr*
Stage *Σ*: stay *1633, H 49, JC*   Triumph] triumph *1633*   23 Then . . . undoe
H 49, O'F, Cy, JC: Lest thou thy love and hate and mee undoe *1633, HK 2, P, B, Gr*
24 Oh . . . yet *O'F, Cy*: Oh . . . O *H 49, JC*: To . . . Oh *1633, HK 2, P, B, Gr*   live, Oh]
live of 1633 uncorrected

    The Curse. *S 96, Cy omit. Title from 1633*: The Curse, *A . . . Curse Σ*: Dirae *P: no title*
HK 2   3 His only,'and only'his] His only, and only his *1633*   8 getting, torne:]
getting torne; *1633*   9 cramps *Σ*: cramp *1633, O'F, P, A 25, S, Gr*   12 fame]
shame *L 74, TCC, P, S*: flame *HK 2; see note*   [*For note 14–16 see opposite*

May he dreame Treason, and beleeve, that hee
Meant to performe it, and confesse, and die,
    And no record tell why:
      His sonnes, which none of his may bee,   20
Inherite nothing but his infamie:
    Or may he so long Parasites have fed,
      That he would faine be theirs, whom he hath bred,
      And at the last be circumcis'd for bread:

The venom of all stepdames, gamsters gall,   25
What Tyrans, and their subjects interwish,
    What Plants, Mynes, Beasts, Foule, Fish,
      Can contribute, all ill which all
Prophets, or Poets spake; And all which shall
    Be'annex'd in schedules unto this by mee,   30
    Fall on that man; For if it be a shee
    Nature before hand hath out-cursed mee.

The Indifferent

I CAN love both faire and browne,
  Her whom abundance melts, and her whom want betraies,
Her who loves lonenesse best, and her who maskes and plaies,
    Her whom the country form'd, and whom the town,
      Her who beleeves, and her who tries,   5
      Her who still weepes with spungie eyes,
  And her who is dry corke, and never cries;
  I can love her, and her, and you and you,
  I can love any, so she be not true.

14–16 (*page 40*) In early . . . begot: *1633, H 40, C 57, H 49, Dob, B*:
                Or may he for her vertue reverence
                One, that hates him onlie for impotence,
                And equall traytors be shee and his sence.
L 74, TC, O'F, HK 2, P, A 25, JC, S: *O'F gives the version of 1633 in the margin with* These
3 sta: in some copyes thus   18 Meant] Went *L 74, TC*,   27 Mynes *Σ*: Myne
1633   28 ill] ill, *1633*   29 spake] spoke *L 74, TC, HK 2, A 25*: speake *H 40,*
Dob, O'F, P, B, S   30 Be'annex'd] Be annex'd *1633*
  The Indifferent. *L 74, Cy, A 25 omit. Title from 1633, TC*   4 and] & *1633*

Will no other vice content you?   10
Will it not serve your turn to do, as did your mothers?
Have you old vices spent, and now would finde out others?
    Or doth a feare, that men are true, torment you?
      Oh we are not, be not you so,
      Let mee and doe you, twenty know.   15
    Rob mee, but binde me not, and let me goe.
    Must I, who came to travaile thorow you,
    Grow your fixt subject, because you are true?

      Venus heard me sigh this song,
And by Loves sweetest Part, Variety, she swore,   20
She heard not this till now; and't should be so no more.
    She went, examin'd, and return'd ere long,
      And said, alas, Some two or three
      Poore Heretiques in love there bee,
    Which thinke to stablish dangerous constancie.   25
    But I have told them, since you will be true,
    You shall be true to them, who'are false to you.

Womans Constancy

Now thou hast lov'd me one whole day,
    To morrow when thou leav'st, what wilt thou say?
Wilt thou then Antedate some new made vow?
      Or say that now
We are not just those persons, which we were?   5
Or, that oathes made in reverentiall feare
Of Love, and his wrath, any may forsweare?
Or, as true deaths, true maryages untie,
So lovers contracts, images of those,

11 Will] Wil *1633*   12 Have you old *H 40, C 57, H 49, Dob, O'F, S 96, B, JC:*
Or have you all old *1633, TC, HK 2, Cy, P, S, Gr; see note*   13 *Omit P*   feare] shame
Dob (b.c.), S 96, HK 2, S   21 and't . . . so *Ed*: and it . . . so *TCD, Dob, S 96, JC: omit*
so *TCC, O'F: omit* and *HK 2, P:* and that it should be so *1633, H 40, C 57, H 49, B, S, Gr;*
see note   23 Some] but *H 40, C 57, H 49, TC, B, S, JC*

Womans Constancy. *S 96, Cy, A 25, JC omit. Title from 1633, TC, O'F*

Binde but till sleep, deaths image, them unloose? 10
Or, your owne end to Justifie,
For having purpos'd change, and falsehood; you
Can have no way but falsehood to be true?
Vaine lunatique, against these scapes I could
Dispute, and conquer, if I would, 15
Which I abstaine to doe,
For by to morrow, I may thinke so too.

The Apparition

WHEN by thy scorne, O murdresse, I am dead,
And that thou thinkst thee free
From all solicitation from mee,
Then shall my ghost come to thy bed,
And thee, fain'd vestall, in worse armes shall see; 5
Then thy sicke taper will begin to winke,
And he, whose thou art then, being tyr'd before,
Will, if thou stirre, or pinch to wake him, thinke
Thou call'st for more,
And in false sleepe will from thee shrinke, 10
And then poore Aspen wretch, neglected thou
Bath'd in a cold quicksilver sweat wilt lye
A veryer ghost then I;
What I will say, I will not tell thee now,
Lest that preserve thee;'and since my love is spent, 15
I'had rather thou shouldst painfully repent,
Then by my threatnings rest still innocent.

The Apparition. *L 74, HK 2 omit. Title from 1633, C 57, H 49, Cy*: An ... *H 40, TC, Dob,*
O'F, S 96, S: Apparition *HK 2, P, A 25*   5 thee, ... vestall,] thee ... vestall *1633*
10 in false] in a false *TC, O'F, P, A 25*: in a fayned *B, JC*   11 And then poore ...
thou] And there ... *Dob, S 96, P, JC*: Then ... *S*: Thou poore ... then *H 40, C 57, H 49,*
TC, Cy   13 I;] I, *1633 uncorrected*   15 thee;'and] thee'; and *1633*   17 rest
still] keepe thee *O'F, Cy, P, A 25, JC*

Loves Usury

FOR every houre that thou wilt spare mee now,
      I will allow,
Usurious God of Love, twenty to thee,
When with my browne, my gray haires equall bee;
Till then, Love, let my body raigne, and let   5
Mee travell, sojourne, snatch, plot, have, forget,
Resume my last yeares relict: thinke that yet
      We'had never met.

Let mee thinke any rivalls letter mine,
      And at next nine   10
Keepe midnights promise; mistake by the way
The maid, and tell the Lady'of that delay;
Onely let mee love none, no, not the sport;
From country grasse, to comfitures of Court,
Or cities quelque choses, let report   15
      My minde transport.

This bargaine's good; if when I'am old, I bee
      Inflam'd by thee,
If thine owne honour, or my shame, or paine,
Thou covet, most at that age thou shalt gaine.   20
Doe thy will then, then subject and degree,
And fruit of love, Love, I submit to thee,
Spare mee till then, I'll beare it, though she bee
      One that loves mee.

Loves Usury. *TC, A 25, JC omit. Title from 1633*   5 raigne] range *Dob, O'F, S 96*
6 snatch] match *Dob, O'F*   12 Lady'of] Lady of *1633*   13 sport;] sport
1633   15 let] let not *Dob, O'F, S 96*   20 covet, most] covet most, *1633; see note*
22 fruit] fruits *C 57, H 49, Dob, O'F, S 96, B*   Love,] Love *1633*

Loves Diet

To what a combersome unwieldinesse
   And burdenous corpulence my love had growne,
  But that I did, to make it lesse,
  And keepe it in proportion,
Give it a diet, made it feed upon   5
That which love worst endures, *discretion.*

Above one sigh a day I'allow'd him not,
Of which my fortune, and my faults had part;
  And if sometimes by stealth he got
  A she sigh from my mistresse heart,   10
And thought to feast on that, I let him see
'Twas neither very sound, nor meant to mee.

If he wroung from mee'a teare, I brin'd it so
With scorne or shame, that him it nourish'd not;
  If he suck'd hers, I let him know   15
  'Twas not a teare, which hee had got,
His drinke was counterfeit, as was his meat;
For, eyes which rowle towards all, weepe not, but sweat.

What ever he would dictate, I writ that,
But burnt my letters; When she writ to me,   20
  And that that favour made him fat,
  I said, if any title bee
Convey'd by this, Ah, what doth it availe,
To be the fortieth name in an entaile?

Loves Diet. JC omits. On leaf torn out from TCD. Title from 1633, Σ: Amoris Dieta *Dob,*
S 96 : The Dyet *A 25*   8 fortune] fortunes *Dob, O'F, S 96, P, A 25*   11 feast]
feede *Dob, O'F, S 96*   12 mee.] mee; *1633*   13 wroung] wrought *HK 2, Cy, P, S*
18 which] that *TCC, Dob, O'F, S 96, HK 2, Cy, P*   19 What ever] Whatsoever
L 74, TCC   dictate] distaste *L 74 (b.c.), TCC, margin of O'F, P*   19 and 20 writ]
wrote *L 74, Dob, O'F, S 96, Cy, S*   20 When] Yf *Dob, O'F*   21 that that] if
that *margin of O'F, Cy, P*

Thus I reclaim'd my buzard love, to flye   25
At what, and when, and how, and where I chuse;
   Now negligent of sport I lye,
   And now as other Fawkners use,
I spring a mistresse, sweare, write, sigh and weepe:
And the game kill'd, or lost, goe talke, and sleepe.   30

Loves Exchange

L<small>O V E</small>, any devill else but you,
   Would for a given Soule give something too.
   At Court your fellowes every day,
Give th'art of Riming, Huntsmanship, and Play,
   For them who were their owne before;
   Onely'I have nothing which gave more,   5
But am, alas, by being lowly, lower.

   I aske not dispensation now
To falsifie a teare, or sigh, or vow,
   I do not sue from thee to draw   10
A *non obstante* on natures law,
   These are prerogatives, they inhere
   In thee and thine; none should forsweare
Except that hee *Loves* minion were.

   Give mee thy weaknesse, make mee blinde,   15
Both wayes, as thou and thine, in eies and minde;
   Love, let me never know that this
   Is love, or, that love childish is.

25 reclaim'd *Σ*: redeem'd *1633, C 57*   27 sport *MSS.*: sports *1633*   29 sweare, write, sigh] sigh, sweare, write *Dob, O'F, S 96*   30 and] or *Dob, O'F, S 96, Cy, P, S*
   Loves Exchange. *L 74, S 96, Cy, A 25, S omit. Title from 1633, TC.*   4 and *MSS.*: or *1633, Gr*   Play] play *1633*   5 who *MSS.*: which *1633, Gr*   6 Onely'I] Onely I *1633*   8 not *Σ*: no *1633, C 57, JC, Gr*: but *TCC*   9 a teare, or sigh, or vow] a teare or vow *H 40, C 57, H 49, TC, O'F (b.c.), JC*: a teare, a sigh, a vowe *HK 2*: a sigh, a teare, a vowe *Dob, P, B; see note*

Let me not know that others know
That she knowes my paine, least that so   20
A tender shame make me mine owne new woe.

If thou give nothing, yet thou'art just,
Because I would not thy first motions trust;
  Small townes which stand stiffe, till great shot
Enforce them, by warres law *condition* not.   25
  Such in loves warfare is my case,
  I may not article for grace,
Having put Love at last to shew this face.

This face, by which he could command
And change th'Idolatrie of any land,   30
  This face, which wheresoe'r it comes,
Can call vow'd men from cloisters, dead from tombes,
  And melt both Poles at once, and store
  Deserts with cities, and make more
Mynes in the earth, then Quarries were before.   35

For this, Love is enrag'd with mee,
Yet kills not. If I must example bee
  To future Rebells; If th'unborne
Must learne, by my being cut up, and torne:
  Kill, and dissect me, Love; for this   40
  Torture against thine owne end is,
Rack't carcasses make ill Anatomies.

Loves Deitie

I LONG to talke with some old lovers ghost,
  Who dyed before the god of Love was borne:
I cannot thinke that hee, who then lov'd most,
  Sunke so low, as to love one which did scorne.

20 paine *MSS.*: paines *1633, Gr*   28 Love] love *1633*   30 th'Idolatrie] the Idolatrie *1633*   36 For this, Love] For, this love *1633*   37 not. If] not; if *1633*
Loves Deitie. *Title from 1633, Σ: no title HK 2, P*

But since this god produc'd a destinie,   5
And that vice-nature, custome, lets it be;
   I must love her, that loves not mee.

Sure, they which made him god, meant not so much:
   Nor he, in his young godhead practis'd it.
But when an even flame two hearts did touch,   10
   His office was indulgently to fit
Actives to passives: Correspondencie
Only his subject was. It cannot bee
   Love, till I love her, that loves mee.

But every moderne god will now extend   15
   His vast prerogative, as far as Jove.
To rage, to lust, to write to, to commend,
   All is the purlewe of the God of Love.
Oh were wee wak'ned by this Tyrannie
To'ungod this child againe, it could not bee   20
   That I should love, who loves not mee.

Rebell and Atheist too, why murmure I,
   As though I felt the worst that love could doe?
Love might make me leave loving, or might trie
   A deeper plague, to make her love mee too,   25
Which, since she loves before, I'am loth to see;
Falshood is worse then hate; and that must bee,
   If shee whom I love, should love mee.

---

8 which] that *H 40, Dob, O'F, S 96*   10 flame] *Omit HK 2* : desire *Cy, P*   12 and 13
passives : . . . was.] passives. . . . was; *1633*   14 till . . . mee] if I love [her] who loves
not mee *O'F* (her *cancelled, as also in l. 21*)   20 To'ungod] To ungod *1633*   21 That
I should love, who *H 40, C 57, H 49, L 74, TC, HK 2, Cy, P, A 25,* . . . love her who . . .
Dob, S 96 : . . . love [her] who *O'F (b.c.)* : . . . love that loves . . . *S* : I should love who *JC* :
I should love her, who *1633, B, Gr*; *see note*   24 might make *Σ* : may make *1633, C 57*
26 Which,] Which *1633*

The Dampe

WHEN I am dead, and Doctors know not why,
  And my friends curiositie
Will have me cut up to survay each part,
When they shall finde your Picture in my heart,
  You thinke a sodaine dampe of love   5
  Will thorough all their senses move,
And worke on them as mee, and so preferre
Your murder, to the name of Massacre.

Poore victories! But if you dare be brave,
  And pleasure in your conquest have,   10
First kill th'enormous Gyant, your *Disdaine*,
And let th'enchantresse *Honor*, next be slaine,
  And like a Goth and Vandall rize,
  Deface Records, and Histories
Of your owne arts and triumphs over men,   15
And without such advantage kill me then.

For I could muster up as well as you
  My Gyants, and my Witches too,
Which are vast *Constancy*, and *Secretnesse*,
But these I neyther looke for, nor professe; 20
  Kill mee as Woman, let mee die
  As a meere man; doe you but try
Your passive valor, and you shall finde than,
Naked you'have odds enough of any man.

The Dampe. *H 40, L 74, HK 2, Cy, A 25 omit. Title from 1633, Σ: no title ℱC*
6 thorough *TCD, Dob*: through *1633, Σ, Gr*   9 victories!] victories; *1633*   15 arts]
acts *P, B, ℱC: TCD corrects arts to acts*   20 neyther] never *1633 uncorrected*
professe;] professe, *1633*   24 Naked *Σ*: In that *1633, TC, Gr*

The Legacie

WHEN I dyed last, and Deare, I dye
    As often as from thee I goe,
  Though it be an houre agoe,
And Lovers houres be full eternity,
I can remember yet, that I   5
  Something did say, and something did bestow;
Though I be dead, which sent mee, I should be
Mine owne executor and Legacie.

I heard mee say, Tell her anon,
  That my selfe, that's you, not I,   10
  Did kill me,'and when I felt mee dye,
I bid mee send my heart, when I was gone;
But I alas could there finde none,
  When I had ripp'd me,'and search'd where hearts
    should lye;
It kill'd mee'againe that I who still was true,   15
In life, in my last Will should cozen you.

Yet I found something like a heart,
  But colours it, and corners had,
  It was not good, it was not bad,
It was intire to none, and few had part.   20
As good as could be made by art
  It seem'd, and therefore for our losses sad,
I thought to send that heart in stead of mine,
But oh, no man could hold it, for twas thine.

The Legacie. *JC omits. Title from 1633*: Legacie *L 74.*   **3** be Σ: be but *1633, C 57,
Dob, HK 2, Gr; see note*   **7** sent] meant *Dob (b.c.), O'F (b.c.), S 96*   **10** that's
... I,] that ... I *H 40, C 57, H 49, B*: that is ... I,) *O'F*: (that is ... I,) *Gr; see note*
11 me,'and] me,and *1633*   **12** gone;] gone, *1633*   **14** ripp'd me] rip'd *L 74, TC, Dob,
O'F, S 96, HK 2, Cy, P*   hearts should *L 74, TC, O'F, HK 2, Cy, P*: ... doe *A 25*: hart did
H 40, C 57, H 49, Dob, S 96, B, S: hearts did *1633, Gr*   lye;] lye, *1633*   **15** mee'againe]
mee againe *1633*   **22** our losses sad] our losse be yee sad *H 40, C 57, H 49, Cy, B, S*
23 thought *L 74, TC, Dob, O'F, HK 2, P*: meant *1633, H 40, C 57, H 49, S 96, Cy, A 25,
B, S, Gr*   that *L 74, TC, O'F, HK 2, Cy, P, A 25*: this *1633, H 40, C 57, H 49, Dob,
S 96, B, S, Gr*

The Broken Heart

HE is starke mad, who ever sayes,
 That he hath beene in love an houre,
Yet not that love so soone decayes,
But that it can tenne in lesse space devour;
 Who will beleeve mee, if I sweare   5
 That I have had the plague a yeare?
Who would not laugh at mee, if I should say,
I saw a flaske of *powder burne a day*?

 Ah, what a trifle is a heart,
If once into loves hands it come!   10
 All other griefes allow a part
To other griefes, and aske themselves but some;
 They come to us, but us Love draws,
 Hee swallows us, and never chawes:
By him, as by chain-shot, whole rankes doe dye,   15
He is the tyran Pike, our hearts the Frye.

 If 'twere not so, what did become
Of my heart, when I first saw thee?
 I brought a heart into the roome,
But from the roome, I carried none with mee;   20
 If it had gone to thee, I know
 Mine would have taught thy heart to show
More pitty unto mee: but Love, alas,
At one first blow did shiver it as glasse.

 Yet nothing can to nothing fall,   25
Nor any place be empty quite,
 Therefore I thinke my breast hath all
Those peeces still, though they be not unite;

The Broken Heart. *Title from 1633.*   8 flaske] flash *C 57, H 49, L 74, TC, Dob,*
O'F (b.c.), S 96, HK 2, Cy, P   10 come!] come? *1633*   12 some;] some, *1633*
15 chain-shot *Σ*: chain'd shot *1633, C 57, H 49, L 74, S 96, B, JC, Gr*   17 did] could
L 74, TC, Dob, O'F, S 96, HK 2, A 25, B: would *Cy, P, S*   20 But] And *L 74, TC,*
HK 2, Cy, P, A 25, B, JC   21 thee] thine *L 74, TC, O'F, HK 2, Cy, P, A 25, B, S*
22 thy *Σ*: thine *1633, B, Gr*   23 alas,] alas *1633*

And now as broken glasses show
A hundred lesser faces, so   30
My ragges of heart can like, wish, and adore,
But after one such love, can love no more.

The Triple Foole

I AM two fooles, I know,
   For loving, and for saying so
      In whining Poëtry;
But where's that wiseman, that would not be I,
      If she would not deny?   5
Then as th'earths inward narrow crooked lanes
Do purge sea waters fretfull salt away,
      I thought, if I could draw my paines,
Through Rimes vexation, I should them allay,
Griefe brought to numbers cannot be so fierce,   10
For, he tames it, that fetters it in verse.

But when I have done so,
   Some man, his art and voice to show,
      Doth set and sing my paine,
And by delighting many, frees againe   15
      Griefe, which verse did restraine.
To Love, and Griefe tribute of Verse belongs,
But not of such as pleases when 'tis read,
      Both are increased by such songs:
For both their triumphs so are published,   20
And I, which was two fooles, do so grow three;
Who are a little wise, the best fooles bee.

30 hundred] thousand L 74, TC, HK 2, Cy, P, A 25, B, S
    The Triple Foole. A 25 omits. Title from 1633, TC.   13 art and voice] act ... TC:
voyce and art Dob, O'F, S 96   14 set (Set 1633)] sitt L 74, TC, Dob, O'F (b.c.), S 96,
Cy, P   20 triumphs] trialls Dob, O'F, S 96, HK 2, P: Tortures Cy

The Flea

MARKE but this flea, and marke in this,
　How little that which thou deny'st me is;
　Mee it suck'd first, and now sucks thee,
And in this flea, our two bloods mingled bee;
　Confesse it, this cannot be said　　　　　　　5
A sinne, or shame, or losse of maidenhead,
　　Yet this enjoyes before it wooe,
And pamper'd swells with one blood made of two,
And this, alas, is more then wee would doe.

　Oh stay, three lives in one flea spare,　　　　10
Where wee almost, nay more then maryed are:
　This flea is you and I, and this
Our mariage bed, and mariage temple is;
　Though parents grudge, and you, w'are met,
And cloysterd in these living walls of Jet.　　　15
　　Though use make thee apt to kill mee,
Let not to this, selfe murder added bee,
And sacrilege, three sinnes in killing three.

　Cruell and sodaine, hast thou since
Purpled thy naile, in blood of innocence?　　　20
　In what could this flea guilty bee,
Except in that drop which it suckt from thee?
　Yet thou triumph'st, and saist that thou
Find'st not thy selfe, nor mee the weaker now;
　　'Tis true, then learne how false, feares bee;　25
Just so much honor, when thou yeeld'st to mee,
Will wast, as this flea's death tooke life from thee.

The Flea. *JC omits. Title from 1633, Σ: no title H 40, L 74, TC, A 25.*　　3 Mee it
suck'd *H 40, L 74, TC, HK 2, Cy, P, A 25, B, S*: It suck'd me *1633, C 57, H 49, Dob, O'F,
S 96, Gr*　　5 Confesse it, *Σ*: Confesse that *A 25*: Thou know'st that *1633, C 57, H 49,
Gr*: Confess it: thou know'st that *Cy*　　6 or . . . or *Σ*: nor . . . nor *1633, C 57, H 49,
Gr*　　shame,] shame *1633*　　11 nay *Σ*: yea *1633, C 57, H 49, Gr*　　are:] are.
1633　　14 and you, w'are met] and you yet we are *Dob, O'F, S 96, Cy, B*: yett we are *P*
16 thee *Σ*: you *1633, C 57, H 49, Gr*　　17 this *Σ*: thie *L 74, TC*: that *1633, C 57,
H 49, Gr*　　21 In what *Σ*: Wherein *1633, C 57, H 49, Gr*

The Will

BEFORE I sigh my last gaspe, let me breath,
   Great love, some Legacies; Here I bequeath
Mine eyes to *Argus*, if mine eyes can see,
If they be blinde, then Love, I give them thee;
My tongue to Fame; to'Embassadours mine eares;   5
   To women or the sea, my teares.
   Thou, Love, hast taught mee heretofore
By making mee serve her who'had twenty more,
That I should give to none, but such, as had too much
     before.

My constancie I to the planets give;   10
My truth to them, who at the Court doe live;
Mine ingenuity and opennesse,
   To Jesuites; to Buffones my pensivenesse;
My silence to'any, who abroad hath beene;
   My mony to a Capuchin.   15
   Thou Love taught'st me, by'appointing mee
To love there, where no love receiv'd can be,
Onely to give to such as have an incapacitie.

My faith I give to Roman Catholiques;
All my good works unto the Schismaticks   20
Of Amsterdam; my best civility
And Courtship, to an Universitie;
My modesty I give to souldiers bare;
   My patience let gamesters share.
   Thou Love taughtst mee, by making mee   25
Love her that holds my love disparity,
Onely to give to those that count my gifts indignity.

The Will. *On leaf torn out from TCD. MSS., except Dob, O'F, S 96, S, omit stanza 3; see note.*
Title from 1633, H 40, C 57, H 49, O'F, HK 2, Cy, P : A Will A 25 : Testamentum Dob, S 96 :
Loves Will L 74, . . . Legacies TCC : His last Will and Testament JC.   6 teares.] teares;
1633   9 That . . . as] Only to give to those that Dob, S, . . . wch O'F, . . . who S 96
10 give;] give, 1633   16 by'appointing] by appointing 1633 : by making Dob, O'F, S 96, S
18 such as] those which Dob, O'F, . . . who S 96, . . . yᵗ S

I give my reputation to those
Which were my friends; Mine industrie to foes;
To Schoolemen I bequeath my doubtfulnesse;   30
My sicknesse to Physitians, or excesse;
To Nature, all that I in Ryme have writ;
    And to my company my wit.
      Thou Love, by making mee adore
Her, who begot this love in mee before,   35
Taughtst me to make, as though I gave, when I did but
    restore.

To him for whom the passing bell next tolls,
I give my physick bookes; my writen rowles
Of Morall counsels, I to Bedlam give;
My brazen medals, unto them which live   40
In want of bread; To them which passe among
    All forrainers, mine English tongue.
      Thou, Love, by making mee love one
Who thinkes her friendship a fit portion
For yonger lovers, dost my gifts thus disproportion.   45

Therefore I'll give no more; But I'll undoe
The world by dying; because love dies too.
Then all your beauties will bee no more worth
Then gold in Mines, where none doth draw it forth;
And all your graces no more use shall have   50
    Then a Sun dyall in a grave.
      Thou Love taughtst mee, by making mee
Love her, who doth neglect both mee and thee,
To'invent, and practise this one way, to'annihilate all three.

28 I ... reputation] My reputation I give *Dob, O'F, S 96, S*   33 wit.] wit; *1633*
34 Love] love *1633*   35 who] that *Dob, O'F, S 96, S*   did] doe *Dob, O'F, S*
49 forth;] forth. *1633*   51 grave.] grave, *1633*   52 making] appointing *Dob, S 96, S*

SONGS AND SONNETS
(II)

Negative Love

I NEVER stoop'd so low, as they
  Which on an eye, cheeke, lip, can prey,
    Seldome to them, which soare no higher
    Then vertue or the minde to'admire,
For sense, and understanding may   5
  Know, what gives fuell to their fire:
My love, though silly, is more brave,
For may I misse, when ere I crave,
If I know yet, what I would have.

If that be simply perfectest   10
Which can by no way be exprest
  But *Negatives*, my love is so.
    To All, which all love, I say no.
If any who deciphers best,
  What we know not, our selves, can know,   15
Let him teach mee that nothing; This
As yet my ease, and comfort is,
Though I speed not, I cannot misse.

Negative Love. *In TC, O'F, A 25: Σ omit. Title from 1633, TC*: Negative Love; or The Nothing *O'F*: The nothinge *A 25.*   5 For] Both *A 25*   8 may I] I may *TC, O'F* (*b.c.*)   11 way] meanes *O'F*

The Undertaking

I HAVE done one braver thing
    Then all the *Worthies* did,
Yet a braver thence doth spring,
    Which is, to keepe that hid.

It were but madnes now t'impart   5
    The skill of specular stone,
When he which can have learn'd the art
    To cut it, can finde none.

So, if I now should utter this,
    Others (because no more   10
Such stuffe to worke upon, there is,)
    Would love but as before.

But he who lovelinesse within
    Hath found, all outward loathes,
For he who colour loves, and skinne,   15
    Loves but their oldest clothes.

If, as I have, you also doe
    Vertue'attir'd in woman see,
And dare love that, and say so too,
    And forget the Hee and Shee;   20

And if this love, though placed so,
    From prophane men you hide,
Which will no faith on this bestow,
    Or, if they doe, deride:

Then you'have done a braver thing   25
    Then all the *Worthies* did,
And a braver thence will spring,
    Which is, to keepe that hid.

The Undertaking. *L 74, S 96, Cy, A 25 omit. Title from 1635:* Platonique Love *TC*
2 *Worthies*] worthies *1633*   3 Yet *MSS.:* And yet *1633, Gr; see note*   7-8 art
... it,] art, ... it *1633*   18 'attir'd] *omit O'F; see note*   woman] women *Dob, O'F*
25 you'have] you have *1633, Gr:* have yow *TCC*   26 did,] did. *1633*

[Image and Dream]

IMAGE of her whom I love, more then she,
  Whose faire impression in my faithfull heart,
Makes mee her Medall, and makes her love mee,
    As Kings do coynes, to which their stamps impart
The value: goe, and take my heart from hence,   5
    Which now is growne too great and good for me:
Honours oppresse weake spirits, and our sense
    Strong objects dull; the more, the lesse wee see.

When you are gone, and Reason gone with you,
    Then Fantasie is Queene and Soule, and all;   10
She can present joyes meaner then you do;
    Convenient, and more proportionall.
So, if I dreame I have you, I have you,
    For, all our joyes are but fantasticall.
And so I scape the paine, for paine is true;   15
    And sleepe which locks up sense, doth lock out all.

After a such fruition I shall wake,
    And, but the waking, nothing shall repent;
And shall to love more thankfull Sonnets make,
    Then if more honour, teares, and paines were spent.   20
But dearest heart, and dearer image stay;
    Alas, true joyes at best are dreame enough;
Though you stay here you passe too fast away:
    For even at first lifes Taper is a snuffe.

Fill'd with her love, may I be rather grown   25
Mad with much heart, then ideott with none.

The Exstasie

WHERE, like a pillow on a bed,
    A Pregnant banke swel'd up, to rest
The violets reclining head,
    Sat we two, one anothers best;

Our hands were firmely cimented   5
    With a fast balme, which thence did spring,
Our eye-beames twisted, and did thred
    Our eyes, upon one double string;

So to'entergraft our hands, as yet
    Was all our meanes to make us one,   10
And pictures on our eyes to get
    Was all our propagation.

As 'twixt two equal Armies, Fate
    Suspends uncertaine victorie,
Our soules, (which to advance their state,   15
    Were gone out,) hung 'twixt her, and mee.

And whil'st our soules negotiate there,
    Wee like sepulchrall statues lay;
All day, the same our postures were,
    And wee said nothing, all the day.   20

If any, so by love refin'd,
    That he soules language understood,
And by good love were grown all minde,
    Within convenient distance stood,

He (though he knew not which soule spake,   25
    Because both meant, both spake the same)
Might thence a new concoction take,
    And part farre purer then he came.

The Exstasie. L 74, Cy omit. Printed without division into stanzas in 1633 and Grierson.
First printed in stanzas by Bennett. Title from 1633, Σ: Exstasie H 40, TC: An Exstacie S.
8 string;] string, 1633   9 to'entergraft] to ingraft Dob, O'F, S 96, HK 2, A 25, B, JC
10 our Σ: the 1633, C 57, H 49, B, Gr   11 on Σ: in 1633, P, Gr   18 lay;] lay, 1633
23 grown] growen 1633   25 knew Σ: knowes 1633, C 57

This Extasie doth unperplex
   (We said) and tell us what we love,   30
Wee see by this, it was not sexe,
   Wee see, we saw not what did move:

But as all severall soules containe
   Mixture of things, they know not what,
Love, these mixt soules, doth mixe againe,   35
   And makes both one, each this and that.

A single violet transplant,
   The strength, the colour, and the size,
(All which before was poore, and scant,)
   Redoubles still, and multiplies.   40

When love, with one another so
   Interinanimates two soules,
That abler soule, which thence doth flow,
   Defects of lonelinesse controules.

Wee then, who are this new soule, know,   45
   Of what we are compos'd, and made,
For, th'Atomies of which we grow,
   Are soules, whom no change can invade.

But O alas, so long, so farre
   Our bodies why doe wee forbeare?   50
They'are ours, though they'are not wee, Wee are
   Th'intelligences, they the spheare.

We owe them thankes, because they thus,
   Did us, to us, at first convay,
Yeelded their forces, sense, to us,   55
   Nor are drosse to us, but allay.

---

31 sexe,] sexe *1633*   42 Interinanimates Σ: Interanimates *1633, C 57, HK 2, S*
51 They'are ours, though they'are not *MSS.*: They are ours, though not *1633*
52 Th'intelligences] The intelligences *1633*   spheare Σ: spheares *1633, Dob*   55 forces,
sense *H 40, H 49, TC, Dob, O'F, A 25, JC*: ... sences *C 57 HK 2*: forces, since *S 96, S*:
forces first *P*: senses force *1633, B*

On man heavens influence workes not so,
  But that it first imprints the ayre,
Soe soule into the soule may flow,
  Though it to body first repaire.   60

As our blood labours to beget
  Spirits, as like soules as it can,
Because such fingers need to knit
  That subtile knot, which makes us man:

So must pure lovers soules descend   65
  T'affections, and to faculties,
That sense may reach and apprehend,
  Else a great Prince in prison lies.

To'our bodies turne wee then, that so
  Weake men on love reveal'd may looke;   70
Loves mysteries in soules doe grow,
  But yet the body is his booke.

And if some lover, such as wee,
  Have heard this dialogue of one,
Let him still marke us, he shall see   75
  Small change, when we'are to bodies gone.

A Feaver

OH doe not die, for I shall hate
  All women so, when thou art gone,
That thee I shall not celebrate,
  When I remember, thou wast one.

But yet thou canst not die, I know;   5
  To leave this world behinde, is death,
But when thou from this world wilt goe,
  The whole world vapors with thy breath.

    59 Soe Σ: For 1633, C 57, H 49   67 That Ed. conj: Which 1633, MSS., Gr; see
note   76 to bodies gone] two bodies growne O'F (b.c.), P: to bodies growne S 96
    A Feaver. A 25 omits. Title from 1633, H 40, C 57, H 49, Dob, S 96: Fever TC, S: The
Fever O'F, Cy, P: Of a fever L 74.   5 know;] know, 1633

Or if, when thou, the worlds soule, goest,
    It stay, 'tis but thy carkasse then,   10
The fairest woman, but thy ghost,
    But corrupt wormes, the worthyest men.

O wrangling schooles, that search what fire
    Shall burne this world, had none the wit
Unto this knowledge to aspire,
    That this her feaver might be it?   15

And yet she cannot wast by this,
    Nor long beare this torturing wrong,
For much corruption needfull is
    To fuell such a feaver long.   20

These burning fits but meteors bee,
    Whose matter in thee is soone spent.
Thy beauty,'and all parts, which are thee,
    Are unchangeable firmament.

Yet 'twas of my minde, seising thee,   25
    Though it in thee cannot persever.
For I had rather owner bee
    Of thee one houre, then all else ever.

A Valediction : forbidding Mourning

As virtuous men passe mildly'away,
  And whisper to their soules, to goe,
Whilst some of their sad friends doe say,
    The breath goes now, and some say, no:

10 'tis] tis *1633*   18 torturing] tormenting *HK 2, JC, S: O'F corrects* torturing *to*
tormenting   19 For much] For more *O'F, HK 2 :* Far more *Cy, P*   22 is soone]
soone is *L 74, O'F, HK 2, Cy, P, JC*   25 'twas] t'was *1633*

    A Valediction : forbidding Mourning. *HK 2 omits. Title from 1633 : omit* A *TC* : . . . against
Mourning *A 25 :* A Valediction *H 40, C 57, H 49, B :* Upon the parting from his Mistresse
Dob, O'F, S 96, S : To his Love upon his departure from her *JC.*   1 mildly'away]
mildly away *1633*   3 Whilst] And *H 40, C 57, H 49, L74, TC, P, A 25, B, S ; see*
note   4 no :] no. *1633*

So let us melt, and make no noise,   5
    No teare-floods, nor sigh-tempests move,
'Twere prophanation of our joyes
    To tell the layetie our love.

Moving of th'earth brings harmes and feares,
    Men reckon what it did and meant,   10
But trepidation of the spheares,
    Though greater farre, is innocent.

Dull sublunary lovers love
    (Whose soule is sense) cannot admit
Absence, because it doth remove   15
    Those things which elemented it.

But we by'a love, so much refin'd,
    That our selves know not what it is,
Inter-assured of the mind,
    Care lesse, eyes, lips, and hands to misse.   20

Our two soules therefore, which are one,
    Though I must goe, endure not yet
A breach, but an expansion,
    Like gold to ayery thinnesse beate.

If they be two, they are two so   25
    As stiffe twin compasses are two,
Thy soule the fixt foot, makes no show
    To move, but doth, if the'other doe.

And though it in the center sit,
    Yet when the other far doth rome,   30
It leanes, and hearkens after it,
    And growes erect, as it comes home.

7 'Twere] T'were *1633*   8 our] of our *L 74, TC, O'F, S 96, Cy, P, B, JC*
9 Moving...brings] Movings... bringe *A 25*: Movings cause *Dob, O'F, S 96*: moving...
cause *JC*   17 by'a] by a *1633*   20 lips, and] *MSS.*: lips *1633*   21 therefore
... are] then ... are but *Dob, O'F, S 96*: therefore ... are but *S*   22 goe] part *Dob,
O'F, S 96, S*   24 Like] As *Dob, O'F, S 96, A 25, JC, S*   28 but] yet *Dob, O'F,
S 96, JC*   30 when] whilst *Dob, O'F, S 96, S*: while *JC*   32 it *H 40, L 74,
TC, Cy, P, B*: yt *C 57, H 49, Dob (b.c.)*: that *1633, O'F, S 96, JC, S, Gr; see note*

Such wilt thou be to mee, who must
Like th'other foot, obliquely runne;
Thy firmnes makes my circle just,   35
And makes me end, where I begunne.

A Valediction : of my Name in the Window

I

MY name engrav'd herein,
   Doth contribute my firmnesse to this glasse,
Which, ever since that charme, hath beene
As hard, as that which grav'd it, was;
Thine eyes will give it price enough, to mock   5
   The diamonds of either rock.

II

'Tis much that Glasse should bee
As all confessing, and through-shine as I,
'Tis more, that it shewes thee to thee,
And cleare reflects thee to thine eye.   10
But all such rules, loves magique can undoe,
   Here you see mee, and I am you.

III

As no one point, nor dash,
Which are but accessarie to this name,
The showers and tempests can outwash,   15
So shall all times finde mee the same;
You this intirenesse better may fulfill,
   Who have the patterne with you still.

34 runne;] runne. *1633*   35 makes] drawes *JC, Hayward; see note*

A Valediction : of my Name in the Window. *L 74, A 25 omit: text in Cy ends at l. 38. Title
from 1633, H 40, C 57, H 49: omit A TC: . . . of his . . . Dob: . . . to my . . . B:* Valediction 4.
Of Glasse. Vpon the engrauing of his name wth a Dyamond in his Mrs Windowe when hee
was to trauell *O'F,* Vpon . . . trauell *S 96:* A Valediction of my name in the Glasse windowe
Cy: Valediction on Glasse *P:* A Valediction of my name engrauen *JC:* The Diamond and
Glasse *S.*   4 was;] was, *1633*   5 eyes *Σ:* eye *1633, C 57, H 49, Gr*
13 nor] or *TCD, Dob, O'F, S 96, HK 2, Cy, P, B, JC, S*   14 accessarie *Σ:* accessaries
1633, Dob, O'F, S, Gr   18 still.] still *1633 uncorrected*

IIII

Or if too hard and deepe
This learning be, for a scratch'd name to teach,   20
  It, as a given deaths head keepe,
  Lovers mortalitie to preach,
Or thinke this ragged bony name to bee
  My ruinous Anatomie.

V

Then, as all my soules bee,   25
Emparadis'd in you, (in whom alone
  I understand, and grow and see,)
  The rafters of my body, bone
Being still with you, the Muscle, Sinew,'and Veine,
  Which tile this house, will come againe.   30

VI

Till my returne repaire
And recompact my scatter'd body so,
  As all the vertuous powers which are
  Fix'd in the starres, are said to flow
Into such characters, as graved bee   35
  When those starres have supremacie,

VII

So since this name was cut
When love and griefe their exaltation had,
  No doore 'gainst this names influence shut;
  As much more loving, as more sad,   40
'Twill make thee; and thou shouldst, till I returne,
  Since I die daily, daily mourne.

---

29 Sinew,'and] Sinew, and *1633*   31–32 returne ... so,] returne, ... so. *1633*:
returne ... so, *1633 uncorrected; see note*   32 scatter'd] scattered *1633*   34 flow]
flow, *1633*   36 those *Σ*: these *1633, C 57, S, Gr*   supremacie,] supremacie: *1633*:
supremacie. *1633 uncorrected*   39 shut;] shut, *1633*   41 'Twill] T'will *1633 uncorrected*

VIII

When thy'inconsiderate hand
Flings out this casement, with my trembling name,
  To looke on one, whose wit or land,   45
  New battry to thy heart may frame,
Then thinke this name alive, and that thou thus
  In it offendst my Genius.

IX

And when thy melted maid,
Corrupted by thy Lover's gold, and page,   50
  His letter at thy pillow'hath laid,
  Disputed it, and tam'd thy rage,
And thou begin'st to thaw towards him, for this,
  May my name step in, and hide his.

X

And if this treason goe   55
To'an overt act, and that thou write againe;
  In superscribing, this name flow
  Into thy fancy, from the pane.
So, in forgetting thou remembrest right,
  And unaware to mee shalt write.   60

XI

But glasse, and lines must bee,
No meanes our firme substantiall love to keepe;
  Neere death inflicts this lethargie,
  And this I murmure in my sleepe;
Impute this idle talke, to that I goe,   65
  For dying men talke often so.

---

43 thy'inconsiderate] thy inconsiderate *1633*   44 out *Σ*: ope *1633*, *O'F*, *S 96*, *S, Gr*
this] the *Dob*, *O'F (b.c.)*, *S 96*, *P*, *B*   45 on] at *O'F*, *S 96*   50 and] or *O'F*, *S 96*, *JC*
53 towards] to *O'F*, *S 96*   55 goe] growe *C 57*, *O'F*, *S 96*, *JC*   56 To'an] To an
1633   60 unaware] unawares *TC*, *Dob*, *O'F*, *HK 2*, *P*, *B*, *JC*, *S*   64 this] thus
O'F, *HK 2*, *P*, *S*

A Valediction : of the Booke

I'LL tell thee now (deare Love) what thou shalt doe
  To anger destiny, as she doth us,
  How I shall stay, though she esloygne me thus,
And how posterity shall know it too;
    How thine may out-endure   5
    Sybills glory, and obscure
    Her who from *Pindar* could allure,
  And her, through whose helpe *Lucan* is not lame,
And her, whose booke (they say) *Homer* did finde, and name.

Study our manuscripts, those Myriades   10
  Of letters, which have past twixt thee and mee,
  Thence write our Annals, and in them will bee,
To all whom loves subliming fire invades,
    Rule and example found;
    There, the faith of any ground   15
    No schismatique will dare to wound,
  That sees, how Love this grace to us affords,
To make, to keep, to use, to be these his Records.

This Booke, as long-liv'd as the elements,
  Or as the worlds forme, this all-graved tome,   20
  In cypher write, or new made Idiome;
Wee for loves clergie only'are instruments.
    When this booke is made thus,
    Should againe the ravenous
    Vandals and Goths inundate us,   25
  Learning were safe; in this our Universe
Schooles might learne Sciences, Spheares Musick, Angels
        Verse.

A Valediction : of the Booke. *L 74, S 96, A 25 omit. Title from TC, Dob, B : omit A C 57,
H 49* : Valediction to his booke *1633* : Valediction 3. of the Booke *O'F* : A Valediction of a
book left in a windowe *JC* : The Booke *Cy, P.*   3 esloygne] Esloygne *1633*   thus,]
thus *1633*   7 *Pindar*] Pindar *1633*   12 bee,] bee *1633*   20 tome,] tome *1633*
21 write *Ed. conj., HK 2, JC* : writ *1633, Σ, Gr* ; *see note*   22 instruments.] instruments, *1633*   25 and Goths inundate *H 40, C 57, H 49, TC, HK 2, Cy, B* : and Goths
invade *Dob, O'F, P, JC, S* : and the Goths invade *1633*

Here Loves Divines, (since all Divinity
    Is love or wonder) may finde all they seeke,
    Whether abstract spirituall love they like,   30
Their Soules exhal'd with what they do not see,
        Or, loth so to amuze
        Faiths infirmitie, they chuse
    Something which they may see and use;
For, though minde be the heaven, where love doth sit, 35
Beauty'a convenient type may be to figure it.

Here more then in their bookes may Lawyers finde,
    Both by what titles Mistresses are ours,
    And how prerogative those states devours,
Transferr'd from Love himselfe, to womankinde,   40
        Who though from heart, and eyes,
        They exact great subsidies,
    Forsake him who on them relies,
And for the cause, honour, or conscience give,
Chimeraes, vaine as they, or their prerogative.   45

Here Statesmen, (or of them, they which can reade,)
    May of their occupation finde the grounds.
    Love and their art alike it deadly wounds,
If to consider what 'tis, one proceed:
        In both they doe excell   50
        Who the present governe well,
    Whose weaknesse none doth, or dares tell;
In this thy booke, such will their nothing see,
As in the Bible some can finde out Alchimy.

Thus vent thy thoughts; abroad I'll studie thee,   55
    As he removes farre off, that great heights takes;
    How great love is, presence best tryall makes,
But absence tryes how long this love will bee;

32 Or, . . . amuze] Or . . . amuze, *1633*   36 Beauty'a] Beauty a *1633*   38 titles]
titles, *1633*   39 those *Σ*: these *1633, C 57, HK 2, Gr*   40 womankinde,] womankinde. *1633*   43 relies,] relies *1633*   47 grounds.] grounds, *1633*   49 proceed :] proceed, *1633*   53 their nothing *C 57, TC, Dob, O'F, B*: there nothing *H 40*,
H 49, Cy, S: they nothing *HK 2*: there nothings *JC*: there something *1633, P*

To take a latitude
Sun, or starres, are fitliest view'd   60
At their brightest, but to conclude
Of longitudes, what other way have wee,
But to marke when, and where the darke eclipses bee?

A Valediction : of Weeping

L ET me powre forth
My teares before thy face, whil'st I stay here,
For thy face coines them, and thy stampe they beare,
And by this Mintage they are something worth,
        For thus they bee   5
        Pregnant of thee;
Fruits of much griefe they are, emblemes of more,
When a teare falls, that thou falls which it bore,
So thou and I are nothing then, when on a divers shore.

        On a round ball   10
A workeman that hath copies by, can lay
An Europe, Afrique, and an Asia,
And quickly make that, which was nothing, *All*,
        So doth each teare,
        Which thee doth weare,   15
A globe, yea world by that impression grow,
Till thy teares mixt with mine doe overflow
This world, by waters sent from thee, my heaven dissolved so.

        O more then Moone,
Draw not up seas to drowne me in thy spheare,   20
Weepe me not dead, in thine armes, but forbeare
To teach the sea, what it may doe too soone;

A Valediction : of Weeping. *A 25 omits. Title from 1633 : omit* A TC : A Valediction *H 40,*
C 57, H 49, B : A Valediction of teares *Dob, S 96, Cy, S :* Valediction 2 of teares *O'F.*
6 thee;] thee, *1633*   8 falls *H 40, C 57, H 49, L 74, TC, HK 2, JC, S :* falst *1633, Dob,*
O'F, S 96, Cy, P, B, Gr : see note   9 shore.] shore *1633*   22 soone;] soone, *1633*

Let not the winde
Example finde,
To doe me more harme, then it purposeth;　　　　25
Since thou and I sigh one anothers breath,
Who e'r sighes most, is cruellest, and hasts the others death.

The Good-morrow

I WONDER by my troth, what thou, and I
　Did, till we lov'd? were we not wean'd till then?
But suck'd on countrey pleasures, childishly?
　Or snorted we i'the seaven sleepers den?
'Twas so; But this, all pleasures fancies bee.　　　　5
If ever any beauty I did see,
Which I desir'd, and got, 'twas but a dreame of thee.

And now good morrow to our waking soules,
　Which watch not one another out of feare;
For love, all love of other sights controules,　　　　10
　And makes one little roome, an every where.
Let sea-discoverers to new worlds have gone,
Let Maps to others, worlds on worlds have showne,
Let us possesse our world, each hath one, and is one.

My face in thine eye, thine in mine appeares,　　　　15
　And true plaine hearts doe in the faces rest,
Where can we finde two better hemispheares
　Without sharpe North, without declining West?

25 purposeth;] purposeth, *1633*

The Good-morrow. *Cy omits. Title from 1633, TC.*　　2 lov'd?] lov'd, *1633*
3 countrey... childishly *1633, H 40, C 57, H 49*; childish... seelily *Σ: see note*　　4 snorted]
slumbred *L 74, TC, HK 2, P, A 25, JC: l. 4 missing in B*　　i'the] in the *1633*　　5 and 8
'Twas ... 'twas] T'was ... t'was *1633*　　10 For] But *L 74, TC, HK 2, P, A 25,
B, S*　　11 one] a *L 74, TC, HK 2, P, A 25, B*　　13 to others, worlds on worlds
Σ: to other... 1633, Gr: to other worlds, one world JC, P, S: in studies, worlds ... A 25
14 our *Σ: one 1633, C 57, H 49, JC, Gr: see note*　　16 true plaine] plaine true *L 74,
TC, HK 2, P, A 25, B*　　17 better *1633, H 40, C 57, H 49, JC: fitter Σ*

What ever dyes, was not mixt equally;
If our two loves be one, or, thou and I   20
Love so alike, that none doe slacken, none can die.

The Anniversarie

ALL Kings, and all their favorites,
   All glory'of honors, beauties, wits,
The Sun it selfe, which makes times, as they passe,
Is elder by a yeare, now, then it was
When thou and I first one another saw: 5
All other things, to their destruction draw,
   Only our love hath no decay;
This, no tomorrow hath, nor yesterday,
Running it never runs from us away,
But truly keepes his first, last, everlasting day.   10

Two graves must hide thine and my coarse,
If one might, death were no divorce.
Alas, as well as other Princes, wee,
(Who Prince enough in one another bee,)
Must leave at last in death, these eyes, and eares,   15
Oft fed with true oathes, and with sweet salt teares;
   But soules where nothing dwells but love
(All other thoughts being inmates) then shall prove
This, or a love increased there above,
When bodies to their graves, soules from their graves
   remove.   20

19 was] is *L 74, TC, HK 2, P, A 25, B*   20 If our two] If both our *L 74, TC,
HK 2, A 25, B*: If our both *P* or] as *H 40*: and *S*: both *O'F, HK 2, P, JC*; *see note*
21 Love ... die *1633, H 40, C 57, H 49*: Love just alike in all; none of these loves can die
Σ; *see note*

The Anniversarie. *L 74, A 25 omit. Title from 1633, TC.*   1 favorites,] favorites
1633 uncorrected   2 glory'of] glory of *1633*   10 his *1633, TC*: the *Σ*; *see note*
12 divorce.] divorce, *1633*   16 oathes,] othes *1633 uncorrected*   17 love] love;
1633

And then wee shall be throughly blest,
But wee no more, then all the rest.
Here upon earth, we'are Kings, and none but wee
Can be such Kings, nor of such subjects bee;
Who is so safe as wee? where none can doe   25
Treason to us, except one of us two.
True and false feares let us refraine,
Let us love nobly,'and live, and adde againe
Yeares and yeares unto yeares, till we attaine
To write threescore: this is the second of our raigne.   30

The Sunne Rising

BUSIE old foole, unruly Sunne,
    Why dost thou thus,
Through windowes, and through curtaines call on us?
Must to thy motions lovers seasons run?
    Sawcy pedantique wretch, goe chide   5
    Late schoole boyes, and sowre prentices,
Goe tell Court-huntsmen, that the King will ride,
Call countrey ants to harvest offices;
Love, all alike, no season knowes, nor clyme,
Nor houres, dayes, months, which are the rags of time.   10

    Thy beames, so reverend, and strong
    Why shouldst thou thinke?
I could eclipse and cloud them with a winke,
But that I would not lose her sight so long:

22 wee *MSS.*: now *1633*; *see note*   rest.] rest *1633 uncorrected*   23–24 and none but
wee/ Can be such Kings *1633*, *TC*: and but wee/ None are such Kings *Σ*   24 nor]
and *H 40, C 57, H 49, HK 2, Cy, JC, S*   28 nobly,'and] nobly,and *1633*
30 threescore:] threescore, *1633*

    The Sunne Rising. *H 40 omits. Title from 1633*: *omit* The *TC*: To the Sunne *C 57, HK 2, Cy*:
Ad Solem *H 49, S 96, JC, S*: Ad solem. A songe *Dob, A 25*: Ad solem. To the Sunne. Song
O'F.   8 offices;] offices, *1633*   10 months] moneths *1633*

If her eyes have not blinded thine,   15
   Looke, and to morrow late, tell mee,
Whether both the'India's of spice and Myne
Be where thou leftst them, or lie here with mee.
Aske for those Kings whom thou saw'st yesterday,
And thou shalt heare, All here in one bed lay.   20

   She'is all States, and all Princes, I,
     Nothing else is.
Princes doe but play us; compar'd to this,
All honor's mimique; All wealth alchimie.
   Thou sunne art halfe as happy'as wee,   25
   In that the world's contracted thus;
  Thine age askes ease, and since thy duties bee
To warme the world, that's done in warming us.
Shine here to us, and thou art every where;
This bed thy center is, these walls, thy spheare.   30

The Canonization

FOR Godsake hold your tongue, and let me love,
   Or chide my palsie, or my gout,
My five gray haires, or ruin'd fortune flout,
With wealth your state, your minde with Arts improve,
   Take you a course, get you a place,   5
   Observe his honour, or his grace,
And the Kings reall, or his stamped face
   Contemplate; what you will, approve,
     So you will let me love.

19 whom] wᶜʰ Dob, O'F, S 96, Cy, P, A 25, JC, S   23 us;] us, 1633
24 alchimie.] alchimie; 1633   26 thus;] thus. 1633

The Canonization. L 74, A 25 omit. B omits stanza 4: ll. 34–45 are on a missing leaf in TCD.
Title from 1633, C 57, H 49, TC, O'F, HK 2, Cy, P: omit The S: Canonizatio Dob, S 96.
4 improve,] improve 1633   7 And MSS.: Or 1633, Gr   8 Contemplate;] Contemplate, 1633

Alas, alas, who's injur'd by my love?   10
   What merchants ships have my sighs drown'd?
Who saies my teares have overflow'd his ground?
When did my colds a forward spring remove?
   When did the heats which my veines fill
     Adde one man to the plaguie Bill?   15
Soldiers finde warres, and Lawyers finde out still
   Litigious men, which quarrels move,
     Though she and I do love.

Call us what you will, wee'are made such by love;
   Call her one, mee another flye,   20
We'are Tapers too, and at our owne cost die,
And wee in us finde the'Eagle and the Dove;
   The Phœnix ridle hath more wit
     By us, we two being one, are it,
So, to one neutrall thing both sexes fit.   25
   Wee dye and rise the same, and prove
     Mysterious by this love.

Wee can dye by it, if not live by love,
   And if unfit for tombes or hearse
Our legend bee, it will be fit for verse;   30
And if no peece of Chronicle wee prove,
   We'll build in sonnets pretty roomes;
   As well a well wrought urne becomes
The greatest ashes, as halfe-acre tombes,
   And by these hymnes, all shall approve   35
     Us *Canoniz'd* for Love.

And thus invoke us; You whom reverend love
   Made one anothers hermitage;
You, to whom love was peace, that now is rage;
Who did the whole worlds soule extract, and drove   40

14 the] those *TC, Dob, HK 2, Cy, P, JC, S*   15 man *Σ*: more *1633, C 57, Gr*
19 wee'are] wee are *1633*   22 Dove;] dove, *1633*   24 we two] we *Dob, O'F, S 96*
it,] it. *1633*   29 tombes] tombe *TC, O'F, HK 2, Cy, P, JC, S*   or *Σ*: and *1633, C 57,*
H 49, Gr   30 legend *Σ*: legends *1633, H 40, C 57, H 49*   35 these] those *Dob,*
O'F, S 96, Cy   39 rage;] rage, *1633*   40 extract *MSS.*: contract *1633, Gr;*
see note   drove] drawe *C 57, H 49, HK 2, Cy, P, B*: have *H 40*

Into the glasses of your eyes,
  So made such mirrors, and such spies,
That they did all to you epitomize,
    Countries, Townes, Courts: Beg from above
      A patterne of your love!   45

Aire and Angels

T WICE or thrice had I lov'd thee,
  Before I knew thy face or name;
So in a voice, so in a shapelesse flame,
Angells affect us oft, and worship'd bee;
  Still when, to where thou wert, I came,   5
Some lovely glorious nothing I did see.
  But since my soule, whose child love is,
Takes limmes of flesh, and else could nothing doe,
  More subtile then the parent is,
Love must not be, but take a body too,   10
  And therefore what thou wert, and who,
    I bid Love aske, and now
That it assume thy body, I allow,
And fixe it selfe in thy lip, eye, and brow.

  Whilst thus to ballast love, I thought,   15
    And so more steddily to have gone,
With wares which would sinke admiration,
I saw, I had loves pinnace overfraught,
  Ev'ry thy haire for love to worke upon
Is much too much, some fitter must be sought;   20

---

41 eyes,] eyes *1633*   44 from] frow *1633*   45 your *Σ*: our *1633*, *C 57*, *H 49*
45 love!] love. *1633*

Aire and Angels. *L 74*, *Cy*, *A 25 omit. Title from 1633*, *Σ*: Fire an Angells *P* : *no title H 40*, *B*.
1 lov'd] loved *1633*   4 bee;] bee, *1633*   5 came,] came *1633*   6 see.] see,
1633   7 since] since, *1633*   11 who,] who *1633*   13 assume] assumes *C 57*,
H 49, *HK 2*, *P*, *JC*: assures *S*   14 lip] lips *Dob*, *O'F*, *S 96*, *B*

For, nor in nothing, nor in things
Extreme, and scatt'ring bright, can love inhere;
    Then as an Angell, face, and wings
Of aire, not pure as it, yet pure doth weare,
    So thy love may be my loves spheare;   25
            Just such disparitie
    As is twixt Aire and Angells puritie,
'Twixt womens love, and mens will ever bee.

Loves Growth

I SCARCE beleeve my love to be so pure
    As I had thought it was,
        Because it doth endure
Vicissitude, and season, as the grasse;
Me thinkes I lyed all winter, when I swore,   5
My love was infinite, if spring make'it more.
But if this medicine, love, which cures all sorrow
    With more, not onely bee no quintessence,
    But mixt of all stuffes, paining soule, or sense,
And of the Sunne his working vigour borrow,   10
Love's not so pure, and abstract, as they use
To say, which have no Mistresse but their Muse,
But as all else, being elemented too,
Love sometimes would contemplate, sometimes do.

And yet not greater, but more eminent,   15
    Love by the spring is growne;
        As, in the firmament,
Starres by the Sunne are not inlarg'd, but showne.

---

22 scatt'ring] scattring *1633*   28 'Twixt] T'wixt *1633 uncorrected*   love] loves *Dob,
O'F, S 96, HK 2, P, JC, S*

Loves Growth. *H 40, L 74, HK 2, A 25 omit. Title from 1633, TC:* Springe *C 57, H 49,
Dob, S 96:* The Spring *O'F, Cy, P, B, S. Printed with first stanza divided after l. 6 in 1633.*
9 paining] vexing *Dob, O'F, S 96, Cy, P, S*   10 working] active *O'F, Cy, P, S: TC
omits l. 10*   11 pure, and] pure an *Dob, O'F, S 96, Cy, P, B, JC, S*   12 which]
who *O'F, Cy, P:* that *S 96:* they *S*   14 do.] do *1633*   15 not *Σ:* no *1633, S, Gr*
18 showne.] showne, *1633*

Gentle love deeds, as blossomes on a bough,
From loves awaken'd root do bud out now.   20
If, as in water stir'd more circles bee
   Produc'd by one, love such additions take,
    Those like to many spheares, but one heaven make,
For, they are all concentrique unto thee;
And though each spring doe adde to love new heate,   25
As princes doe in times of action get
New taxes, and remit them not in peace,
No winter shall abate the springs encrease.

Loves Infiniteness

IF yet I have not all thy love,
   Deare, I shall never have it all;
I cannot breath one other sigh, to move,
   Nor can intreat one other teare to fall.
All my treasure, which should purchase thee,   5
   Sighs, teares, and oathes, and letters I have spent,
Yet no more can be due to mee,
   Then at the bargaine made was ment.
If then thy gift of love were partiall,
That some to mee, some should to others fall,   10
   Deare, I shall never have Thee All.

Or if then thou gav'st mee all,
   All was but All, which thou hadst then,
But if in thy heart, since, there be or shall,
   New love created bee, by other men,   15

20 awaken'd] awakened *1633*   23 to many *Σ*: so many *1633*, *S*, *Gr*: the *P*
24 thee;] thee, *1633*   28 the] this *O'F, Cy, P, S*

Loves Infiniteness. *L 74, TC, Cy, omit. Title adapted from* Lovers Infiniteness *1633*: Mon
Tout *A 25*.   1 thy] your *H 40, C 57, H 49, Dob, B, S*   2 all;] all, *1633*
3 move,] move; *1633*   5 All *MSS*.: And all *1633, Gr*; *see note*   6 Sighs, teares,] . . .
teares *1633*: Teares, sighs *HK 2, P, A 25*   8 ment.] ment, *1633*   12 gav'st]
gavest *1633*   14 heart] breast *HK 2, P, A 25*

Which have their stocks intire, and can in teares,
  In sighs, in oathes, and letters outbid mee,
This new love may beget new feares,
  For, this love was not vowed by thee.
And yet it was, thy gift being generall,   20
The ground, thy heart is mine, what ever shall
  Grow there, deare, I should have it all.

Yet I would not have all yet,
  Hee that hath all can have no more,
And since my love doth every day admit   25
  New growth, thou shouldst have new rewards in store;
Thou canst not every day give me thy heart,
  If thou canst give it, then thou never gav'st it:
Loves riddles are, that though thy heart depart,
  It stayes at home, and thou with losing sav'st it: 30
But wee will have a way more liberall,
  Then changing hearts, to joyne them, so wee shall
    Be one, and one anothers All.

A Lecture upon the Shadow

STAND still, and I will read to thee
  A Lecture, Love, in loves philosophy.
These three houres that we have spent,
  Walking here, two shadowes went

16 Which] Who *Dob, O'F, S 96, HK 2, P, A 25*   17 and] in *Dob, HK 2, P, B, JC, S*
19 thee.] thee, *1633*   20 it] is *1633*   21 is] was *O'F, S 96, HK 2, P, A 25*
25–26 love ... admit ... growth] heart ... begett ... love *HK 2, P, A 25*   28 it, then]
it now *HK 2, P, A 25*   28 and 30 gav'st ... sav'st] gavest ... savest *1633*
29–30 Loves ... it] Except mine come when thine doth parte/ And, in such giving it thou
savest it *HK 2*: ... And so in giving ... *P, A 25*: Perchance mine ... And by such losing
it ... *JC*   31 have] find *HK 2, P, A 25*   32 joyne] coyne *HK 2*: winne *P, A 25*
  A Lecture upon the Shadow. *Cy omits. First printed in 1635. Title from 1650*: Song *1635*:
Lecture vppon the shaddowe *TC*: Shaddowe *Dob, S 96*: The Shadow *O'F, P*: Loves Phylo-
sophie *JC*: Loves Lecture *S*.   3 These] Those *H 40, C 57, H 49, S 96, B, JC*   that]
which *H 40, C 57, H 49, Dob, O'F, S 96, A 25, B, JC, S*   4 Walking] In walking
H 40, C 57, H 49, Dob, S 96, B, JC, S   here, two] here; Two *1635*

Along with us, which we our selves produc'd;   5
But, now the Sunne is just above our head,
    We doe those shadowes tread;
And to brave clearenesse all things are reduc'd.
    So whilst our infant loves did grow,
      Disguises did, and shadowes, flow   10
From us, and our care; but, now 'tis not so.

That love hath not attain'd the high'st degree,
Which is still diligent lest others see.

    Except our loves at this noone stay,
We shall new shadowes make the other way.   15
    As the first were made to blinde
    Others; these which come behinde
Will worke upon our selves, and blind our eyes.
If our loves faint, and westwardly decline;
    To me thou, falsly, thine,   20
And I to thee mine actions shall disguise.
    The morning shadowes weare away,
    But these grow longer all the day,
But oh, loves day is short, if love decay.

Love is a growing, or full constant light;   25
And his first minute, after noone, is night.

The Dreame

DEARE love, for nothing lesse then thee
   Would I have broke this happy dreame,
      It was a theame
   For reason, much too strong for phantasie,

9 loves] love *H 40, C 57, H 49, Dob, O'F, S 96, B, JC, S; see note*   10 flow] flow,
1635   11 care *Σ*: cares *1635, L 74, TC, P, Gr*: eares *HK 2, O'F*   12 high'st]
least *H 40, H 49, Dob, O'F, S 96, B, JC, S*: last *C 57*   14 loves] love *H 40, C 57, H 49,*
Dob, O'F, S 96, P, B, JC, S   19 If our loves] . . . love *Dob (b.c.), O'F, S 96*: If once
love *H 40, C 57, H 49, B, JC*: If Love once *S*   26 first *MSS.*: short *1635*

The Dreame. *H 40, JC omit. A 25 omits stanza 3. Title from 1633, C 57, H 49, TC*:
Dreame *L 74, Dob, O'F, S 96, HK 2, S*: A Dreame *Cy, P.*

Therefore thou wakd'st me wisely; yet   5
My Dreame thou brok'st not, but continued'st it,
Thou art so true, that thoughts of thee suffice,
To make dreames truth; and fables histories;
Enter these armes, for since thou thoughtst it best,
Not to dreame all my dreame, let's do the rest.   10

As lightning, or a Tapers light,
Thine eyes, and not thy noise wak'd mee;
            Yet I thought thee
(For thou lov'st truth) an Angell, at first sight,
But when I saw thou saw'st my heart,   15
And knew'st my thoughts, beyond an Angels art,
When thou knew'st what I dreamt, when thou knew'st
            when
Excesse of joy would wake me, and cam'st then,
I doe confesse, it could not chuse but bee
Prophane, to thinke thee any thing but thee.   20

Comming and staying show'd thee, thee,
But rising makes me doubt, that now,
            Thou art not thou.
That love is weake, where feare's as strong as hee;
    'Tis not all spirit, pure, and brave,   25
If mixture it of *Feare, Shame, Honor,* have.
Perchance as torches which must ready bee,
Men light and put out, so thou deal'st with mee,
Thou cam'st to kindle, goest to come; Then I
Will dreame that hope againe, but else would die.   30

7 true Σ: truth *1633, C 57, H 49, L 74, TC, Gr; see note*   8 truth *C 57, H 49, TCD,
S 96*: truths *1633, L 74, TCC, O'F, HK 2, Cy, P, A 25, Gr*: true *Dob, B, S; see note*
10 do Σ: act *1633, TC, Gr*: to *Cy, P*   14 (For thou . . .) an] (Thou . . .) but an
C 57, H 49, L 74, TC   14 and 15 lov'st . . . saw'st] lovest . . . sawest *1633*
19 doe Σ: must *1633, Gr*   it] I *HK 2, Cy, P, A 25, B, S*   20 Prophane]
Prophaness *C 57, H 49, L 74, TC, Dob, O'F (b.c.), S 96; see note*   24 feare's as] feare
is *TCD*: feares are *Dob, O'F, S 96, HK 2, P, B, S*   26 have.] have; *1633*   28 deal'st]
doest *Dob, O'F, S 96, B, S*   29 Then] Thus *C 57, H 49, L 74, TC*   30 but] or
Dob, HK 2, Cy, P   would] will *C 57, H 49*

Loves Alchymie

SOME that have deeper digg'd loves Myne then I,
Say, where his centrique happinesse doth lie:
   I have lov'd, and got, and told,
But should I love, get, tell, till I were old,
I should not finde that hidden mysterie;   5
     Oh, 'tis imposture all:
And as no chymique yet th'Elixar got,
   But glorifies his pregnant pot,
   If by the way to him befall
Some odoriferous thing, or med'cinall,   10
So, lovers dreame a rich and long delight,
But get a winter-seeming summers night.

Our ease, our thrift, our honor, and our day,
Shall we, for this vaine Bubles shadow pay?
     Ends love in this, that my man,   15
Can be as happy,'as I can; If he can
Endure the short scorne of a Bridegroomes play?
     That loving wretch that sweares,
'Tis not the bodies marry, but the mindes,
   Which he in her Angelique findes,   20
   Would sweare as justly, that he heares,
In that dayes rude hoarse minstralsey, the spheares.
Hope not for minde in women; at their best
Sweetnesse and wit, they' are but *Mummy*, possest.

Loves Alchymie. *Title from 1633*: Mummie *Σ*: *no title* P, *A 25*.   10 med'cinall]
medicinall *1633*   19 marry] marrowe *Dob*, S 96, HK 2; *see note*   23 women]
woman H 49, L 74, TC, O'F, S   23–24 best/ Sweetnesse and wit, they'are but
Mummy,] best,/ Sweetnesse, and wit they'are, but, *Mummy*, *1633*; *see note*
811835   G

Farewell to Love

WHILST yet to prove,
  I thought there was some Deitie in love,
   So did I reverence, and gave
Worship, as Atheists at their dying houre
Call, what they cannot name, an unknowne power,   5
   As ignorantly did I crave:
        Thus when
Things not yet knowne are coveted by men,
Our desires give them fashion, and so
As they waxe lesser, fall, as they sise, grow.   10

   But, from late faire
His highnesse sitting in a golden Chaire,
   Is not lesse cared for after three dayes
By children, then the thing which lovers so
Blindly admire, and with such worship wooe;   15
   Being had, enjoying it decayes:
        And thence,
What before pleas'd them all, takes but one sense,
And that so lamely, as it leaves behinde
A kinde of sorrowing dulnesse to the minde.   20

   Ah cannot wee,
As well as Cocks and Lyons jocund be,
   After such pleasures? Unlesse wise
Nature decreed (since each such Act, they say,
Diminisheth the length of life a day)   25
   This; as shee would man should despise
        The sport,
Because that other curse of being short,
   And onely for a minute, made to be
Eager, desires to raise posterity.   30

Farewell to Love. *In O'F, S 96 : omit Σ. First printed in 1635. Title from 1635, MSS.*
2 love,] love *1635*   10 sise] rise *S 96*   23 pleasures? Unlesse] pleasures, unlesse *1635*
29 minute,] minute *1635*   29–30 be/ Eager, desires] be,/ ⟨Eagers desire⟩ *Gr*; *see note*

Since so, my minde
Shall not desire what no man else can finde,
  I'll no more dote and runne
To pursue things which had, indammage me.
And when I come where moving beauties be,   35
  As men doe when the summers Sunne
      Growes great,
Though I admire their greatnesse, shun their heat;
Each place can afford shadowes. If all faile,
'Tis but applying worme-seed to the Taile.   40

Twicknam Garden

BLASTED with sighs, and surrounded with teares,
  Hither I come to seeke the spring,
  And at mine eyes, and at mine eares,
Receive such balmes, as else cure every thing;
  But O, selfe traytor, I do bring   5
The spider love, which transubstantiates all,
  And can convert Manna to gall,
And that this place may thoroughly be thought
True Paradise, I have the serpent brought.

'Twere wholsomer for mee, that winter did   10
  Benight the glory of this place,
  And that a grave frost did forbid
These trees to laugh, and mocke mee to my face;
  But that I may not this disgrace
Indure, nor leave this garden, Love let mee   15
  Some senslesse peece of this place bee;

34 had, indammage S 96 : had indammag'd 1635, O'F, Gr
  Twicknam Garden. Title from 1633, TC, Dob, O'F, P, S: In a Garden B; see note.
4 balmes . . . cure] balmes . . . cures L 74, TCD : balme . . . cures TCC, Dob, O'F, S 96, HK 2,
Cy, P, B, S   thing;] thing, 1633   8 may] might TC, HK 2, A 25, B, JC, S
12 grave] gray Dob, O'F, S 96, Cy, JC : gray grave S   did] would L 74, TC, HK 2, Cy,
P, S   13 laugh,] laugh 1633   15 leave this garden Σ: omit H 40, C 57, H 49: yet
leave loving 1633, Gr; see note   16 peece] parte L 74, TC, HK 2, Cy, P, S

Make me a mandrake, so I may grow here,
Or a stone fountaine weeping out my yeare.

Hither with christall vyals, lovers come,
  And take my teares, which are loves wine,   20
  And try your mistresse Teares at home,
For all are false, that tast not just like mine;
  Alas, hearts do not in eyes shine,
Nor can you more judge womans thoughts by teares,
  Then by her shadow, what she weares.   25
O perverse sexe, where none is true but shee,
Who's therefore true, because her truth kills mee.

A Nocturnall upon S. Lucies Day, being the shortest day

'TIS the yeares midnight, and it is the dayes,
  Lucies, who scarce seaven houres herself unmaskes,
    The Sunne is spent, and now his flasks
    Send forth light squibs, no constant rayes;
      The world's whole sap is sunke: 5
The generall balme th'hydroptique earth hath drunk,
Whither, as to the beds-feet, life is shrunke,
Dead and enterr'd; yet all these seeme to laugh,
Compar'd with mee, who am their Epitaph.

Study me then, you who shall lovers bee   10
At the next world, that is, at the next Spring:
    For I am every dead thing,
    In whom love wrought new Alchimie.
      For his art did expresse

17 grow] grone *H 40, H 49, TC* (*TCD corrects* grow *to* groan), *Gr; see note*   18 my]
the *L 74, TC, Dob, O'F, S 96, HK 2, Cy, P, A 25, JC*   24 womans *H 40, H 49, L 74,
TC, A 25, B*: womens *1633, C 57, Dob, O'F, HK 2, Cy, P, JC, S*

A Nocturnall &c. *In TC, O'F: omit Σ. Title from 1633, MSS.*   1 'Tis] Tis *1633*
4 no] not *O'F*   7 beds-feet,] beds-feet *1633*   13 Alchimie] Alchimee *1633 uncorrected*

A quintessence even from nothingnesse,   15
From dull privations, and leane emptinesse:
He ruin'd mee, and I am re-begot
Of absence, darknesse, death; things which are not.

All others, from all things, draw all that's good,
Life, soule, forme, spirit, whence they beeing have;   20
    I, by loves limbecke, am the grave
    Of all, that's nothing. Oft a flood
        Have wee two wept, and so
Drownd the whole world, us two; oft did we grow
To be two Chaosses, when we did show   25
Care to ought else; and often absences
Withdrew our soules, and made us carcasses.

But I am by her death, (which word wrongs her)
Of the first nothing, the Elixer grown;
    Were I a man, that I were one,   30
    I needs must know; I should preferre,
        If I were any beast,
Some ends, some means; Yea plants, yea stones detest,
And love; All, all some properties invest;
If I an ordinary nothing were,   35
As shadow,'a light, and body must be here.

But I am None; nor will my Sunne renew.
You lovers, for whose sake, the lesser Sunne
    At this time to the Goat is runne
    To fetch new lust, and give it you,   40
        Enjoy your summer all;
Since shee enjoyes her long nights festivall,
Let mee prepare towards her, and let mee call
This houre her Vigill, and her Eve, since this
Both the yeares, and the dayes deep midnight is.   45

---

16 emptinesse :] emptinesse *1633*; *see note*   20 have;] have, *1633*   31 know;]
know, *1633*   34 love; All] love, all *1633*   invest;] invest, *1633*   36 shadow,'a]
shadow, a *1633*   41 all;] all, *1633*   44 Eve] eve *1633*

The Dissolution

SHEE'IS dead; And all which die
  To their first Elements resolve;
And wee were mutuall Elements to us,
      And made of one another.
My body then doth hers involve,   5
And those things whereof I consist, hereby
In me abundant grow, and burdenous,
      And nourish not, but smother.
My fire of Passion, sighes of ayre,
Water of teares, and earthly sad despaire,   10
      Which my materialls bee,
But neere worne out by loves securitie,
Shee, to my losse, doth by her death repaire,
      And I might live long wretched so
But that my fire doth with my fuell grow.   15
      Now as those Active Kings
Whose foraine conquest treasure brings,
Receive more, and spend more, and soonest breake:
This (which I am amaz'd that I can speake)
      This death, hath with my store   20
      My use encreas'd.
And so my soule more earnestly releas'd,
Will outstrip hers; As bullets flown before
A latter bullet may o'rtake, the pouder being more.

The Dissolution. *In TC, O'F: omit Σ. Title from 1633, MSS.*   10 earthly] earthy
O'F   12 neere *MSS.*: ne'r *1633*   23 flown] flowen *1633*

The Blossome

LITTLE think'st thou, poore flower,
  Whom I'have watch'd sixe or seaven dayes,
And seene thy birth, and seene what every houre
Gave to thy growth, thee to this height to raise,
And now dost laugh and triumph on this bough,   5
      Little think'st thou
That it will freeze anon, and that I shall
To morrow finde thee falne, or not at all.

  Little think'st thou poore heart
    That labour'st yet to nestle thee,   10
And think'st by hovering here to get a part
In a forbidden or forbidding tree,
And hop'st her stiffenesse by long siege to bow:
      Little think'st thou,
That thou to morrow, ere that Sunne doth wake,   15
Must with this Sunne, and mee a journey take.

  But thou which lov'st to bee
    Subtile to plague thy selfe, wilt say,
Alas, if you must goe, what's that to mee?
Here lyes my businesse, and here I will stay: 20
You goe to friends, whose love and meanes present
      Various content
To your eyes, eares, and tongue, and every part.
If then your body goe, what need you'a heart?

  Well then, stay here; but know,   25
    When thou hast stayd and done thy most;
A naked thinking heart, that makes no show,
Is to a woman, but a kinde of Ghost;

The Blossome. *H 40, L 74, HK 2, Cy, P omit. Title from 1633, Σ: no title A 25.*
2 I'have] I have *1633*   10 labour'st *Σ: labours 1633, C 57, H 49*   15 that] the *Dob,*
O'F, S 96   21 love] loves *TC, Dob, S 96, A 25, B, JC, S*   23 and tongue *Σ:*
omit S: and tast 1633   24 need you'a *Σ: . . . yow have a JC: need your 1633*

How shall shee know my heart; or having none,
   Know thee for one?   30
Practise may make her know some other part,
But take my word, shee doth not know a Heart.

  Meet mee at London, then,
  Twenty dayes hence, and thou shalt see
Mee fresher, and more fat, by being with men, 35
Then if I had staid still with her and thee.
For Gods sake, if you can, be you so too:
   I would give you
There, to another friend, whom wee shall finde
As glad to have my body, as my minde.   40

The Primrose

V PON this Primrose hill,
  Where, if Heav'n would distill
A shoure of raine, each severall drop might goe
To his owne primrose, and grow Manna so;
And where their forme, and their infinitie   5
  Make a terrestriall Galaxie,
  As the small starres doe in the skie:
I walke to finde a true Love; and I see
That 'tis not a mere woman, that is shee,
But must, or more, or lesse then woman bee. 10

  Yet know I not, which flower
  I wish; a sixe, or foure;
For should my true-Love lesse then woman bee,
She were scarce any thing; and then, should she
Be more then woman, shee would get above 15
  All thought of sexe, and thinke to move
  My heart to study'her, not to love;

38 would Σ: will _1633_, _C 57_

 The Primrose. _H 40, L 74, HK 2, Cy, P, A 25, JC_ omit. _Title from 1633_, MSS.: The
Primrose, being at Mountgomery Castle, upon the hill, on which it is situate _1635_; _see note._
17 study'her, not Σ: study her and not _1633, S 96, B, Gr_; _see note_

Both these were monsters; Since there must reside
Falshood in woman, I could more abide,
She were by art, then Nature falsify'd.   20

    Live Primrose then, and thrive
    With thy true number, five;
And women, whom this flower doth represent,
With this mysterious number be content;
Ten is the farthest number; if halfe ten   25
    Belonge unto each woman, then
    Each woman may take halfe us men;
Or if this will not serve their turne, Since all
Numbers are odde, or even, and they fall
First into this, five, women may take us all.   30

The Relique

WHEN my grave is broke up againe
    Some second ghest to entertaine,
(For graves have learn'd that woman-head
To be to more then one a Bed)
    And he that digs it, spies   5
A bracelet of bright haire about the bone,
    Will he not let'us alone,
And thinke that there a loving couple lies,
Who thought that this device might be some way
To make their soules, at the last busie day,   10
Meet at this grave, and make a little stay?

    If this fall in a time, or land,
    Where mis-devotion doth command,
    Then, he that digges us up, will bring
    Us, to the Bishop, and the King,   15

---

22 number,] number *1633*   25 number;] number, *1633*   26 Belonge *Σ*:
Belongs *1633, C 57*   27 men;] men, *1633*   30 this,] this *1633*

    The Relique. *H 40, L 74, HK 2, Cy, P omit. Title from 1633, Σ: no title A 25.*
9 thought . . . some *1633, TC:* hop'd . . . a *Σ*   14 Then, he that digges us *1633, TC:*
Hee that doth digge it *Σ*

To make us Reliques; then
Thou shalt be'a Mary Magdalen, and I
A something else thereby;
All women shall adore us, and some men;
And since at such times, miracles are sought,   20
I would that age were by this paper taught
What miracles wee harmlesse lovers wrought.

First, we lov'd well and faithfully,
Yet knew not what wee lov'd, nor why,
Difference of sex no more wee knew,   25
Then our Guardian Angells doe;
Comming and going, wee
Perchance might kisse, but not between those meales;
Our hands ne'r toucht the seales,
Which nature, injur'd by late law, sets free: 30
These miracles wee did; but now alas,
All measure, and all language, I should passe,
Should I tell what a miracle shee was.

The Funerall

WHO ever comes to shroud me, do not harme
        Nor question much
That subtile wreath of haire, which crowns mine arme;
The mystery, the signe you must not touch,
        For 'tis my outward Soule,   5
Viceroy to that, which then to heaven being gone,
        Will leave this to controule,
    And keepe these limbes, her Provinces, from dissolution.

17 Thou shalt *1633*, *TC*: Yow shal *Σ*   be'a] be a *1633*   20 times *Σ*: time *1633*,
C 57, *H 49*, *A 25*, *Gr*   21 that age were *TC*: have that age *1633*, *Σ*, *Gr*   25–26 no
more wee knew,/ Then our Guardian *1633*, *TC*: wee never knew/ More then our Guardian
C 57, *H 49*, *A 25*, *JC*, *S*: wee never knew/ No more then . . . *Dob*, *O'F* (*omitting* our), *S 96*,
B; *see note*   26 doe;] doe, *1633*   27 wee] wee, *1633*   28 between *1633*,
TC: betwixt *Σ*   meales;] meales. *1633*: meales *1633 uncorrected*   29 the] those *TC*
30 free:] free, *1633*   32 measure] measures *TCD*

The Funerall. *H 40*, *HK 2*, *A 25*, *JC omit. Title from 1633, MSS.*   3 mine *Σ*: my
1633, *C 57*, *Cy*, *S*, *Gr*   6 then to *MSS.*: unto *1633*

For if the sinewie thread my braine lets fall
      Through every part,   10
Can tye those parts, and make mee one of all;
These haires which upward grew, and strength and art
      Have from a better braine,
Can better do'it; Except she meant that I
      By this should know my pain,   15
As prisoners then are manacled, when they'are condemn'd
      to die.

What ere shee meant by'it, bury it with me,
      For since I am
Loves martyr, it might breed idolatrie,
If into others hands these Reliques came;   20
      As 'twas humility
To'afford to it all that a Soule can doe,
      So, 'tis some bravery,
That since you would save none of mee, I bury some of
      you.

12 These Σ: Those *1633*, *C 57*, *O'F*, *P*: The *S*   16 condemn'd] condem'nd *1633*
17 with Σ: by *1633*, *Cy (b.c.)*   22 To'afford] To afford *1633*   24 save *H 49*, *L 74*,
TC, *Cy*, *P*, *B*: have *1633*, *C 57*, *Dob*, *O'F*, *S 96*: *omit S*

DUBIA

POEMS INCLUDED IN EDITIONS FROM 1633 TO 1669

Sapho to Philaenis

WHERE is that holy fire, which Verse is said
⠀⠀To have, is that inchanting force decai'd?
Verse that drawes Natures workes, from Natures law,
⠀⠀Thee, her best worke, to her worke cannot draw.
Have my teares quench'd my old Poetique fire;⠀⠀⠀⠀⠀5
⠀⠀Why quench'd they not as well, that of desire?
Thoughts, my mindes creatures, often are with thee,
⠀⠀But I, their maker, want their libertie.
Onely thine image, in my heart, doth sit,
⠀⠀But that is waxe, and fires environ it.⠀⠀⠀⠀⠀⠀10
My fires have driven, thine have drawne it hence;
⠀⠀And I am rob'd of Picture, Heart, and Sense.
Dwells with me still mine irksome Memory,
⠀⠀Which, both to keepe, and lose, grieves equally.
That tells me'how faire thou art: Thou art so faire,⠀⠀⠀15
⠀⠀As, gods, when gods to thee I doe compare,
Are grac'd thereby; And to make blinde men see,
⠀⠀What things gods are, I say they'are like to thee.
For, if we justly call each silly man
⠀⠀A litle world, What shall we call thee than?⠀⠀⠀⠀20
Thou art not soft, and cleare, and strait, and faire,
⠀⠀As Down, as Stars, Cedars, and Lillies are,
But thy right hand, and cheek, and eye, only
⠀⠀Are like thy other hand, and cheek, and eye.

Sapho to Philaenis. *First printed in 1633. Text in 1633 is heavily italicized. MSS.: TCC,
TCD, O'F, P, A 25, JC. Title from 1633, TC, O'F, P.*⠀⠀⠀3 workes] worke O'F
8 maker,] maker; *1633*⠀⠀⠀10 fires environ] fire envyrons O'F, A 25⠀⠀⠀17 thereby;
And] thereby. And *1633 uncorrected*

Such was my *Phao* awhile, but shall be never,   25
    As thou, wast, art, and, oh, maist thou be ever.
Here lovers sweare in their Idolatrie,
    That I am such; but Griefe discolors me.
And yet I grieve the lesse, least Griefe remove
    My beauty,'and make me'unworthy of thy love.   30
Plaies some soft boy with thee, oh there wants yet
    A mutuall feeling which should sweeten it.
His chinne, a thorny hairy'unevennesse
    Doth threaten, and some daily change possesse.
Thy body is a naturall Paradise,   35
    In whose selfe, unmanur'd, all pleasure lies,
Nor needs perfection; why shouldst thou than
    Admit the tillage of a harsh rough man?
Men leave behinde them that which their sin showes,
    And are as theeves trac'd, which rob when it snows.   40
But of our dallyance no more signes there are,
    Then fishes leave in streames, or Birds in aire.
And betweene us all sweetnesse may be had;
    All, all that Nature yields, or Art can adde.
My two lips, eyes, thighs, differ from thy two,   45
    But so, as thine from one another doe;
And, oh, no more; the likenesse being such,
    Why should they not alike in all parts touch?
Hand to strange hand, lippe to lippe none denies;
    Why should they brest to brest, or thighs to thighs?   50
Likenesse begets such strange selfe flatterie,
    That touching my selfe, all seemes done to thee.
My selfe I'embrace, and mine owne hands I kisse,
    And amorously thanke my selfe for this.
Me, in my glasse, I call thee; But, alas,   55
    When I would kisse, teares dimme mine eyes, and
      glasse.

---

26 and, oh, mayst thou be ever *O'F*: . . . mayst be ever *1633, TC, Gr*: and oh shalt be for
ever *P*: and maist thou be for ever *A 25, JC; see note*   30 beauty,'and] beauty, and *1633*
31–54 *Omit P, A 25, JC*   33 hairy'unevennesse] hairy unevennesse *1633*   40 are]
are, *1633*   53 I'embrace] I embrace *1633*

O cure this loving madnesse, and restore
    Me to mee; thee, my halfe, my all, my more.
So may thy cheekes red outweare scarlet dye,
    And their white, whitenesse of the Galaxy,   60
So may thy mighty,'amazing beauty move
    Envy'in all women, and in all men, love,
And so be change, and sicknesse, farre from thee,
    As thou by comming neere, keep'st them from me.

The Expostulation

To make the doubt cleare, that no woman's true,
    Was it my fate to prove it strong in you?
Thought I, but one had breathed purest aire,
And must she needs be false because she's faire?
Is it your beauties marke, or of your youth,   5
Or your perfection, not to study truth?
Or thinke you heaven is deafe, or hath no eyes?
Or those it hath, smile at your perjuries?
Are vowes so cheape with women, or the matter
Whereof they'are made, that they are writ in water,   10
And blowne away with winde? Or doth their breath
(Both hot and cold at once) make life and death?
Who could have thought so many accents sweet
Form'd into words, so many sighs should meete
As from our hearts, so many oathes, and teares   15
Sprinkled among, (all sweeter by our feares

58 thee *MSS.*: shee *1633*   59 cheekes red outweare] cheekes outweare all *P*:
cheekes outweare the *JC*   60 May blisse and thee be one eternally *P*: *omit line JC*
61 mighty,'amazing] mighty amazing *1633*

The Expostulation (Elegy XV *Gr*). *First printed in 1633*: *also in Jonson's* Underwoods,
1640. *Paragraphing supplied. MSS.*: (*on leaf torn out from TCD*), *N*, *Dob*, *O'F*, *S 96*, *Cy*, *P*.
Title from 1635.   2 strong] full *Und*   3 breathed purest] breath'd the purer *Und*
8 it] she *Dob*, *O'F* (*b.c.*), *S 96*, *Cy*, *P*   hath, smile] has, winke *Und*   10 they'are]
they are *1633*   12 cold at once)] cold) at once *1633*   make] threat *Und*   14 Form'd
into] Tun'd to our *Und*   15 As] Blowne *Und*   16 sweeter] sweetned *Dob*, *O'F*,
S 96

And the divine impression of stolne kisses,
That seal'd the rest) should now prove empty blisses?
Did you draw bonds to forfet? signe to breake?
Or must we reade you quite from what you speake,   20
And finde the truth out the wrong way? or must
Hee first desire you false, would wish you just?
  O I prophane, though most of women be
This kinde of beast, my thought shall except thee;
My dearest love, though froward jealousie,   25
With circumstance might urge thy'inconstancie,
Sooner I'll thinke the Sunne will cease to cheare
The teeming earth, and *that* forget to beare,
Sooner that rivers will runne back, or Thames
With ribs of Ice in June would bind his streames,   30
Or Nature, by whose strength the world endures,
Would change her course, before you alter yours.
  But O that treacherous breast to whom weake you
Did trust our Counsells, and wee both may rue,
Having his falshood found too late, 'twas hee   35
That made me *cast* you guilty, and you mee,
Whilst he, black wretch, betray'd each simple word
Wee spake, unto the cunning of a third.
Curst may hee be, that so our love hath slaine,
And wander on the earth, wretched as *Cain*,   40
Wretched as hee, and not deserve least pitty;
In plaguing him, let misery be witty;
Let all eyes shunne him, and hee shunne each eye,
Till hee be noysome as his infamie;
May he without remorse deny God thrice,   45
And not be trusted more on his Soules price;
And after all selfe torment, when hee dyes,
May Wolves teare out his heart, Vultures his eyes,

Swine eate his bowels, and his falser tongue
That utter'd all, be to some Raven flung,   50
And let his carrion coarse be'a longer feast
To the Kings dogges, then any other beast.

   Now I have curst, let us our love revive;
In mee the flame was never more alive;
I could beginne againe to court and praise,   55
And in that pleasure lengthen the short dayes
Of my lifes lease; like Painters that do take
Delight, not in made worke, but whiles they make;
I could renew those times, when first I saw
Love in your eyes, that gave my tongue the law   60
To like what you lik'd; and at maskes and playes
Commend the selfe same Actors, the same wayes;
Aske how you did, and often with intent
Of being officious, be impertinent;
All which were such soft pastimes, as in these   65
Love was as subtilly catch'd, as a disease;
But being got it is a treasure sweet,
Which to defend is harder then to get:
And ought not be prophan'd on either part,
For though 'tis got by *chance*, 'tis kept by *art*.   70

His Parting from Her

SINCE she must go, and I must mourn, come Night,
Environ me with darkness, whilst I write:
Shadow that hell unto me, which alone
I am to suffer when my Love is gone.

51 coarse] coarse, *1633*   be'a] be a *1633*   52 dogges, . . . beast.] dogges; . . .
beast; *1633*   53 I have *Dob, O'F, S 96, Cy, P, Und*: have I *1633, N, Gr*   58 Delight,
not . . . worke] Not . . . works delight *Dob, O'F, S 96*   whiles] whilst *Dob, O'F, S 96, Und*
61 and] or *Und*   62 Actors] Actor *Dob, O'F, S 96*   64 be] grow *Und*

  His Parting from Her (Elegy XII *Gr*). *First printed in full in 1669: a short version (ll. 1–4,
45–56, 67–82, 95–104) was printed in 1635 and subsequent editions to 1654. Paragraphing
supplied. MSS.: O'F, S 96; H 40*, P; B. Title from 1635–69: At his Mistris departure B.*
1 Night,] night *1669*   4 Love] soule *1635*

Alas the darkest Magick cannot do it,   5
Thou and greate Hell to boot are shadows to it.
Should *Cinthia* quit thee, *Venus*, and each starre,
It would not forme one thought dark as mine are.
I could lend thee obscureness now, and say,
Out of my self, There should be no more Day,   10
Such is already my felt want of sight,
Did not the fires within me force a light.

Oh Love, that fire and darkness should be mixt,
Or to thy Triumphs soe strange torments fixt?
Is't because thou thy self art blind, that wee   15
Thy Martyrs must no more each other see?
Or tak'st thou pride to break us on the wheel,
And view old Chaos in the Pains we feel?
Or have we left undone some mutual Right,
Through holy fear, that merits thy despight?   20
No, no. The falt was mine, impute it me,
Or rather to conspiring destinie,
Which, since I lov'd for forme before, decreed,
That I should suffer when I lov'd indeed:
And therefore now, sooner then I can say   25
I saw the golden fruit, 'tis rapt away.
Or as I'had watcht one drop in a vast stream,
And I left wealthy only in a dream.
Yet Love, thou'rt blinder then thy self in this,
To vex my Dove-like friend for mine amiss: 30
And, where my own glad truth may expiate
Thy wrath, to make her fortune run my fate.
So blinded Justice doth, when Favorites fall,
Strike them, their house, their friends, their followers all.

5-44 *Omit 1635, B*   6 Thou and *MSS.*: And that *1669*   7 thee,] thee *1669*
8 are.] are *1669*   9 thee *H 40**: them *1669, O'F, S 96, P*   11 felt want *MSS.*:
self-want *1669*   12 fires *Σ*: fire *1669, P*   14 soe *MSS.*: such *1669*   17 the
MSS.: thy *1669*   20 Through holy fear, that merits thy despite *O'F, H 40**: ... that
causes ... *S 96*: ... that meriteth thy spight *P*: That thus with parting thou seek'st us to
spight *1669*   21 was *Σ*: is *1669, P*   it me *Σ*: it to me *1669, S 96, Gr*   23 Which
... decreed *O'F, S 96, H 40**: Which (since I lov'd) for me before decreed *1669, P*
25 now, sooner *MSS.*: sooner now *1669*   26 rapt *MSS.*: wrapt *1669*   27 I'had]
I had *1669*   a *MSS.*: the *1669*   30 mine *Σ*: my *1669, P, Gr*   31 my own glad
MSS.: my one sad *1669*: my own sad *Gr*   34 followers *H 40*, P*: favourites *1669, O'F, S 96*

Was't not enough that thou didst dart thy fires   35
Into our blouds, inflaming our desires,
And made'st us sigh and glow, and pant, and burn,
And then thy self into our flame did'st turn?
Was't not enough, that thou didst hazard us
To paths in love so dark, so dangerous: 40
And those so ambush'd round with houshold spies,
And over all, thy towred husbands eyes
That flam'd with oylie sweat of jealousie:
Yet went we not still on with Constancie?
Have we not kept our guards, like spie on spie?   45
Had correspondence when the foe stood by?
Stoln (more to sweeten them) our many blisses
Of meetings, conference, embracements, kisses?
Shadow'd with negligence our most respects?
Varied our language through all dialects,   50
Of becks, winks, looks, and often under-boards
Spoak dialogues with our feet far from our words?
Have we prov'd all these secrets of thy Art,
Yea, thy pale colours, inward as thy heart?
And, after all this passed Purgatory,   55
Must sad divorce make us the vulgar story?
First let our eyes be rivited quite through
Our turning brains, and both our lips grow to:
Let our armes clasp like Ivy, and our fear
Freese us together, that we may stick here,   60
Till Fortune, that would rive us, with the deed
Strain her eyes open, and it make them bleed:

37 glow *MSS.*: blow *1669*   38 flame *MSS.*: flames *1669*   40 so dangerous *MSS.*:
and dangerous *1669*   42 all,] all *1669*   thy] the *H 40**   towred husbands eyes *H 40**:
husbands towred ... *O'F, S 96, P*: husbands towring ... *1669, Gr; see note*   43 That
flam'd with oylie *MSS.*: Inflam'd with th'ouglie *1669*   jealousie:] jealousie, *1669*
44 with *MSS.*: in *1669*   45 Have we not kept our guards *O'F, S 96, P*: Have not
we ... *H 40**: Have we for this kept guards *1669, B*   on] o'r *1635*   46 when
MSS.: whilst *1669, Gr*   49 most *MSS., 1635*: best *1669*   52 from our] from
1635, B   53 these *S 96, H 40*, P, B*: the *1669, O'F*   thy *H 40**: our *1669, Σ, Gr*
54 Thy pale colours, inward as thy heart *O'F, S 96, H 40**: ... Colour'd ... *P*: thy pale inwards, and thy panting heart *1669, Gr*   57–66 *Omit 1635, B*   61 and 65 Fortune]
fortune *1669*   61 rive *O'F, S 96, H 40**: reave *P*: ruine *1669*   .us,] us *1669*
62 her *S 96, H 40**: his *1669, O'F, P*   it make them *S 96, H 40**: make them for to *P*:
yet make them *1669, O'F*   bleed :] bleed *1669*

For Love it cannot be, whom hitherto
I have accus'd, should such a mischief doe.

    Oh Fortune, thou'rt not worth my least exclame,   65
And plague enough thou hast in thine owne shame.
Do thy great worst, my friend and I have armes,
Though not against thy strokes, against thy harmes.
Rend us in sunder, thou canst not divide
Our bodies so, but still our souls are ty'd,   70
And we can love by letters still and gifts,
And thoughts and dreams; Love never wanteth shifts.
I will not look upon the quickning Sun,
But straight her beauty to my sense shall run;
The ayre shall note her soft, the fire most pure;   75
Water suggest her clear, and the earth sure.
Time shall not lose our passages; the Spring
Shall tell how fresh our love was in beginning;
The Summer how it ripen'd in the eare;
And Autumn, what our golden harvests were.   80
The Winter I'll not think on to spite thee,
But count it a lost season, so shall shee.

    And dearest Friend, since we must part, drown night
With hope of Day, burthens well born are light.
Though cold and darkness longer hang somewhere,   85
Yet *Phoebus* equally lights all the Sphere.
And what he cannot in like portions pay,
The world enjoyes in mass, and so we may.
Be then ever your selfe, and let no woe
Win on your health, your youth, your beauty: so   90
Declare your self base fortunes Enemy,
No less by your contempt then constancy:

66 thine *MSS.*: thy *1669*, *Gr*   shame *MSS.*: name *1669*   67 Do thy great
worst] Fortune, doe thy worst *1635*, *B*   69 Rend] Bend *1635*   70 but still *MSS.*:
but that *1669*, *Gr*   72 shifts.] shifts, *1669*   76 Water *H 40**, *P*: Waters *1669*,
O'F, *S 96*   sure.] sure; *1669*   77–78 *Omit P*   77 Spring] spring *1669*
78 Shall tell how fresh our love was in beginning *H 40**: *omit* was *O'F*: Shall tell our love
was fresh in the beginning *S 96*: How fresh our love was in the beginning *1669*, *Gr*
79 ripen'd in the eare *Σ*: ripened in the yeare *1635*, *B*: inripened the yeare *1669*
83–94 *Omit 1635*, *B*   85 Though *H 40**, *P*: The *1669*, *O'F*, *S 96*   87 he *MSS.*:
we *1669*   portions *H 40**: portion *O'F*, *S 96*, *P*: Portion *1669*   88 mass] Mass
1669   89 ever your] your fayrest *H 40**, *P*   92 by your contempt then constancy
S 96, *H 40**: be . . . constancy *O'F*, *P*: be your contempt then her inconstancy *1669*

That I may grow enamour'd on your mind,
When mine own thoughts I there reflected find.
For this to th'comfort of my Dear I vow,   95
My Deeds shall still be what my words are now;
The Pole shall move to teach me ere I start;
And when I change my Love, I'll change my heart;
Nay, if I wax but cold in my desire,
Think, heaven hath motion lost, and the world, fire: 100
Much more I could, but many words have made
That, oft, suspected which men would perswade;
Take therefore all in this: I love so true,
As I will never look for less in you.

Julia

HARKE newes, ô envy, thou shalt heare descry'd
My *Julia*; who as yet was ne'r envy'd.
To vomit gall in slander, swell her vaines
With calumny, that hell it selfe disdaines,
Is her continuall practice; does her best,   5
To teare opinion even out of the brest
Of dearest friends, and (which is worse than vilde)
Sticks jelousie in wedlock, her owne childe
Scapes not the showres of envie; To repeate
The monstrous fashions, how, were,'alive to eate   10
Deare reputation. Would to God she were
But halfe so loath to act vice, as to heare
My milde reproofe. Liv'd *Mantuan* now againe,
That fœmall Mastix, to limme with his penne

94 mine *MSS.*: my *1669, Gr*   there reflected *MSS.*: here neglected *1669*   95 For
Σ: And *1669, B*   96 words *H 40*, P*: deeds *1669, O'F, S 96*   97 Pole *O'F, S 96*:
Poles *1669, H 40*, P, B, Gr*   ere] when *O'F, S 96*   102 oft,] oft *1669*   would
Σ: could *P*: most *1669*

Julia (Elegy XIII *Gr*). *First printed in 1635. MSS.: B, O'F. Title from 1635, B, O'F.*
2 as yet was ne'r] was ne're as yet *B*   5 practice;] practice, *1635*   7 vilde *B, O'F*:
vile *1635*   9 envie;] envie, *1635*   10 were, 'alive] were, alive *1635*   14 limme]
lymm out *B*

This she *Chymera*, that hath eyes of fire,   15
Burning with anger, anger feeds desire,
Tongu'd like the night-crow, whose ill boding cries
Give out for nothing but new injuries,
Her breath like to the juice in *Tenarus*
That blasts the Spring, though ne'r so prosperous,   20
Her hands, I know not how, us'd more to spill
The food of others, then her selfe to fill.
But oh her minde, that *Orcus*, which includes
Legions of mischiefs, countlesse multitudes
Of formlesse curses, projects unmade up,   25
Abuses yet unfashion'd, thoughts corrupt,
Mishapen Cavils, palpable untroths,
Inevitable'errours, self-accusing loathes:
These, like those Atoms swarming in the Sunne,
Throng in her bosome for creation.   30
I blush to give her halfe her due; yet say,
No poyson's halfe so bad as *Julia*.

A Tale of a Citizen and his Wife

I SING no harme good sooth to any wight,
To Lord or foole, Cuckold, begger or knight,
To peace-teaching Lawyer, Proctor, or brave
Reformed or reduced Captaine, Knave,
Officer, Jugler, or Justice of peace,   5
Juror or Judge; I touch no fat sowes grease,
I am no Libeller, nor will be any,
But (like a true man) say there are too many.
I feare not *ore tenus*; for my tale,
Nor Count nor Counsellour will redd or pale.   10

17 Tongu'd] Tongued *1635*   20 Spring *B*: springs *1635*, *O'F*, *Gr*   prosperous,]
prosperous. *1635*   24 mischiefs *B*, *O'F*: mischief *1635*   28 Inevitable'errours]
inevitable errours *1635*   loathes] oathes *B*, *Gr*   31 give her halfe] give but half *B*:
give half *O'F*   yet] only this *B*: but this *O'F*
     A Tale &c. (Elegy XIV *Gr*). *First printed in 1635: MSS.: B, Dob, O'F.*   9 tenus;]
tenus, *1635*   10 will redd *B*: shall redd *O'F*: will looke redd *1635*, *Dob*

A Citizen and his wife the other day
Both riding on one horse, upon the way
I overtooke, the wench a pretty peate,
And (by her eye) well fitting for the feate.
I saw the lecherous Citizen turne backe   15
His head, and on his wifes lips steale a smacke,
Whence apprehending that the man was kinde,
Riding before, to kisse his wife behinde,
To get acquaintance with him I began
To sort discourse fit for so fine a man: 20
I ask'd the number of the Plaguy Bill,
Ask'd if the Custome Farmers held out still,
Of the Virginian plot, and whether Ward
The traffique of the Midland seas had marr'd,
Whether the Brittaine *Burse* did fill apace,   25
And likely were to give th'Exchange disgrace;
Of new-built *Algate*, and the *More-field* crosses,
Of store of Bankerouts, and poore Merchants losses
I urged him to speake; But he (as mute
As an old Courtier worne to his last suite)   30
Replies with onely yeas and nayes; At last
(To hit his element) my theame I cast
On Tradesmens gaines; that set his tongue agoing:
Alas, good sir (quoth he) *There is no doing*
In Court nor City now; she smil'd and I,   35
And (in my conscience) both gave him the lie
In one met thought: but he went on apace,
And at the present time with such a face
He rail'd as fray'd me; for he gave no praise,
To any but my Lord of *Essex* dayes;   40
Call'd those the age of action; true (quoth Hee)
There's now as great an itch of bravery,

14 feate.] feate, *1635*   16 lips *MSS.*: lip *1635, Gr*   steale] seale *Dob, O'F*
18 behinde,] behinde. *1635*   21 Plaguy *MSS.*: Plaguing *1635*   Bill,] Bill. *1635*
22 Ask'd if] Whether *Dob, O'F*   Custome] custome *1635*   24 Midland *MSS.*: Iland
1635: I⟨n⟩land *Gr*   32 hit *MSS.*: fit *1635, Gr*   33 agoing:] a going, *1635*
35 *In . . . now*] roman in *1635*   38 time] times *Dob, O'F*   41 those . . . Hee *MSS.*:
that . . . I *1635*

And heat of taking up, but cold lay downe,
For, put to push of pay, away they runne;
Our onely City trades of hope now are   45
Bawd, Tavern-keeper, Whore and Scrivener;
The much of Priviledg'd kingsmen, and the store
Of fresh protections make the rest all poore;
In the first state of their Creation,
Though many stoutly stand, yet proves not one   50
A righteous pay-master. Thus ranne he on
In a continu'd rage: so void of reason
Seem'd his harsh talke, I sweat for feare of treason.
And (troth) how could I lesse? when in the prayer
For the protection of the wise Lord Mayor,   55
And his wise brethrens worships, when one pray'th,
He swore that none could say Amen with faith.
To get him off from what I glow'd to heare,
(In happy time) an Angel did appeare,
The bright Signe of a lov'd and wel-try'd Inne,   60
Where many Citizens with their wives have bin
Well us'd and often; here I pray'd him stay,
To take some due refreshment by the way.
Looke how hee look'd that hid the gold (his hope)
And at returne found nothing but a Rope,   65
So he on me, refus'd and made away,
Though willing she pleaded a weary day:
I found my misse, shook hands, yet praid him tell
(To hold acquaintance still) where he did dwell;
He barely nam'd the street, promis'd the Wine.   70
But his kinde wife gave me the very Signe.

43 cold lay downe] cold good donne *Dob, O'F*   46 Bawd . . . Whore *MSS.*: Bawds,
Tavern-keepers, Whores *1635*   Scrivener;] Scriveners, *1635*   47 kingsmen *B*: Kings-
man *O'F*: kinsmen *1635, Dob*   the store *O'F*: store *1635, B, Dob*   52 continu'd]
continued *1635*   55 Mayor] Major *1635*   56 pray'th] prayeth *1635*   58 him off
MSS.: him *1635*   glow'd] glowed *1635*   61 have *Dob, O'F*: had *1635, B*   bin] beene
1635   65 at] at's *Gr*   66 on *MSS.*: at *1635*   me,] me: *1635*   67 day *MSS.*:
stay *1635*   68 shooke *MSS.*: strucke *1635, Gr*   yet *MSS.*: and *1635, Gr*

Variety

THE heavens rejoyce in motion, why should I
  Abjure my so much lov'd variety,
And not with many youth and love divide?
Pleasure is none, if not diversifi'd:
The sun that sitting in the chaire of light   5
Sheds flame into what ever else seemes bright,
Is not contented at one Signe to Inne,
But ends his year and with a new beginnes.
All things doe willingly in change delight,
The fruitfull mother of our appetite: 10
Rivers the clearer and more pleasing are,
Where their fair spreading streames run wide and farr;
And a dead lake that no strange bank doth greet,
Corrupts it self and what doth live in it.
Let no man tell me such a one is faire,   15
And worthy all alone my love to share.
Nature in her hath done the liberall part
Of a kinde Mistresse, and imploy'd her art
To make her loveable, and I aver
Him not humane that would turn back from her: 20
I love her well, and would, if need were, dye
To doe her service. But followes it that I
Must serve her onely, when I may have choice?
The law is hard, and shall not have my voice.
The last I saw in all extreames is faire,   25
And holds me in the Sun-beames of her haire;

Variety (Elegy XVII *Gr*). *First printed without title among poems added on extra leaves in*
1650. MSS.: *A 10, HK 1, HK 2, JC. Title*: Variety *Gr*.   1 motion, why] motion
why *1650*   2 so much lov'd] soe beloved *A 10, HK 1, HK 2*   3 love *MSS.*:
lov'd *1650*   4 diversifi'd :] diversifi'd *1650*   6 what ever else seems *HK 2*: what
else seems *HK 1*: what else is not so *A 10*: what else so ever doth seem *1650, JC, Gr*
12 fair-spreading] broad silver *A 10*   farr *Σ*: faire *HK 1*: cleare *1650*   13 bank *Ed*:
banks *HK 2*: bark *1650, Σ, Gr; see note*   14 self and] self: kills *A 10*   16 And
only worthy to be past compare *A 10*   19 aver *MSS.*: ever *1650*   20 Him ...
that would turn back] ... would returne *HK 1*: He is ... would turne *HK 2*: ... that could
not fancy *A 10*   24 Of other beauties, and in change rejoice *A 10; included by Grierson*
as l. 24; see note   24–36 Omit *A 10*

Her nymph-like features such agreements have
That I could venture with her to the grave:
Another's brown, I like her not the worse,
Her tongue is soft and takes me with discourse.   30
Others, for that they well descended are,
Do in my love obtain as large a share;
And though they be not fair, 'tis much with mee
To win their love onely for their degree.
And though I faile of my required ends,   35
The'attempt is glorious and it self commends.
How happy were our Syres in ancient time,
Who held plurality of loves no crime!
With them it was accounted charity
To stirre up race of all indifferently;   40
Kindred were not exempted from the bands:
Which with the Persian still in usage stands.
Women were then no sooner ask'd then won,
And what they did was honest and well done.
But since this title honour hath been us'd,   45
Our weake credulity hath been abus'd;
The golden laws of nature are repeald,
Which our first Fathers in such reverence held;
Our liberty's revers'd, our Charter's gone,
And we made servants to opinion,   50
A monster in no certain shape attir'd,
And whose originall is much desir'd,
Formlesse at first, but growing on it fashions,
And doth prescribe manners and laws to nations.
Here love receiv'd immedicable harmes,   55
And was dispoiled of his daring armes.
A greater want then is his daring eyes,
He lost those awfull wings with which he flies;

29 brown,] brown *1650*   31 are *MSS.*: were *1650*   37 time *Σ*: times *1650*,
JC, Gr   38 crime!] crime? *1650*   41 Kindred *MSS.*: Kindreds *1650, Gr*
43 ask'd] asked *1650*: woo'd *A 10*   45 title *MSS.*: little *1650*   48 first Fathers]
great grandsires *A 10*   49 liberty's *Σ*: liberty *1650, JC*   revers'd our *A 10,*
HK 2: revers'd and *1650, HK 1, JC*   50 we] we're *A 10, Gr*   52 whose origi-
nall] one whose origin *A 10*   53 growing] goeing *A 10, Gr*   it *MSS.*: its *1650*
54 manners and laws to] Lawes, Manners, unto *A 10*   56 armes.] armes, *1650*

His sinewy bow, and those immortall darts
Wherewith he'is wont to bruise resisting hearts.   60
Onely some few strong in themselves and free
Retain the seeds of antient liberty,
Following that part of Love although deprest,
And make a throne for him within their brest,
In spight of modern censures him avowing   65
Their Soveraigne, all service him allowing.
Amongst which troop although I am the least,
Yet equall in perfection with the best,
I glory in subjection of his hand,
Nor ever did decline his least command: 70
For in whatever forme the message came
My heart did open and receive the flame.
But time will in his course a point discry
When I this loved service must deny,
For our allegiance temporary is,   75
With firmer age returnes our liberties.
What time in years and judgement we repos'd,
Shall not so easily be to change dispos'd,
Nor to the art of severall eyes obeying;
But beauty with true worth securely weighing,   80
Which being found assembled in some one,
Wee'l love her ever, and love her alone.

60 bruise] wound *A 10*   hearts.] hearts; *1650*   62 seeds of antient] seede of
pristine *A 10*   63 Love] love *1650*   65 censures] censure *A 10, HK 2*
69 of his] under's *A 10*: to his *HK 2*   70 Nor . . . decline] Never declining from *A 10*
71–78 *Omit A 10*   72 flame. *Σ*: same; *1650*: same. *Gr*   74 deny,] deny. *1650*
78 dispos'd,] dispos'd *1650*   79 obeying;] obeying, *1650*   80 securely] sincerely
HK 2: unpartially *A 10*   81 being] having *A 10, HK 2*   one,] one *1650*   82 Wee'l
love her ever *HK 1, HK 2*: . . . leave . . . *1650, JC*: Would love for ever *A 10*

Sonnet. The Token

SEND me some token, that my hope may live,
Or that my easelesse thoughts may sleep and rest;
Send me some honey to make sweet my hive,
    That in my passions I may hope the best.
I beg noe ribbond wrought with thine owne hands,   5
    To knit our loves in the fantastick straine
Of new-toucht youth; nor Ring to shew the stands
    Of our affection, that as that's round and plaine,
So should our loves meet in simplicity;
    No, nor the Coralls which thy wrist infold,   10
Lac'd up together with congruity,
    To shew our thoughts should rest in the same hold;
No, nor thy picture, though most gracious,
    And most desir'd, because best like the best;
Nor witty Lines, which are most copious,   15
    Within the Writings which thou hast addrest.
Send me nor this, nor that, t'increase my store,
But swear thou thinkst I love thee, and no more.

Self Love

HE that cannot chuse but love,
    And strives against it still,
Never shall my fancy move;
    For he loves 'gaynst his will;

Sonnet. The Token. *First printed in 1649. MSS.: O'F, S 96; B, Cy, HK 1, P. Title from 1649:* Ad Lesbiam *S 96.* 1 token *O'F, S 96, B, HK 1:* Tokens *1649, Cy, P* 4 passions] passion *S 96, HK 1, Gr* 5 noe *MSS.:* nor *1649* 9 simplicity;] simplicity. *1649* 11 with *O'F, S 96, B, HK 1:* in *1649, Cy, P, Gr* 12 hold;] hold *1649* 14 desir'd, because best like the best *O'F, S 96, B, HK 1:* . . . because 'tis like . . . *Cy, P:* desired 'cause tis like thee best *1649* 17 store *MSS.:* score *1649*

Self Love. *First printed without title and without division into stanzas among poems added on extra leaves in 1650. MSS.: JC, O'F. Title from Chambers First printed in stanzas by Bennett* 4 'gaynst *MSS.:* against *1650*

Nor he which is all his own,   5
    And can at pleasure chuse,
When I am caught he can be gone,
    And when he list refuse.

Nor he that loves none but faire,
    For such by all are sought;   10
Nor he that can for fouleness care,
    For his Judgement then is nought:

Nor he that hath wit, for he
    Will make me his jest or slave;
Nor a fool, for when others . . .,   15
    He can neither. . . .

Nor he that still his Mistresse payes,
    For she is thrall'd therefore:
Nor he that payes not, for he sayes
    Within, shee's worth no more.   20

Is there then no kinde of men
    Whom I may freely prove?
I will vent that humour then
    In mine owne selfe love.

Song

STAY, O sweet, and do not rise,
  The light that shines comes from thine eyes;
The day breaks not, it is my heart,
Because that you and I must part.
    Stay, or else my joys will die,   5
    And perish in their infancie.

6 can at pleasure *JC*:... all pleasure *O'F*: cannot pleasure *1650*   11 fouleness
O'F: foul ones *1650, JC, Gr*   14 slave;] slave *1650*   15 fool,] fool *1650*
16 He can neyther want nor crave *O'F*   17 payes *MSS.*: prays *1650*   19 payes
not,] payes, not, *1650*   20 Within,] Within *1650*

Song. *Printed in John Dowland's* A Pilgrim's Solace, *1612, as the first stanza of a poem
in two stanzas, and alone in Orlando Gibbons,* Madrigals and Motets, *1612. It was printed as
the first stanza of 'Break of Day' (p. 35) in 1669. It appears similarly placed in S 96, and in
A 25 it is written in the margin against 'Break of Day' with a mark to show it should be the
first stanza.*

COMMENTARY

Note on Versification

Donne's verse can be regarded as strictly syllabic if we recognize the great use that he makes of elision and synalœpha. Assimilated syllables are not necessarily suppressed in reading but they are metrically worthless, like grace-notes in music that do not disturb the time. In the edition of 1633 great care was taken to distinguish contracted and uncontracted forms and to supply an elision mark when the editor judged it necessary between final and initial vowels; but no attempt was made to indicate when an unstressed medial syllable was to be suppressed. Donne allows himself considerable play here, trusting to his reader's ear, and there is normally no difficulty in recognizing when a syllable is suppressed and when it is given metrical value; cf. 'The Bait', l. 11:

> × / × / × × × / ×
> Will am|orous|ly to | thee swimme,

and 'Recusancy', l. 18:

> / × × / × / × / × /
> Am'rous|ly twink|ling beck'ns | the gidd|ie flie.

I have attempted to apply the principles on which the copy for *1633* was prepared consistently. The care with which it was prepared is clear from the fact that in over 2,000 lines of verse it has only been necessary to make a contraction, supply an elision mark, or remove those wrongly made or supplied, some fifty times.

As well as the normal licence in English syllabic verse of an extra weak final syllable, and the Chaucerian licence of an occasional defective first foot, Donne allows himself the licence, usually only found in dramatic verse, of a defective medial foot. This occurs when a line has a marked dramatic pause; see, for example, 'Going to Bed', l. 17:

> × × / × / / × /
> Off with | those shoes: || and | then safe|ly tread.

Except in a few of the songs Donne's metres are basically iambic, but he shows great boldness in not keeping accent and in weighting some lines by using several feet with level stress; see, for example, 'On his Mistress', l. 54:

> × / / / × / / / ×
> Assayld, | fight, tak|en, stabb'd, | bleede, fall, | and dye,

or 'The Sun Rising':

> × / / / × / × / × /
> Nor houres, | dayes, months, | which are | the rags | of time

and

> × / × / / / × /
> And thou | shalt heare, | All here | in one | bed lay.

In marking the reading of a line I mark feet with normal stress ×/, feet with inverted stress /×, feet with level stress //, and feet with very light stress ××. I mark this last because I believe it is our sense of the foot as a metrical reality that enables us to accept rhythmic variation as not inconsistent with a metrical norm, and that in many lines we need to give metrical stress some value to bring out the meaning as well as to preserve the music. There is a good example of how attention to metrical stress can bring out meaning in 'The Sun Rising', l. 23. The line is usually read as:

$$\text{Princes} \mid \text{doe but} \mid \text{play us;} \mid \text{compar'd} \mid \text{to this;}$$

but if we read by metrical stress we get a stronger point as well as Donne's characteristic emphasis on the personal pronoun:

$$\text{Princes} \mid \text{doe but} \mid \text{play us;} \mid \text{compar'd} \mid \text{to this.}$$

Great care was also taken in *1633* over the setting of the lyrics, by indentation to show length of line and rhyme scheme. But the practice here was neither thorough nor wholly consistent. Mr. R. E. Bennett, in his modernized text, is the only editor who has attempted to set Donne's lyrics so as to bring out the form of the stanzas. I have followed his example and profited much by studying his text. The lyrics in my first group present few difficulties: to indent by length of line will also be to indent by rhyme scheme. But some of the lyrics of the second group present a problem since the pattern by length of line runs athwart the pattern by rhyme scheme. I have usually preferred to bring out the pattern by line length at the cost of suppressing the pattern by rhyme.

ELEGIES

MSS.: Group I (*C 57, D, H 49, Lec, SP*); Group II (*A 18, N, TCC, TCD*); *DC*;
    Group III (*Dob, Lut, O'F, S 96*); *W*; *Cy, O, P*; *A 25, D 17, JC*; *B, K, S*.
Miscellanies: *Hd, S 962*.

The twenty-four collections listed above contain a more or less full count of the fourteen Elegies that I accept as canonical. For convenience I have added to them two miscellanies: *Hd* which includes twelve, and *S 962* which includes ten. The use of the formula 'Σ— . . .' at the beginning of the commentary on a poem denotes that the poem can be found in all these twenty-six manuscripts except those specified.

The presence of a poem in *L 74*, which contains eight, or in a miscellany is noted at the beginning of the commentary on that poem.

Nine of the fourteen Elegies were printed in *1633*, eight from a manuscript of Group I and one from a manuscript of Group II. The text in *1633* is good; but it requires correction when it follows its manuscript source in error and when, occasionally, it attempts correction itself.

The text of the remaining five Elegies, which were 'excepted' by the licenser, is taken from *C 57*, the manuscript nearest to that used to supply the copy for *1633*; see Textual Introduction, pp. xci–xciii.

The great majority of the variants in the text of the *Elegies* are trivial and should be attributed to scribal corruption. For the establishment of the text the important witnesses are Groups I, II, III, and *W*. Of these *W* has the highest authority and in cases where there is a choice of reading I have usually accepted *W*.

None of the Elegies printed in *1633* was given a title and very few are found with a title other than 'Elegy' in manuscript. The edition of *1635* supplied titles for all but two of the eleven Elegies that appear there. I have kept the titles of *1635* and the titles given to the three Elegies that were printed subsequently and added titles of my own to the two left untitled in *1635*.

The *Elegies* are printed in the order in which they occur in *W*, except that the ninth, 'Love's Progress', which is not found in the set in *W*, *A 25*, *D 17*, *JC*, has been inserted in what seems an appropriate place. I prefer the order of the set in *W* to the order of the similar set in Group I because of the high extrinsic authority of *W* and because it brings together at the close the three most serious poems. Owing to our differing judgements on the canon, my numbering would necessarily have had to be different from Grierson's. I have thought it best to print in what I think is the best order, not to renumber, and to give Grierson's number in the apparatus to facilitate reference.

The Bracelet (p. 1)

MSS.: *Σ — A 18*, *TCC*. Also in *L 74*.
Miscellanies: *CCC* (extracts), *EH*, *HK 1*, *HK 2**, *Hol*, *La*, *RP 117 (2)*; Brit. Mus. MSS. *Egerton 2230*, *Sloane 1792*; Bodleian MSS. *Ashmole 36, 37*, *Don c 54*, *Eng. Poet. e 14*, *Rawl. Poet. 160* and *212*; St. John's Coll. Cambridge MS. *U 26*; Folger MSS. *V a 170* and *262*; Harvard MS. *Eng. 686*; Rosenbach MS. *239/22*.

'The Bracelet' was 'excepted' by the licenser for *1633* and was first printed in *1635*, although no authority had been obtained. The text in *1635* was taken from a poor manuscript. It shares some bad readings with *Cy* and *P* and has others that I have not found elsewhere. Grierson printed from *1635*, emending its punctuation considerably but on the whole retaining its readings. The text here is based on *C 57*.

The reading of *C 57* has been rejected on eight occasions. On three (ll. 3, 7, 11) it reads with *Lec* against the other members of Group I and on two (ll. 38, 54) it is in error with Group I. For the choice of reading in ll. 23, 92, and 96, see notes. Punctuation presents a problem in l. 77; see note.

In *1635* and in some, but not the best, manuscripts the poem is in paragraphs. Since paragraphing is a help to the reader of a long poem, but the paragraphing in the edition and the manuscripts is not uniform or logically consistent, I have adopted with supplementation the paragraphing of the edition.

Drummond reports that 'The Bracelet' was a favourite poem of Jonson's:

> He esteemeth John Done the first poet in the World in some things his verses of the Lost Chaine, he heth by Heart & that passage of the calme, that dust and feathers doe not stirr, all was so quiet. affirmeth Done to have written all his best pieces err he was 25 years old (Jonson, *Works*, i. 135).

Professor F. P. Wilson suggested that Jonson was here declaring a preference for Donne's earlier manner and saying that Donne's best poems were those he wrote before he was twenty-five (i.e. before 1597), such as 'The Bracelet' and 'The Calm' (*Elizabethan and Jacobean*, 1945, pp. 54–55). I should like to propose a date not much after 1593 for 'The Bracelet'.

'The Bracelet' owes little, if anything, to Ovid. It is close to the *Satires* in its realism, and its fantastic virtuosity in punning relates it to drama rather than to Ovidian Elegy. Grierson, commenting on l. 55, observed:

> Donne would almost seem to have read or seen . . . the old play of *Soliman and Perseda* (pr. 1599). There, the lover, having lost a carcanet, sends a cryer through the streets and offers one hundred crowns reward.

Soliman and Perseda is ascribed on good grounds to Thomas Kyd, and a 'lost chain' is the main subject of its first two acts. Perseda gives a 'carkanet', or chain of gold, to her lover Erastus. He loses it and his servant bargains with a cryer to cry the loss through the streets. It has been found, meanwhile, by Ferdinando who gives it to his mistress, Lucina. Perseda sees her wearing it and bitterly reproaches Erastus. He wins it back from Lucina by means of false dice, and Ferdinando, meeting him on his return from her house wearing it, challenges him and is fatally wounded. The reproaches of Perseda at the loss of her chain, the abject despair of the loser, and the fatal consequences of the quarrel over it might well have struck a satirical young law-student as highly absurd. The 'seely old moralitie' of ll. 5–6 occurs in the play, as well as the use of a cryer to cry the lost chain through the streets, and there is possibly a reminiscence in the curse on the 'wretched finder' of the play's sensational denouement, where Soliman is poisoned by kissing the lips of the dead Perseda. With Donne a suggested source never provides more than a starting-point. I suggest the starting-point of 'The Bracelet' was the impulse to mock a foolishly romantic play. Whether or not *Soliman and Perseda* is by Kyd it must be dated by manner and style not later than Kyd's death in 1594, and probably rather earlier. If I am right to see a connexion, 'The Bracelet' should be dated early in the 1590's.

There appears also to be a topical reference to the misfortunes that befell Kyd in 1593; see note to ll. 101–2. Another passage that seems to be related to events in 1593 is that on the sly working of Spanish pistoles in France and, particularly, Scotland. This was a main concern of the Parliament of that year;

see note to ll. 39–41. A slighter point is that the zest with which Donne's mercenary lover launches his attack on French crowns points to a period before this tedious jest had become a commonplace. Donne makes his own jests as a rule and may even have the unenviable distinction of having been the first person to make this one; see notes to ll. 23 and 24.

While none of these arguments is in itself conclusive, the support they give to each other is impressive and leads me to date 'The Bracelet' *c.* 1593–4, at the time when Donne was writing his first *Satires*.

l. 5. *moralitie*: signification.

l. 6. *That as those links are tyed our love should be.* 'Tyed' has overwhelming authority; only *Cy* reads with *1635*. The consensus of I, II, and *W* establishes 'love' as the true reading against 'hearts' (III — *Dob*) which echoes the 'moralitie' in the play. Cf.

> Till when, receiue this precious Carcanet,
> In signe that, as the linkes are interlaced,
> So both our hearts are still combind in one. . . .
> (*Soliman and Perseda*, II. i. 22–24.)

ll. 9–22. *O shall twelve righteous Angels, &c.* The reign of Elizabeth was marked by a 'financial operation of unexampled magnitude', the restoration of the coinage; see W. Cunningham, *The Growth of English Industry and Commerce*, 1907, ii. 127–42. The bulk of the money coined in England was silver and its re-coining was completed by 1560. The amount of gold coined was small, the commonest gold coins being the angel (or angel-noble) and the royal (or rose-noble), which had risen in value to 10*s.* Since gold was an international currency, there was a considerable amount of foreign currency in circulation. This was revalued against English silver, crowns (French, Kaisers, and Burgundians) at 6*s.* and pistoles (Spanish, Venetian, and Flemish) at 5*s.* 10*d.* There were also foreign coins closely resembling the English angels. These were declared to be worth no more than 9*s.* 3*d.* at best, and the worst of them to be worth as little as 7*s.* The complaints against these 'bad angels' are stated in a proclamation of 1587:

> Forasmuch as a great part of our moneys of Gold of our Realme of England, and such Gold of forraine countries, which are now currant within our said Realme, are by the sinister and unlawfull dealings of wicked persons, not onely caried out of our Realme to forraine countreys, and there by divers meanes diminished of their value, and from thence returned hither, and payed in lieu of lefull coyne for the commodities of our countreys, and some other of them embased by clipping, sowthering and other unlawfull practises of their due fines, so that both the one sort and the other (by the meanes aforesaide) are brought much inferiour to their first true value and goodnesse . . . (Cunningham, ii. 138–9).

The obvious quibble on 'good and bad angels' is a favourite with dramatists in the latter half of the 1590's. Here and in ll. 69–78 it is transformed by Donne's fantastic ingenuity in seeing analogies. Both passages are soaked in Biblical phraseology and are full of theological implications.

l. 10. *leaven of vile soder*: debasing element of soldering metal. Cf. 'the leaven of the Pharisees' (Matt. xvi. 6) and 'the leaven of malice and wickedness' (1 Cor. v. 8). Broken, chipped, and cracked coins were patched by soldering.

l. 11. *fault.* 'way' (*1635*) is without manuscript support. I retain 'fault' (I and II) as more applicable to a defect in a coin than 'taint' (III, *W*).

ll. 13–15. *Angels, which heaven commanded,* &c. Cf. 'He shall give his angels charge over thee' (Ps. xci. 11, Matt. iv. 6). The speaker may have in mind all that Raphael did for Tobias.

ll. 17–22. There is a flippant use in this passage of that doctrine of the Atonement that holds that Christ bore men's sins and their punishment as their substitute: cf. 'He took not on him the nature of angels', Heb. ii. 16.

l. 22. *burnt and tyed in chaines.* Cf. 'In Adamantine Chains and penal Fire' (*Paradise Lost*, i. 48), based on 2 Pet. ii. 4 and Jude 6.

ll. 23–42. A reform of the French currency was contemplated in the 1570's, but the wars prevented its being carried out. Neither France nor Spain could show anything comparable to the Elizabethan achievement. Donne is not usually thought of as a patriot; but in this contrast between 'good' English coins and 'bad' foreign ones, as elsewhere in the *Elegies*, he shows the common Elizabethan pride in English ways and the common contempt for foreign.

l. 23. *Were they but Crownes of France, I cared not.* Donne normally uses contracted forms for the past tense and participle of weak verbs; but here, as in 'Farewell to Love' (l. 13), the metre requires 'carèd'.

  A. W. Ward's statement that the Clown's allusion to French crowns in *Dr. Faustus* would have been unintelligible in Marlowe's day, which Greg cited to argue that the A text contains unoriginal matter (*Dr. Faustus*, 1950, p. 32), is unacceptable. Although there was an increase in commerce between France and England from 1595, proclamations show that French crowns circulated freely throughout the reign of Elizabeth.

l. 24. *their naturall country rot*: their native country's rot. For the idiom, see *O.E.D.*, 'country', III.13. The jest on French crowns and the 'French disease' is exploited at length by Nashe in the 'Epistle Dedicatorie' to *Have with You to Saffron Walden*, 1596. Professor F. P. Wilson told me that he was not aware of an earlier datable example of this jest. It occurs in *A Midsummer Night's Dream*, I. ii. 86 and elsewhere in Shakespeare.

l. 26. *leane . . . pale . . . lame.* The order of the epithets in the text (I, III, *W*) gives the best climax: the coins are thin, made of 'pale' metal, and 'lame' through loss of parts by clipping.

ll. 27 and 30. *most Christian . . . as Catholique as.* The King of France was styled *Rex Christianissimus* from 1464 and was always so addressed by the Pope. The King of Spain's traditional title 'His Most Catholic Majesty' is said to have been granted to Ferdinand of Aragon in 1492 for his reconquest of Granada. See *Oxford Dictionary of the Christian Church*, 1957, pp. 275 and 252.

l. 29. *Spanish Stamps, still travailing*. 'Stamp', from meaning the design impressed on a coin, came to be used for the coin itself; see *O.E.D.*, 'stamp', sb. III.12.b, and 15. The ubiquity of Spanish gold is a common complaint. Grierson cites Raleigh, *Discovery of Guiana*, 1596:

> It is his [the king of Spain's] Indian gold that endangereth and disturbeth all the nations of Europe; it purchaseth intelligence, creepeth into councils, and setteth bound loyalty at liberty in the greatest monarchies of Europe (*Works*, ed. Oldys and Birch, 1829, viii. 388).

l. 31. *unlick'd beare-whelps*. For discussion of the notion, surviving in the metaphor 'lick into shape', that 'a Bear brings forth her young informous and unshapen, which she fashioneth after by licking them over', see Sir Thomas Browne, *Pseudodoxia Epidemica*, book iii, chap. vi.

Pistolets: Spanish écus.

l. 32. *availes or lets*. The singular verbs must be explained by attraction to the preceding noun 'cannon-shot'.

l. 34. *many-angled figures*. The figure most commonly used in conjuring was the pentagram or five-pointed star.

ll. 39–41.   *and have slily made*
       Gorgeous France *ruin'd, ragged, and decay'd,*
       Scotland, *which knew no state, proud in one day*. . . .

The activity of Spain in France and Scotland was a main concern of the Parliament of 1593. The opening speech of the Lord Keeper, Sir John Puckering (printed *Eng. Hist. Rev.* xxxi. 128–34), told at length how the King of Spain was taking every opportunity to revenge the defeat of the Armada. 'In France at first he fought with his money, but with other mens weapons, and at there perill, corrupting with his Indian treasure', now he was sending his armies there too.

> So that partlie by the terror of these sundrie forces, partlie by the helpe of the french Rebells waged by his money, and the assistance of sundrie principall townes and citties, which if they were not corrupted by his golde, would never have shut their gates against their naturall kinge . . . he attempteth . . . to commaunde all that late most flourishing kingdome.

After speaking of the danger of invasion by way of Brittany, Puckering turned to the danger from Scotland: 'Lastly in Scotland he hath of late endeavoured by corrupcion of his monye and pensions, to make a partie there readye to receaue an armye.' This theme was taken up by Burghley in the Lords who clinched his argument by revealing details of Spanish intrigue in Scotland, the affair of the 'Spanish Blanks'. He told of Philip's offer to send an army of 25,000 men to the west of Scotland that summer and to pay the wages of 10,000 Scots. See J. E. Neale, *Elizabeth and her Parliaments, 1584–1601,* 1957, pp. 246–7 and 301–2.

The ruin of France by the wars of Religion was a standing warning to Englishmen of the horrors of civil war. With the conversion of Henry of Navarre in 1593, his entry into Paris in 1594 and recognition by the Pope, the tide turned towards recovery. After 1595 Donne's reference would lose its point.

The beggary of Scotland had been made embarrassingly clear at James's wedding in 1589. I cannot propose a precise interpretation of 'proud in one day', and can only suggest it means 'rich overnight', the contrast being between the ruin of once wealthy France and the sudden enriching of poverty-stricken Scotland.

l. 42. *And mangled seventeen-headed* Belgia. This is probably a general reference to the destructiveness of the war in the Low Countries; but 'mangled' might be taken as 'hacked apart' and refer to the division of the seventeen provinces into a Southern and a Northern Union in 1579.

ll. 43–46. The basic theory of alchemy was that all minerals contained the same *prima materia,* called the 'mercury of the philosophers', or 'soul of mercury'. This 'soul' could be extracted, or 'out-pulled' by fire and upon it was projected the tincture, or stone of the philosophers, to produce gold. Cf. 'The Comparison', ll. 35–37 and note.

ll. 55–68. Cf. *Soliman and Perseda,* I. iv, where a cryer is sent through the streets to cry a lost chain. Resorting to conjurers in such cases was frequent. There is a case recorded in 1593 when a Mrs. Shelley is reported to have 'had a conference at Cambridge . . . with Fletcher of Gonville and Caius College, said to be skilful in astronomy and moved him to set a figure how she should recover certain jewels'. She told another woman that she 'wanted to take up with a cunning man for something she had lost' and spoke 'afterwards of the planets and houses' (*C.S.P. Dom.,* 17 Feb. 1593). Such 'figures' can be found in John Melton's *Astrologaster or the Figure-Caster* (1620), which contains, as its title-page states, 'the Arraignment of Artless Astrologers, and Fortune-tellers that cheat many ignorant people under the pretence of foretelling things to come, of telling things that are past, finding out things that are lost . . .'. The author visits a conjurer, pretending to have lost a chain of gold of 300 links in Westminster Hall. Collections of magical recipes give directions how to proceed in recovering stolen goods; see British Museum MS. Add. 36674, item 6: 'How experyments for thinges that are stolen ought to be wroughte.'

ll. 59–60. *Conjurer . . . paper.* This is a peculiarly shocking example of what Professor Lewis has dubbed 'Simpsonian rhyme', with a weak tenth syllable rhyming with a weak eleventh; see P. Simpson, 'The Rhyming of Stressed with Unstressed Syllables in Elizabethan Verse' (*M.L.R.* xxxviii, 1943).

l. 60. *Which with fantastique schemes fullfills much paper.* The misreading 'scenes'
for 'schemes' occurs in *Dr. Faustus* (A text, l. 81) and was declared unintelligible by Boas and Greg. 'Schema' and 'Figura' are interchangeable terms in
magical works. Cf. 'Satire I', l. 60, 'heavens Scheme'. Manuscript authority is
overwhelmingly on the side of 'fullfills', and the *Concordance* shows Donne's
fondness for using 'fulfil' in its now archaic sense of 'fill up'; see *O.E.D.*,
'fulfil', I.a.

l. 61. *tenements*: rows of houses. Cf.

> Searching for things lost, with a sive, and sheeres,
> Erecting *figures*, in your rowes of *houses*. . . .
> (*The Alchemist*, I. i. 95–96)

The heavens were divided into twelve 'houses' or 'mansions', each presided
over by a sign of the Zodiac. A 'Scheme' or 'Figure' of the heavens can be
found in Melton's *Astrologaster* (facing p. 12). It is a rectangle divided into
eighty-four compartments by setting the seven planets along the top and the
twelve houses down the side. In each compartment trades and occupations
are placed, some respectable, some plainly not, and some dubious. In the last
two classes may be put Highwaymen, Cutpurses, Roaring Boys, Brothers of
the Sword, Laundresses, and Chambermaids.

l. 62. *And with whores, theeves and murtherers stuft his rents.* Like a slum-landlord,
the conjurer has packed shady characters into his 'rents', that is, property let
out. Melton's table may suggest that Donne had in mind persons placed in the
compartments there; but Melton himself, possibly echoing Donne's jest, has
a passage suggesting the reference is to the conjurer's clients:

> These twelve Houses are the Tenements most commonly such Astrologers as you
> your selfe doe let out to simple people, whereby they purchase to themselves much
> money, and to their Tenants much sorrow (p. 35).

ll. 71–72. *So, in the first, fall'n Angels . . . ill.* Of the three kinds of knowledge,
natural, speculative, and affective (that is, leading to the love of God), the
fallen angels retained the first and, to a certain degree, the second; but were
wholly deprived of the third, since 'voluntas dæmonum obstinata est in
malo'. See Aquinas, *S.T.*, Iᵃ pars, q. lxiv, art. 1–2, cited by Grierson.

l. 76. *For forme gives being; . . .* In Aristotelian and Scholastic philosophy 'form'
is the essential determinant principle of a thing. The bestowal of form on
matter 'gives being'.

l. 77. *Pity these Angels yet; . . .* I have adopted the pointing of II, III, and *W*
against that of I and *Dob* (which here reads against the other members of
Group III), but have strengthened the comma to a semicolon. Grierson placed
the stop before 'yet', arguing that the meaning was: 'Pity these Angels, for yet
(i.e. until they are melted down) they, as good angels, are superior in dignity
to Vertues, Powers and Principalities among the bad angels.' But there seems
no reason for taking it that Donne is thinking of bad angels here. I prefer to

understand 'Pity these angels while there is still time'; see *O.E.D.*, 'yet', II.5.b.

The order of angelic beings is Seraphim, Cherubim, and Thrones; Dominions, Virtues, and Powers; Principalities, Archangels, and Angels. The point of Donne's jest is that whereas the Angels of Heaven are inferior to the three orders he names, his golden Angels are more powerful and more honoured than earthly Virtues, Powers, and Princes.

ll. 83–84. *Good soules . . . Good Angels.* In the old philosophy the whole universe was regarded as living and everything had a 'soul' or animating principle. The original meaning of ἄγγελος was 'messenger', later specialized to 'messenger from God'.

ll. 91–110. Cf. 'The Curse' (p. 40). The model for these 'curses' is the pseudo-Virgilian 'Dirae' and Ovid's poem against Ibis.

l. 92. *So much that I'almost pity thy estate.* This is a lame line at best. It seems certain that it must have begun 'So much that . . .' or 'So much as . . .', and that 'So as' (*O'F*), 'So that' (*Cy, P*), and 'So much' (*B*) are attempts to regularize by dropping a syllable. The reading 'state' (I, III–*Lut* and *O'F, W, A 25, JC*) appears to be an attempt to regularize the line at the other end. It gives a ten-syllable line which cannot be scanned:

> So much that I almost pity thy state.

This is made worse in Group I by the omission of 'almost'. I print the line as it appears in Group II, adding an elision mark before 'almost'.

l. 93. *Gold being the heaviest metall.* This was true until the discovery of platinum.

l. 96. I have preferred the reading of Group II and *W* to that of Groups I and III.

ll. 101–2.   *Or libells, or some interdicted thinge,*
                     Which negligently kept thy ruine bringe.

Thomas Kyd was arrested on 12 May 1593 on suspicion of being guilty of 'a libell that concerned the State', and when his room was searched a fragment of a 'disputation' was discovered among his papers that laid him open to the more deadly charge of atheism. He was examined and put to the torture. In his letter to Puckering he wrote:

When I was first suspected for that libell that concern'd the state, amongst those waste and idle papers (which I carde not for) & which unaskt I did deliver up, were founde some fragments of a disputation toching that opinion, affirmd by Marlowe to be his, and shufled with some of myne (unknowne to me) by some occasion of our wrytinge in one chamber twoe yeares synce.

See *The Works of Thomas Kyd*, edited by F. S. Boas, 1901, pp. lxv-lxxiii and cviii. It is difficult not to see a reference in Donne's lines to Kyd's negligent keeping of a dangerous document.

ll. 112–14   *Gold is restorative; restore it then.*
Or if with it thou beest loath to depart
Because 'tis cordiall, would 'twere at thy heart.

Grierson cites Burton, *Anatomy*, part 2, subsect. 4:

Men say as much of Gold, and some other Minerals, as these have done of pretious stones. *Erastus* still maintains the opposite part. *Disput. in Paracelsum* cap. 4. *fol.* 196. he confesseth of gold, *that it makes the heart merry, but in no other sense but as it is in a misers chest: at mihi plaudo simul ac nummos contemplor in arca,* as he said in the Poet, it so revives the spirits, and is an excellent receit against Melancholy,

For Gold in Physick is a cordial
Therefore he loved Gold in special.

Burton after quoting Chaucer (*Prologue*, ll. 443–4) goes on to say that Erastus 'discommends and inveighs against' *Aurum potabile,* supporting him in the margin by a quotation from 'our Dr. *Guin*' ('Metallica omnia . . . nec tuto nec commode intra corpus sumi'), and ending '*Erastus* concludes their Philosophical stones and potable gold, &c. *to be no better then poyson*'.

I take it that Donne's final couplet means: 'If you aren't willing to give it up I hope it poisons you.' Cf. Problem 14, 'Why doth Gold not soyl the fingers?': 'Doth it direct all venom to the heart?'

At one time time when Bishop *Morton* gave him (Donne) a good quantity of Gold (then a usefull token) saying, *Here Mr.* Donne, *take this, Gold is restorative*: He presently answered *Sir, I doubt I shall never restore it back again*: and I am assured that he never did (R.B., *Life of Morton*, 1669).

The Comparison (p. 5)

MSS.: *Σ* — Group I, *DC*, *Lut*, *S 962*. Also in *L 74*.
Miscellanies: *CCC* (extract), *Grey*, *HK 1*, *RP 117*(2); Bodleian MSS. *Eng. Poet. e 14*, *Rawl. Poet. 142* (extracts); Emmanuel Coll. MS. *1 3 16*; Folger MS. *V a 125*.

If the text in *1633* was taken from a Group II manuscript it had a worse text of this poem than any extant manuscript of the group. On five occasions (ll. 7, 13, 14, 48, 51) *1633* has no manuscript support; on three (ll. 26, 34, 46) it has only random support; and on one (l. 4) it reads with Group III against Group II and *W*. I have abandoned the edition on all nine occasions; except in ll. 4, 7, 26, and 46 I agree with Grierson in doing so.

On four occasions (ll. 6, 9, 16, 37) I have preferred the reading of *W* to that of *1633* and Group II, where (except in l. 37) Grierson retained the reading of *1633*. In l. 5 I reject one of Grierson's rare conjectural emendations. In l. 41 I suspect that the reading of *1633* (which both Grierson and I retain) is an editorial patch. See notes.

'The Comparison' owes nothing to Roman Elegy. It ingeniously blends in one poem the Petrarchan and anti-Petrarchan tradition in Italian poetry. The

Petrarchan catalogue of a mistress's beauties had provoked in parody cata-
logues of deformities, a famous and much imitated example being Berni's
sonnet on an old hag: 'Chiome d'argento fine, irte, ed attorte.' The brutality
and offensiveness of English poems on ugly women, such as Corbett's and
John Stephens's poems on 'Mistress Mallet', and Henry King's on 'Mistress
Gabrina', can partly be ascribed to the vigour with which Donne has infused
into Italian wit the coarseness of Horace's eighth and twelfth Epodes. For a
mid-seventeenth-century imitation of 'The Comparison', see *Seventeenth-
Century Songs*, edited by J. P. Cutts and F. Kermode (University of Reading,
1956).

l. 2. *muskats*: musk-cats.
  trill: trickle (obsolete).

ll. 5–6.   *And on her necke her skin such lustre sets,*
                   They seeme no sweat drops, but pearle carcanets.

'Coronets' (*1633*, II and III), which Grierson retained, led him to conjecture
that Donne wrote 'brow', intending to contrast his mistress's brow with that
of his enemy's mistress, and that 'an early copyist' substituted 'necke'. As all
the manuscripts read 'necke' the reading cannot be rejected; and 'coronets'
is better explained as a misreading of 'carcanets' than by postulating with
Grierson alternatives in the author's own copy.

l. 8. *spermatique*. The accent is on the first syllable, as in Drayton's line:
          Pamper'd with meats, full spermatike and fat.

ll. 9 and 16. *that*. I prefer the emphatic 'that' (*W*) to 'the' which *1633* derives
from Group II.

l. 9. *needs lawlesse law*. Cf. the legal maxim 'Necessitas non habet legem'.

l. 10. *Sanserra's starved men*. The extremities to which the citizens of Sancerre
were reduced in the nine months during which the Protestants were besieged
there in 1573 are described by Jean de Léry, *Histoire Memorable de la Ville de
Sancerre*, La Rochelle, 1574. See D. C. Allen (*M.L.N.*, 1953) for extended
quotations. Léry tells how men tried 'si les cuirs de bœufs, de vaches, peaux
de moutons & autres (mesmes seichans par les greniers) pourroyent suppléer
au lieu de chair & des corps)'; and how, when hides were exhausted, old books,
parchments, harness, and children's leather belts were boiled down. In a
sermon preached in 1622 Donne can still refer to this as the type of the
horrors of siege: 'How many Sancerraes he hath delivered from famins'
(*Sermons*, v. 71).

ll. 13–14.   *And like vile lying stones in saffrond tinne,*
                     Or warts, or wheales, they hang....
I concur with Grierson in preferring the reading of all manuscripts to 'vile
stones lying' (*1633*), and the plural 'they hang' to the superficially more
grammatical reading 'it hangs' (*1633*). It is true that 'sweaty froth' requires a

singular verb, but the comparisons with 'stones', 'warts', and 'wheales' have replaced the singular with the plural idea of sweat drops. Both readings in *1633* are, in my view as in Grierson's, sophistications.

'Vile lying' means 'base deceiving'. That is, the stones are as false as their setting, which is pretending to be gold but is only tin painted yellow.

ll. 15–16. I do not know why Donne assumes that the golden apple of the contest on Mount Ida and the apple of the Fall were perfectly spherical.

l. 19. *Thy head*: the head of thy mistress. Donne continues to use this ellipsis for the rest of the poem.

ll. 23–24.   *Like Proserpines white beauty-keeping chest,*
                 Or Joves best fortunes urne, is her faire brest.
The last labour of Psyche was to take down to Hell a box (*pyxis*) and beg from Proserpina a little beauty for Venus (*The Golden Ass*, book vi). I do not know why Donne assumes the 'beauty-keeping' *pyxis* to have been white; but in Giulio Romano's fresco of the scene in the Palazzo del Tè in Mantua the *pyxis* which Proserpina is handing back to Psyche is a white urn. The two urns of Jove, containing good and bad fortune (*Iliad*, xxiv. 527), are inscribed *kalon* and *kakon* in Renaissance emblem books: see Boissard, *Emblematum Liber*, 2nd edn., Metz, 1588, p. 31, and Bocchi, *Symbolicae Quaestiones*, 2nd edn., Bologna, 1574, no. viii.

ll. 35–37. *Then like the Chymicks*, &c. Cf. 'The Bracelet', ll. 43–46, for a more sceptical view of alchemy. The reference here is to the intense heat needed for 'projection'.

l. 37. *durt*. I agree with Grierson in rejecting the reading of *1633* which follows Group II in obvious error, 'part' having been picked up from the line below.

l. 41. *to that Ætna*. Group II and *W* (with *A 25*) omit 'to', which gives a defective line. 'That flaming Etna' (*JC*) gives an eleven-syllable line with the unstressed eleventh syllable rhyming with a stressed tenth. This is a possible licence; but it seems highly unlikely that *JC* has preserved the true reading. *JC* depends on *W* and would seem to be here patching a defective line. I agree with Grierson in retaining *1633*, which is supported by Group III, but I think it likely that the edition and the manuscripts that concur with it have feebly patched a defective line.

l. 46. *As one which gath'ring flowers, still fear'd a snake*. 'Latet anguis in herba' (Virgil, *Ecl*. iii, 93) would seem to be the source of the common Elizabethan image of the serpent under the 'innocent flower'.

l. 54. *She, and comparisons are odious*. The proverb 'Comparisons are odious' goes back to at least the fifteenth century; its popular currency is attested by Dogberry's malapropism.

The Perfume (p. 7)

MSS.: Σ — K. Also in L 74.

Miscellanies: *CCC*, *HN*, *Hol*, *RP 117* (*2*); Brit. Mus. MSS. *Egerton 2230*, *Sloane 1792*; Bodleian MSS. *Eng. Poet. e 14*, *Malone 19* (ll. 1–50); Emmanuel Coll. MS. 1 3 16; Folger MS. *V a 125*; Rosenbach MSS. *239/22* and *1083/17*.

The text in *1633* follows the text of Group I very closely even to the omission of ll. 7–8.

I have rejected the reading of *1633* on seven occasions. In l. 42 it follows *C 57*, *Lec* against the other manuscripts of Group I which agree with II and *W*; in l. 40 it follows Group I against II, III, and *W*; and in ll. 22 and 37 it has only accidental support. In ll. 9, 15, and 21 I have preferred *W* supported by II to *1633*, I and III; see notes. On all seven occasions my text differs from Grierson's.

This vigorous monologue, addressed by a young dandy to his partner in an amorous misadventure, translates the tone and spirit of Ovid's Elegies into Elizabethan terms. The porter of ll. 31–36 may be a descendant of the janitor Ovid pleads with (*Amores*, I. vi) but the actors in this little drama are the persons of romantic comedy viewed satirically: the young girl 'mewed up' by her suspicious parents takes the place of the wife watched by her jealous husband or the *meretrix* with rival lovers of Roman Elegy.

l. 2. *escapes*: peccadilloes, but used by Shakespeare in a stronger sense for breaches of chastity.

l. 6. *Hydroptique*: dropsical. The normal form of the adjective from 'hydropsy' would be 'hydropic'. The earliest use of 'hydroptic', an erroneous formation on the model of 'epileptic', cited in *O.E.D.* is from one of Donne's letters and the word occurs no less than six times in his poems.

ll. 7–8.   *Though he had wont to search with glazed eyes,*
                    As though he came to kill a Cockatrice,
This couplet, omitted by an obvious eye-slip to l. 9 in the manuscripts of Group I is missing in *1633*.

Grierson took 'glazed' to mean 'glaring', referring to *Julius Caesar*, I. iii. 20–22 for the sense 'glare' and to the Shakespearian use of the past for present participle. It seems more likely that the father peers through eyes 'bleared' by age and sickness, or possibly he is peering through spectacles.

Pliny relates that the Cockatrice, or Basilisk, can kill by its glance alone (*Nat. Hist.* xxix. 66). A later development of this legend, wrongly fathered on Pliny, was that the basilisk's glance kills only if it sees a man before it is seen by him; if it is seen first it falls dead itself. See Albertus Magnus, *De Animalibus*, ed. Stadler, Munster, 1916–20, xxv. 18. This error (of destruction depending on 'priority of aspection') is discussed by Browne, *Pseudodoxia Epidemica*, book iii, chap. vii.

ll. 9 and 15. *have . . . take.* I have adopted the subjunctives of *W* and II. Grierson noted that it was undoubtedly Donne's practice to use the subjunctive in concessive clauses and that he had found only seven examples of the indicative (including these two) against over ninety of the subjunctive.

l. 10. *Thy beauties beautie, and food of our love.* Grierson takes it that the young man is cynical here; but he may be only quoting the father's accusation that he is after the girl's money.

l. 21. *And to trie.* I adopt the reading of *W* and II, supported by *O'F* and *S 96*. It gives a ten-syllable line that, though awkward, can be scanned:

$$\overset{/}{\text{And to}} \mid \overset{\times\ /}{\text{trie if}} \overset{\times}{\mid} \overset{\times}{\text{thou}} \overset{/}{\text{long,}} \mid \overset{\times}{\text{doth}} \overset{/}{\text{name}} \mid \overset{/}{\text{strange}} \overset{/}{\text{meates,}}$$

The reading of *1633* and I gives a line with a defective third foot:

$$\overset{\times\ /}{\text{To trie}} \mid \overset{\times}{\text{if}} \overset{/}{\text{thou}} \mid \overset{/}{\text{long,}} \mid \overset{\times}{\text{doth}} \overset{/}{\text{name}} \mid \overset{/}{\text{strange}} \overset{/}{\text{meates,}}$$

There are examples of lines of this kind in the *Divine Poems* and in other Elegies; see Gardner, *Divine Poems*, p. 62 and notes to 'Going to Bed', ll. 17 and 43, 'Change', l. 23, and 'On his Mistress', l. 49. In all these examples there is a marked pause which compensates for metrical deficiency; but here there is no reason for a pause at 'long'.

ll. 27–38. The 'little brethren' and the 'serving-man' are joint subjects of the verb 'could'.

l. 27. *like Fairey Sprights.* The simile might have been suggested by the close of *A Midsummer Night's Dream* where the fairies trip through the house to bless the lovers.

l. 29. *ingled*: fondled. 'Nigled' (*H 49* and II) and 'iuggled' (*B*), both with the sense of 'tricked' give less good sense and may be regarded as misreadings of 'ingled'. 'Dandled' (III) presents a genuine alternative.

l. 34. *Rhodian Colossus.* The statue of Apollo at Rhodes, said by Pliny to have been seventy cubits high, was one of the seven wonders. It was traditionally held that its feet rested on two moles, forming the entrance to the harbour, and ships passed between its legs.

l. 43. *When.* 'Then' (III) makes easier sense, connecting this couplet with what follows; but the weight of authority is behind 'When'. It may be taken as a connective, meaning 'And then'. I follow Grierson in strengthening the stop after 'shivered'.

l. 52. *my opprest shoes, dumbe and speechlesse were.* 'Pressing', the *peine forte et dure*, was inflicted on those arraigned for felony who stood mute and refused to plead.

ll. 53–70. The attack on perfume reads like a parody of a scholastic disputation with its use of theological and philosophic arguments, and its rebutting of possible defences.

l. 57. *Base excrement of earth.* Cf. Touchstone on civet: 'the very uncleanly flux of a cat', *As You Like It*, III. ii. 60.

l. 64. *things that seeme, exceed substantiall*: either 'Semblance is more highly valued than substance', or 'There are more things with the semblance of worth than with the reality'.

ll. 67–68. *You'are loathsome all*, &c. 'You are altogether loathsome when un-compounded: are we to love bad things when they are joined together and hate them when separated?' This is the reverse of Sidney's argument in defence of tragi-comedy: 'if severed they be good, the conjunction cannot be hurtful'.

ll. 69–70. *If you were good*, &c. It is the nature of 'the good' to be stable and universal. Cf. Paradox 4: 'That good is more common than ill', where it is said that '*Good* . . . hath this for nature and perfection to bee common.'

Jealosie (p. 9)

MSS.: *Σ — S 962.*
Miscellanies: *Grey, RP 117 (2)*; Brit. Mus. MS. *Harleian 3511.*

The text in *1633* agrees with that in Groups I and II and *W*. I adopt, with Grierson, the reading of the manuscripts in l. 25 and have adopted a manuscript spelling in l. 34. For the Group III readings in ll. 21 and 30, see notes.

The Roman world is more obviously present here than in 'The Perfume'. Grierson cites *Amores*, I. iv. 15–32 and 51–54, where Ovid instructs his mistress in the art of making love under her husband's eyes and tells her to ply him with wine unti lhe falls asleep, to illustrate ll. 19–22. The legacy-hunters (ll. 9–10) and the slave anticipating his freedom belong to Rome rather than to Elizabethan London and to Roman Satire rather than to Elegy.

l. 1. *Fond*: foolish.

l. 4. *a sere-barke*: a dry crust. Cf.

> a most instant tetter bark'd about
> Most lazar-like, with vile and loathsome crust,
> All my smooth body.   (*Hamlet*, I. v. 71–73)

l. 21. *great.* Here, and more strikingly in l. 30, Group III presents a genuine alternative reading.

l. 30. *Wee play'in another house, what should we feare?* 'We into some third place retyred were' (III, *Cy, P, B*) is weaker. It is not easy to explain 'some third place', unless we take 'board' and 'bed' as two. I hesitate to ascribe the Group III readings here and in l. 21 to authorial revision and would prefer to postulate some defect in the copy on which these manuscripts depend.

l. 33. *Thames right side*: the South Bank. Although Southwark was a ward of the City of London, it was notoriously unruly. The rest of the South Bank was outside the Lord Mayor's jurisdiction.

[Recusancy] (p. 10)

MSS.: All collections. Also in *L 74.*
Miscellanies: *EH, Grey, RP 117 (2), TCD (2)*; Brit. Mus. MS. *Harleian 3511.*

Three minor corrections have been made in the text of *1633*: in l. 6 where it misreads 'which' for 'with'; in l. 26 where it follows *C 57, Lec* against all other manuscripts; and in l. 28 where it follows Group I in reading plural for singular. In l. 41 I agree with Grierson in retaining *1633*; see note.

The long description of a stream changing its course is one of the rare examples of Donne basing a conceit on natural observation. It was imitated by Carew in 'An Eddy' (*Poems*, ed. Dunlap, 1949, p. 14) and possibly by John Weever in *Faustus and Melliflora*, 1600 (sig. B2ᵛ) where phrases that seem to echo Donne enlarge a passage based on the *Arcadia*.

Title: The compiler of *1635* left this and the following Elegy without a title. I have supplied one from the striking final couplet.

l. 2. *Whom honours smoakes at once fatten and sterve.* 'Fatten', giving the paradox 'fatten and sterve', which anticipates the oxymoron 'Poorely enrich't' in the next line, is stronger than 'flatter' (II, *Cy, P,* and *S 96* reading against its group).
    honours smoakes: vain delusions of honour; see *O.E.D.*, 'smoke', 4.d and e. Under e, 'Denoting a clouding or obscuring medium', *O.E.D.* cites *The French Academy*, book ii, 1594: 'Their eies dimmed with some smoake of honours' (p. 333). The clients of rich men grow fat through idleness while they starve on the delusive promises of their 'word and looks'; or, possibly, they are 'swoln with wind', like the hungry sheep of *Lycidas*, from eating 'the air promise-crammed'.

l. 4. *thy loving bookes*: thy register of lovers. Cf. 'to be on the books of a society' and 'to be in someone's good books'.

ll. 5–7. *As those Idolatrous flatterers,* &c. The Kings of England for many years bore in their style the kingdom of France, and Mary Stuart from 1558–66 bore in hers the kingdoms of England and Ireland.

ll. 8–9.   *Such services I offer as shall pay*
                                Themselves, I hate dead names:
The reflexive is used in a passive sense. 'Dead names' may be on the analogy of 'dead letter', based on the contrast of letter and spirit in Rom. vii. 6 and 2 Cor. iii. 6. He does not wish to be her servant merely in name. Or the reference

may be to the names of dead men which a captain kept on his muster-roll; cf. 'Satire 1', l. 18: 'Bright parcell gilt, with forty dead mens pay.'

l. 10. *in Ordinary*: regular, as opposed to 'extraordinary'. The phrase was added to official designations to distinguish those who regularly carried out a function from those who did so occasionally and purely as a formality.

ll. 17–19. *so the tapers beamie eye*, &c. The attraction of butterflies to a candle is a favourite love-emblem in Renaissance emblem books; see 'The Canonization', ll. 20–21, and note.

l. 35. *thy deepe bitternesse*: either 'the bitterness deep within thee', under a show of sweetness; or 'the deep bitterness thou causest in me'.

ll. 35 et seq. Cf. Ovid, *Remedia Amoris*, 655–72.

l. 37. *scorne*. 'Scorne' is a general *contemptus mundi*, product of 'despaire' and a concomitant of 'love-melancholy'; 'disdaine' is a merely particular contempt for her.

l. 41. *bred*. I agree with Grierson in retaining *1633*, though it is only supported by *W* and *A 25*. The 'editor' of *1633* rightly corrected his Group I manuscript here, seeing that a past tense is required: 'Though (when you were kind) hope bred faith and love, taught by experience to hope nothing from you I shall give up faith and love.' 'Breede' (I, II, and III) would be in accordance with Donne's practice of using the subjunctive in concessive clauses if the present were possible. It was adopted in *1635*.

l. 45. *Recusant*. The general sense of the word is 'one who refuses to acknowledge authority'; but at this period the word was normally used for a papist who refused to attend his parish church. One who stays away by his own free will cannot be harmed by being forbidden to come. Cf. 'It is not a *Recusancie*, for I would come, but it is an *Excommunication*, I must not' (Sparrow, *Devotions*, p. 13).

[Tutelage] (p. 12)

MSS.: *Σ — S 96*.

Miscellanies: *EH, HK 1, HK 2*, RP 117 (2)*; Bodleian MS. *Malone 19*; Folger MS. *V a 162*; Harvard MS. *Eng. 686*; Rosenbach MS. *239/22*.

This Elegy may owe something to Tibullus, I. vi. 5–14, though it is more innocent. Only 'Jealousy' among Donne's *Elegies* is concerned with adultery.

Title: The compiler of *1635* omitted to supply a title for this Elegy, perhaps because the text suggests no obvious word.

l. 1. *Natures lay Ideot*: ignorant simpleton by nature.

l. 2. *sophistrie*: probably in the obsolete sense of 'trickery or craft'.

l. 7. *by the'eyes water call a maladie.* The usual method of diagnosing a disease was by 'casting the patient's water'; the mistress was taught to diagnose the seriousness of a passion by examining her suitors' tears. Cf. 'Twickenham Garden', ll. 19–22.

ll. 9–10. *the Alphabet | Of flowers*: the rudiments of the language of flowers. Grierson quotes from Weekley, *Romance of Words*, 1912, p. 134: '*Posy*, in both its senses, is a contraction of *poesy*, the flowers of a nosegay expressing by their arrangement a sentiment like that engraved on a ring.'

l. 13. *Remember since*: remember the time when. See *The Winter's Tale*, v. i. 219, for the same idiom.

l. 15. *household charmes, thy husbands name to teach.* Burton tells how young maids only desire:

> ... if it may be done by art, to see their husbands picture in a glass, they'l give any thing to know when they shall be married, how many husbands they shall have, by *Cromnyomantia*, a kind of Divination with onions laid on the Altar on Christmas Eve, or by fasting on S. *Annes* Eve or night, to know who shall be their first husband ... (*Anatomy*, part 3, sect. 2, memb. 4, subs. 1).

ll. 21–22.   *That from the worlds Common having sever'd thee,*
                     Inlaid thee,
For a full discussion of these lines, see Eric Jacobsen, 'Donne's Elegy VII', *English Studies*, xlv, 1964. Dr. Jacobsen takes 'inlaid' as from 'lay-in' 'to enclose or reserve (a meadow) for hay' (*O.E.D.*, 'lay', v. 53 e). The girl, when unmarried, was a common and untilled. Her husband has enclosed her, but only to produce a coarse and barren crop. The lover had made of her a 'blisfull paradise', or *hortus conclusus*, only to have his pupil snatched from him before he could enjoy the fruits of his labours, and by someone incapable of cultivating the land.

l. 22. *neither to be seene, nor see.* Donne adapts a famous line from Ovid, *Ars Amatoria*, i. 99. Ladies at the playhouse:

> Spectatum veniunt, veniunt spectentur ut ipsae.

l. 24. *paradise*: pleasure garden, such as 'the Lord God planted'. Her 'graces and good words' are his creation, like the animals of Eden.

l. 25. *words.* 'Works' would appear to have arisen independently in Group I, *TCC*, and *Dob*, owing to the influence of 'graces'. The editor of *1633* presumably corrected his Group I manuscript by recourse to his Group II manuscript which read with *TCD*.
    'Good words' takes us back to l. 13. Taught by him she can now both flatter and praise.

l. 28. *Frame and enamell Plate, and drinke in Glasse*: fashion and adorn with enamel vessels of gold and silver and drink myself out of glass. Cf. Falstaff's retort to the Hostess's lament that she 'must be fain to pawn' her plate: 'Glasses, glasses, is the only drinking' (*2 Hen. IV*, II. i. 136–9).

l. 29. *Chafe waxe for others seales.* For the play on the obscene meaning of 'seals', cf. 'Going to Bed', l. 32, and 'The Relic', ll. 29–30.

Loves Warre (p. 13)

MSS.: All collections.

Miscellanies: *CCC, EH, Grey, HK 2*, RP 117 (2)*; Brit. Mus. MS. *Add. 30982*; Bodleian MS. *Eng. Poet. e 14*; Folger MSS. *V a 103* and *345*.

This, the second of the Elegies in Group I, was excepted by the licenser. It was first printed in 1802. Grierson printed from *W*. The text here is from *C 57*. I have adopted readings from *W* twice in l. 19, and abandoned *C 57* also in ll. 31 and 38. Apart from accidents my text agrees with Grierson's.

The contrast between the wars of Mars and the wars of Venus is a stock theme in Roman Elegy; cf. Ovid, *Amores*, I. ix, 'Militat omnis amans, et habet sua castra Cupido', and Tibullus, I. x. In its use of topical reference Donne's Elegy is nearest to two Elegies of Propertius (III. iv and v). In the first Propertius refers to the opening of the campaign against Parthia in 20 B.C., wishes it success and hopes that he may 'reclined on the bosom of his beloved' watch Caesar pass in triumph through Rome; ending that the soldiers who won it can keep the booty, he will be content to cheer them. The second is a more sustained repudiation of war:

> Pacis Amor deus est, pacem veneramur amantes:
> sat mihi cum domina proelia dura mea.

The date of 'Love's War' would seem to be before 1596 as, among the wars mentioned, there is no reference to the Cadiz expedition in which Donne took part. Grierson noted this and suggested that the reference to 'Spanish journeys' would be topical in 1595, the year of Raleigh's voyage to Guiana. But the reference is surely general, to the lack of profit to the 'gentlemen adventurers' who went privateering to the Spanish Main; see note to ll. 17–18. The reference to Henry IV's conversion as being 'of late' (l. 10) points to a date rather earlier than 1595. I would suggest the poem was written in 1594.

It had been found very difficult to recruit for the expedition to France of 1592 and Burghley notes that 'the Realm here is wearie to see the Expense of theare People for forein service'. After Henry's conversion in July 1593, the Normandy garrison remained until the end of the year and was then transported to Ostend to be part of the regular English garrison in the Netherlands. The troops in Brittany remained and were joined by a fresh expedition, partly from the Netherlands, and partly from Portsmouth in 1594. These were withdrawn early in 1595 and by the end of February in that year:

France was left for the first time for more than four years without English troops on her soil. Negotiations for military support were frequently renewed during the remaining eight years of Elizabeth's reign, but no considerable body of troops again crossed the Channel. The relations of the two countries were purely diplomatic and commercial (E. P. Cheyney, *History of England from the Defeat of the Armada to the Death of Elizabeth*, 1914, i. 277–306).

Donne's lover would hardly think of fighting in France after the close of 1594.

Title. Grierson took over Waldron's title, but gave it an archaic spelling. *B*, the only manuscript with a title, takes its 'Making of Men' from the final couplet. The number of manuscript titles thus derived suggests that Donne's contemporaries did not share the view of some modern critics that his beginnings are better than his endings.

l. 3. *scrupulous*: hedged about with conditions that create scruples. War has laws, but not love.

l. 4. *free City*. A free city may open its ports and gates at its own will.

ll. 5–6. *In Flanders*, &c. Fighting in Flanders (used for the Low Countries generally), with mutinies of unpaid Spanish troops, and disputes between the Spanish authorities and the Estates in the Southern Provinces, and open revolt in the Northern, was continuous in the 1590's. Donne declares that the rights and wrongs are confused and it is impossible to tell whether the master is a tyrant, oppressing his subjects, or whether the subjects are rebelling against lawful authority. The lack of sympathy here, and in the reference to 'mutinous Dutch' in 'Satire III', l. 17, with the Protestant cause in the Low Countries need not be ascribed to lingering Catholic sympathies. Donne shares it with most of his contemporaries:

> The whole policy of the English government towards the revolted Netherlands was dominated by the requirements of the war with Spain. There is no indication of religious, social, political or economic sympathy with the rising Dutch state (Cheyney, op. cit. i. 296–7).

Professor R. B. Wernham, whom I have consulted over Donne's allusions to foreign affairs, was struck by how markedly he echoes 'official policy', which in this matter he writes to me:

> . . . was not to make the Dutch independent but to restore the whole Netherlands to their ancient liberties, get the Spanish army out, and then leave them under the nominal suzerainty of Spain, who alone would be strong enough to defend them against France when France recovered. Elizabeth was still, vainly, urging this as late as 1598.

ll. 7–8. *Only wee knowe, that which all Ideots say,*
  They beare most blowes which come to part the fraye.

What 'all Ideots say' must be a proverb. No proverb resembling this has survived. But cf. Sidney, *Lady of May* (*Works*, ed. Feuillerat, ii. 209): '*Rombus* . . . fully perswaded of his owne learned wisedome, came thither, with his authority to part their fray; where for aunswer he received many unlearned blowes.'

ll. 9–12. *France in her lunatique giddiness*, &c. Flightiness was a common charge against the French, traditional enemies of the English. It was made topical in the 1590's by the treatment of English forces fighting in France, changes in French policy after the death of Henry III, the conversion of Henry IV in July 1593, and the extent of Henry's indebtedness to England. Elizabeth had financed him to the tune of nearly £400,000. The first repayment of this debt, and that a trifling one, was not made until 1603.

ll. 13–16. *Sick Ireland*, &c. This description fits well the uneasy period from 1594 to 1596 when Tyrone's rebellion was brewing. Spenser's *Short View*, written early in 1596, argues at length the view Donne puts through his medical metaphor, that drastic action is required.

l. 17. *And Midas joyes our Spanish journeys give.* See A. L. Rowse, *The Expansion of Elizabethan England*, 1955, pp. 296–7, for a summary of the economics of privateering: 'it was the professionals, not the amateurs, who profited.' The 'gentlemen-venturers' are like Midas, whose touch turned all to gold but who starved all the same; see Ovid, *Metamorphoses*, xi.

l. 22. *prison*. Cf. Burton, 'What is a ship but a prison?' (*Anatomy*, part 2, sect. 3, memb. 4) and Johnson, 'No man will be a sailor who has contrivance enough to get himself into a jail; for being in a ship is being in a jail, with the chance of being drowned' (Boswell, *Life of Johnson*, ed. Powell, 1934, i. 348).

l. 37. *engines*. The word was used at this time for all offensive weapons and not merely for those mechanically operated.

l. 44. *To warres, but stay, swords, armes and shot.* The line is a foot short. Since no variants exist in the manuscripts to suggest emendation, it must be left.

To his Mistris Going to Bed (p. 14)

MSS.: *Σ* — *DC*, *Hd*. Also in *L 74*.
Miscellanies: *Grey*, *HK 1*, *Hol* (fragment), *RP 117* (*2*); Brit. Mus. MSS. *Add. 19268* and *30982*, *Harleian 6931*, *Sloane 542* and *1792*; Bodleian MSS. *Ashmole 38*, *Don. b 9*, *Eng. Poet. c 50*, *e 97*, and *f 25*, *Rawl. Poet. 160*; Folger MSS. *V a 103*, *124*, *170*, and *345*; Rosenbach MS. *239/27*; Osborn MS. *B 12 5*.

This Elegy was not printed in *1633*. It first appeared in *1669* printed from a manuscript related to *Cy*, *O*, *P*, but having some poor readings of its own and others in common with inferior manuscripts such as *B*. Grierson was forced on a good many occasions to abandon the reading of the first edition; but since he based his text upon it and preferred it whenever possible his text differs a good deal from mine which is based on *C 57*; see ll. 4, 5, 10, 11, 13, 15, 17, 24 (*bis*), 26, 36, 43, 46. In most cases it is clear from the apparatus that my reading is the reading of Groups I and II and *W* and that Grierson's is the reading of *1669* supported by manuscripts of little authority. Where this is not so a note is supplied; see notes to ll. 17, 31, 43, 46.

The amount of variation recorded is partly due to the fact that the text in *1669* was taken from the kind of manuscript whose trivial variations and patent errors would not normally be cited in a critical apparatus. But there is also a certain amount of disagreement between the main groups, though none of it of a nature to suggest authorial revision. Revision has been suggested as an explanation of the variant in l. 46, but the manuscripts in which the variant occurs are of very doubtful authority.

In *Amores*, I. v Ovid tells how, as he lay in bed in the heat of the day, Corinna came to visit him, how he tore away her garments and having admired her naked beauty took her to his bed. Donne has translated this into the dramatic present and written an impassioned monologue, 'a piece of frank naturalism, redeemed from coarseness by passion and poetic completeness' (Saintsbury). The same praise could not be given to some of the imitations of this Elegy; see, for instance, Thomas Jordan, 'To Leda his coy Bride, on the Bridall Night' (*Poetical Varieties*, 1637), and *Roxburghe Ballads*, ed. Ebsworth, vii. 458. Carew's 'A Rapture' (*Poems*, ed. Dunlap, 1949) is an original masterpiece in the same tradition.

l. 5. *zone*. The singular is required both for sense and to avoid a further sibilant in the line. The reference is either to the 'zone or girdle of Orion' (*O.E.D.*, 'zone', sb. 3. c), or to the outermost circle of the universe, within the Primum Mobile, the sphere of the fixed stars.

l. 7. *that spangled brest-plate*. The stomacher, which covered the chest under the laced bodice, was often richly ornamented with jewels.

l. 9. *that harmonious chime*. The lady is wearing a chiming watch.

l. 17. *Off with those shoes: and then safely tread*. I concur with Grierson in rejecting 'softly' (I, *JC, Cy, P, 1669*) as an error arising from 'soft' in the following line. I differ from him in adopting the abrupt 'Off with' (I, II, and III), which repeats the opening of ll. 5 and 11, in place of 'Now off with' (*W, A 25, JC et al.*). The line I print is a syllable short. It can be scanned with a defective fourth foot:

Off with | those shoes: | and then | safe|ly tread.

But the strong pause at the colon suggests that a better scansion would regard the third foot as defective, or virtually non-existent, and take it that its deficiency received rhythmic compensation from a dramatic pause:

Off with | those shoes: ‖ and | then safe|ly tread.

Cf. l. 43:

Must see reveal'd. ‖ Then | since I | may knowe.

'Off with those shoes you weare' (III) and 'Off with your hose and shoes' (*S*) are plainly attempts to regularize the line in Groups I and II. The line in *W* has its full complement of syllables; but it is both less vigorous and rhythmically unsatisfactory:

Now off | with those | shoes and | then safe|ly tread.

It could be argued that this is the original reading and that the omission of 'Now' was due to the influence of ll. 5 and 11. I prefer the explanation that the line in *W* has also been regularized. The parallel in l. 43 suggests that in this dramatic monologue Donne was availing himself of a licence common in dramatic verse.

l. 22. *Ill spirits walk in white.* White is normally the garb of 'good spirits'; but since the devil is sometimes 'transformed into an angel of light' (2 Cor. xi. 14) white is no proof of a spirit's goodness.

l. 27. *my new found lande.* Modern Newfoundland was only one of many 'new found lands'. The title was not restricted to the island at the mouth of the St. Lawrence until the seventeenth century.

l. 31. *in these bonds.* To 'enter into' a bond is the more common form; but since, even if we elide 'enter' into', we get an awkward line, I have preferred 'enter in' (*W*, *A 25*, *JC*) for which there are Shakespearian parallels.

In *B*, where this poem occurs at the close in a different hand from that of the bulk of the manuscript, the writer has written against this line 'why may a man not write his owne Epithalamion if he can doe it so modestly'.

l. 32. *my seal shall be.* Cf. 'Tutelage', l. 29, and 'The Relic', ll. 29–30.

ll. 34–35. 'As souls must cast off the body to taste the fullness of joy, so bodies must cast off their clothes.' See Aquinas, *S. T.*, Iᵃ pars, IIᵃᵉ partis, q. lxix, art. ii, where it is concluded that the full reward of the blessed is after death and that in this life they have only a foretaste of bliss. For the praise of nakedness, cf. Propertius, II. xv.

ll. 35–36. Since it was Hippomenes who cast the golden balls in the path of Atalanta to distract her from the race (Ovid, *Metamorphoses*, x), Donne's simile which equates women with Hippomenes and men with Atalanta is not altogether happy.

ll. 39–40.   *Like pictures, or like bookes gay coverings made*
                For laymen,
There is a glance here at the view commonly ascribed to Papists that images and pictures are 'lay-mennes bokes' (Norton, *Calvin's Institutes*, 1561, I. xi) as well as at the ignorant rich man who values his books for their binding.

l. 42. *imputed grace.* The Reformation dispute over Justification turned on whether the merits of Christ are imparted, as Catholics held, or merely 'imputed' by a kind of legal fiction. By using the Protestant term Donne implies the distinction between the few 'elect' and the mass of the reprobate, and also pays women a hyperbolical compliment: all merit and grace is from them.

l. 43. See note to l. 17. As there, the line has been filled out in various manuscripts.

l. 46. *Here is no pennance, much lesse innocence.* Grierson preserved the reading of *1669*: 'There is no pennance due to innocence.' He thought that the line I print was the original reading and that the reading of *1669* was 'a softening of the original to make it compatible with the suggestion that the poem could be read as an epithalamium', quoting the marginal note in *B* cited above in the note to l. 31. He presumably ascribed the 'softening' to Donne. Apart from un-reliable miscellanies the reading of *1669* is found only in *Lut, O'F, JC, Cy, O, P, B,* and *S. JC* (reading here against *W* and *A 25*, with whom in the *Elegies* it usually agrees) may well be the source of this reading. *Lut* and *O'F*, reading here against the other Group III manuscripts, show contact with the tradi-tion in *Cy, O,* and *P* as they do occasionally elsewhere. The agreement of Groups I, II, and III (less *Lut, O'F*) with *W* establishes 'much lesse' as the true reading, and I cannot regard the variant as anything but scribal in origin. The notion that the poem could be an epithalamium need hardly be taken seriously. The lady is plainly, like the lady of 'Love's War', a 'faire free City'; white, the colour of penitence and virginity, is not for her. The initial address 'Come, Madame, come' and the fact that she is obviously very expensively dressed suggests that she is one of the 'cities quelque choses' ('Love's Usury', l. 15).

Loves Progress (p. 16)

MSS.: *Σ — DC, Dob, W, S 962.*
Miscellanies: *Grey, RP 117* (2); Bodleian MS. *Rawl. Poet. 116*; Emmanuel Coll. MS. *1 3 16*; Rosenbach MS. *239/18.*

'Love's Progress' is not included in the set of Elegies in *W, A 25, D 17, JC,* but a text is found later on in *A 25, D 17, JC.* The objection of the licenser prevented its appearance in *1633* and it was first printed in *1669*. It is impossible to suggest a relation between the text of *1669* and that in any extant manuscript. Grierson based his text on *1669* but emended it con-siderably. My text is based on *C 57.* Its differences from Grierson's are mainly trivial: see ll. 2, 4 (*bis*), 18, 20, 40, 52, 63, 70, and 82. Most of these are places where I prefer the reading of Groups I, II, and *W* to that of *1669*; but the readings in ll. 4, 20, and 82 need discussion; see notes.

This outrageous poem is a paradox, arguing that since the beauty of a woman is not what a lover desires in her the foot should be studied rather than the face. There may be some connexion between this Elegy and Nashe's indecent *The Choice of Valentines* where a similar voyage from the foot up is described. A tepid poem obviously inspired by Donne's argument can be found in *Wit Restored*, 1659, and was printed by Dobell, under the title of 'On a Good Legg and Foot' in *The Poetical Works of William Strode*, 1907 (p. 108).

l. 4. *wee'overlicke.* The abbreviated form 'o'relicke' (*1669* and some inferior manuscripts) gives a line that only scans if we leave 'wee o're' unelided which is contrary to Donne's usual practice. I follow the best manuscripts in reading 'over' and have supplied an elision mark.

For the allusion, see note to 'The Bracelet', l. 31.

ll. 7–8. 'Would not a Calf be a monster that developed a face like a man's though that face were, in itself, better than its own?'

l. 9. *Perfection is in unitie.* The 'perfect' is one, single, and unmixed. By a parody of logic Donne argues from this unexceptionable premise that if we love 'one thing' in woman we love 'the perfect'.

l. 16. *our new Nature, use.* Cf. 'Love's Deity', l. 6: 'that vice-nature, custome'.

l. 18. *but one*: only one thing, contrasted with 'all these' (things).

l. 20. *they are.* Grierson accepted the reading of *1669* 'they're', which gives a line of ten syllables but with the stress falling on all the unimportant words:

$$\text{They lóve} \mid \text{them fór} \mid \text{that bý} \mid \text{which they're} \mid \text{not théy.}$$

There is no manuscript authority for the elision, though elision in such circumstances is usual in Donne. Since the line runs more vigorously if we regard 'them' as an extra unaccented syllable in the first foot ('em'), I have at the risk of inconsistency accepted 'they are' as unelided:

$$\text{They lóve'them} \mid \text{for thát} \mid \text{by whích} \mid \text{they áre} \mid \text{not théy.}$$

ll. 27–28. *Search every spheare, &c.* No planet in its sphere or constellation in the firmament is named after Cupid. Not being a celestial God he must be presumed to be infernal.

l. 30. *where gold and fyre abound.* The service of Cupid demands gold in the purse as well as fire in the heart, so he may well be sought underground.

ll. 31–32. *Men to such Gods, &c.* Grierson cites Eusebius, *Praeparatio Evangelica*, iv. 9 (trans. Gifford, 1903), where Eusebius quotes from a lost work of Porphyry on the sacrifices appropriate to celestial, terrestrial, and infernal gods:

> For gods infernal bury deep, and cast
> The blood into a trench.

See Migne, *P.G.* xxi, col. 254; and cf. a story told by Valerius Maximus (ii. 4. 5).

ll. 33–36. The 'Centrique part', or centre, of the universe is the earth. For Donne's analogy, cf. *Measure for Measure*, I. iv. 43–44:

> Even so her plenteous womb
> Expresseth his full tilth and husbandry.

l. 38. *as infinite as it.* Cf. Prov. xxx. 15–16.

l. 47. *the first Meridian.* Cf. 'The ancient Cosmographers do place the division of the East and Western Hemisphere, that is the first term of longitude in the Canary or fortunate Islands.... But the Moderns have altered that term, and

translated it unto the Azores or Islands of St. *Michael.*' (*Pseudodoxia Epidemica,*
VI. vii.) In a sermon preached in 1627 Donne, as here, assumes the first
Meridian runs through the Canaries; see *Sermons,* vii. 310.

l. 52. (*Not faint Canarye but Ambrosiall*). Canary is a light, sweet wine: ambrosia,
the fabled drink of the Gods.

l. 58. *The Remora, her cleavinge tongue.* The remora, or sucking fish, was believed
to be able to stop any ship to which it attached itself, as a woman's tongue
will delay her lover's progress to the desired port.

ll. 61–62. *The Sestos and Abydos,* &c. Hero lived in Sestos and Leander in Abydos,
on the opposite shores of the Hellespont.

l. 65. *India:* used allusively at this time as a source of wealth.

l. 78. *the devill never can change his.* It was popularly held that the devil could
never disguise his cloven foot. Cf. *Othello,* v. ii. 288: 'I look down towards his
feet—but that's a fable.'

ll. 79–80. Professor Wind informs me that Scarlatini, *Homo Symbolicus,* 1695
(pp. 319 ff. and 325 ff.), lists a series of authorities, chiefly theological, for
regarding the foot as an emblem of *firmitas* or *soliditas.*

ll. 81–84. Grierson followed *1669* in reading 'began' for 'begun' and accepted
its punctuation with a colon after 'refin'd'. The weight of manuscript authority is overwhelmingly on the side of 'begun' and of taking 'we see' as paren-
thetical and 'the kisse' as the object of 'refin'd'.

'Politeness, we see, refined our habits in kissing.' The kiss on the face
is the kiss between equals. To kiss the hand is to acknowledge superiority; to
kiss the knee is a sign of feudal service; to kiss the foot is a sign of total subservience. 'In English satires, from a cut in Foxe's *Martyrs* in 1576 to a poster
against Gladstone in 1885, kissing of the papal toe recurs as a sign of abject
subservience to Rome' (M. Dorothy George, *English Political Caricature to
1792,* 1959, p. 5). Kissing the Pope's foot seems to be first attested in the
ninth century (Duchesne, *Liber Pontificalis,* ii. 107).

ll. 87–89. *For as free spheares,* &c. The speed at which the spheres move, making
a complete circuit of the heavens every twenty-four hours, is contrasted with
the speed of birds which, being sublunary, have to contend with the element
of air.

l. 92. *Two purses.* A purse was originally a small bag capable of being drawn
tightly together at the mouth by 'purse-strings', hence 'pursing of the lips'.
Donne plays here on the notion of the lips as the mouth of one purse and the
obscene colloquial use of 'purse'.

l. 96. *Clyster:* enema.
    meate: food.

Change (p. 19)

MSS.: All collections. Also in *L 74*.

Miscellanies: *HK 2**, *RP 117(2)*, *Wel*; Brit. Mus. MS. *Egerton 923*; Folger MS. *V a 103*.

The text in *1633* departs from Group I in l. 15, either because it has accepted a reading from Group II, or because it has made independently the same mistaken correction. In ll. 23 and 32 it is without manuscript support. On all three occasions I differ from Grierson in rejecting *1633*; see notes.

Donne wrote a prose paradox on the same theme: 'A Defence of Women's Inconstancy.' The poetic treatment differs from the prose in the distinction drawn between feminine promiscuity and masculine discrimination in libertinage. The two main literary sources of the naturalism expressed here and elsewhere in Donne's verse are the speech of Myrrha in Ovid's *Metamorphoses*, x. 320 et seq., and Tasso's 'O bella età del oro', from the first act of *Aminta*.

ll. 3–4.   *Yea though thou fall backe, that apostasie*
              Confirme thy love;

Cf. *Romeo and Juliet*, I. iii. 43: 'Thou wilt fall backward when thou hast more wit.' Carrying on the religious metaphors of 'faith' and 'good workes', Donne punningly takes 'falling back' as 'apostasie'. The word can have the general sense of 'abandonment of principle', the lady confirming her love by apostatizing from virtue; or it may be taken that in giving herself to him she apostatizes from an earlier lover. Or, possibly, the jest is that since nobody can apostatize who has not believed 'falling back' is a proof of having loved.

ll. 5–6.   *Women are like the Arts, forc'd unto none,*
              Open to' all searchers, unpriz'd, if unknowne.

Cf. '*Candidae musarum januae*. The dores of the muses be without envy, that is to say learned persons ought freely, gently and without envye admit other unto them that desire to be taught or informed of them.' Also, '*Occultae musices nullus respectus*'. See Taverner, *Proverbs of Erasmus*, 1539; quoted from the edition of 1569, ff. 12ᵛ, 23ᵛ.

ll. 11–14. Montaigne expatiates on the view that women are 'much more capable and violent in Loves-effects' than men in the long essay 'Upon some Verses of Virgil' (iii. 5), printed in 1588 and much expanded in the edition of 1595.

l. 15. *our clogges, and their owne.* Grierson accepted 'not their owne' (*1633*). This may have been adopted from Group II, or may show accidental agreement with Group II, *Lut, O'F* in correction of a misunderstood idiom. The authority for 'and' is very strong and it yields the sense required. A contrast is wanted between man who is fastened to a woman, as a slave is to a galley, and woman who is not fastened to man and may go where she pleases. If we read 'not their owne', we do not get this contrast but the meaningless 'they are clogs on us, not on themselves'. If we read 'and their owne', we must take the phrase absolutely: 'They are our clogs, and their own mistresses.' Cf. *The Tempest*, v. i. 213: 'When no man was his own', i.e. 'his own master'.

l. 23. *Likenesse glues love.* Cf. '*Simile gaudet simili*' and '*Similitudo mater amoris*', both ascribed to Aristotle by Taverner (*Proverbs of Erasmus*, 1539).

Then if soe thou doe. The line as printed has overwhelming manuscript authority. It is a syllable short in the third foot:

$$\text{Likenesse} \mid \text{glues love:} \mid \text{Then} \mid \text{if soe} \mid \text{thou doe.}$$

Cf. notes to 'Going to Bed', ll. 17 and 43. *Lut, O'F* and *S 96* add a conjunction to fill out the line: 'And then if. . . .', The reading of *1633*, 'And if that. . .', is patently a similar patch.

l. 24. *like and love.* The idiom 'to like and love' is so common (cf. 'His Picture', l. 16) that we must take 'like' here as a pun, the word standing both for the infinitive of 'to like' and for the adjective 'alike'.

ll. 27–28.　　　　*And soe not teach, but force my' opinion*
　　　　　　　　To love not any one, nor every one.

'Force' would seem to be used in the sense in which we 'force' a text of Scripture, making it bear a sense beyond its own. If he is as promiscuous as she he will not teach (by example) his true belief, but falsify it; for his true belief is that one should neither love one single woman nor every woman.

l. 32. *worse.* There seems no reason to preserve 'more' (*1633*) against the *consensus* of the manuscripts.

ll. 35–36, Cf. Spenser on 'Mutabilitie':

　　　　For, all that moueth, doth in *Change* delight.

With characteristic sophistry Donne confuses things that cannot exist without movement or 'change', such as music, with Eternity which is 'contrayr to *Mutabilitie*' being its term or end.

The Anagram (p. 21)

MSS.: $\Sigma - K$. Also in *L 74*.
Miscellanies: *EH, Grey, Hol, RP 117 (2), Sp, Wel*; Brit. Mus. MSS. *Add. 22118* and *30982, Egerton 2421, Sloane 542*, and *1792*; Bodleian MSS. *Add. B 97, Don. d 58, Eng. Poet. e 14* and *e 37; Rawl. Poet. 160*; Emmanuel Coll. MS. *1 3 16*; St. John's Coll. Cambridge MS. *U 26*; Folger MSS. *V a 97, 103, 170, 245, 319*, and *322, V b 43, W a 118*; Harvard MS. *Eng. 686 (bis)*; Rosenbach MS. *239/22*.

The text in *1633* follows Group I, but omits ll. 53–54 found in all manuscripts. On two occasions, l. 4 (where it follows Group I) and l. 49 (where it follows *C 57*), I differ from Grierson in rejecting the edition. I also differ from him in l. 7 in moving an editorial elision mark; see note.

'The Anagram' easily outstrips 'The Bracelet' and 'Going to Bed' as a favourite poem in miscellanies. Drummond noted its resemblance to Tasso's 'Sopra la bellezza' (*Rime*, no. xxxvii): 'Compare Song: *Marry and Love*, &c. with *Tasso's stanzas agaiust beauty*; one shall hardly know who hath the best' (*Works*, 1711, p. 226). The first four stanzas of Tasso's poem are a conventional attack on the deceptiveness of beauty; in the last two he expresses the wish for an ugly mistress:

> Let my mistress be ugly, and let her have a huge nose which casts a shadow as far as her chin; let her mouth be large enough to hold anything, her teeth be few and far between and her eyes set crooked—the teeth of ebony and the eyes silvery; and may what appears and what is hidden correspond to these excellencies. I shall have no fear of her being loved by anyone else, or followed, or admired; I shall not be alarmed if she looks at anyone else or if she sighs and seems sad. I shall not always be calling her proud, ungrateful, perverse and unyielding. Her thoughts will be like my thoughts; she will be wholly mine and I wholly hers.

For the tradition to which this 'praise of ugliness' belongs, see H. K. Miller, 'The Paradoxical Encomium', *M.P.*, 1956, and J. B. Leishman, *The Monarch of Wit*, 1951, pp. 74–81, where Tasso and Donne are compared.

Donne blends with the paradoxical praise of ugliness another strain deriving from Berni's scoffing sonnet on an old woman; see note to 'The Comparison' (p. 119). Berni, like his imitator Sidney in his praise of Mopsa, puts the right qualities in the wrong places. His hag has silver hair frizzed round a yellow face, her eyes, instead of her teeth, are pearly, her eyebrows, rather than her breast, are of snow, and so on.

A shortened and corrupt version of 'The Anagram' appears in *Parnassus Biceps*, 1656, and the poem was imitated by Kynaston in 'To Cynthia on a Mistress for his Rivals' (Saintsbury, *Minor Caroline Poets*, ii. 157).

l. 7. *haire is red. 1633* elides to 'haire's' which gives a ten-syllable line. I prefer to follow the manuscripts and take it that the second syllable of 'yellow', pronounced 'yeller', is elided. This gives a line with the required emphasis:

> $$\overset{\times}{\text{What}} \overset{/}{\text{though}} \mid \overset{\times}{\text{her}} \overset{/}{\text{cheeks}} \mid \overset{\times}{\text{be}} \overset{/}{\text{yellow,'}} \overset{(\times)}{} \overset{\times}{\text{her}} \overset{/}{\text{haire}} \overset{\times}{\text{is}} \overset{/}{\text{red.}}$$

ll. 17–21. Grierson cites Du Bartas in Sylvester's translation:

> As six sweet Notes, curiously varied
> In skilfull Musick, make a hundred kindes
> Of Heav'nly sounds, that ravish hardest mindes . . .:
> Or, as of twice-twelve *Letters*, thus transpos'd,
> This World of Words, is variously compos'd.
>   (First Week, Second Day)

He suggests that Du Bartas's source is probably Lucretius, I. 824–7.

The 'Gamut' is the scale of seven notes, made up by adding a ground note 'Gamma' to the ancient hexachord, the 'six sweet notes' of Du Bartas. The notes of the hexachord were named 'ut', 're', 'mi', &c.; 'Gamut' is a contraction of 'gamma ut'.

l. 22. *Things simply good, can never be unfit*: things good in themselves can never be useless, or can never be incapable of joining well together. Cf. note to 'The Perfume', ll. 67–68 (p. 124).

ll. 25–26. *All love is wonder*. I have not been able to find the origin of this axiom which Donne makes the major premiss of his false syllogism.

l. 35. *husbands*: husbandmen. For the *double entendre* cf. note to 'Love's Progress', ll. 33–36 (p. 134).

l. 37. *Plaister*: a soothing or healing remedy.

l. 40. *Marmosit*. 'Marmoset' was used at this time as a term of abuse or contempt for a man; *O.E.D.* cites Brathwait (1615), 'Her apple-squire, or wanton Marmosite'. But it is probably intended literally here as in Marston's *Scourge of Villainy*, satire III: 'She hath her monkey. . . .'

ll. 41–42. *When Belgiaes citties*, &c. 'When the cities of the Low Countries flood the country around them. . . .' The most famous examples of the opening of the dikes to save besieged cities were Alkmaar in 1573 and Leyden in 1574.

l. 50. *a tympanie*: a morbid swelling or tumour.

ll. 53–54.   *Whom Dildoes, Bedstaves, and her Velvet Glasse*
                   Would be as loath to touch as Joseph was:

This couplet, present in all manuscripts, was omitted *causa pudoris* in 1633 and first printed in 1669.

There are plentiful references to these *succedanea*, or 'instruments' as they are commonly termed, a usage neglected by *O.E.D.* whose first reference to 'dildo' (1610) is far too late. See Nashe, *The Choice of Valentines*, ll. 239 et seq., and Marston, *Scourge of Villainy*, Satire III, ll. 31–33 and 121–4.

as Joseph was: when he fled from Potiphar's wife (Gen. xxxix).

On his Mistris (p. 23)

MSS.: Σ — Cy.
Miscellanies: *HK 2**, *RP 117 (2)*, *Wel*; Bodleian MS. *Eng. Poet. e 14*; Folger MS. *V a 262*; Rosenbach MS. *1083/16*.

It was probably ll. 33–41 that caused this poem to be excepted against. Although no authority had been obtained it was printed in 1635. There can be no doubt that the source of the text there was *O'F*. Three of the readings of 1635 are only found in *Lut* and *O'F*; further, 1635 never reads against these manuscripts and it reproduces much of the characteristic punctuation of *O'F*. The text here is based on *C 57* and differs considerably from Grierson's which consistently follows *1635*; see ll. 7, 9, 12, 18, 37, 40, 46, 49, and notes to these lines.

I have abandoned *C 57* on seven occasions; in ll. 24, 39, and 51 where it reads against the other Group I manuscripts in minor error; and in ll. 28, 35 (see note), 37, and 46, where the witness of Groups I and II and *W* is divided and I regard Group I as having the weaker reading.

The situation of a woman accompanying her lover disguised as his page is a commonplace of romantic literature. Grierson notes an occurrence in real life when Elizabeth Southwell, disguised as his page, accompanied Robert Dudley abroad in 1605. In Arthur Brook's *Romeus and Juliet* (1562) Juliet pleads with her lover to be allowed to follow him into exile disguised. Shakespeare's Juliet makes no such romantic suggestion. Donne's mistress, with her nurse over-hearing her nightmare, reminds us of Juliet, and it is difficult to parallel out-side the drama the intensity of this valediction and not to connect its opening adjuration with the sense of fate that hangs over Shakespeare's treatment of lovers cruelly parted.

In Hazlitt's essay 'On Persons one would Wish to have Seen' 'B' (Lamb), indignant at the suggestion that Donne's meaning was *'uncomeatable'*, 'seizing the volume, turned to the beautiful "Lines to his Mistress", dis-suading her from accompanying him abroad, and read them with suffused features and a faltering tongue'. The title in *B* which connects the poem with Ann More is a tribute to its verisimilitude and to the fame of Donne's romantic marriage, but has no other value.

l. 3. *remorse*: pity.

ll. 7, 12, and 18. On these three occasions *1635* reads with *Lut* and *O'F* against all other manuscripts, except that in l. 12 *Lut* and *O'F* are joined by *S*. Grierson suggested that 'fathers' (*1635*, *O'F*) for 'parents' in l. 7 arose from the identification of the lady addressed with the motherless Ann More. It seems highly improbable that at the date at which this reading would seem to have arisen (*Lut* and *O'F* were both written after Donne's death) the fact that Donne's bride had no mother would have been remembered. 'Fathers' (who are notoriously wrathful with unsuitable wooers of their daughters) looks like an obvious scribal substitution for 'parents'. Similar insignificant variants are 'wayes' (*1635*, *O'F*) for 'meanes' in l. 12 and the transposition of words in l. 18.

l. 9. *those*. The agreement of Groups I, II, and *W* establishes this reading.

ll. 21–23. *Nor tame wilde Boreas harshness*, &c. In all versions of the myth known to me Boreas, the north wind, carried off Orithea to his home in Thrace where she bore him twin sons; see Ovid, *Metamorphoses*, vi. 682–713. In the *Phaedrus* Socrates refers to a rationalization of the myth which said that the girl was blown off a cliff by a blast of the north wind and hence the fable of her rape by a god arose. This hardly explains Donne's allusion since it rationalizes away the roughly amorous god. Donne may have confused two stories, the rape of Orithea and a story Burton tells:

> Constantine in the eleventh book of his husbandry, *cap.* 11. hath a pleasant tale of the Pine tree; she was once a fair maid, whom *Pineus* and *Boreas* two corrivals, dearly sought; but jealous *Boreas* broke her neck (*Anatomy*, part 3, sect. 3, memb. 1, subs. 1).

ll. 24–25. 'Whether things turn out well or badly, it is madness to have endured dangers not thrust upon us.'

l. 27. *Dissemble.* There is a zeugma here, the verb being used in two senses, the current sense 'hide' and the obsolete sense 'simulate'. 'Hide nothing, nor simulate a boy.'

ll. 28–30. *bee not strange,* &c. If she disguises herself she will deceive only herself.

l. 29. As in 'The Anagram', l. 7, see note, there is an extra unmetrical syllable before the pause which could be elided.

$$\overset{\times}{\text{To}} \overset{/}{\text{thy}} \mid \overset{/}{\text{selfe}} \overset{/}{\text{onely}}; \parallel \overset{(\times)}{\text{All}} \overset{/}{\text{will}} \mid \overset{\times}{\text{spye}} \overset{/}{\text{in}} \mid \overset{\times}{\text{thy}} \overset{/}{\text{face}}. \dots$$

l. 31. *Apes*: fools.

ll. 33–42. For the traditional characteristics of the French, Italians, and Dutch (Germans), cf. the old rhyme quoted by Browne, *Religio Medici*, ii. 4:

> Le mutin Anglois, et le bravache Escossois;
> Le bougre Italian, & le fol François;
> Le poultron Romain, le larron de Gascongne,
> L'Espagnol superbe, & l'Aleman yvrongne.

ll. 33–34. *Men of France, changeable Camelions,*
            Spittles of diseases, shops of fashions,

For the changeability of the French, see note on 'Love's War', l. 9. The diseases treated in spital-houses were venereal; cf. 'Even Spittles will give me souldiers to fight for me, by their miserable example against that sin' (*Sermons,* iv. 55). French changeableness in fashions is commented on by Du Bartas:

> Heer's nothing constant: nothing still doth stay. . . .
> Much like the *French,* (*or like our selves, their Apes*)
> Who with strange habit do disguise their shapes;
> Who loving novels, full of affection,
> Receive the Manners of each other Nation;
> And scarcely shift they shirts so oft, as change
> Fantastick Fashions of their garments strange.
> (Sylvester, *Du Bartas,* First Week, Second Day.)

l. 35. *Loves fuellers.* I agree with Grierson in reading 'Loves' though the weight of authority is with 'Lives'. It is easy to misread one for the other. The reading is established and the sense explained by reference to the same sermon quoted in the note above and later in the note to l. 44. It would almost seem as if Donne had been re-reading this poem of his youth when preparing this sermon, preached 8 March 1622 at Whitehall:

If mine enemie meet me betimes in my youth, in an object of tentation, (so *Josephs* enemie met him in *Putifars* Wife) yet if I doe not adhere to this enemy, dwell upon a delightfull meditation of that sin, if I doe not fuell, and foment that sin, assist and encourage that sin, by high diet, wanton discourse, other provocation, I shall have reason on my side, and I shall have grace on my side, and I shall have the History of a thousand that have perished by that sin, on my side; Even Spittles . . . (*Sermons*, iv. 55).

l. 37. *Will quickly knowe thee,' and knowe thee; and alas.* There can be no doubt that this is the line that Donne wrote and that the reading of *1635*, taken from O'F, is a patch of the defective line found in Group I and other manuscripts. Grierson thought this, but preserved the reading of *1635* out of repugnance for 'the sudden brutal change in the sense of the word "knowe"', though he owned that it was in Donne's manner.

l. 40. *haunt.* The Group III reading 'hunt', which *1635* took from O'F, does not fit the behaviour of the Sodomites who, when Lot was entertaining the two angels, 'compassed the house round' (Gen. xix. 4). Lot might well have used to them the words of Brabantio to Roderigo: 'I have charg'd thee not to haunt about my doors' (*Othello*, I. i. 98).

l. 42. *spungie hydroptique Dutch.* The more the dropsical man drinks the more he thirsts.

l. 44. *England is only' a worthy gallerie.* The 'gallery' is the long room or corridor in a palace where suitors wait for admission to the presence-chamber. Donne frequently in his sermons uses the metaphor of this world as a gallery to the presence-chamber of Heaven; see *Sermons*, iii. 203 and iv. 240, cited by Grierson. The closest parallel to the poem is in the sermon already quoted from twice where, having spoken of the 'Heaven of Heavens' as 'the Presence Chamber of God himselfe' which awaits 'the presence of our bodies', Donne turns to this world as 'one house' and says 'Let this Kingdome, where God hath blessed thee with a being, be the Gallery, the best roome of that house' (*Sermons*, iv. 47 and 49).

l. 46. *Our greate King call thee into his presence.* All the versions of this line are lame. The line printed here is from *W*, *A 25*, *JC*, *S*. Groups I and II agree with *W* in reading 'Our greate', but both read 'to' for 'into'. This gives in Group I a line of nine syllables that is hopelessly unmetrical. Group II has mended the line by adding the auxiliary 'do', but this does not help the rhythm. Group III, which also reads 'to' for 'into', achieves ten syllables by reading 'greatest'. I think we must regard the lines in II and III as patched and that an editor has no choice but to accept the line in *W* or attempt emendation on his own judgement.

l. 49. *blesse.* Grierson retained the reading of *1635* and Group III, 'nor blesse', though he owned that the reading of Groups I and II and *W* was 'probably original'. For the absence of a syllable at a medial pause, see notes to 'Going to Bed', l. 17. The line as printed is very forceful:

$$\overset{\times}{\text{Nor}} \overset{/}{\text{praise,}} \mid \overset{\times}{\text{nor}} \overset{/}{\text{dis}}\vert\overset{/}{\text{praise}} \overset{'}{\text{mee,}} \parallel \overset{/}{\text{blesse,}} \overset{\times}{\text{nor}} \overset{/}{\text{curse.}} \dots$$

ll. 52–53. Mr. Leishman suggested to me that the vividness of these lines might owe something to Virgil's tenth Eclogue (ll. 46–48):

> Tu procul a patria (nec sit mihi credere tantum)
> Alpinas ah dura nives et frigora Rheni
> Me sine sola vides.

l. 54. See note on versification (p. 109) for the scansion of this line.

l. 55. *Augure mee better chance.* Cf. the song 'Sweetest love, I doe not goe' and 'A Valediction: of Weeping' for this fear that his mistress's 'ill-divining soul' may provide an ill omen. In these two poems Donne, as here, makes no attempt to prove the 'flatterye':

> That absent lovers one in th'other bee.

His Picture (p. 25)

MSS.: *Σ* — *Dob.* Also in *L 74.*
Miscellanies: *HK 2*, RP 117 (2)*; Brit. Mus. MSS. *Egerton 2230, Harleian 3511*; Bodleian MS. *Rawl. Poet. 160; Folger MS. V a 103.*

On two occasions (ll. 8 and 16) *1633* follows Group II against Group I. Grierson accepted *1633.* I regard the Group II readings as sophistications. I also think that the variant readings in l. 8 provide a striking example of progressive corruption from a single original whose reading is preserved in *W et al.* whereas Grierson thought the variants arose from the author's revisions. I also differ from Grierson in ll. 6 and 20. See notes to ll. 6, 8, 16, and 20.

One need not believe that Donne actually handed a miniature to a mistress before sailing to connect this poem with his participation in the attack on Cadiz in 1596.

l. 1. *Here take my Picture.* The speaker is presumably handing his mistress a miniature to wear, as Olivia hands hers to the supposed Cesario: 'Here; wear this jewel for me; 'tis my picture' (*Twelfth Night*, III. iv. 198). Isaac Oliver's miniature of Donne, dated 1616, is at Windsor Castle. Laurence Binyon's suggestion that the Marshall engraving, prefixed to the *Poems* of 1635 and reproduced here facing p. 1, is a copy of a miniature by Hilliard is generally accepted. It is dated 1591, *Aet.* 18. The Lothian portrait (facing p. 29) was probably painted not far from the time that this poem was written; but it is hardly of the size to hand to a lady.

l. 4. *When wee are shadowes both.* 'Shadow' was often used for 'portrait'; see

O.E.D., 'shadow', sb. 6.b, and cf. Randolph, 'Upon his Picture' (*Poems,* ed. G. Thorn-Drury, 1929, p. 79):

> Behold what frailty we in man may see,
> Whose Shaddow is lesse given to change then hee.

The portrait is like the speaker now; it will be even more so when he, like it, is a 'shadow', or ghost.

l. 6. *Perchance.* I accept the reading of *W, A 25, JC* against *1633* and all the other manuscripts, which read 'Perhaps'. There is no other example of 'perhaps' in the *Concordance.*

l. 8. *With cares rash sodaine hoarinesse o'rspread.* Grierson thought that the variants in this line had arisen from the poet's rewriting of it. He accepted *1633*, which follows Group II, though feeling sure that Donne had not written the line as it stands there. I believe that the line printed above is the line that Donne wrote and that all other versions of it have arisen from a misreading of 'hoarinesse' (spelt 'horines') as 'stormes'. This misreading gives us the defective line found in Group I, *S 96* and *Cy*:

> With cares rash sodaine stormes ore sprede.

Group II has patched this to

> With cares rash sodaine stormes, being o'erspread.

This reading was adopted in *1633*, the compiler finding the line defective in his Group I manuscript. *P* (usually dependent on the text in *Cy*) and *B* (often agreeing with *Cy* and *P*) patch the line by adding 'cruel', but insert the word in different places:

> With cares rash cruell sudeine stormes orespread *P*
> With cares rash sudden cruel stormes oreprest *B*

B's error of 'oreprest' for 'o'rspread', which destroys the rhyme, is found also in *S.*

The reading of *W, A 25, D 17, JC* which I print is found also in *Lut* and *O'F* which read here against *S 96* (the poem is missing in *Dob*). This is an example of intelligent editing by the compiler of *Lut* who on other occasions deserts the tradition of Group III which he mainly follows.

ll. 14 and 15. *reach*: affect (me or his judgement of me).

l. 16. *like' and love.* I have adopted the reading of all manuscripts except those of Group II which *1633* here follows, but have supplied an elision mark to indicate that in this common idiom 'and' may be regarded as metrically worthless. 'Should now love lesse' (*1633* and II) though smoother is less idiomatic.

ll. 17–20. The comparison between milk for babes and meat for grown men (1 Cor. iii. 1–2 and Heb. v. 13–14) is frequently used in devotional literature to distinguish the love of Christ in His Manhood from love of Christ as God and Man; see my note 'John Donne: A Note on Elegie V', *M.L.R.*, 1944, for a discussion. The speaker hopes that his mistress will assert that when her love was childish it was nursed on his outward beauty, but that now, when it is mature and strong, it is able to feed on the 'meat' of his inner self, something too hard for the inexperienced in love to apprehend.

l. 20. *to'disus'd*. Grierson expanded 'disus'd' (*1633*) to 'disusèd' and made the line an alexandrine. Apart from the fact that Donne rarely uses uncontracted forms of the past participle and there is no other example of an alexandrine in his poems in couplet, this gives a feeble line. I prefer, as in l. 16, to regard the line as having a metrically worthless syllable:

$$\times \quad / \quad \times \quad / \quad \times \quad (\times) \; / \quad \times \quad / \quad / \quad /$$
To feed | on that, | which to'dis|us'd tasts | seemes tough.

A Funeral Elegy (p. 26)

MSS.: Σ — Group II, *DC*, *Dob*, *A 25*, *Hd*, *S 962*.
Miscellanies: *HK 1*, *HN*.

In both the Group I manuscripts and in *W*, *D 17*, *JC* this poem appears with the Love Elegies. It was printed from a Group I manuscript as 'Elegie VI' in *1633*. It was moved in *1635* and put with the Epicedes and Obsequies under the title 'Elegie on the L. C.'. I print it here with the other Elegies with which it occurs in manuscript on the grounds that Donne had precedent in Ovid for including a funeral poem among Love Elegies and either anticipated or followed Campion in doing so; and that in style and manner it is very unlike the funeral poems that Donne wrote from 1609 onwards.

Most of the titles added in *1635*, when not taken from manuscript, look like editorial inventions; but this title, and the expansion of the title of 'The Primrose', though they are not found in any extant manuscript, can hardly be inventions. In Giles Oldisworth's copy of *1639* (see Keynes, p. 162) 'the L. C.' is expanded to 'Lord Cary'. This could only mean Henry Cary, first Baron Hunsdon, the Lord Chamberlain, who died in 1596. The identification cannot be accepted. The poem is patently not concerned with a great nobleman who, in addition to having held high office, was first cousin to the Queen. Only his family mourn the dead man, not the nation or the monarch, and all that is praised is the dead man's virtues. Grierson recognized this in rejecting an earlier suggestion that the poem was on 'the Lord Chancellor' (i.e. Egerton), and suggested that it was an early experiment in epicede 'on the death of someone, we cannot now say whom, perhaps the father of the Woodwards or some other of Donne's early correspondents and friends'.

I believe that Grierson was right in suggesting that it is the father of 'L. C.' who is dead and that, as Campion included a poem 'Ad. Ed. Mychelbourne' on the death of a friend's sister in his Latin Elegies, so Donne included in his 'book of Elegies' a poem 'To L. C.' on his father's death. The editor of *1635*, finding this title attached to the poem and influenced by the fact that the great majority of Donne's Epicedes are 'On' persons of rank might very easily misinterpret the initials as standing for 'the Lord C.' and alter 'To L. C.' to 'On the L. C.'.

I wish to suggest that the poem was written to Lionel Cranfield on the death of his father Thomas Cranfield in 1595. Although there is no evidence that Donne knew Cranfield before 1611 when they were both present at the feast at the Mitre Tavern, the fact that eight of those present at the feast were Inns of Court men, including Christopher Brooke, gives colour to the notion that Cranfield as a young merchant might have had contact with Donne's circle at Lincoln's Inn. Mr. Shapiro tells me that although he knows of no evidence for acquaintance between Donne and Cranfield before the Mitre feast he knows none that makes it an impossible suggestion. My reasons for proposing that 'L. C.' is Cranfield are that there is no other friend or acquaintance of Donne with these initials and that the lines:

> though no familie
> Ere rigg'd a soul for heavens discoverie
> With whom more Venturers more boldly dare
> Venture their states, with him in joy to share,

point to the dead man as having been a merchant concerned with foreign trade. Thomas Cranfield was an original member of the Baltic Company. Professor Tawney thinks that his will suggests that 'in his later years, his export business may not have fared too well' (R. H. Tawney, *Business and Politics under James I*, 1958, pp. 9–11). Donne's lines, declaring that the family might safely 'venture their states' on the dead man's prospects of heaven, look like a graceful reference to a not wholly successful business career.

The same initials 'L. C.' occur puzzlingly in a large manuscript miscellany, *HK 1*, written in the margin against the poems of a collection, largely by Donne, written in double columns; see Textual Introduction, pp. lxxix–lxxx. The initials cannot possibly stand for the author of the poems. Their presence suggests that the scribe was copying poems from a book belonging to 'L. C.'. Here again the only friend of Donne's with these initials, who might well have a collection of his poems, is Cranfield.

The Autumnall (p. 27)

MSS.: *H 40*; Group I (*C 57, D, H 49, Lec, SP*); Group II (*A 18, N, TCC, TCD*); Group III (*Dob, Lut, O'F, S 96*); *O, P; A 25, D 17, JC; B, K, S*.
Miscellanies: *EH, Grey, Hd, HK 2*, RP 117 (2), S 962, TCD (2), Wel*; Brit. Mus. MS. *Egerton 2725*; Bodleian MSS. *Eng. Poet. e 14, Rawl. Poet. 160*; Emmanuel Coll. MS. *1 3 16*; Folger MSS. *V a 97* and *103*.

'The Autumnal' is not included in the set of Elegies in the Group I manuscripts or in the similar set in *W, A 25, D 17, JC*. It appears among the *Songs and Sonnets* in the Group I manuscripts and is found in the related set of lyrics in *H 40*. It was printed in *1633* in the middle of the volume, between

'The Comparison' (which the compiler of *1633* found in his Group II manuscript) and the lyric that I have called 'Image and Dream', which appears in the Group I manuscripts written continuously, as if it were in couplets, among the *Songs and Sonnets*. All three poems are headed 'Elegie'. In *1635* they were moved from their no-man's land of *1633* to join the *Elegies*.

The text in *1633* is indented and very heavily italicized. I have printed it in block setting and removed the italics except in the first couplet where they have point.

The text of *1633* has been abandoned in ll. 8, 47, and 50, where it reads against all the manuscripts and in l. 6 where it has only accidental support. Except in l. 50 I agree here with Grierson. I differ from him in abandoning *1633* in ll. 3 and 44 where it follows Group I against Groups II and III.

Readings in the apparatus are given from eight manuscripts only: *H 40*; *L 74*; *C 57* and *H 49*; *TC* (*TCC* and *TCD*); *Dob* and *O'F*. These are sufficient to establish the text. There are no variants of interest in the less reliable manuscripts.

For discussion of the date of the poem see Appendix C, 'Lady Bedford and Mrs. Herbert', where it is suggested that a date around 1600 is probable.

'The Autumnal' is a witty series of variations on an ancient theme. Professor Mario Praz (*Secentismo e Marinismo*, Florence, 1925, p. 128), while asserting that the praise of mature charms was too common a topic in the Renaissance for it to be possible to suggest a single source, drew attention to an epigram in the Greek Anthology:

> Your autumn excels anothers spring, and your winter is warmer than another's summer (V. 258).

Mrs. Duncan-Jones (*M.L.R.*, April 1961) pointed out that in the Planudean text, the only one known in the sixteenth and early seventeenth centuries, these two lines formed the complete epigram and that the preceding four lines, praising the lady's wrinkles and mature breasts, are only found in the Palatine text; but she pointed to another epigram (VII. 217) as a source for Donne's conceit of love sitting in the lady's wrinkles, and for the contrast between her 'torrid and inflaming time' and her milder warmth now. This epigram, which was famous because Diogenes Laertius attributed a version to Plato, she quotes in a Latin translation from Henri Estienne's edition of Diogenes, Paris, 1570, p. 103.

> Archeanassa mihi est meretrix Colophonia, seris
>   Cuius et in rugis sedit acerbus amor.
> Quas miseri flammas, per quanta incendia abistis
>   Libata illa quibus prima iuventa fuit.

Title: Apart from *Lut* and *O'F* none of the manuscripts of Groups I, II, and III connect the poem with Mrs. Herbert. *L 74* has a note 'Widdow Her' in the margin. *B* has 'An autumnall face: on the Ladie Sʳ Ed Herbart mothers Ladie Danvers'; but *S 96* suggests another name with 'Elegie Autumnall on the Ladie Shandoys'. *O* and *P* call the poem simply 'Widdowe' and *S* gives it the title 'A Paradox of an ould woman'.

ll. 1–2. Bacon ('Of Beauty') supports the claim of age against youth by an adage 'Pulchrorum autumnus pulcher', a misquotation of 'Pulchrorum etiam autumnus pulcher est' (Erasmus, *Adagia*). The saying occurs three times in Plutarch. Since Bacon uses his misquotation to support the view that autumn is the most beautiful of the seasons and North mistranslates Plutarch to give the same sense, the adage seems to have become assimilated to the epigram from the Anthology quoted above. Mrs. Duncan-Jones points out that Plutarch's anecdote in the *Life of Alcibiades* in which the saying figures could have been found by Donne in Aelian where he could also have found the story of Xerxes and the plane tree.

l. 3. *your.* *1633* follows Group I in reading 'our' which is inconsistent with the idiomatic use of the second person plural in ll. 4 and 24.

l. 6. *Affection.* I agree with Grierson in rejecting the plural of *1633* which has only the accidental support of *Lut, O'F.* It is possibly an example of editorial sophistication, to provide a parallel to 'Reverences' mistakenly regarded as a plural.

l. 8. *shee's gold.* The reading of *1633* ('they'are gold') gives nonsense as her 'first yeares' are now past.

I presume Donne thinks of the 'Golden Age' as the age of innocence. By experience, or assaying, she has herself now been proved to be gold. Gold, being the purest of metals, is unimpaired ('ever new') by being 'tried'.

ll. 9–10. 　　　　　*That was her torrid and inflaming time,*
　　　　　　　　　　This is her tolerable Tropique clyme.

The 'torrid zone' is bounded by the tropics of Cancer and Capricorn, a little over 23° north and south of the equator. As the next couplet makes clear, the lady has not arrived at the temperate zone, but at a region that is 'tolerable' or 'habitable' (the choice of reading is indifferent), though still very warm.

l. 13. *graves*: trenches or furrows. Cf. Shakespeare, Sonnet ii:

　　　　When forty winters shall besiege thy brow
　　　　And dig deep trenches in thy beauty's field. . . .

Donne makes the same play on the sense of 'graves' in a sermon:

　If when they are filling the wrinkles, and graves of their face, they would remember, that there is another grave, that calls for a filling with the whole body . . . (*Sermons*, vi. 269).

l. 16. *like an Anachorit.* Cf. *The Second Anniversary*, ll. 169–72:

　　　　Thinke that no stubborne sullen Anchorit,
　　　　Which fixt to a pillar, or a grave, doth sit
　　　　Bedded, and bath'd in all his ordures, dwels
　　　　So fowly as our Soules in their first-built Cels.

Anchorites, as distinct from hermits who might wander, were fixed to one place. Legouis, in a note on *The Second Anniversary*, refers to a certain 'Baradatos, qui habita de longues années une sorte de niche creusée dans le sol (Théodoret, *Histoire religieuse*, ch. xvii)'. Donne adapts, possibly from the Anthology, the conceit of love sitting in the lady's wrinkles, adding the hyperbole that he makes there a thing of beauty, a tomb, not a mere grave.

l. 20. *his standing house*: his permanent dwelling as distinct from houses he visits while 'on progress' through his kingdom.

ll. 23–24. In all her conversation there is both delight and instruction, so that it is suitable for all hearers who may enjoy which they choose.

l. 25. *under-wood*: small bushes, coppice wood or brushwood growing beneath high timber trees. It flares up and burns out quickly compared with slow-burning timber.

ll. 26–28. 'In youth, love, like wine, overheats the blood; it comes at a better time when our other appetites have lost their strength.' Cf. the note to the phrase 'love's fuellers' in the Elegy 'On his Mistress', p. 141.

ll. 29–32.   Xerxes *strange Lydian love, the Platane tree,*
                   Was lov'd for age, none being so large as shee,
                   Or else because, being yong, nature did blesse
                   Her youth with ages glory, Barrennesse.

Grierson refers to Herodotus (vii. 31) for the story of how Xerxes found in Lydia a plane tree which because of its beauty he decked with gold ornaments and entrusted to a guardian. He also cites Aelian, *Variae Historiae*, ii. 14, who ascribes Xerxes' passion to the tree's size. In popular encyclopedias, such as Maplet's *A Greene Forrest*, 1567, and Swan's *Speculum Mundi*, 1635, the story is taken from Aelian and the tree's size is insisted on. Mrs. Duncan-Jones (*N. and Q.*, February 1960) explained the reference to the 'barrennesse' of the plane-tree, an idea found in William Browne's *Britannia's Pastorals* (book ii, song iv) as well as here. She quotes Evelyn (*Sylva*, 1664, II. iv) as saying of the plane 'I know it was anciently accounted ἄκαρπος', citing a Greek author in support. She suggests that Donne and Browne were probably familiar with the idea from the *Georgics* (ii. 69–70):

                   inseritur vero et fetu nucis arbutus horrida,
                   et steriles platani malos gessere valentes.

For a fuller discussion see R. L. Sharp (*N. and Q.*, June 1962) who suggests that the pseudo-Aristotelian *De Mundo* (*c.* vi) is the ultimate authority for the notion that the plane is *akarpos* or *sterilis*.

Donne's argument is that Xerxes loved the plane either for its age which he deduced from its huge size, or because, though young, it possessed the attribute of age, barrenness. Gosse absurdly misread the passage as implying that the lady was 'not so slender' as she had been (ii. 229).

l. 44. *Antiques*. The jest requires the plural noun rather than the adjective 'Antique' (*1633*, I), which may have arisen as a correction of 'Antiquityes' (*H 40*) or by attraction to 'Ancient'. The attraction has worked the other way in *Lut, O'F* which read 'Ancients . . . Antiques'.

The 'living Deaths-heads' are not merely ancient, they are grotesques. 'Antic' (from Italian *antico*) and 'antique' (from Latin *antiquus*) were spelt alike at this period and both were stressed on the first syllable. Originally used as an architectural term, equivalent to 'grotesque', 'antic' came to be applied to those who performed grotesque roles. Death's heads grin like antics. Cf. Shakespeare's reference to Death in *Richard II*, III. ii. 162:

> And there the antic sits
> Scoffing his state and grinning at his pomp.

l. 47. *naturall lation*. The obsolete astronomical term 'lation', for the movement of a body from one place to another, caused trouble to many scribes. *HK 2, O*, and *P* read 'natur-alation', *S* reads 'Naturallatyon', and *JC* gives up and leaves a blank after 'naturall'. The reading 'natural statyon' (*C 57, Lec, Dob, Lut, O'F*) is plainly a misreading of an unfamiliar word and gives a sense opposite to that required. 'Motion natural' (*1633*) has no manuscript support. We may assume it to be a shot at sense made by the editor faced with 'natural statyon' in his Group I manuscript. He either did not consult his Group II manuscript, or, if he did, made no sense of 'lation'.

l. 50. *ebbe on*. 'Ebbe out' (*1633*) looks like a substitution of a more familiar phrase for the reading in the text which is found in all manuscripts.

SONGS AND SONNETS

MSS.: *H 40*; Group I (*C 57, D, H 49, Lec, SP*); *L 74*; Group II (*A 18, N, TCC, TCD*); *DC*; Group III (*Dob, Lut, O'F, S 96*); *HK 2, Cy, O, P; A 25, B, D 17, JC, K, S.*
Miscellanies: *S 962*.

The number of lyrics present in these twenty-six collections of Donne's poems varies from the full fifty-four (found in *O'F* alone) to twenty-five. For convenience I have added to the collections one large miscellany, *S 962*, since it contains forty-nine. The presence or absence of a poem from any of these twenty-seven manuscripts is noted at the beginning of the commentary on that poem. When a poem is present in the great majority the formula '*Σ* — . . .' is used. When a poem is found in only a few manuscripts those in which it appears are listed, followed by the formula 'omit *Σ*'. On a few occasions when the manuscripts divide evenly a full list is given. The presence of a poem in a miscellany other than *S 962* is also noted at the beginning of the commentary on that poem.

All but two of the *Songs and Sonnets* were printed in *1633*, forty-four from a manuscript closely resembling *C 57* and *Lec*, and eight from a manuscript of

Group II. Whoever prepared the copy for *1633* adopted most of the titles found in Group II and at times adopted readings from his Group II manuscript into the text of poems taken from his Group I manuscript. He also made a certain number of corrections apparently on his own judgement. The evidence that leads me to regard the text of *1633* as sophisticated, is set out in the Textual Introduction, pp. lxxxvi–lxxxviii. Departures from the text of *1633* and occasions where my text differs from Grierson's are summarized in a textual note at the beginning of the commentary on each poem where attention is also called to readings that receive discussion.

No general title was given to the lyrics in the edition of 1633. The title 'Songs and Sonets', under which they were collected in the second edition of 1635, was adapted from the heading 'Sonnets and Songes' which *O'F* (the main source of the additional poems in the second edition) took from its parent manuscript *Lut*. It signified simply 'love lyrics'. Few of the individual lyrics have titles, and fewer still the same title, in all manuscripts. Textual analysis suggests that Donne did not normally give his lyrics any title and that we owe the majority of the established titles to whoever compiled the collection in the Group II manuscripts. Titles found in manuscript are given in the apparatus. If a manuscript is not cited as having a title it should be assumed that the poem appears there without title or with a mere heading such as 'Song', 'Sonnet', or 'Elegy'.

The poems are printed here in two groups and arranged within these groups so as to bring together poems linked by theme, metrical form, and style. Arguments for thus dividing the lyrics and for dating the first group before 1600 and the second after 1602 are given in the essay on 'The Canon and Date of the *Songs and Sonnets*', pp. li–lxii. For a justification for a rearrangement of the poems on grounds of convenience, see pp. v–vi.

SONGS AND SONNETS

(I)

Song (p. 29.)

MSS.: *Σ — K*.

Miscellanies: *Grey, Hol, RP 117 (2)*; Brit. Mus. MSS. *Add. 5956, Egerton 2013*; Bodleian MS. *Eng. Poet e 37*; Folger MSS. *V a 103* and *162*; Rosenbach MS. *243/4.*

I agree with Grierson in retaining, but with some misgiving, the reading of *1633* in l. 11; see note.

There is a good deal of trivial and erroneous variation in the manuscripts outside Groups I and II. Group III adds 'grace notes' to avoid medial hiatus in ll. 21 and 24; and *JC* (with *D 17*) has a variant text, reading in ll. 5–8

> Who ever heard a Mermayd singing
> Or found a cure for Envies stinging
>   Let him finde
>   What winde . . .;

in l. 13

> Till age white hayre doe strawe . . .;

in l. 14

> And thou returnst come tell me . . .;

and in ll. 23–27

> Though shee were true when you last met her
> And last so till yow had writt your letter
>   Yet shee
>   Would bee
> False ere I came. . . .

The weakening of the emphatic stress in the first verse and the destruction of the metre in ll. 23–24 make it impossible to regard these variants as anything but corruptions, probably memorial in origin. There are similar variants in the song 'Sweetest Love, I do not goe'; see notes.

   Grierson noted a poem modelled on Donne's and ascribed to him in MS. Harleian 6057 which was printed in *The Treasury of Music. By Mr. Lawes and others* (1669):

> Goe catch a star that's falling from the sky
> Cause an immortal creature for to die;
> Stop with thy hand the current of the seas,
> Post ore the earth to the Antipodes;
> Cause times return and call back yesterday,
> Cloake January with the month of May;
>   Weigh out an ounce of flame, blow backe the winde
>   And then find faith within a womans minde.

There is a similar poem, called 'Impossibilities', ascribed to 'John Coventry' in MS. Ashmole 47 (no. 132), and printed in the 1637 edition of Camden's *Remains* (p. 417):

> Embrace a sunbeam and on it
> The shadow of a cloud beget. . . .

The listing of impossibilities (*adunata*) is a well-known device in classical poetry, usually going with oaths of fidelity in the formula 'Sooner will . . .'; see Propertius, II. xv. 29–36 and Ovid, *Tristia*, I. viii. 1–10, imitated in 'The Expostulation', ll. 27–32.

   For the theme of the poem, cf. Nashe, *Anatomy of Absurdity* (1588):

Democritus accounted a faire chaste woman a miracle of miracles, a degree of immortality, a crowne of tryumph, because shee is so harde to be founde (*Works*, i. 13).

McKerrow was unable to find a source for this apothegm. For a reply to Donne's poem see William Habington, *Castara, the Second Part*, 1635, 'Against them who lay Unchastity to the Sex of Women'.

For a setting of the poem, see Appendix B, 'Musical Settings of Donne's Poems'. In spite of having been set it does not appear to have circulated widely in manuscript. The first two stanzas were, however, printed in the *Poems* of Francis Beaumont (1653) under the heading 'A Song'.

l. 1. *Goe, and catche a falling starre.* Cf. the Somerset Epithalamium, ll. 204–5:

> As he that sees a starre fall, runs apace,
> And findes a gellie in the place. . . .

l. 2. *Get with child a mandrake roote.* The mandrake had a forked root and was thus held to resemble the human form. It was valued in antiquity as a soporific, an aphrodisiac, and a promoter of fertility in women. Donne in 'The Progress of the Soul' (Stanza XV) adds a further property when he declares

> His apples kindle, his leaves, force of conception kill.

See D. C. Allen, 'Donne on the Mandrake', *M.L.N.* lxxiv, 1959, for information on the lore of the mandrake.

l. 11. *to see. 1633* appears to have made an obvious correction of the defective line in Groups I and II. The true reading has possibly been preserved in Group III (*Dob, S 96*) which reads 'goe see', giving an imperative to balance 'Ride': 'If you are already gifted with the power to see marvels, go and see the invisible.' The manuscripts that agree with *1633* may do so accidentally through having made the same correction in the defective line in Group II with which they are all textually connected.

ll. 12–13. Miss K. M. Lea (*Elizabethan and Jacobean Studies*, 1959, pp. 51–52) has suggested this may be an echo of *Orlando Furioso*, xxvii. 123–4, where Rodomonte rails at the inconstancy of women and the poet intervenes to say that he is sure good women can be found but none have so far come his way. Still he will not give up and before he dies, before more white hairs come, he will continue his search in the hope that one day he will be able to say that one woman has kept her word.

l. 23. The tune makes the point:

$$\overset{/}{\text{Though}}\ \overset{\times}{\text{shee}}\ |\ \overset{/}{\text{were}}\ \overset{\times}{\text{true,}}\ |\ \overset{/}{\text{when}}\ \overset{\times}{\text{you}}\ |\ \overset{/}{\text{met}}\ \overset{\times}{\text{her.}}$$

The Message (p. 30)

MSS.: *Σ* — *H 40, L 74, K.*
Miscellanies: *CCC, Hd, HK 2*, La, RP 117 (2), Wel*; Brit. Mus. MSS. *Add. 10309* and *19268, Egerton 2421*; Bodleian MS. *Eng. Poet. e 37*; Emmanuel Coll. MS. *1 3 16*; Camb. Univ. Lib. MS. *Ee V 23*; Folger MSS. *V a 103* and *339*; Rosenbach MS. *243/4*.

I agree with Grierson in rejecting *1633* in l. 14; but differ from him in retaining its reading in l. 11; see notes.

The absence of this poem from the key collections in *H 40* and *L 74* may account for some variation from the normal manuscript groupings, *Cy* not agreeing here with *O*, *P*.

For a setting of the poem see Appendix B, 'Musical Settings of Donne's Poems'.

l. 11. *Which if it be taught by thine.* I retain, against Grierson, the reading of *1633* (I, II, *Dob*, *S 96*, *Cy*, *S*). Grierson adopted the reading of *Lut*, *O'F*, 'But if . . .'. He refused to believe that Donne could have written 'Which', and declared roundly: 'If "But" is not Donne's own reading or emendation it ought to be, and I am loath to spoil a charming poem by pedantic adherence to authority in so small a point.' It is impossible, having regard to the agreement of I, II, *Dob*, *S 96*, to regard 'But' as anything but an emendation in *Lut* to avoid the repetition that Grierson disliked. The remaining manuscripts rewrite the line to make it conform to l. 3, *HK 2* and *A 25* showing a first stage in a process completed in *P*, *B*, *JC*.

l. 14. *crosse.* I agree with Grierson in adopting the reading of all the manuscripts for 'breake' (*1633*). Possibly the editor misguidedly took 'crosse' as having some religious significance and played for safety in substituting 'breake'.

l. 19. *laugh and joy, when.* *1633* here adopts the reading of Group II, supported by *P*, *B*, *JC*. It is certainly preferable to the lame reading of Group I, *Dob*, *S 96*, *Cy*, *S*: 'laugh when that thou'. *Lut*, *O'F* read 'joy and laugh' and *HK 2* has an attractive but obviously unauthoritative reading 'lie and laugh'. It would seem that all manuscripts outside Group II, *P*, *B*, *JC* depend upon an exemplar in which 'and joy' had been dropped or was illegible. *Lut*, *O'F* supply the words but transpose the verbs, *HK 2* makes a brilliant shot, while Group I makes a weak patch.

Song (p. 31)

MSS.: *Σ — L 74*, *Cy*.
Miscellanies: *Hd*, *HK 2**, *La*, *RP 117 (2)*, *Wel*; Brit. Mus. MS. *Harleian 6918*; Bodleian MS. *Eng. Poet. e 14*; Folger MS. *V a 103*; Harvard MS. *Eng. 626 F.* Rosenbach MS. *1083/16*.

In both Group I and Group II the first four lines of each stanza are written as two long lines and the sixth and seventh as one. I have not undone the work of the editor of *1633* as his setting brings out the rhyme scheme.

As in the 'Mandrake' song *JC* (with *D 17*) has variants that are patently the result of memorial corruption, reading in ll. 14–15

Since (Dearest) I doe make
Speedier iourneyes and doe take . . .;

and in ll. 17–19

> Oh how feeble is mans powre
> If that his fortune fall?
> It cannot add another howre . . .;

and in l. 40 'separated' for 'parted'. The presence of variants of this type makes me unwilling to consider seriously any readings in *JC*, however plausible, that are unsupported in the main groups.

Walton, in describing Donne's parting from his wife in 1611, puts words from this poem into her mouth, declaring that she said 'her divining soul boded her some ill in his absence'. This is an example of his skill in using phrases from Donne's works rather than a reason for dating the poem.

For contemporary settings, see Appendix B, 'Musical Settings of Donne's Poems'.

ll. 6–8. The reading of *Lut, O'F* is a good example of intelligent editing in *Lut*, since it makes the first stanza correspond to the others. *1635* adopted this reading from *O'F*, but *1669* reverted to the reading of *1633*.

ll. 21–24. 'But if misfortune come we side with it and teach it how to protract itself, so that it triumphs over us.'

ll. 25–32. In both Greek and Latin the same word ('psyche' or 'anima') means either 'breath' or 'soul', so that the notion of the soul being breathed out in sighs is natural in classical poets. That sighs 'waste life' is an old belief, sometimes found in the form that each sigh costs a drop of blood; cf. 'blood-consuming sighs', 'blood-drinking sighs', and 'blood-sucking sighs' (*2 Henry VI*, III. ii. 61 and 63, and *3 Henry VI*, IV. iv. 22).

l. 32. *the best of mee*: my life, my soul.

l. 33. *thy divining heart*. Cf. Juliet's 'O God, I have an ill-divining soul!' (*Romeo and Juliet*, III. v. 54) and note on the Elegy 'On his Mistress', l. 55 (p. 143).

The Baite (p. 32)

MSS.: *Σ — L 74, Dob, A 25, B, K, S.*
Miscellanies: *Grey, HK 2*, La, RP 117* (2); Brit. Mus. MSS. *Add. 19268, Harleian 3511, Sloane 542*; Bodleian MSS. *Ash. 47, Eng. Poet. e 97, Rawl. Poet. 84*; Folger MS. *V a 96*; Huntington MS. *HM 172*; Rosenbach MS. *243/4*.

1633 has two obvious misprints: ll. 18 and 23. I differ from Grierson in adopting a manuscript reading in l. 6; see note.

Marlowe's 'The Passionate Shepherd to his Love' was printed (stanzas 1, 2, 3, and 5 only) in *The Passionate Pilgrim*, 1599, and in six stanzas in *England's Helicon*, 1600, where it is followed by 'The Nymph's Reply', generally accepted as Raleigh's. Donne's imitation may be inspired by two verses in an anonymous parody of Marlowe's poem which follows 'The Nymph's Reply' in *England's Helicon* and is, like it, ascribed to 'Ignoto':

> The seate for your disport shall be
> Over some River in a tree,
> Where silver sands, and pebbles sing,
> Eternall ditties with the spring.
>
> There shall you see the Nimphs at play,
> And how the Satires spend the day,
> The fishes gliding on the sands:
> Offering their bellies to your hands.

Walton, in *The Compleat Angler* (1653), makes his milkmaid sing Marlowe's song and her mother sing Raleigh's answer. Later he puts 'The Bait' into the mouth of Venator as

a Coppie of Verses that were made by Doctor *Donne*, and made to shew the world that hee could make soft and smooth Verses, when he thought them fit and worth his labour.

The text, as in poems quoted in *The Life of Donne*, has variants that we must ascribe to Walton's inaccuracy or invention.

For the tune Donne's poem was written to, given in Corkine's *Second Book of Airs*, 1612, see Appendix B, 'Musical Settings of Donne's Poems'.

l. 6. In spite of poor manuscript authority I adopt 'thine' as it is in accordance with Donne's practice to avoid the hiatus in 'thy eye'.

l. 22. *out-wrest*: drag out.

l. 23. *curious*: exquisitely made.

sleave-silke: silk capable of being 'sleaved', that is, divided into fine filaments to make artificial flies.

Communitie (p. 33)

MSS.: *Σ* — *A 25*, *D 17*, *JC*.
Miscellanies: *Hd*, *HK 1*, *TCD* (2); Brit. Mus. MS. *Egerton 2230*.

I agree with Grierson in rejecting *1633* in l. 3 where it follows Group I in error; but differ from him in adopting the reading of the great majority of manuscripts in l. 21.

Although the point made is different, this paradoxical song recalls the fourth Paradox, 'That good is more common than evill':

And of *indifferent* things many things are become perfectly good by being *common*, as *customes* by use are made binding *Lawes*. But I remember nothing that is therefore *ill*, because it is *common*, but *Women*, of whom also; *They that are most common, are the best of that Occupation they professe.*

l. 5. *prove*: test.

l. 6. *fancy*: amorous inclination.

l. 14. *Good is as visible as greene.* Visibility, according to Aristotle, depends on colour, and 'green' is presumably chosen as the commonest colour in nature. Cf. Paradox 4, where 'good' is said to have 'this for *nature* and *perfection* to bee *common*. . . . It dares appeare and spread, and glister in the *World*, but *evill* buries it selfe in night and darknesse.'

Confined Love (p. 34)

MSS.: *Σ* — *H 40, S 96, A 25, K.*
Miscellanies: *HK 1.*

I differ from Grierson in adopting the reading of all the manuscripts in l. 6. Groups I and II agree in an obviously wrong tense in l. 12 and l. 17. The editor of *1633* rightly corrected his manuscript sources on both occasions.

Like the next poem this is spoken by a woman and, though no setting has been found, is a song. It can only be scanned with a strongly marked tune in mind. It is appropriate that Donne should put this piece of frank naturalism into a woman's mouth, for the literary origin of this line of argument is Myrrha's speech in Ovid's *Metamorphoses* (x. 320–55):

> coeunt animalia nullo
> cetera dilectu, nec habetur turpe iuvencae
> ferre patrem tergo, fit equo sua filia coniunx,
> quasque creavit init pecudes caper, ipsaque, cuius
> semine concepta est, ex illo concipit ales (324–28).

Breake of Day (p. 35)

MSS.: *Σ* — *Cy, O, K.*
Miscellanies: *Grey, HK 2*, Hol, RP 117 (2), Wel*; Brit. Mus. MSS. *Add. 10309, 15227, 19268,* and *30982, Egerton 2230, Harleian 3511* and *4888, Sloane 542*; Bodleian MSS. *Don d 58, Eng. Poet. f 25*; Folger MS. *V a 103*; Harvard MS. *Eng. 686*; Rosenbach MS. *243/4.*

There are two traditions here, one found in *H 40* and Group I and the other in *L 74*, Group II and *HK 2* with its dependants. (The Group III manuscripts do not read together.) *1633* follows Group I, except in l. 2 where it supplies 'therefore' from Group II and in l. 5 where it corrects an error common to Groups I and II. Since there seems no reason for preferring one tradition to the other, I retain with Grierson the text of *1633*.

In *S 96* the first stanza is preceded by a stanza beginning 'Stay, oh sweet, and do not rise' (printed among the *Dubia* on p. 108). The same stanza is written in the margin against 'Break of Day' in *A 25*, with a mark to show it should appear as the first stanza of the poem. It was so printed in *1669*. It occurs also alone in manuscripts containing Donne's poems. It was printed, as the first stanza of a poem in two stanzas, in 1612 in Dowland's *A Pilgrim's Solace*, and alone, in the same year, in Orlando Gibbon's *Madrigals and Motets*. Whether or not Donne wrote it, it cannot be combined with 'Break of Day'; its metre is different and it is spoken by a man.

'Break of Day' is spoken by a woman and is thus in the tradition of popular, not courtly, song. It descends from the Provençal *aube*, the dialogue of lovers parted by the dawn.

For the setting in William Corkine's *Second Book of Airs*, 1612, see Appendix B, 'Musical Settings of Donne's Poems'.

ll. 9–12. *were . . . lov'd . . . had.* It seems more probable that the subjunctive after a conditional clause and the past tenses of indirect speech preserving sequence would be changed in transmission to the present 'is . . . love . . . hath' (*L 74*, II, *HK 2*, &c.) than that the reverse change should take place.

ll. 13–18. *Must businesse thee from hence remove,* &c. Grierson quotes:

It is a good definition of ill love, that St. *Chrysostom* gives, that it is *Animae vacantis passio*, a passion of an empty soul, of an idle mind. For fill a man with business, and he hath no room for such love (*Sermons*, iv. 121).

The Computation (p. 36)

MSS.: *Σ* — *H 40*, Group I, *L 74*, *S 96*, *Cy*, *A 25*, *D 17*, *JC*.

This and the following two poems, love-epigrams on the theme of parting, are not in the manuscripts of Group I or collections of Donne's lyrics in *H 40* and *L 74*. The editor of *1633* could have found all three in his Group II manuscript.

The Group II manuscripts preserve a distinct text of this poem which employs the familiar second person singular instead of the plural. Although Donne varies a good deal between 'thou' and 'you', sometimes (as in 'The Flea') varying within a single poem, in the songs and epigrams he habitually uses 'thou'. I retain, with Grierson, the text of *1633* which follows Group II, except that it supplies l. 7 which is missing in the extant Group II manuscripts.

The sum works out at 2,400 years, that is, a hundred years for each hour since they parted.

l. 8. In the last thousand years even the thought of her was forgotten, being too distant for recollection.

ll. 9–10. Since he died at the moment of their parting he lives on immortally as a mere ghost.

The Expiration (p. 37)

MSS.: *Σ* — *H 40*, Group I, *L 74*, *Cy*.
Miscellanies: *CCC*, *Hd*, *Hol*; Bodleian MSS. *Eng. Poet. c 50*, *Mus. School F 575*.

1633 reads with Group II against the majority of other manuscripts in ll. 1, 4 (*bis*), and 9; see notes.

For the setting in Ferrabosco's *Airs*, 1609, see Appendix B, 'Musical Settings of Donne's Poems'. This is the earliest appearance of one of Donne's poems in print.

l. 1. *breake*. *1633* follows Group II, which has the support of *D 17*, *JC* only. The text that Ferrabosco set agrees with all the other manuscripts in reading 'leave'. 'Breake' is the more powerful word; but 'leave' is the more musical, giving extra, though perhaps excessive, alliteration in the first line.

l. 2. *sucks two soules, and vapors both away*. Cf. a Verse-Letter to Wotton (Grierson, i. 180): 'Sir, more then kisses, letters mingle Soules.' The notion that the soul is in the breath (see note to 'Sweetest Love, I do not goe', p. 155) leads naturally to the notion that kisses mingle souls. For many examples of this conceit in classical poetry, see S. Gaselee, 'The Soul in the Kiss', *Criterion*, April 1924, where the first example cited is an epigram ascribed to Plato (*Greek Anthology*, v. 78) quoted with a paraphrase by Aulus Gellius. Donne refers to this in a sermon on the text 'Kiss the Son, lest he be angry':

> As in death there is a transmigration of the soule, so in this spirituall love, and this expressing of it, by this kisse, there is a transfusion of the soule too: And as we find in *Gellius* a Poem of *Platoes*, where he sayes he knew one so extremely passionate, *Ut parum affuit quin moreretur in osculo*, much more it is true in this heavenly union, expressed in this kisse, as S. *Ambrose* delivers it, *Per osculum adhæret anima Deo, et transfunditur spiritus osculantis* (*Sermons*, iii. 320).

The only English example of the conceit before Donne that Gaselee gives is from Marlowe's *Dr. Faustus*:

> Sweet Helen, make me immortal with a kiss.—
> Her lips suck forth my soul: see where it flies!—
> Come, Helen, come, give me my soul again.

l. 4. *our selves . . . happiest*. 'Sowles' (III) is an obvious error, the word having been caught from l. 2. It seems to have arisen independently in other manuscripts, since *HK 2*, on which *O* and *P* usually depend, reads 'selves' with Group II. 'Happiest' (*1633*, II) may be only a scribal or memorial strengthening of 'happy'.

l. 5. *ask'd*. The agreement of Groups II and III establishes this reading. 'Aske' (*1633*, *HK 2*, &c.) has probably arisen from misreading of 'd' as 'e', which is easy in secretary hand.

l. 9. *Oh*. This reading (*1633*, II, *D 17*, *JC*) seems preferable to the purely logical 'Or'. It is more in keeping with the emotional tone of the poem and repeats its dominant vowel.

Witchcraft by a Picture (p. 37)

MSS.: *Σ* — *H 40*, Group I, *L 74*, *A 25*, *K*, *S*.
Miscellanies: *Grey, Hol., H 40*, RP 31*.

Since this is one of the poems common to *H 40** and *RP 31* (see Textual Introduction, p. lxv) I do not count it as one of the collection of lyrics incorporated in *H 40*.

ll. 1–7. Cf.

So we have used the image of God, as witches are said to do the images of men; by wounding or defacing the image, they destroy the person (*Sermons, i.* 160).

The conceit that the lover's image reflected in his mistress's eye is drowned by a tear is elaborated in 'A Valediction of Weeping'.

l. 8. *sweet salt teares*. Cf. 'The Anniversary', l. 16. It is possible that 'sweetest' (III, *HK 2*, &c.) is the true reading and that 'sweet salt' (*1633*, II, *B*, *S*) is due to reminiscence of the line in 'The Anniversary'.

A Jeat Ring Sent (p. 38)

MSS.: Group II, *Lut, O'F, W, S 962*: omit *Σ*.
Miscellanies: Brit. Mus. MSS. *Add. 21433* and *25303*; Harvard MS. *Eng. 686*.

This is the only one of the *Songs and Sonnets* to be found in the Westmoreland manuscript, Rowland Woodward's copy of Donne's poems. It occurs together with a verse-letter to Woodward ('If as mine is, thy life a slumber be') in MS. Add. *25303*. As, apart from the two sets of 'Holy Sonnets', all the poems in *W* are poems that can be dated with varying degrees of certainty before 1598, it seems safe to regard this poem as an early one.

In *Every Man in his Humour*, II. iv. 35, Stephen, the gull, is distressed at losing his purse because it contained 'the jet ring mistris Mary sent me'. Jet was a favourite material for cheap rings which were often lined with silver for posies to be engraved; see 'Posies for a jet ring lined with silver' in Manningham's *Diary*, ed. J. Bruce, 1868, p. 83.

l. 1. *so black*: so constant. Cf. the proverb 'Black can take no other hue'.

l. 8. *fling me'away*. To 'jet', meaning to 'throw, cast, or toss' (*O.E.D.*, 'jet', vb. 2, II.3) is the first element in 'jettison' and 'jetsam'.

The Paradox (p. 38)

MSS.; *L 74*, Group II, *Lut, O'F, S 96, S, S 962*: omit *Σ*.
Miscellanies: *Hd, HK 1, H 40*, RP 31*.

1633 follows Group II in error in ll. 14 and 20.

This poem is comparatively rare in manuscript. It usually occurs with, or close to, a very similar poem 'Who so termes Love a fire'. In the Group II manuscripts 'No Lover saith, I love' occurs without title, followed immediately by this second poem, called 'A Paradox'. In *Lut, O'F* 'No Lover saith, I love' occurs among the *Songs and Sonnets* and the other poem occurs among the miscellaneous poems in couplet (many spurious) which *Lut, O'F* include as *Elegies*. In *HK 1* both poems occur in the second collection of poems marked by the mysterious initials 'L. C.', most of which are by Donne (see Textual Introduction, p. lxxix). Both are included in the miscellany common to *H 40** and *RP 31*, the first being untitled, as in Group II, and the second called 'A Paradox. Love is no fier'. I give the text of the second poem from *TCD*.

> Who so termes Loue a fire, may like a Poet
> Faine what hee will, for certaine cannot showe it.
> For fire nere burnes, but when the fuell's neare
> But Loue doth at most distance most appeare.
> Yet out of fire water did neuer goe
> But teares from loue aboundantlie doe flowe.
> Fire still mounts vpward; but Loue ofte descendeth:
> Fire leaues the midd'st: Loue to the Center tendeth.
> Fire dryes, and hardens: Loue doth mollifie.
> Fire doth consume, but loue doth fructifie.
>   The powerfull Queene of Loue faire Venus came
> Descended from the Sea, not from the flame;
> Whence passions ebb and flowe, and from the braine
> Run to the heart like streames, and back againe.
> Yea Loue ofte fills mens breasts with melting snowe
> Drowning their Loue-sick minds in flouds of woe.
> What is Loue water then? it may bee soe;
>   But he saith truth, who saith hee doth not knowe.

The two poems, linked by manuscript tradition, are linked by theme and manner. Possibly they are rival attempts by Donne and a friend to write paradoxes to prove that 'Love cannot be known': the one arguing that since Love slays and dead men tell no tales, nobody can know what Love is; the other that the most common description of it is plainly false but its opposite is unprovable. The superior vivacity of 'No Lover saith, I love' justifies the editor of *1633* in printing it and in rejecting its fellow.

ll. 1–6. No true lover talks about his love and no outsider can judge it, for every lover thinks that nobody else can love as he does. Since love kills, nobody can say he *did* love. The dead do not speak.

l. 10. *he that saith twice*: he that says we die twice. The syntax of this poem is notably compressed.

l. 14. *the lights life*: the sun, the source of light.

l. 20. *I lye*. The point of the jest, that he is merely an epitaph and tomb and the possible pun (that he is still not telling the truth) is lost if we read 'dye' (*1633*, *L 74*, *TC*, *S*).

The Prohibition (p. 39)

MSS.: *Σ — H 40, C 57, Lec, L 74, A 25, K, S*.
Miscellanies: *CCC, Hd, HK 1, H 40*, RP 31*.

I agree with Grierson in adopting manuscript readings in ll. 5, 18, and 22, though I differ from him in the punctuation of l. 22: I differ from him in preferring manuscript readings in ll. 23–24; see notes.

The poem is missing in *C 57, Lec*, the Group I manuscripts nearest to that used for *1633*. As the edition prints not only the third stanza but also l. 5, both of which are missing in the Group II manuscripts, the compiler of *1633* either had at his disposal a third manuscript (in addition to his Group I manuscript and the Group II manuscript by which he supplemented it) or his Group II manuscript had been corrected.

The third stanza is omitted in Group II, *Dob* and *S 96*. It appears in *B* headed 'T. R.', the first two stanzas being headed 'J. D.'; and in *Hd* the first two stanzas are headed 'J. D.' but the third is headed 'Answeare'. It is possible that Donne wrote an epigrammatic poem in two stanzas and that 'T. R.' 'capped' it by resolving the dilemma they posed. 'T. R.' is probably Sir Thomas Roe to whom poems are ascribed in manuscript. He is suggested as the author of 'The Expostulation' in *O'F* and, according to a note in *C 57*, 'A Litany' was 'To Sir Thomas Roe'.

l. 5. This line is missing in Group II and in those Group I manuscripts (*D, H 49, SP*) that include the poem. In most of the manuscripts that preserve it there is an obvious error (*mee* for *thee*) which *1633*, in its lame version, incorporated.

l. 11. *officer*: executioner.

ll. 13–14. She will lose the glory of leading him captive.

l. 18. *neythers*. The reading of *1633, HK 2, P, B*, 'ne'r their', is an obvious misreading of 'neyther' which *Cy* has unmetrically emended, the writer recognizing that the sense required 'neither' or 'neither's'.

l. 22. *So shall I live, thy Stage, not Triumph bee*. Grierson took 'live' as a shortened form of 'alive' and punctuated 'So shall I, live, . . .'. It seems simpler to take it as a verb, cognate with 'bee'.

If he lives he will be the stage on which she can perpetually display her power over him instead of triumphing once and for all. The culmination of a Roman Triumph was the slaughter of the captives.

ll. 23–24.   *Then, least thy love, hate and mee thou undoe,*
    Oh let mee live, yet love and hate mee too.

Grierson retained the reading of *1633* which has the support of *HK 2, P, B.* These are in general unreliable manuscripts. The reading I adopt is that of the better manuscripts and makes the final couplet repeat the formula of the final couplets of the first and second stanzas. Each of the first two stanzas ends with a couplet beginning with the words 'Then, least . . .' and ending with the opening line of its stanza.

The Curse (p. 40)

MSS.: *Σ — S 96, Cy.* Also in *Q* (Queen's College, Oxford, MS.), following the *Satires,* 'The Storm' and 'The Calm'.
Miscellanies: Grey, *Hd, HK 1, HK 2*, RP 117* (2); Brit. Mus. MS. *Egerton 2230;* Bodleian MS. *Ash. 38;* Emmanuel Coll. MS. *1 3 16.*

I agree with Grierson in correcting *1633* in l. 27 where it reads singular for plural; but differ from him in making a similar correction in l. 9.

Two authentic versions of ll. 14–16 are preserved in the manuscripts. For discussion of them see note.

'The Curse' appears as a single lyric in the Queen's College, Oxford, manuscript of the *Satires* and also appears at the beginning of *HK 1,* attached to 'The Bracelet', among a collection of poems by miscellaneous authors. These appearances are consistent with the date we should assign to it on internal evidence. Its affinities are with the *Satires* and the *Elegies.* It is on a classical model to which Puttenham devoted a chapter: 'A certaine auncient forme of poesie by which men did use to reproch their enemies' (I. xxix). The chapter concludes: 'They were called *Dirae,* such as *Virgill* made against *Battarus,* and *Ovide* against *Ibis.*' Characteristically, Donne employs this classical form on a stock medieval theme, cursing that bugbear of the courtly lover the *losengour* or tale-bearer. See R. A. Bryan, 'John Donne's Use of the Anathema', *J.E.G.P.,* 1962, for examples of religious cursing.

There is an 'Answere to Dr. Donne's curse' in MS. Rawlinson Poetical 147 (f. 83), printed in the works of William Browne of Tavistock, ed. Goodwin, 1894, ii. 197.

Title. Except for *HK 2,* all manuscripts give this poem a title: 'The Curse', 'A Curse', and 'Dirae' (*O, P,* and Q).

ll. 3–5. The sense required is 'May the little money he has and only that money incline some creature unapt for love to love him'; but the word

order would make 'some dull heart' the subject of 'may dispose'. In this case
'dispose' must be used intransitively with a passive or reflexive sense: 'May
some dull heart dispose itself to love his little money and only his money.'

l. 12. *fame*: reputation. 'Shame' (*L 74*, *TCC*) gives easier sense, since we can
feel a 'touch of shame' as of 'conscience'. But it looks like a sophistication of
a difficult reading, influenced by the occurrence of 'shame' in l. 8.

'May he feel no wound in his conscience, but only in his reputation.' He is
not to have the benefit of repentance.

ll. 14–16.   *In early and long scarcenesse may he rot,*
                    For land which had been his, if he had not
                    Himselfe incestuously an heire begot:

                                        (*1633*, H 40, Group I, *Dob*, B)

All other manuscripts read:

                    Or may he for her vertue reverence
                    One, that hates him onlie for impotence,
                    And equall traytors be shee and his sence.

There can be no doubt that both versions are Donne's. It seems probable that
the second is the earlier. It is the version found in *Q* and *HK 1* where 'The
Curse' appears as a solitary lyric circulating with the *Satires* in the one
case and 'The Bracelet' in the other. Also the last words recall a theme of
Latin Elegy; cf. Ovid, *Amores*, III. vii, and the equally indecent fifth Elegy of
Maximian.

I can suggest no source for the version that appears in *1633*; but the situation Donne wishes for is referred to by Marston in his tenth Satire, 'To his
very friend, Master E. G.', added in the second edition of *The Scourge of
Villainy* in 1599:

              And tell me, Ned, what might that gallant be,
              Who, to obtain intemperate luxury,
              Cuckolds his elder brother, gets an heir,
              By which his hope is turned to despair?
              In faith (good Ned) he damn'd himself with cost;
              For well thou know'st full goodly land was lost.
                                        (*Works*, ed. Bullen, 1887, iii. 368.)

The most recent editor of *The Scourge of Villainy*, Mr. Arnold Davenport,
cannot propose a classical source and suggests that this is a topical reference
to a current scandal. This seems improbable as Marston uses the same situation later in his play *The Fawn* (printed 1606), where Herod Frappatore
cuckolds his elder brother, Sir Amoroso Debile-Dosso, and by getting his wife
with child loses the inheritance he had hoped for (Bullen, ii. 184–5). This
rather sordid example of a biter bit seems a little too neat for real life. (A
modern novelist, Miss Compton-Burnett, has built a novel, *A Heritage and its
History*, 1959, on a similar situation.) I would suggest the situation originated
in the satiric imagination of Donne and that Marston took it from him.

Edward Guilpin (the E. G. to whom Marston dedicated his Satire) imitated Donne's *Satires* in his *Skialetheia*, 1598, and may well have been the intermediary by whom a copy of 'The Curse' came into Marston's hands. If this suggestion were accepted it would date the poem as written before 1599 and provide us with our earliest allusion to one of the *Songs and Sonnets*.

l. 22. *Parasites*. Like the legacy-hunters and the slave expecting freedom in 'Jealousy', these 'parasites' come from the satirists' Rome rather than Elizabethan London.

l. 24. *be circumcis'd for bread*. There are many references to men captured by the Barbary pirates being forced by necessity to 'turn Turk'; but this seems more probably to refer to currying favour with Jewish money-lenders. They, like 'parasites', were not a feature of the Elizabethan scene.

The Indifferent (p. 41)

MSS.: Σ — *L 74*, *Cy*, *A 25*.
Miscellanies: *Hd*; Brit. Mus. MS. *Add. 10309*; Folger MS. *V a 162*.

1633 adopts a reading from Group II in l. 12 and retains a reading of Group I in l. 21, on both occasions printing a line that is two syllables longer than the corresponding line in the first stanza. I differ from Grierson in rejecting *1633* on both occasions. In l. 23 *1633* reads with Group III against Groups I and II and, with Grierson, I retain it, but with some misgivings; see notes.

l. 1. *I can love*, &c. Cf. Ovid, *Amores*, II. iv.

l. 12. *Have you old vices spent*, &c. 'Or have you all old' (*1633*, II, *HK 2*, &c.) gives an extra foot and destroys the vigorous repetition of the same idea in the first three lines of the stanza: that constancy is a newfangled modern vice. It seems likely that 'Or' was caught from the line below and the resulting unmetrical line mended by the insertion of the weak and unnecessary 'all'.

l. 19. *song*. The lilting rhythms of the first stanza justify the appellation. The second stanza modulates very skilfully towards the speech rhythms of the third.

l. 21. *and't should be so no more*. This half-line caused trouble in the manuscripts. The line printed here (*TCD*, *Dob*, *S 96*, *JC*) is, I believe, the line that Donne wrote. It is regular if 'and it' is contracted. *TCC*, *Lut*, *O'F* regularize by omitting 'so'; *HK 2* and *P* by omitting 'and'. *H 40*, Group I, *B*, *S* regularize the metre by adding 'that' ('and that it . . .') but at the cost of a flat line that is two syllables too long. It must be conceded that since it is the same line (the third) in both the second and third stanzas where the reading is in question on metrical grounds, there is a possibility that Donne varied his pattern after the first stanza. The weakness of the two lines in their lengthened form makes me unwilling to accept this argument.

l. 23. *Some.* There is no question but that the weight of authority is on the side of 'But' (*H*, *40* I, and II). It is, however, so awkward to read 'But two or three ...' at the opening of a sentence in which 'but' is repeated as a conjunction, that I retain the reading of *1633* on the rather weak ground that the first 'But' may have arisen from anticipation of the second.

Womans Constancy (p. 42)

MSS.: *Σ — Cy, A 25, D 17, JC, K.*
Miscellanies: *CCC, Grey, Hol.*

In this and the following poem, both dramatic monologues, Donne abandons couplet and stanza form for the verse-paragraph. I do not know of an English precedent.

The Apparition (p. 43)

MSS.: *Σ — L 74, HK 2, K.*
Miscellanies: *Grey, Hd, HK 2*, RP 117(2),Wel*; Brit. Mus. MSS. *Harleian 3511, Sloane 1792*; Bodleian MSS. *Ash. 36 and 37, Eng. Poet. c 50*; Folger MS. *V a 103*; Rosenbach MSS. *239/23* and *243/4.*

There is a great deal of trivial variation in the text of this poem in manuscript, particularly in ll. 8, 10, and 11. *Lut, O'F* show independence of Group III, reading with *O* and *P*, once in patent error. In l. 11 Groups I and II agree in error, destructive of rhyme, which *1633* corrects to a reading found in *Lut, O'F, A 25, B.* The correction is obvious and was probably made independently in *1633.* The great majority of the variants are too insignificant to be recorded, or are patently wrong.

For comment on this poem's blending of traditions, see Introduction, pp. xxi–xxii.

Loves Usury (p. 44)

MSS.: *Σ — Group II, A 25, D 17, JC.*
Miscellanies: *Hd, HK 1.*

I differ from Grierson in the punctuation of l. 20; see note.

Group III reads against *H 40*, Group I, and *L 74* in ll. 5, 6, and 15. The agreement of *H 40* and *L 74* with Group I makes it likely that Group III is misreading. In l. 22 I retain the singular of *1633* against the plural of Groups I and III, again because it has the support of *H 40* and *L 74*.

ll. 7–8. 'Take up with a woman abandoned last year as if we had never met before.'

ll. 9–11. He wants to anticipate his rival's midnight assignation by turning up at nine. The rival's letter may be a letter from or to the rival.

   at next nine: at the following nine o'clock, that is, as soon as possible after getting hold of the letter.

l. 11. *mistake*. There is an obvious equivoque here: he will 'take' the maid 'for' (and instead of) the mistress.

l. 12. *tell the Lady*. Ovid is less impudent. Cf. *Amores*, II. vii and viii, where he defends himself against Corinna's charge that he has slept with Cypassis her maid, and in the next poem cajoles and threatens the girl to obtain a continuance of her favours.

l. 13. *no, not the sport*. The plea is that he may be carefree in his pleasures, no more the slave of lust than of love.

ll. 14–16.   *From country grasse, to comfitures of Court,*
                    Or cities quelque choses,

Cf. 'Community', l. 22: 'Chang'd loves are but chang'd sorts of meat.' The country girl, the court lady, and the city madam are dismissed as raw pasture, preserved sweetmeats, and dressed-up trifles. 'Quelque choses', in its more usual form 'kickshaws' is first recorded in *O.E.D.* in 1598 (Florio) and 1597(?) (*2 Henry IV*). The term is contemptuous, for fancy foreign dishes as opposed to substantial English ones, and is used here as a hit at the affectation of rich citizens' wives.

l. 15. *report*: mere rumour (of a possible intrigue).

l. 20. *Thou covet, most at that age thou shalt gaine*. This is the punctuation of *H 40*, Group I, *L 74*, *Lut*, *O'F*, and *B*. (*Dob*, *S 96*, and *S* put a stop after 'age'.) The pointing of *1633* ('Thou covet most, . . .'), which Grierson retained, has no manuscript support. The sense required is that whether Love covets honour, shame, or pain he will gain most of what he covets from an old man.

Loves Diet (p. 45)

MSS.: *Σ* — *TCD* (leaf torn out), *D 17*, *JC*.
Miscellanies: *Grey*, *Hd*, *HK 1*, *La*, *RP 117* (2); Bodleian MSS. *Eng. Poet. c 50* and *53*; Emmanuel Coll. MS. *1 3 16*; Folger MSS. *V a 96*, *125*, and *345*; Huntington MS. *HM 172*; Rosenbach MS. *1083/16*.

I agree with Grierson in rejecting *1633* in l. 25 where it follows *C 57, Lec* against all other manuscripts, and in l. 27 where it has no manuscript support.

l. 12. *meant to mee*: intended for me. Although there is no authority for the idiom 'meant to' for 'meant for' in *O.E.D.* I do not feel the difficulty in accepting it that Mr. Hayward, who proposed emendation, did.

l. 25. *buzard*: an inferior kind of hawk useless for falconry, hence, a blockhead, or dunce.

l. 29. *spring a mistresse*: as a falconer springs or starts up a bird for the hawk to chase.

Loves Exchange (p. 46)

MSS.: *Σ — L 74, S 96, Cy, A 25, K, S, S 962.*
Miscellanies: *Hd, HK 1.*

I differ from Grierson in adopting the reading of all the MSS. in ll. 4, 5, and 20, and of the great majority in l. 8, where *1633* follows *C 57, Lec.* Both Grierson and I retain the reading of *1633* in l. 9; see note.

ll. 8–14. *I aske not dispensation now*, &c. In *Biathanatos* (p. 48), Donne, discussing dispensations from oaths and vows, refers to Aquinas: 'implere votum est de lege naturae et est etiam praeceptum legis divinae' (*S.T.*, II^a pars, II^ae partis qq. lxxxviii and lxxxix).

a non obstante: 'a licence from the Crown to do that which could not lawfully be done without it' (Wharton's *Law Dictionary*). Cf. '*Nature* is the *Common law* by which God governs us, and *Miracle* is his *Prerogative*. For Miracles are but so many *Non-obstantes* upon Nature' (Simpson, *Essays*, p. 81). The presence of *non-obstante* clauses in letters-patent granting privileges, monopolies, and licences protected the holders against being sued in the courts of Common Law 'since these courts could not proceed with cases concerning the prerogative without the Crown's consent, while patentees had recourse to the Privy Council and the Star Chamber, whose duty it was to defend and enforce the royal prerogative' (J. E. Neale, *Elizabeth and her Parliaments 1584–1601*, 1957, p. 352). The question was a burning one in the Parliament of 1597–8 and the struggle against patents and monopolies came to a climax in the Parliament of 1601 in which Donne sat. Cf. 'Love's Deity' and 'A Valediction: of the Book'.

Love, as a monarch, grants privileges exempting his favourites from obedience to the law of nature which demands that oaths should be kept: cf. *Romeo and Juliet*, II. ii. 92:

> at lovers' perjuries
> They say Jove laughs;

and its source, Ovid, *Ars Amatoria*, i. 631–4.

l. 9. *or sigh.* I retain *1633* with some doubt. The agreement of *H 40* with Groups I and II in omitting 'or sigh' suggests Donne wrote a short line here. He has, in this and the following stanza, varied from the other stanzas by making the fourth line octosyllabic. The manuscripts that agree with *1633* may be merely agreeing in an obvious expansion.

l. 15. *Give mee thy weaknesse.* The religion of Cupid parodies the devout Christian's refusal to ask for other reward than to share the weakness of his God.

ll. 24–25. *Small townes,* &c. The publication of Alberico Gentili's *De Jure Belli,* 1588 and 1589, gave rise to a number of other books on the laws of war in the 1590's. Gentili, an Italian Protestant exile, was Professor of Law at Oxford. In Book II, chaps. 16 and 17, Gentili declares that once artillery has been brought up to a weak place ('si ad infirma loca deducuntur bombardae') there can be no question of terms of surrender.

l. 27, *article*: make stipulations.

l. 42. *Rack't carcasses make ill Anatomies.* The companies of Surgeons and Barbers from the reign of Henry VIII were permitted to take yearly for dissection the bodies of four persons condemned and put to death for felony. Later they seem to have had the right to the bodies of all, except traitors, executed at Tyburn. Strype describes a yearly anatomy lecture lasting for three days before students; this 'yearly anatomy' is alluded to by Nashe in *The Unfortunate Traveller* (*Works,* ii. 304; see also i. 196, 19–20 and note). Cf. Donne's verses on Coryate, ll. 53–54 (Grierson, i. 173):

> Worst malefactors, to whom men are prize,
> Do publike good, cut in Anatomies.

Loves Deitie (p. 47)

MSS.: All collections.
Miscellanies: *Hd, TCD* (2); Folger MSS. *V a 103* and *345*; Rosenbach MS. *1083/16.*

I agree with Grierson in rejecting *1633* in l. 24 where it follows *C 57, Lec* against all other manuscripts. I differ from him in rejecting its reading in l. 21; see note.

Suckling's 'Oh! for some honest Lovers ghost' is a characteristically Caroline variation on Donne's poem.

ll. 5–6. Cupid, parodying Jove, brings forth a destiny of his own whose authority has been legalized by custom which is 'second nature'; cf. 'Consuetudo est altera natura'.

l. 10. *even*: equal.

l. 12. *Actives to passives*: males to females, Cf. note to 'Air and Angels', ll. 26–28.
The adverb 'indulgently' makes clear that Love's office is not concerned with
joining soul to soul.

ll. 12–13.   *Correspondencie*
                           Only his subject was.

'Subject' may be used in its general sense for a person's particular business or
craft, or in its legal sense as a thing over which a right is exercised. Similarly,
'Correspondencie' may be used in the sense of agreement or harmony, so that
Love's business is to make perfect matches; or in the sense of communication
or intercourse of every kind. The second sense in each case fits better with the
development of ideas in the next stanza. 'His office was indulgently to join
males to females: his sphere of authority was only the mutual exchanges of
love.'

l. 14. *till I love her, that loves mee. Lut*, followed as usual by *O'F*, remodels this
line on the pattern of l. 7 and l. 21, by making it end with a negative clause.
This produces an extra-metrical syllable 'her' which both place in square
brackets and which the corrector of *O'F* then struck out.

l. 15. *moderne*: new-fangled.

l. 16. *prerogative*. Cf. notes to 'Love's Exchange', ll. 8–14, and to 'A Valediction:
of the Book', ll. 37–45.

l. 18. *All is the purlewe of the God of Love.* The right to declare land forest was a
part of the royal prerogative, and forests were exempt from common law and
under the law of the forest. 'Purlieu' was land that had been disafforested
under the Charter of the Forest in 1217 but which remained in some respects,
such as preservation of game, still subject to forest law. See John Manwood,
A Treatise and Discourse of the Laws of the Forest, 1592, second edition 1598,
chapter xx 'Of the Purallee'. Attempts by the Crown to assert rights over the
purlieus were a permanent source of discontent up to the Long Parliament.
I am unable to suggest any particular year when this reference would be
topical and have not found evidence to support Arthur Wilson's statement
that at the beginning of James's reign 'the liberty of hunting must be forbidden, the King's Game preserved, and a strict Proclamation threatens the
disobeyer' (*History of Great Britain*, 1653, p. 11).

Love, a minor god with a well-defined sphere, is now imitating the King of
the Gods and extending his prerogative over neighbouring regions where his
rights are at best dubious. He now exercises power where there is no 'correspondencie', and where the lover burns with passion, lusts after, writes to,
and extols a lady who feels no 'even flame'.

l. 21. *That I should love, who loves not mee.* Manuscript authority is overwhelmingly in support of this reading. Group III inserts an extra-metrical 'her'
which in *Lut* and *O'F* is set in square brackets. *1633*, which has the support

of only *B* (and *O'F* after correction), has similarly followed the pattern of ll. 7 and 14, but has omitted 'That' to regularize the line.

ll. 24–28. *Love might make me leave loving*, &c. Cf. 'Twickenham Garden', l. 15 and ll. 26–27, where the lady is also true to another.

The Dampe (p. 49)

MSS.: *Σ*— *H 40, L 74, HK 2, Cy, A 25, K.*
Miscellanies: *Grey, Hd, HK 1*; Bodleian MS. *Eng. Poet. f 25.*

I differ from Grierson in rejecting *1633* in l. 24 and in adopting a form from manuscript in l. 6; see notes.

For comment on Grierson's suggestion that this poem may be connected with Mrs. Herbert, see Appendix C, 'Lady Bedford and Mrs. Herbert'.

ll. 1–3. Cf. '*Abraham Hoffemanus lib.* 1. *amor. conjugal. cap 2. pag.* 22 relates out of *Plato*, that *Empedocles* the Philosopher was present at the cutting up of one that died for love' (Burton, *Anatomy*, part 3, sect. 2, memb. 4, subs. 1).

l. 5. *dampe*: an exhalation of a noxious kind.

l. 6. *thorough*. I adopt a form found in manuscript, *causa metri*. Cf. 'The Indifferent', l. 17, for an example of Donne's use of the dissyllabic form.

l. 7. *preferre*: raise, or promote.

ll. 11–12 and 19–20. The giants, enchantresses, and witches of medieval romance are blended with the abstractions of courtly allegory in which the lady is guarded by Danger (or Disdain) and Honour and the lover aided by Fidelity and Secrecy. Moral qualities are thus reduced to figments of the imagination. Cf. 'A Valediction: of the Book', ll. 44–45, where honour and conscience are dismissed as chimeras. Their common reference to Goths and Vandals also relates the two poems.

ll. 21–24. For the assumption that women are 'apter to'endure then men' see note to 'Change', ll. 11–14 (p. 136).
    passive valor, cf. 'Love's Deity', l. 12.

l. 24. *Naked*. It is just possible that the tamer reading of Group II ('In that') which was adopted in *1633*, is a softening made by Donne; but it seems unlikely since the poem, as a whole, is beyond propriety.

The Legacie (p. 50)

MSS.: *Σ*— *D 17, JC.*
Miscellanies: *CCC, EH, Grey, Hd, Hol, La, RP 117 (2), TCD (2)*; Brit. Mus. MS. *Egerton 2230*; Bodleian MS. *Rawl. Poet. 116*; Emmanuel Coll. MS. *1 3 16*; Folger MS. *V a 345*; Rosenbach MS. *1983/16.*

There are two distinct traditions here, one in *H 40* and Group I, the other in *L 74* and Group II. (The witness of Group III is divided.) *1633* adopts one reading (l. 22) from Group II but otherwise follows Group I, emending one of its readings in l. 14. I prefer the version in *L 74*, Group II, and adopt its readings in ll. 14 and 23 (*bis*) where Grierson retained *1633*. I also differ from him in l. 3 where *1633* follows *C 57*, *Lec* against the other Group I manuscripts; see notes. In l. 10 I retain a contraction that Grierson expanded and have supplied contraction marks in ll. 11 and 15.

A line quoted from this poem is the earliest known quotation from one of the *Songs and Sonnets*. Katherine Thimelby wrote to her lover (*c.* 1635):

How infinite a time will it seme till I se you: for lovers hours are full eternity. Doctor Dun sayd this, but I think it (*Tixall Letters*, ed. A. Clifford, 1815, i. 147).

l. 3. *Though it be an houre agoe.* The agreement of *H 40*, *D*, *H 49*, with *L 74*, Group II establishes this reading. The absence of a weak initial syllable is a common licence in poems that are near to song. The reading of *1633* (*C 57*, *Dob*, *HK 2*), 'Though it be but ...', gives eight syllables at the cost of sense. The point is that even though it was as long as an hour ago he can still remember.

l. 7. *Though I be dead, which sent me.* His ghost is speaking; cf. 'The Computation' and 'The Expiration'.

ll. 9–12. I retain the contraction 'that's' in l. 10. It has good manuscript support and gives a livelier line with stresses falling where they are needed. As in l. 3 the absence of a weak initial syllable does not disturb the metre.

I agree with Chambers against Grierson that the 'something' he said was only 'Tell her anon that myself did kill me'; and that, having said this and feeling himself *in extremis*, he then bestowed 'something': his heart.

l. 14. The extra-metrical reflexive 'me' has been dropped in *L 74* and Group II, but their reading 'hearts should' gives better sense than 'hart did' (*H 40* and Group I) which *1633* emended to 'hearts did'.

l. 18. *colours it, and corners had.* These are presumably 'false colours' and 'dark corners'. She is a mistress of simulation and dissimulation.

l. 20. *It was intire to none, and few had part.* It was neither given wholly to one lover nor shared among many. She combines fickleness with coldness.

l. 22. *for our losses sad.* *1633* here deserts Group I and adopts the Group II reading. It is a better reading, since a sudden address to a plural audience, 'for our loss be ye sad', seems unlikely. It is difficult to give any precise meaning to 'our loss' or 'our losses' and I suspect there is a corruption here.

Since she has his good heart, it is not easy to see what her 'loss' is. It is best not to take it that he is 'sad' because *he* has lost his heart and *she* his legacy; but that 'sad' qualifies 'losses'. 'Therefore, to make up for our partings I thought ...'.

l. 23. *thought . . . that.* The readings of *L 74*, Group II, which I have adopted suit the imagined situation better than 'meant . . . this' (*1633, H 40*, Group I). 'Meant' is rather too purposeful and 'this' implies he could 'hold' the slippery heart.

The Broken Heart (p. 51)

MSS.: All collections.
Miscellanies: *Grey, Hd, La, RP 117* (2); Brit. Mus. MSS. *Add. 10309* and *30982, Egerton 2230*; Bodleian MS. *Eng. Poet. e 14*; Univ Lib. Camb. MS. *Add. 5778*; Folger MS. *V a 103*; Rosenbach MS. *1083/16*.

As in 'The Legacy', *H 40*, Group I, read against *L 74*, Group II (ll. 17, 20, 21, 30). *1633* follows Group I and I concur with Grierson in retaining its readings.

l. 15. *chain-shot*: cannon balls chained together. Either 'chain' or 'chained' is possible. Donne uses the form adopted in a sermon in which he echoes this poem:

But as the *Woe* is denounced in the second acceptation against Hypocrites, so it is a chain-shot, and in every congregation takes whole rankes (*Sermons*, ii. 355).

ll. 17, 20, and 21. *did . . . But . . . to thee.* 'Did' is an easier reading than 'could' which can only be taken as idiomatic for 'could have'. 'But' makes what seems a necessary antithesis, and 'to thee' seems more natural than 'to thine' which anticipates the point of the next line.

l. 24. *first.* Since *L 74* agrees with all the other manuscripts in reading 'first', the reading of Group II, 'fierce', cannot be considered.

l. 30. *hundred.* Although the hyperbolic 'thousand' is in Donne's manner, I retain 'hundred' since it seems more likely that a copyist would enlarge than diminish.

The Triple Foole (p. 52)

MSS.: *Σ — A 25.*
Miscellanies: *Grey, Hd, HN*; Brit. Mus. MS. *Harl. 4888*; Folger MS. *V a 103*.

ll. 6–7. *Then as th'earths inward narrow crooked lanes*, &c. The problem of why seas were salt and rivers fresh was much debated in antiquity. This theory of the filtration of sea-water by its passage through the earth, mentioned but rejected by Aristotle (*Meteorologia*, 354b and 355b), was adopted by Seneca (*Quaestiones Naturales*, III. v) and became the standard explanation, agreeing with Jerome's gloss on Eccles. i. 7. It appears in all popular encyclopedias which stress the 'endless winding channels' (Seneca) and the 'occultas venas' (Jerome) through which the water must pass to be purged of its salinity.

The Flea (p. 53)

MSS.: *Σ* — *D 17, JC.*
Miscellanies: *CCC, Grey, RP 117 (2)*; Brit. Mus. MS. *Egerton 2230*; Bodleian
MSS. *Malone 19, Rawl. Poet. 172*; Folger MS. *V a 103* and *170*; Rosenbach
MS. *243/4.*

The text in Group I is distinct from that in *H 40* and all other manuscripts
and *1633* followed it without alteration. The Group I, *1633* text seems to me
less vivid and idiomatic and I have preferred to its readings those of the other
manuscripts. My text thus differs from Grierson's in ll. 3, 5, 6, 11, 16, and 21.

In *1635* 'The Flea' was taken from its place in *1633* to stand first of the
Songs and Sonnets. Grierson suggested that this was because it was 'greatly
admired as a masterpiece of wit' and mentions that it was the first of the pieces
translated by Huyghens and was 'selected for special commendation by some
of his correspondents'. Search of miscellanies does not suggest that it was
exceptionally popular in England. I presume Huyghens translated it first
because he was working from the edition of *1635*.

The flea was a popular subject for erotic verse all over Europe in the sixteenth century. The main model was the late medieval 'Carmen de Pulice',
ascribed to Ovid, in which the poet envying the flea the liberties it takes with
his mistress's person wishes to be transformed into one. The subject was also
taken up by writers of facetious *encomia*, following the 'Encomium Pulicis'
(1519) of Calcagnini. In 1579 Etienne Pasquier, visiting Mme Des Roches at
Poitiers, observed a flea on the bosom of Mademoiselle Catherine. The event
was commemorated in *La Puce de Madame Des Roches* (1582), a collection of
over fifty poems on fleas in French, Spanish, Italian, Latin, and Greek. Neo-
Latin poems on fleas can be found in a vast storehouse of jocose *encomia*, the
Amphitheatrum Sapientiae Socraticae Joco-Seriae by Caspar Dornavius (Hanover,
1619). Poems on fleas fall monotonously into two types. The poet either
wishes to be a flea or he envies the flea its death at his mistress's hands and on
her bosom. The latter type can be seen in two madrigals by Drummond of
Hawthornden, translated from Tasso (*Rime*, Venice, 1608) where he substituted a flea for Tasso's gnat (*Works*, ed. Kastner, 1913, i. 125). See Marcel
Françon, 'Un Motif de la Poésie Amoureuse au xvɪᵉᵐᵉ siecle', *P.M.L.A.* lvi
(1941) and, for mock *encomia*, A. S. Pease, 'Things without Honour', *Class.
Phil.* xxi (1926). Donne's originality transforms this well-worn subject by
making the flea bite both him and his mistress, thus making it a symbol not
of the lover's desire but of the desired union. Instead of a languid, erotic fancy,
he gives us a witty, dramatic argument.

l. 3. *Mee it suck'd first*. The inversion throws the stress where it is needed, on
the two personal pronouns.

l. 4. *our two bloods mingled bee*. Cf. 'To mingle friendship far is mingling bloods

(*Winter's Tale*, I. ii. 109). In Aristotelian physiology coition was thought to be a 'mingling of bloods'; see *De Generatione Animalium*, and cf. 'The Progress of the Soul', stanza L.

l. 16. *thee*. The reversion to the familiar singular pronoun marks a change from the pleading and respectful tone of the opening of the second stanza, marked by the change to the plural form. 'Thee' also gives an effective internal rhyme.

The Will (p. 54)

MSS.: *Σ* — *TCD* (leaf torn out).
Miscellanies: *CCC, Grey, Hd, HK 1, La, RP 117*(*2*); Brit. Mus. MSS. *Add. 10309* and *27407, Egerton 2230*; Bodleian MS. *Malone 19*; St. John's Coll. Camb. MS. *U 26*; Folger MS. *V a 125*.

The third stanza appears in manuscript in Group III, *S*, the late miscellany *S 962*, and (as a marginal addition) in *L 74* and *HK 1*. In the other stanzas Group III and *S* differ slightly from all other manuscripts. *1633*, which prints the third stanza, agrees in the rest of the poem with Groups I and II.

Grierson suggested that the third stanza was omitted as liable to misinterpretation. This argument which might tell with an author intending publication hardly applies to a writer circulating his poems among friends. The third stanza is, in any case, not more open to misinterpretation by dullards than the second. An eye-slip could well cause its omission since both the second and third stanza begin with 'My' and end with a line beginning with the same four words. But if this explanation were accepted it would mean that all the manuscripts except Group III and *S* descend from one corrupt copy, unless we can believe that the same mistake happened independently in two or more copies.

I think it more probable that this stanza is an addition to a poem originally in five stanzas that made no attempt to repeat the pattern of the last line of the first stanza in the succeeding ones. The third stanza is modelled on the second and may have been supplied as an alternative, as Donne wrote an alternative to three lines in 'The Curse'. In the manuscripts that preserve the third stanza the first, like the second and third, ends with the formula 'Only to give to . . .'. We have thus in Group III and *S* a poem in six stanzas of which the first three end with variations on the same pattern and the last three abandon the pattern. This is very unlike Donne's craftsmanship. I have therefore not adopted the Group III reading in l. 9 which is, I believe, a scribal adjustment to bring the first stanza into line with the next two. I print the six stanzas although I think it possible that the second and third are alternatives.

l. 3. *Argus*. He had a hundred eyes.

l. 5. *My tongue to Fame.* Fame, or Rumour, was presented, as in the prologue to *2 Henry IV*, as 'painted full of tongues'.

l. 10. *planets.* They were often called the errant, or wandering stars.

l. 14. *My silence to'any, who abroad hath beene.* Cf. Bacon's advice: 'And in his Discourse, let him be rather advised in his Answers, then forward to tell Stories' ('Of Travel').

l. 15. *Capuchin*: a Friar of the order of the new rule founded in 1528 and named from his pointed *capuche* or hood. The earliest recorded use of the word in *O.E.D.* is 1599 (Marston, *The Scourge of Villainy*), and it was in this year that the first Capuchin fathers landed in England. They were immediately arrested and imprisoned and after three years expelled from the country. But the word was in use earlier and it would be unwise to take Donne's reference as topical in view of Nashe's reference to 'the most beggerly new erected Order of the Fryer Capuchines' in *Pierce Penniless* (1592).

l. 19. *Roman Catholiques.* The earliest use of this term recorded in *O.E.D.* is 1605.

ll. 20–21.   the Schismaticks
                          Of Amsterdam;
Grierson refers to *The Alchemist* where Tribulation Wholesome, a Pastor of Amsterdam, refers to himself and his brethren as 'we of the *Separation*'.

ll. 21–22.   *my best civility*
                   And Courtship, to an Universitie;
For a kindly view of the traditional uncouthness of scholars, see Earle, *Microcosmography*, 'A Down-right Scholar':

   He is good metal in the inside, though rough and unscoured without, and there-fore hated of the courtier.... He is exceedingly censured by the inns-of court men, for that heinous vice of being out of fashion.

l. 23. *to souldiers bare*: to soldiers who have none of it, or, possibly, whose rags hardly cover them. The bragging soldier is a stock comic type, and the poverty of discharged soldiers a commonplace.

l. 26. *disparity*: something unequal (to her deserts).

l. 29. *Mine industrie to foes.* The malice of others is a spur to endeavour. Cf. 'A Litany', stanza XXVI, where the petition is that the severity of magistrates, preachers, and our enemies may make us 'to amendment, hear them'.

l. 40. *brazen medals*: Roman bronze coins, valued by collectors but useless to the starving. The word 'medal' for a coin that was not current remained in use until the eighteenth century. Donne's allusions here, in the *Sermons*, and in *Essays in Divinity*, show his interest in antiquarianism. He can be regarded as an early connoisseur of painting; his interest in 'medals' suggests that he may have been a collector himself. See Simpson, *Essays*, pp. 43–44 and 56.

l. 42. *mine English tongue.* Cf.

What thinke you of this English tongue, tell me, I pray you? It is a language that wyl do you good in England but passe Dover it is woorth nothing (*Florio's First Fruits*, ed. A. del Re, 1936, p. 123).

ll. 43–45. We must assume from l. 53 that the lady is chaste, since she neglects Love itself as well as the speaker. The point of the stanza as a whole is that he has been taught to give what is inappropriate ('disproportioned') since the recipient is incapable of using it. The lady is incapable of anything but friendship, suitable as a portion for older men, but not for 'younger lovers'.

SONGS AND SONNETS

(II)

This second group of lyrics is distinguished from the first in its literary sources and in its stanza forms, as well as in its elaboration of conceits; see Introduction, pp. li–lxii.

Negative Love (p. 56)

MSS.: Group II, *DC*, *Lut*, *O'F*, *A 25* (and Camb. Univ. Library MS. *Add. 29*): omit *Σ*.
Miscellanies: *Hd*.

Apart from its appearance in *A 25*, and a Cambridge manuscript that duplicates part of *A 25*, this poem would seem to owe its survival to the compiler of the collection in the Group II manuscripts. It passed from one of these, with other poems also found elsewhere only in Group II, to *Lut* and thence to *O'F*.

Although its lightness of tone and octosyllabic metre relate this poem to the songs and epigrams in the first group, its theme (which is a Neo-Platonic commonplace) relates it closely to poems in the second. It poses the question to which 'Air and Angels' attempts an answer, and plays with the idea that 'Farewell to Love' repudiates, that there is 'some Deitie in love'.

Ficino declared:

The passion of a lover is not quenched by the mere touch or sight of a body, for it does not desire this or that body, but desires the splendour of the divine light shining through bodies, and is amazed and awed by it. For this reason lovers never know what it is they desire or seek, for they do not know God Himself, whose subtle incense has infused into His works a certain sweet aroma of Himself; by this aroma we are certainly every day aroused. We sense the aroma certainly, but we cannot distinguish its flavour, and so when we yearn for the indistinguishable flavour itself, being charmed by its sensible aroma, certainly we do not know what we desire and what we suffer. Hence also it always happens that lovers somehow both worship and fear the sight of the beloved (*Commentary*, pp. 140–1).

The notion that lovers desire 'un non so che' appears without philosophical trimmings in popular Neo-Platonism also; see *La Seconda Parte delle Lezzioni di M. Benedetto Varchi*, Florence, 1561, sig. C8. A characteristically French variation on the theme is Ronsard's Madrigal 'L'homme est bien sot qui aime sans cognoistre' (*Oeuvres*, ed. Laumonier, Paris, 1914–19, i. 247).

l. 2. *eye, cheeke, lip.* Cf. 'Air and Angels', l. 14, where the lover allows Love to assume his mistress's body and fix itself in her 'lip, eye, and brow'.

ll. 5–6.   *For sense, and understanding may*
                             Know, what gives fuell to their fire:

In *The Courtier* Castiglione makes Bembo declare that we can only desire things known, and that to every faculty by which we know there is joined a faculty by which we desire:

> And because in our soule there be three manner waies to know, namely, by sense, reason, and understanding: of sense there ariseth appetite or longing, which is common to us with brute beasts: of reason ariseth election or choice, which is proper to man: of understanding, by the which man may be partner with Angels, ariseth will.

Reason enables man to choose between 'inclining to sense or reaching to understanding' (pp. 303–4). Rejecting both sense and understanding which know their objects, Donne exalts an irrational love, foolish but more glorious, that desires without knowing what it desires.

ll. 10–12.   *If that be simply perfectest*
                             Which can by no way be exprest
                             But Negatives, my love is so.

The absolutely simple and perfect cannot be defined except in terms of what it is not. Cf. Aquinas, *S.T.*, Iª pars, q. iii, 'De Dei Simplicitate':

> Cognito de aliquo an sit, inquirendum restat, quomodo sit, ut sciatur de eo quid sit. Sed quia de Deo scire non possumus quid sit, sed quid non sit: non possumus considerare de Deo quomodo sit, sed potius quomodo non sit.

l. 13. *To All, which all love.* If the capital, which has some manuscript support, is right we can take 'All' as the totality of created things, 'τὸ πᾶν'; cf. 'A Litany', l. 74. More probably the 'all' which 'all love' is the sum of a mistress's perfections; cf. 'Air and Angels', ll. 19–20:

> Ev'ry thy haire for love to worke upon
> Is much too much. . . .

Either way Donne is declaring that he is *sui generis* among lovers.

l. 15. *What we know not, our selves.* There is a glance here at the mystical doctrine that it is by knowledge of ourselves that we can come to knowledge of God. Grierson cites an undatable sermon:

> All creatures were brought to *Adam*, and, because he understood the natures of all those creatures, he gave them names accordingly. In that he gave no name to himselfe,

it may be by some perhaps argued, that he understood himselfe less then he did other creatures (*Sermons*, ix. 256).

Cf. also Raleigh, *History of the World*, preface:

Man . . . that is ignorant of the essence of his owne soul, and which the wisest of the naturalists (if Aristotle be he) could never so much as define, but by the action and effect, telling us what it works, . . . but not what it is, which neither he, nor anyone else doth know, but God that created it . . . (*Works*, ed. Oldys and Birch, 1829, ii. xlvi).

The Undertaking (p. 57)

MSS.: *Σ* — *L 74, S 96, Cy, A 25, S 962.*
Miscellanies: *Hd, HK 1.*

The edition of *1633* adds a superfluous 'And' in l. 3 and omits to mark an elision in l. 25, thus destroying a pleasing variation in the first and last stanzas. There is another departure from metrical regularity in l. 18; see note.

Apart from 'The Relic' this is the only poem that is 'Platonic' in the vulgar sense of the term. It is also the only lyric in ballad measure. See note to ll. 5–12 for an argument for dating it after 1599.

Title. The editor of *1633* did not in this case take the title ('Platonique Love') from his Group II manuscript, but supplied a title of his own.

l. 1. *braver*: more glorious, Cf. 'Negative Love', l. 7.

l. 2. *the* Worthies. Although Caxton in the preface to the *Morte d'Arthur* says it is universally known that the Worthies were Hector, Alexander, Julius Caesar, Joshua, David, Judas Maccabeus, Arthur, Charlemagne, and Godfrey of Boulogne, there is a good deal of variety in their number and names. They were favourite figures in pageants, as in *Love's Labour's Lost*, where they would boastfully announce their claims to fame. Donne claims to have surpassed them in achievement, and even more in not boasting.

ll. 5–12. *It were but madness now t'impart*, &c. Cf. 'To the Countess of Bedford' (Grierson, i. 219):

> You teach (though wee learne not) a thing unknowne
> To our late times, the use of specular stone,
> Through which all things within without were shown.

> Of such were Temples. . . .

Cf. also:

The *heathens* served their Gods in Temples, *sub dio*, . . . and, where they could, in Temples made of *Specular stone*, that was transparent as glasse, or crystall, so as they which walked without in the streets, might see all that was done within (*Sermons*, vii. 397).

Pliny has many references to *lapis specularis* (which Holland renders as 'Talc, which is a kind of transparent glass stone'), and describes the art of cutting it into leaves as thin as can be desired (*Nat. Hist.* xxxvi. 22. 45. 160). Immediately after this he tells of a stone hard as marble, white, and transparent, called Phengites, of which Nero built the Temple of Fortune. It has been suggested that Donne confused the two passages and that he was also identifying 'specular stone' with ancient Selenite; see D. C. Allen, *M.L.N.* lxi, and J. P. Wendell, ibid. lxiii.

All that Donne says about 'specular' stone can be explained by reference to one very popular work, Guido Panciroli's *Rerum Memorabilium Libri Duo*, written in Italian but first published in a Latin translation at Hamburg in 1599. Panciroli's first book contains notes on substances known to the ancients but unknown to the moderns and, as well as finding there a chapter headed *De Specularibus*, Donne would find in a note on incombustible oil the story of the lamp in Tullia's tomb that he used in the Somerset Epithalamium. Panciroli's second book deals with things known to the moderns but unknown to the ancients. Donne refers to this in *Ignatius His Conclave* where he cites '*Pancirollo*' with a marginal note 'De rebus nuper inventis'.

Panciroli gives a marginal reference to Pliny's description of the cutting of 'specular stone', says that Nero built the Temple of Fortune with it, adds that anyone within the temple could be seen by those without, and ends by saying that the substance is unknown today, the point of Donne's stanza:

Specularia seu speculares lapides materia quaedam lucida erant ut S. Basilius scribit, & instar aeris transparens. Hanc veteres fenestris imponebant, ut nos vitrum. De his specularibus apud Plinium extat & in jure civile. Nero sacellum sive templum Fortunae ex specularibus construxit: in quo qui erat, extrinsecus absque ullo obstaculo conspiciebatur: ac, ut Plinius scriptum reliquit, portis etiam clausis, Lux ibi inclusa, non transmissa videbatur. Speculares hodie non reperiuntur.

If this is accepted as the source of Donne's references to 'specular stone', 'The Undertaking' must be dated after 1599.

l. 18. *Vertue'attir'd in woman see.* The additional foot in this line offended the compiler of *Lut* who regularized by omitting 'attir'd'. *O'F* follows *Lut*, and from *O'F* the reading 'Vertue in woman see' was adopted in *1635* and stood in all editions until Grierson's.

l. 22. *From prophane men you hide.* Cf. 'A Valediction: forbidding Mourning', ll. 7–8:

> 'Twere prophanation of our joyes
> To tell the layetie our love.

The notion of love as an esoteric mystery to be hidden from the 'profanum vulgus' is characteristic of the poems in this second group of the *Songs and Sonnets*.

[Image and Dream] (p. 58)

MSS.: Σ — *HK 2, Cy, A 25, K.*
Miscellanies: *Hd, HK 1, HK 2**.

This poem, printed without division into stanzas and headed 'Elegie', occurs in *1633* in the middle of the volume, following 'The Comparison' and 'The Autumnal'. In *1635* all three poems were moved to join the *Elegies*, this one becoming 'Elegie X' and being given the title 'The Dreame'. It occurs among the *Songs and Sonnets* in the Group I manuscripts but is written continuously, as if it were in couplets, as it is in all the manuscripts. The first editor to print it in stanzas was Mr. R. E. Bennett.

Title. Except in *S 96* where it is called 'Picture' the poem appears in manuscript without title other than 'Elegie'. To avoid confusion with the other lyric called 'The Dream', I have given it a fuller title which expresses the contrast on which the poem is based.

It is a commonplace among Neo-Platonists that the lover may fashion in imagination an image of the beloved more beautiful than the image his senses perceive in her presence; see Ficino, *Commentary*, pp. 188–9, and Castiglione, p. 317. A more precise source can be suggested for this poem: the third dialogue in the *Dialoghi d'amore* of Leone Ebreo, written 1501–2 and published at Rome in 1535. At the opening of the dialogue Philo, the lover, is rebuked by his mistress, Sophia, for passing without seeing her and replies that his mind was rapt in the contemplation of the image of her beauty. Sophia asks how 'can that be impressed so effectively on the mind, which, when present, cannot even find entrance through the eyes'; and Philo owns that it was through his eyes that her radiant beauty pierced the faculties of perception and imagination and passed 'into the very midst of my heart and into the depth of my mind'. Sophia is still surprised that her actual presence should be unnoticed and Philo retorts that she would not have blamed him if he had been asleep. She agrees since sleep is able 'to occlude all perception', and asks what else can 'still the senses but sleep, which is a semi-death'. Philo replies that 'the ecstasy or distraction caused by a lover's thoughts' is 'more than semi-death'. A discussion follows on the distinction between ecstasy, when the mind is rapt in the contemplation of what truly is, and sleep, when the mind is invaded by dreams. Philo then accuses Sophia of destroying him, because the image of her beauty is so overpowering that it arouses insatiable desire (Leone Ebreo, pp. 197–205 and 229–31).

Donne has blended with this conception of the image of the beloved, more potent than her presence, which overwhelms the spirits and senses to produce a semi-death, the well-known theme of the sensual love-dream in which the lover finds in sleep the satisfaction which his mistress refuses to him waking.

l. 1. *more then she.* Cf.

> *Sophia*: The image of my person has more sway over you than my person itself.
> *Philo*: It is more potent: because the image within our mind is stronger than that from without, since, being within, it has already become master over the whole of its domain (Leone Ebreo, p. 229).

l. 3. *Medall*: a disk of metal stamped with a figure and worn as a charm or love-token, and also a coin struck to commemorate an event and, thus, ancient as distinct from current coins. This last sense leads Donne to a favourite idea of the stamp imparting value to a coin; cf. 'A Valediction: of Weeping' and 'To Mr. Tilman'.

ll. 7–8. Weak-spirited men cannot support positions of dignity and the bright or the loud blinds or deafens us to everything else. The greater an object the less we can see beside it. Cf.

> *Philo*: The poison of your venom is harder to counteract than any bodily poison. And as the latter goes straight to the heart and does not leave until it has consumed all the spirits which follow it thither... so your image keeps its perpetual lodging in my mind, drawing to itself all the powers and spirits, and together with these would cut off my whole life' (ibid., p. 230). Also 'The spirits are withdrawn with the soul and collected, either in the midst of the head, the seat of all knowledge, or in the centre of the heart, the abode of desire, leaving the eyes bereft of sight, the ears of hearing, and the other organs of feeling and movement' (ibid., p. 204).

ll. 9–10. The Heart, the seat of Reason, is the organ that mediates between the Brain, the seat of Understanding, and the Liver, the organ of the sensual faculties; see note to 'Negative Love' ll. 5–6. In Reason's absence the lower faculty of Fancy, bred of sensual desires, takes control as a Queen in the absence of the King. Cf. Adam's explanation of dreams in *Paradise Lost*, v. 110–13.

ll. 11–15. Fancy, which plays with images communicated through the senses and stored in memory, presents only sensual pleasures, joys not too great for the lover's capacity. Since in waking life these joys only exist in imagination he possesses her as truly in dream as in waking, with the advantage that he does not feel the pain of his actual unsatisfied desire. Cf. Rochester, 'The Mistress':

> Fantastick Fancies fondly move,
> And in frail Joys believe,
> Taking false Pleasure for true Love;
> But Pain can ne're deceive.

l. 17. *a such fruition*: such an enjoyment. The idiomatic inversion of 'such a' occurs also in 'A Litany', l. 34.

ll. 21–24. Satisfaction in life is as brief as a dream. Cf. 'Farewell to Love': 'Being had, enjoying it decays.' The shortness of human life will take his heart away only too soon. Life's taper in its beginning is no more than a mere 'candle-end'. 'Snuff' is used in the same sense in Satire II, ll. 82–83.

ll. 25–26. Ecstasy, born of rational contemplation of her image, is better than irrationality. The lover prefers the better way of being 'out of his senses'.

The Exstasie (p. 59)

MSS.: *Σ* — *L 74, Cy, K, S 962.*
Miscellanies: *RP 117 (2).*

I concur with Grierson in rejecting the reading of *1633* in ll. 25, 42, and 59, where it follows its Group I manuscript in error, and in ll. 51, 52, and 55, where it has random or no support. I differ from Grierson in rejecting *1633* also in l. 10, where it follows Group I against other manuscripts, and l. 11, where it has the support of *P* only. In l. 67 I have made a conjectural emendation; see note.

Coleridge said of 'The Ecstasy': 'I should never find fault with metaphysical poems, were they all like this, or but half as excellent' (*Miscellaneous Criticism*, ed. Raysor, 1936, p. 138); and Ezra Pound commenting on it exclaimed:

Platonism believed. The decadence of trying to make pretty speeches and of hunting for something to say temporarily checked. Absolute belief in the existence of an extracorporal soul, and of its incarnation. Donne stating a thesis in precise even technical terms (*A B C of Reading*, 1934, p. 126).

None of Donne's poems has received more discussion than 'The Ecstasy'. For a summary of the debate and for illustrative passages from Neo-Platonists, see Appendix D, 'The Ecstasy'. I have confined myself in the commentary to annotation and attempted to avoid matter that is disputed.

'The Ecstasy' belongs to a tradition exemplified by Sidney's Eighth Song in *Astrophel and Stella*, Fulke Greville's *Caelica 75*, Lord Herbert's 'Ode upon a Question Moved' and Wither's *Fair Virtue*, sonnet 3. These poems, which are all in simple verse-forms, have in common a May landscape in which two lovers walk, a period of silent communion and a long casuistical dialogue on love. See George Williamson, 'The Convention of *The Exstasie*', *Seventeenth-Century Contexts*, 1960.

Title. The agreement of all manuscripts in attaching the word 'Ecstasy' to this poem suggests that Donne gave this poem its title.

l. 6. *a fast balme*: either a steadfast, or a fastening, warm moisture. Cf. *Othello*, III. iv. 33–40, where Othello comments on Desdemona's 'moist hand': 'this argues fruitfulness and liberal heart', and *Venus and Adonis*, ll. 25–28:

> With this she seizeth on his sweating palm,
> The precedent of pith and livelihood,
> And, trembling in her passion, calls it balm,
> Earth's sovereign salve to do a goddess good.

ll. 7–8. *Our eye-beames*, &c. The debate as to whether sight was by extramission (beams from the eye striking the object) or by intramission (beams from the object imprinting an image on the eye) was unsettled at the Renaissance; see Agrippa, *De Vanitate*, *c*. 23, and Donne, *Sermons*, ix. 247:

> No man knows so, as that strong arguments may not be brought on the other side, how he sees, whether by reception of species from without, or by emission of beames from within.

Leone Ebreo reconciles the two views, saying that the eye transmits beams to the object but that the representation of the object on the pupil is also necessary, and that, further, the eye must direct its beam a second time to make the form on the pupil tally with the object (p. 215). This passage may have suggested to Donne his two conceits of the twisting of the beams and the reflection of each in the other's pupils.

ll. 11–12. *And pictures*, &c. The small image of oneself reflected in the pupils of another person was called a 'baby', from a pun on *pupilla*. For lovers thus to 'look babies' was a common idiom.

ll. 13–16. *As 'twixt two equal Armies*, &c. Visually, and by the verbal link of the repeated 'twixt', the two equal armies should be the bodies between which the souls, like envoys, negotiate. The point of the simile is then simply in the word 'suspend': 'our souls hung in the air between our bodies as Victory does in an allegorical painting'. But the point of the simile may be the absolute equality and immobility of the souls: 'Just as when two armies are locked in battle so that neither can advance or retreat, so our souls hung motionless face to face in the air.'

l. 15. *to advance their state*: to increase their dignity.

l. 18. *Wee like sepulchrall statues lay*. I find a difficulty here. Are the lovers who were sitting holding hands and gazing in each other's eyes now lying side by side like two figures on a tomb? Or are they only like 'sepulchrall statues' in their unchanging postures?

l. 27. *concoction*: the process by which metals and minerals are refined by heat from an impure to a perfect or mature state. The listener will be even more 'refin'd' after he has heard the 'dialogue of one'.

l. 29. *This Extasie*. In a letter, cited by Grierson, Donne speaks of ecstasy as 'a departing, and secession, and suspension of the soul' (*Letters*, p. 11), and at the beginning of *Ignatius His Conclave* writes 'I was in an *Extasie*, and

> My little wandring sportful Soule,
> Ghest, and Companion of my body

had liberty to wander through all places.' The essential notion of ecstasy is the enfranchisement of the soul which, freed from the body, obtains knowledge directly without the use of the senses or discursive reason. In his *Sermons* Donne is contemptuous or sceptical of such illumination; see *Sermons*, i. 186 and 253, vii. 334, ix. 170, x. 145–6, and:

> Some men draw some reasons, out of some stories of some credit, to imprint a

belief of *extasie*, and *raptures*; That the body remaining upon the floore, or in the bed, the soul may be gone out to the contemplation of heavenly things (*Sermons*, vi. 101).

l. 30. The lovers learn in ecstasy what is hidden from other lovers: 'what we love'. Cf. note to 'Negative Love' (p. 177); and 'A Valediction: forbidding Mourning', ll. 17–18, and 'The Relic', l. 24.

l. 31. *sexe*. Cf. 'The Primrose', l. 16, where Donne also uses this word in its modern sense for all the desires and impulses that arise from differentiation of sex. No earlier example is recorded in *O.E.D.*

l. 32. *what did move*: both what impelled and what attracted.

ll. 33–34. *But as all severall soules*, &c. Leone Ebreo explains that the soul, although 'one and indivisible' has different functions and

> ...is not uniform, but is intermediate between the intellectual and corporeal world.... It must therefore have a nature compounded of spiritual intelligence and corporeal mutability, for otherwise it could not animate bodies (pp. 204 and 206).

For the notion that we are ignorant of the nature of our own souls, see note to 'Negative Love' l. 15 (p. 178).

l. 35. *Love, these mixt soules, doth mixe againe*. Donne may mean 'As all separate souls are mixed, so the "abler soule" is made by mixture.' Or, he may be referring to a process preliminary to the union of the souls by which each is first 're-mixed' by being drawn into unity; cf. Leone Ebreo:

> When, therefore, the spiritual mind, ... through the force of desire, retires within itself to contemplate a beloved and desired object, it draws every part of the soul to itself, gathering it into one indivisible unity' (p. 204)

and

> At certain times, however, the soul withdraws within itself and returns to its intellectual nature when it connects and unites with the pure intellect above it (p. 206).

l. 36. *And makes both one, each this and that*. It is a Neo-Platonic commonplace that love makes 'of one person—two; and of two persons—one', and that 'two persons who love each other mutually are not really two persons', but 'only one, or else four':

> Each one being transformed into the other becomes two, at once lover and beloved; and two multiplied by two makes four, so that each of them is twain, and both together are one and four (Leone Ebreo, pp. 31 and 260).

ll. 37–40. *A single violet*, &c. Cf. the Funeral Sermon on Lady Danvers:

> But in that *ground*, her Fathers *family*, shee grew not many yeeres. Transplanted young from thence, by marriage, into another *family* of *Honour*, as a flower that doubles and multiplies by transplantation, she multiplied into *ten Children* (*Sermons*, viii. 87).

This implies merely that transplantation will produce more flowers; but in the poem it is the 'strength, the colour, and the size' of the single flower that 'redoubles' and 'multiplies'. I believe that Donne is referring to the fact that

transplantation will produce double from single flowers. There are many references to this in the period and some writers appear to ascribe it not to its true
cause, the richness of the new soil producing a superabundance of petals, but
to 'commixtion of seeds' in the earth. Some such notion of a union of single
flowers to produce double flowers may be behind Donne's analogy. For references to making flowers grow double by transplantation, see Bacon, *Natural
History*, Century VI, section 513, and Century V, section 478, Giambattista
Porta, *Magia Naturalis*, translated as *Natural Magick*, 1658, p. 70, and Puttenham, *The Arte of English Poesie*, ed. Willcock and Walker, 1936, pp. 303–4.

l. 44. *Defects of lonelinesse controules*: overcomes the imperfections of separateness.
Cf. *Paradise Lost*, viii. 422–5.

> But Man by number is to manifest
> His single imperfection, and beget
> Like of his like, his Image multipli'd,
> In unitie defective. . . .

l. 50. *forbeare*: avoid or shun.

l. 52. *spheare*. The singular form is necessitated by the rhyme.
   Leone Ebreo illustrates the love that superior feels for inferior by a long
passage on the love that intelligences bear for the spheres that they govern.
Cf. note to 'Air and Angels', l. 25 (p. 205).

l. 53. *thus*: by the joining of hands and the interchange of eye-beams described
in ll. 5–8.

l. 55. *Yeelded their forces, sense, to us*. The reading of *1633* ('senses force'), which
has only accidental support from *B*, is plainly a sophistication of the misreading in *C 57* ('forces sences').
   The 'forces' of the body are the powers of the sensitive soul, movement and
perception. These the bodies yielded up as the souls of the lovers met in
ecstasy.

ll. 57–58. *On man heavens influence, &c.* It was a fundamental Paracelsian doctrine
that the influence of the stars was mediated by the air and was the 'smell,
smoke, or sweat' of the stars mixed with the air (*Paramirum*, I viii, *Der Bücher
und Schrifften*, Basle, 1589–90, i. 15).

ll. 61–64. *As our blood labours, &c.* Grierson cites Burton:

   Bloud, is a hot, sweet, temperate, red humor, prepared in the *Meseraicke* veines, and
made of the most temperate parts of the *Chylus* in the Liver . . . from it *Spirits* are first
begotten in the heart. . . . Spirit is a most subtile vapour, which is expressed from
the *Bloud*, & the instrument of the soule, to perform all his actions; a common tye or
medium betwixt the body and the soul. . . . Of these spirits there be three kinds. . . .
The *Natural* are begotten in the *Liver* and thence dispersed through the Veins, to
perform those natural actions. The *Vital Spirits* are made in the *Heart* of the *Natural*,
which by the Arteries are transported to all the other parts. . . . The *Animal spirits*
formed of the *Vital*, brought up to the Brain, and diffused by the Nerves, to the

subordinate Members, give sense and motion to them all (part 1, sect. 1, memb. 2, subs. 2).

Cf. also:

In the constitution and making of a natural man, the body is not the man, nor the soul is not the man, but the union of these two makes up the man; the spirits in a man which are the thin and active part of the blood, and so are of a kind of middle nature, between soul and body, those spirits are able to doe, and they doe the office, to unite and apply the faculties of the soul to the organs of the body, and so there is a man (*Sermons*, ii. 261–2).

l. 63. *need*: are necessary (*O.E.D.*, 'need', vb. I.3).

l. 67. *That sense may reach and apprehend*. Against the *consensus* of *1633* and all manuscripts I have emended 'Which' to 'That'. Copyists tend to treat the two forms of the relative as interchangeable, and I am assuming that 'Which' was substituted under the mistaken notion that 'That' was the relative and not the conjunction. The relative here gives poor sense because 'sense' does not 'reach and apprehend' affections and faculties but 'reaches and apprehends' the objects of perception by means of affections and faculties. If we read 'That' (in order that) the action of the souls parallels the action of the blood. Cf. Leone Ebreo who teaches that the mind

... must issue from within the body to its external parts and to the organs of sense and movement in order that man may approach the objects of sense in the world around him, and it is then that we are able to think at the same time as we see, hear, and speak (p. 201).

The blood strives to produce the spirits, or powers of the soul, which are necessary to unite the intellectual and corporal in man. Conversely souls must descend to the affections and faculties of the body in order that man's sense organs may become rational.

A Feaver (p. 61)

MSS.: Σ — *A 25*, *K*.
Miscellanies: *Hd*, *HK 1*, *HK 2**, *Grey*, *TCD* (2).

The hyperbole of the destruction of the world by the death of a mistress derives from Petrarch; see *Rime*, 268, 326, 338, and 352. The conceit that a virtuous woman is the 'worlds soule' is fully developed in *The First Anniversary*.

ll. 13–14.　　　*O wrangling schooles, that search what fire*
　　　　　　　　Shall burne this world,

The belief that the world would end by fire, based on 2 Pet. iii, received much support from Stoic philosophers and the Fathers took over their debates on the nature of the fire. See Aquinas, *S. T.*, IIIᵃ pars, supp., q. lxxvi; under article iii, 'Utrum ignis ille, quo mundus purgabitur, sit eiusdem speciei cum igne elementari', he gives three contrary opinions. For an account of speculation on the final conflagration in the sixteenth and seventeenth centuries, see D. C. Allen, 'Three Notes on Donne's Poetry', *M.L.N.* lxv, 1950.

l. 18. *torturing.* If the Latin or French stress is given the line runs smoothly

$$\overset{\times}{\text{Nor}} \overset{/}{\text{longe}} \mid \overset{/}{\text{beare}} \overset{\times}{\text{this}} \mid \overset{\times}{\text{tortur}} \overset{/}{\text{|ing}} \overset{\times}{\text{wrong.}}$$

With the usual stress the line is harsh and the reading 'tormenting', found in some manuscripts of weak authority, is an obvious attempt to smooth it and avoid two successive inverted stresses:

$$\overset{\times}{\text{Nor}} \overset{/}{\text{longe}} \mid \overset{/}{\text{beare}} \overset{\times}{\text{this}} \mid \overset{/}{\text{tortur}} \overset{\times}{\text{|ing}} \overset{\times}{\text{wrong.}}$$

ll. 21–24. *These burning fits but meteors bee,* &c.

Meteors were imperfect mixtures of the four Elements. They were confined to the region of Air in the sublunary universe, since changing weather conditions could not conceivably transpire in the immutable regions beyond the Moon. The contrast between the transitoriness of meteors and the permanence of the heavens provided the argument for Donne's reassurance of health to his mistress in a fever (S. K. Heninger, *Handbook of Renaissance Meteorology*, Duke University Press, 1960, p. 4; see also pp. 200–1 for a discussion of the poem).

l. 25. *of my minde*: of my opinion.
seising: taking possession of; legally owning.

A Valediction: forbidding Mourning (p. 62)

MSS.: *Σ* — *HK 2, K.*
Miscellanies: *EH, HK 1, Grey, La, Sp*; Brit. Mus. MSS. *Add. 10309, Egerton 2230, Harleian 3511* and *4888, Sloane 1792*; Bodleian MSS. *Ash. 51, Eng. Poet. e 14* and *e 37, Rawl. Poet. 142*; Emmanuel Coll. MS. *1 3 16*; Folger MS. *V a 170.*

I agree with Grierson in correcting *1633* from the manuscripts in l. 20, and differ from him in preferring a manuscript reading in l. 32. Group III (supported by *S*) reads independently in ll. 9, 21, 22, 24, 28, and 30. The variants are trivial in themselves, but their number is striking and suggests that there may be two slightly different authentic versions of this poem. Mr. Hayward adopted an attractive reading from *Sp* in l. 36; see note.

In the fourth edition of his *Life of Donne* (1675) Walton quotes this poem in full as 'a Copy of Verses' given by Donne to his wife when he left her in 1611 to go abroad with the Drury's and adds 'I beg leave to tell, that I have heard some Criticks, learned, both in Languages and Poetry, say, that none of the Greek or Latine Poets did ever equal them'. Reasons for rejecting Walton's story and date are given in the Introduction, p. xxix. Walton's text has some variants which may be due to his inaccuracy in quotation or to his having a manuscript copy more corrupt than any extant manuscript. In view of his dependence throughout the *Life* on printed sources this latter suggestion is improbable. The variants are clearly corruptions and I have not recorded them.

Title. I follow Grierson in punctuating the titles of all four Valedictions in the same way, with a colon separating the general and the specific title.

l. 3. *Whilst.* The weight of manuscript authority is on the side of 'And', but it could so easily have been caught from the line above that I retain the reading of *1633* and Group III.

l. 8. *To tell the layetie our love.* In spite of the hiatus, unusual in Donne, I prefer the reading of *1633*, H *40*, Group I, to 'of our love' (*L 74*, II). The witness of Group III is divided. The reading of Group II gives a smoother line but at the expense of adding an unnecessary preposition which takes metrical stress.

ll. 9–12. Earthquakes cause damage and inspire fear; men calculate what harm they have done and what they portend. The 'trepidation' (or libration) of the ninth, the crystalline, sphere, which communicates its movement to all the spheres beneath it, is imperceptible and harmless. The crystalline sphere was postulated to account for the phenomenon of the precession of the equinoxes.

The contrast between the corruptible regions below the moon, in which such phenomena as earthquakes (classed by the Elizabethans as meteors) occur, and the incorruptible heavens above her sphere leads to the contrast between 'Dull sublunary lovers love' and 'refin'd' love.

l. 13. *sublunary.* The stress is on the first syllable.

l. 14. *Whose soule is sense*: whose animating principle is sensual desire.

l. 16. *elemented*: composed.

l. 18. *That our soules know not what it is.* Cf. 'Negative Love'.

l. 19. *Inter-assured.* Donne's fondness for the prefix 'inter', denoting reciprocal action, is strikingly apparent in *O.E.D.*

ll. 25–36. *If they be two, &c.* A pair of compasses was a well-known emblem, familiar from the device of the firm of Plantin which displays a hand emerging from a cloud and holding a pair of compasses, with the motto '*Labore et Constantia*'. Professor Praz (*Secentismo e Marinismo*, Florence, 1925, p. 109) pointed out a use of the image in a madrigal by Guarini (no. xcvi), and Professor Wilson (*Elizabethan and Jacobean*, 1945, pp. 30 and 133) quoted a use of the image very like Donne's from Hall's *Epistles, The Second Volume*, 1608, Decade I, Epistle 1, p. 6:

An heart truly faithful cannot but have an hand Christianly bountiful: Charity and Faith make up one perfect pair of compasses, that can take the true latitude of a Christian heart: Faith is the one foot, pitch't in the centre unmovable, whiles Charity walks about, in a perfect circle of beneficence: these two never did, never can go asunder.

Guarini's madrigal 'Risposta dell'amante' is a reply by a lover departing for foreign countries to his mistress's fears that he might forsake her, expressed in the preceding madrigal:

> Con voi sempre son io
> Agitato, ma fermo,
> E se'l meno v'involo, il più vi lasso;
> Son simile al compasso,
> Ch'un piede in voi, quasi mio centro, i'fermo,
> L'altro patisce di fortuna i giri,
> Ma non può far, che'n torno a voi non giri.

It seems highly probable that Donne developed the image from Guarini. He employed it again in the 'Obsequies to the Lord Harington' (ll. 105–10) and more than once in his *Sermons*; see Josef Lederer, 'John Donne and the Emblematic Practice', *R.E.S.*, xxii, July 1946.

l. 32. *it*. The agreement of *H 40* and *L 74* makes me prefer 'it' to 'that' (*1633*). This may well be a misreading of the spelling 'yt' found in Group I.

l. 35. *makes*. The reading 'draws', which Mr. Hayward adopted from *Sp*, occurs also in *HK 1*, *Sloane 1792* and Bodleian MS. *Eng. Poet e 37*. It is also found in *JC* (and *D 17*) which I suspect to be the source of the reading. In face of the agreement of *H 40*, *L 74*, I, II, and III it is impossible to reject 'makes'. Repetition is by no means uncharacteristic of Donne's style.

ll. 35–36. The fixed foot both makes the circle perfect and brings the wandering foot back to itself.

A Valediction: of my Name in the Window (p. 64)

MSS.: *Σ — L 74*, *A 25*.
Miscellanies: *HK 1*.

I have departed from *1633* on four occasions: in l. 36 where it follows *C 57*, in l. 5 where it follows Group I, and in ll. 14 and 44 where it reads against Groups I and II. On each occasion I differ from Grierson.

This Valediction differs from all Donne's other poems of parting in that the lover is concerned to admonish rather than to console. He plainly fears his mistress will not be constant.

l. 1. *My name*. The notion that there is some magic power in proper names is common in magical works; see Cornelius Agrippa, *Occult Philosophy*, translated by J. F., 1651, book i, chapter lxx: 'Of the vertue of proper names.' The diamond also had magical properties. Maplet (*A Green Forest*, 1567) says of it: 'Iorach calleth it an other eie: such certaintie and truth giveth it in things done in its presence.'

l. 3. *that charme*: that magical act. The carving of his name makes the glass an amulet or charm.

l. 6. *of either rock*: of the old or the new rock. Diamonds are thus classified in the standard work of the day, Boetius de Boot's *Gemmarum et Lapidum Historia*, Hanover, 1609: 'Orientales a locis ubi inveniuntur, distinguuntur. Alii enim de rupe veteri, alii de rupe nova nominantur . . .' (p. 54).

l. 8. *through-shine*: transparent.

l. 13. *nor*. I retain *1633* because Group I, which it follows, has the support of *H 40*.

l. 14. *accessarie*. Manuscript authority is on the side of the adjective rather than the plural noun of *1633*.

ll. 17–18. The lady may the better attain to the perfect constancy of her absent lover by having always before her as model his unchanging name.

ll. 21–22.   *It, as a given deaths head keepe,*
                     Lovers mortalitie to preach,

Chambers notes that the fashion of wearing death's heads in rings, by way of a *Memento Mori*, is said to have been set by Diane de Poitiers. He cites Beaumont and Fletcher, *The Chances*, I. vi:

> As they keep deaths-heads in rings
> To cry *memento* to me.

The name will serve as a perpetual reminder that they are parted, parting being death to lovers.

l. 24. *my ruinous Anatomie*. Cf. 'In this Chapter . . . we have *Iobs* Anatomy, *Iobs* Sceleton, the ruins to which he was reduced' (*Sermons*, ix. 214).

ll. 25–27. *Then, as all my soules bee*, &c. The three souls in man are the intellectual, the sensitive, and the vegetable. 'Paradise', in Luke xxiii. 43, was sometimes interpreted as heaven, sometimes as an intermediate state of happiness where the souls of the just awaited the general resurrection. For Donne's interest in the question of what happened to the soul at death, see Gardner, *Divine Poems*, pp. xliv–xlvii and 114–17.

l. 28. *the rafters of my body, bone*. Grierson cites 'First, *Ossa*, Bones . . .; They are these Beames, and Timbers, and Rafters of these Tabernacles, these Temples of the Holy Ghost, these bodies of ours' (*Sermons*, v. 352).

ll. 31–32.   *Till my returne repaire*
                     And recompact my scatter'd body so,

The punctuation is that of *1633* before correction. It was corrected to a comma after 'returne' and a full stop at 'so', making this a command to the lady. It is difficult to see how, during his absence, she could 'repaire and recompact' his body merely by cherishing his soul and keeping his skeleton with her. The punctuation I adopt gives an adverbial clause with its verbs in the subjunctive. I take it that stanzas VI and VII form a unit, summed up by the statement that she should, until he returns, 'daily mourne'. I have, therefore, replaced the colon at the end of l. 36 by a comma. The construction of the sentence is clumsy, but the general sense is clear. 'Until my return thus reconstitutes my body, as the powers of the stars are communicated to characters carved when they are in the ascendant, so, since this name was cut under the influence of love and grief, do not shut out its influence.'

ll. 32–36. The basic doctrine of astrology was that all material things made by man receive the influence of those constellations that are in the ascendant when they are made, and that they never lose this celestial energy until they are corrupted or destroyed. This doctrine underlies the practice of 'image-making' in early medicine.

l. 44. *out.* 'Ope' (*1633*, *Lut*, *O'F*, *S 96*, *S*) is a less vigorous reading than 'out', which suggests the lady leaning out to look at her suitor below, and Donne does not elsewhere use the shortened form of 'open'.

l. 48. *Genius*: originally a presiding or tutelary spirit allotted to a man at birth and hence his essential self.

l. 52. *disputed it*: argued the matter.

l. 57. *In superscribing*: in addressing (the letter); see *O.E.D.*, 'superscribe', 2.

l. 65. *this idle talke.* Cf. 'I may die yet, if talking idly be an ill sign' (*Letters*, p. 57).

A Valediction: of the Booke (p. 67)

MSS.: Σ — *L 74*, *S 96*, *A 25*.
Miscellanies: *HK 1*.

I have departed from *1633* on four occasions: in l. 39 where it follows *C 57*, in ll. 25 and 53 where I agree with Grierson in preferring the reading of the majority of the manuscripts (see notes); and in l. 21 where I have made a conjectural emendation (see note).

For reason for dating this poem after 1602, see note to ll. 5–9.

l. 3. *esloygne.* The spelling 'esloign' for 'eloin' was current until the mid-seventeenth century and the word remained in general currency until considerably later. Although Donne cannot be accused of archaism, the word with its legal associations has a flavour of preciosity.

ll. 5–9. François de Billon, in his famous and popular attempt to prove the superiority of women *Le Fort inexpugnable de l'honneur du Sexe Feminin*, Paris, 1555 (pp. 27–30), cites the ancient Sybils and in the following chapter (designed to prove the genius of women in invention and composition) mentions Corinna

and Polla Argentaria, the wife of Lucan. The ultimate source for the triumph
of Corinna over Pindar is Aelian (*Var. Hist.* xiii. 25) and the source for the
tradition that Lucan's wife assisted him to complete the *Pharsalia* appears to
be a letter of Apollinaris Sidonius (*Epist.*, 2, 10, 6).

De Billon is unaware of any tradition that a woman wrote the works of
Homer. This tradition is not Latin but Byzantine. It is found in the *Myrio-
biblion* of Photius, first printed at Augsburg in 1601 and translated into Latin in
1606, and is also referred to by Eustathius of Thessalonica in the preface to his
enormous commentary on the *Odyssey*, printed with his commentary on the
Iliad at Rome, 1542–50, reprinted at Basle, 1559–60, but not translated into
Latin. It was given currency by Lipsius in the first chapter of his *De Bibliothecis Syntagma*, Antwerp, 1602. Wishing to prove that the ancient Egyptians
kept libraries in their temples, he refers to an accusation of plagiary that a
certain Naucrates made against Homer and gives as his reference 'Eustat. in
Praefat. Odyss.'. Naucrates alleged that Homer coming to Egypt found the
books of a woman called Phantasia, who had written the *Iliad* and the
Odyssey and had deposited them in the temple of Vulcan at Memphis. Homer
saw them, put his name to them and published them ('Homerum igitur
vidisse, sibi adscripsisse, et edidisse'). Lipsius's reference to so remote an author
as Eustathius shows that the story had no currency in his day. I cannot explain
why Samuel Butler ascribes it to Diogenes Laertius (*Characters*, &c., ed.
Waller, 1908, p. 429); it is possible it may be referred to in some of the copious
annotations in seventeenth-century editions of Diogenes, though I have not
found it.

Unless an earlier reference to the story can be found, Donne's allusion to
this striking example of female genius must date the poem after 1602.

ll. 10–18. The age of Elizabeth was a great age of antiquarian scholarship.
Donne's awareness of the intellectual currents of his age can be seen in this
advice to a mistress to be 'Love's Antiquary'.

l. 13. *subliming*: purifying. By sublimation solids having been vapourized by
heat are reconverted to solids by cooling, impurities being purged in the
process.

l. 15. *the faith of any ground*: the orthodoxy of any fundamental doctrine.

l. 16. *schismatique*. The stress on the first syllable was retained until the early
nineteenth century.

l. 18. *Records*. Love has given them grace to make, preserve, and use these
archives and to be his 'witnesses'; see *O.E.D.*, 'record', sb. I.3.c for this last
obsolete Biblical sense.

ll. 19–22.   *This Booke, as long-liv'd as the elements,*
              Or as the worlds forme, this all-graved tome,
              In cypher write, or new made Idiome;
              Wee for loves clergie only' are instruments.

Against the agreement of all good manuscripts with *1633* I have emended 'writ' to 'write' in l. 21. If we preserve the past participle we must take the first three lines as an absolute clause as Grierson did, removing the semicolon after 'Idiome' and transferring it to the next line. Grierson rendered the sense as: 'This Book once written, in cipher or new-made idiom, we are thereby (in these letters) the only instruments for Love's clergy. . . .' This misses the point of 'only' which qualifies 'clergie' not 'instruments'. It also obscures the fresh point the stanza makes: that the book is to be written in a secret alphabet or secret language so that only the clergy can read it. This point seems too important to be communicated by a participle. With the emendation of 'writ' to 'write' the sequence of ideas is clear and the lines are easily punctuated. She is to study, then she is to write, and further she is to write in cipher or a specially minted language. The mysteries of love are not for the profane laity.

The Book will last as long as the world or longer. The 'elements' are the matter of the world upon which form has been imposed. This form of the world is its eternal idea subsisting in the mind of the Creator. The Book is to be 'all-graved', or indelibly written. This figurative use of 'graved', commonly used for what is permanently impressed on the mind or heart, seems to have puzzled scribes since the reading 'Tombe' for 'Tome' occurs sporadically in the manuscripts.

ll. 24–25   *Should againe the ravenous*
                              Vandals and Goths inundate us,

I agree with Grierson in rejecting the reading of *1633*: 'and the Goths invade'. This appears to be a sophistication of the reading found in *Dob, Lut, O'F, O, P, JC, S*, patching their short line by the addition of the definite article. It is an example of the sporadic contact there seems to be between the copy for *1633* and the tradition in Group III. Grierson cites in defence of 'inundate', Donne's reference to the 'Inundation of the *Goths* in *Italy*' (Simpson, *Essays*, p. 61) and refers to Isa. viii. 7–8 where the Assyrian invasion is spoken of as a river over-flowing (Vulgate 'inundans'). *O.E.D.* cites Puttenham as its first example of this figurative use: 'the notable inundations of the Hunnes and Vandalles.'

l. 26. *Universe*: university. Since 'university' was frequently used for 'universe' at this period, I assume that Donne regards the words as interchangeable, although there is no example given of this use of 'universe' in *O.E.D.*

l. 27. *Angels Verse*. I presume that Angels are thought of as expert in versing because of the tradition of angelic song.

l. 32. *amuze*: puzzle.

l. 36. *type*: the earthly counterpart of a heavenly reality which it 'figures' or represents.

ll. 37–45. *Here more then in their bookes*, &c. Donne sat in the Parliament of 1601

in which discontent over monopolies, patents, and privileges reached its
height. There was strong pressure to bring all such grants to the test of the
Common Law. This was as strongly opposed by those who argued that this
would touch the royal prerogative. The same clash arose over subsidies,
special grants levied in time of need, which it was claimed were also a matter
of prerogative. See J. E. Neale, *Elizabeth and her Parliaments, 1584–1601*, 1957,
pp. 369–93 and 411–22.

'Here, rather than in their law-books, lawyers will find what entitles lovers
to the possession of their mistresses and how their rights are eaten into by
prerogative, transferred by Love, as sovereign, to the race of women. Women,
although they demand extraordinary payments of devotion and tears from
their lovers, disappoint the expectations of those who depend on them, giving
as reason the claims of honour or conscience, figments as worthless as themselves or their prerogative.'

'States' is used in its legal sense of 'the interest which anyone has in a
property; right or title to a property'. It seems probable that 'rely' is also
used in an obsolete legal sense: 'to hold of, be a vassal of'. 'Forsake' is used in
the obsolete sense of 'fail, or disappoint the expectations of'. Women are
not accused of infidelity, but of refusing to their lovers what they have a
right to expect. Since the speaker and his mistress have not restricted themselves to 'abstract spiritual love', lawyers will find in the Book 'rule and
example' by which to condemn current practice.

For other allusions to the question of prerogative, see 'Love's Exchange' and
'Love's Deity' and notes (pp. 168 and 170).

ll. 46–52. *Here Statesmen,* &c. 'Here politicians . . . will find the essential rudi-
ments of their profession. Neither love nor statecraft can be defined. In both
present success is the criterion of excellence, and to have the reputation of
strength.' Cf. 'Negative Love', 'A Valediction: forbidding Mourning', and
'The Relic' for the notion that lovers do not know what they love or what
love is.

ll. 53–54.   *In this thy booke, such will their nothing see,*
                     As in the Bible some can finde out Alchimy.

I regard the agreement of *O* and *P* with *1633* in reading 'there something' as
coincidental. It is an obvious sophistication of an at first sight difficult reading.

Statesmen will find their own 'nothing' in the 'nothing' of the lovers in the
same way as Alchemists find support for their doctrines in the Bible. Grierson
cites

And as our Alchymists can finde their whole art and worke of Alchymy, not onely
in *Virgil* and *Ovid*, but in *Moses* and *Solomon* . . . (*Sermons*, vii. 191).

He also quotes Montaigne, *Apologie de Raimond Sebond* (*Essays*, ii. 12).

Unlike the lawyers who will use the book to establish the true laws of love, statesmen will use it to find justification for their own lack of principle and opportunism.

l. 55. *vent*. Cf. *Twelfth Night*, IV. i, where Feste mocks at Sebastian for using this word. Donne's language throughout this poem seems strained.

ll. 59–63. Grierson comments: 'The latitude of a spot may always be found by measuring the distance from the zenith of a star whose altitude, i.e. distance from the equator, is known.' He also states that the method of estimating longitude by eclipses was first discovered by noting that an eclipse which took place during the battle of Arbela was observed at Alexandria an hour later. See R. Gemma Frisius, translated into French by Claude de Bossière, 1582, for methods of calculating longitude by eclipses.

Grierson rightly observes that the comparison 'rests on a purely verbal basis. "Longitude" means "length", "latitude", "breadth". Therefore longitude is compared with the duration of love. . . . There is no real appropriateness.'

A Valediction: of Weeping (p. 69)

MSS.: Σ — A 25, K.
Miscellanies: HK 1.

I differ from Grierson in rejecting the reading of *1633* in l. 8; see note.

The basic conceit is that an image reflected in a tear is an emblem of death by drowning; cf. 'Witchcraft by a Picture'. At the beginning the lover weeps and attempts to justify indulgence in grief; but when his mistress begins to weep too (l. 17) his mood changes and the poem becomes a valediction 'forbidding mourning', employing arguments used in 'Sweetest Love, I do not goe'.

l. 8. *falls*. The reading of *1633*, 'falst', occurs also in Group III, *Cy, O, P, B*. I regard it as an obvious correction of what might easily be taken to be a false concord.

'When a tear falls the image of thee that it bore falls with it and is dissolved. In the same way thou and I are dead when parted by the sea between us.'

ll. 10–13. The workman has copies, not originals, of maps beside him which he pastes onto a round ball to make a 'globe'. Cf.

Though the labour of any ordinary Artificer in that Trade, will bring East and West together, (for if a flat Map be but pasted upon a round Globe, the farthest East, and the Farthest West meet, and are all one) . . . (Donne to Sir Robert Carr, 1624, *Tobie Mathew Collection*, p. 306).

l. 12. *Asia*. This was pronounced as a trisyllable; cf. *Tamburlaine*, Pt. 2, IV. iii. 1·

Holla, ye pampered jades of Asia.

ll. 17–18. The lady is now weeping too and her tears, mingling with his, drown the world that her image printed on his tears had created. She is his 'heaven' from which these floods pour down, a heaven dissolved into water.

ll. 19–20. As her tears drown the image of her, so his tears will destroy his image. He implores her not to draw tears from him that will drown him as her tears have drowned her. She is 'more then Moone' because the moon is only mistress of the tides. She can draw seas up into her sphere.

l. 21. Speech stress and metrical stress pull against each other here. The line depends on our giving the metrical stress, which as often in Donne falls on the personal pronouns, sufficient weight:

$$\text{Weepe me} \mid \text{not dead,} \mid \text{in thine} \mid \text{armes, but} \mid \text{forbeare.}$$

ll. 26–27. For the idea of the soul in the breath, cf. 'The Expiration' and note (p. 159). We may take it either that the breath of the lovers is commingled as are their tears, or that, since their souls are one, each sighs out the other's soul. For the idea that each sigh costs a drop of blood, see note to 'Sweetest Love, I do not goe' (p. 155).

The Good-morrow (p. 70)

MSS.: Σ — Cy.
Miscellanies: Hd, Grey, TCD (2); Brit. Mus. MS. Egerton 2230; Emmanuel Coll. MS. 1 3 16; Folger MS. V a 103; Rosenbach MS. 1083/16.

There are clearly two traditions in manuscript, H 40 and Group I reading against L 74, Group II, HK 2, P, A 25 in ll. 3, 4, 10, 11, 16, 17, 19, 20, and 21. In ll. 3, 17, and 21 H 40 and Group I stand alone (except for the support of JC in l. 17). Otherwise they have the support of Group III.

The text of 1633 follows Group I and I agree with Grierson in retaining it, except for two minor corrections: in l. 13 where 'other' (1633) appears to be a misprint for 'others', and in l. 14 where 1633 follows Group I in reading 'one' where H 40 and all other manuscripts (except JC) read 'our'.

Two of the three readings peculiar to H 40 and Group I (ll. 3 and 21) are difficult to explain on any other hypothesis than the author's revision of his text. In both cases the reading of H 40 and Group I is the more forceful and, therefore, presumably, the later. The same is true of the reading in l. 4, where H 40 and Group I have the support of Group III. In the remaining readings it is difficult to argue for the superiority of either version. If we accept the version in H 40 and Group I, printed in 1633, as the final version, the textual situation could be explained on the hypothesis that Donne made alterations in the original copy of the poem and did not write out a fair copy of his final version. The ancestor of L 74, Group II, &c., would then be a copy of the original poem; the ancestor of Group III a copy of the corrected version which incorporated most but not all the corrections; and the ancestor of *H 40* and Group I would be a copy that included all the second thoughts. Or it might be held that there were three stages and that the readings peculiar to *H 40* and Group I were 'third thoughts'.

ll. 1–3. As in 'His Picture', ll. 17–20, Donne has borrowed from devotional literature the Pauline contrast between milk for babes and meat for grown men.

l. 3. *suck'd on countrey pleasures, childishly.* This reading (*1633, H 40,* I) is so much stronger than the weakly repetitive 'childish pleasures seelily' that it must be either the original of which the other is a corruption or an improvement made by the author. I incline to the second explanation because corruption does not seem a sufficient explanation either here or in l. 21 for transposition as well as alteration of words.

countrey pleasures: rustic, hence unrefined pleasures. Cf. 'country grasse', 'Love's Usury', l. 14, also 'To Sir Henry Wotton' (Grierson, i. 180–2), l. 61: 'A dramme of Countries dulnesse.' There may be a hint of what Hamlet intends in his *riposte* to Ophelia: 'Do you think I meant country matters?' If so, the lady, as well as her lover, has enjoyed such pleasures.

l. 4. *snorted*; snored. This reading (*1663, H 40,* I, III) is again far more vivid than 'slumbred' (*L 74,* II, &c.).

the seaven sleepers den. Under the persecution of Decius seven noble youths took refuge in a cave where their pursuers walled them up to starve to death. A miraculous slumber fell upon them which lasted 187 years. See the close of chapter xxxiii of Gibbon's *Decline and Fall* for the sources of this 'memorable fable'.

l. 5. *But this*: except for this.

ll. 6–7. *If ever any beauty I did see,* &c. Cf. Shakespeare, Sonnet xxxi, 'Thy bosom is endeared with all hearts'. Professor Praz cited a parallel from Tasso, *Rime,* I. xlii:

> L'altre bellezze, ove m'insidia amore,
> Sono imagini vostre e vostri raggi.

ll. 12–14. *Let sea-discoverers,* &c. This, again, is a commonplace of Elizabethan poetry; cf. Spenser, Amoretti xv: 'Ye tradefull Merchants, that with weary toyle.'

maps: probably 'maps' of the heavens showing new spheres. Cf. Holy Sonnet, 'I am a little world made cunningly':

> You which beyond that heaven which was most high
> Have found new sphears, and of new lands can write. . . .

l. 14. *Let us possesse our world, each hath one, and is one.* I do not doubt that the reading of *1633* ('one world') reproduces an error in Group I. The 'world' of each is the other. Since they are 'one' they possess one world which is 'ours', but there are also four worlds, since each 'hath one and is one'; see note to 'The Ecstasy', l. 36 (p. 185).

l. 17. *two better hemispheares.* Presumably, as Grierson says, looking in each other's eyes each beholds only a hemisphere, since the whole world cannot be at once visible.

l. 19. *What ever dyes, was not mixt equally.* Grierson cites Aquinas:

Non invenitur corruptio nisi ubi invenitur contrarietas; generationes enim et corruptiones ex contrariis et in contraria sunt (*S.T.*, I³ pars, q. lxxv, art. 6).

ll. 20–21. 'If our two loves are wholly united in one love, or, if they are always alike and at the same pitch, neither can perish.'

As in l. 3 it seems impossible to explain the variants in these two lines on any other theory than that of the poet's rewriting an unsatisfactory line. Neither version provides a close worthy of the poem's opening. Conditional clauses must always suggest an element of doubt.

The Anniversarie (p. 71)

MSS.: *Σ — L 74, A 25, K.*
Miscellanies: *Hd, HK 1, Grey.*

On two occasions (ll. 10 and 23–24) Group II reads against all other manuscripts and its readings have been adopted by *1633.* I follow Grierson in retaining *1633* here and also in rejecting *1633* in l. 22; see notes.

l. 1. *All Kings, &c.* When read with 'The Sun Rising' and 'The Canonization' this poem seems likely to have been written, as they were, when James was on the throne. It breathes the same scorn for the Court from which Donne was an exile.

l. 2. *honors.* Although there is no example in *O.E.D.* of such a use without the personal pronoun, taken with 'beauties' and 'wits', 'honors' must mean persons of honour. Cf. 'The Canonization', l. 6: 'Observe his honour.'

l. 10. *his: its.* The personal pronoun sounds more natural than the definite article here. As in ll. 23–24 *1633* follows Group II. I retain *1633* because this poem is not found in *L 74.* As among the poems that Group II adds to those it shares with *L 74* there are some unfinished poems, we may presume that the compiler of the larger collection had access to Donne's papers. Since in one of the 'Holy Sonnets' Group II alone preserves what is certainly a rewriting of a line, I regard texts in this section of the Group II manuscripts as likely to be final versions. See Textual Introduction, pp. lxviii–lxx.

ll. 11–12. *Two graves, &c.* Their love is clandestine. They may not, as married lovers may, expect to be 'married in the dust'; see Introduction, p. xxix.

l. 17. *dwells:* resides permanently.

l. 18. *inmates*: temporary lodgers.

prove: experience.

l. 20. The concept of the soul as buried in the body is unusual in Donne and is quickly repudiated in the next stanza.

ll. 21–22.   *And then wee shall be throughly blest,*
              But wee no more, then all the rest.

1633 stands alone in reading 'But now no more . . .'. This is a clear example of unintelligent correction of the manuscript reading by whoever prepared the copy for *1633*. Reading only the first two lines of the stanza, thinking that an antithesis was required to 'then', and taking 'wee', no doubt, as erroneously caught from the line above, he substituted 'now' to the destruction of the sense. The point of the stanza as a whole is that the bliss they enjoy now on earth is preferable to the bliss they will enjoy in heaven since *now* they are better off than 'all the rest', *then* they will enjoy only a common felicity.

Grierson points out that the Scholastics did not hold that all in heaven were equally blest, but that each was blest according to his capacity and so all were equally content; see Aquinas, *S. T.*, Supp., q. xciii, art. v. The scholastic distinction was between 'gaudium' which was equal and 'beatitudo' which was not. The joy was equal because in heaven each rejoices in others' good as well as in his own. Donne's point is a true one: there is no place in heaven for the *égoïsme à deux* of this poem.

ll. 23–24.   *Here upon earth, we'are Kings, and none but wee*
              Can be such Kings,
I retain the reading of *1633* and Group II. All other manuscripts read

              Here upon earth we'are Kings, and but wee
              None are such Kings,

This gives a line with a missing medial syllable:

              Here up|on earth, | we'are Kings,|| and | but wee.

There are a good many parallel examples of this licence in Donne's poems; see note to 'The Perfume', l. 21 (p. 123). But it seems unlikely that a copyist would recast two lines to avoid metrical hiatus and this may more probably be an example of a minor alteration by Donne to give a smoother, if less forceful, line.

The Sunne Rising (p. 72)

MSS.: *Σ* — *H 40.*
Miscellanies: *Grey*; Folger MS. *V a 103.*

This poem is remarkably free of textual variation. The fact that there are a certain number of the *Songs and Sonnets* of which this can be said lends support

to the theory that when variants that are not obviously corruptions are found
they have arisen from the author's alterations, since there seems no reason
why poems with the same textual history should differ widely in the care
with which they were copied.

Grierson refers to Ovid, *Amores*, I. xiii:

> Iam super oceanum venit a seniore marito
> flava pruinoso quae vehit axe diem.
> 'Quo properas, Aurora? . . .
> quo properas, ingrata viris, ingrata puellis?'

He adds 'a comparison of Ovid's simple and natural images and reflections
with Donne's passionate but ingenious hyperboles will show exactly what
Testi meant by his contrast of the homely imagery of classical and the metaphysical manner of Italian love poetry'. Coleridge said of this poem: 'Fine,
vigorous exultation, both soul and body in full puissance' (*Miscellaneous
Criticism*, ed. Raysor, 1936, p. 136).

l. 1. *Busie old foole*. Ovid mocks Aurora for her haste to leave the bed of her
aged lover Tithonus. Donne mocks the sun as an aged busybody.

unruly: straying beyond bounds. The sun in interfering where he has no
legitimate right.

ll. 5–6.

> *Sawcy pedantique wretch, goe chide*
> *Late schoole-boyes, and sowre prentices,*

Cf. Ovid, ibid., ll. 17–18:

> tu pueros somno fraudas tradisque magistris,
> ut subeant tenerae verbera saeva manus.

Donne has perhaps caught from Marlowe's translation the epithet, which
makes the sun a tetchy schoolmaster:

> Thou cousenst boyes of sleepe, and doest betray them
> To *Pedants* that with cruell lashes pay them.

l. 7. *Goe tell Court-huntsmen, that the King will ride*. As Professor Praz was the
first to point out, this is clearly a topical jest at King James's passion for
hunting which, to his attendants' disgust, involved early rising.

l. 8. *Call countrey ants to harvest offices*: call farm-drudges to the tasks of harvest-
ing. Cf. Ovid, ibid., ll. 15–16:

> prima bidente vides oneratos arva colentes,
> prima vocas tardos sub iuga panda boves.

l. 9. *all alike*: always the same.

l. 10. *rags of time*. Cf. the Christmas Sermon of 1624:

> We begin with that which is elder then our beginning, and shall over-live our end,
> The mercy of God. . . . The names of first or last derogate from it, for first and last
> are but ragges of time, and his mercy hath no relation to time, no limitation in time,
> it is not first, nor last, but eternall, everlasting (*Sermons*, vi. 170).

The passage might equally have been cited to illustrate 'The Anniversary', ll. 9–10. The two poems are very close in thought and expression.

l. 17. *both the'India's of spice and Myne*: the East and West Indies. Cf. Donne's letter to Sir Robert Carr in 1624:

> Your way into *Spain* was Eastward, and that is the way to the land of Perfumes and Spices; their way hither is Westward, and that is the way to the land of Gold, and of Mynes (*Tobie Mathew Collection*, p. 305).

l. 23. For the scansion of this line, see note on Versification, p. 110.

l. 24. *alchimie*: glittering dross; see *O.E.D.*, 'alchemy', 4.

l. 25. *halfe as happy'as wee*. His satisfaction is a solitary one.

l. 27. *Thine age askes ease*. Cf. Ovid, *Metam.* ii. 385–7, where Phoebus after the death of Phaeton complains of his endless unrequited toil:

> 'satis' inquit 'ab aevi
> sors mea principiis fuit inrequieta, pigetque
> actorum sine fine mihi, sine honore laborum.

l. 30. *thy center*: the centre of your universe, the earth about which you must revolve.

The Canonization (p. 73)

MSS.: *Σ — L 74, A 25*.
Miscellanies: *Grey, Hd, HK 1, La, RP 117 (2), TCD (2)*.

In addition to correcting a misprint in l. 44, I have abandoned *1633* on six occasions. In l. 15 it follows *C 57* and *Lec* against all other manuscripts. In ll. 29 and 45 it follows Group I against *H 40*, II and III; and in l. 30 it follows Group I supported by *H 40*. Grierson abandoned *1633* in ll. 30 and 45, but retained it in ll. 15 and 29. In ll. 7 and 40 *1633* has no manuscript support. Grierson retained its readings which I reject as sophistications; see notes.

As in 'The Sun Rising' Donne has transformed an Ovidian theme. In *Amores*, II. x Ovid tells a friend who had said that it was impossible to love two women at once that he now does so, boasts of the superiority of a life devoted to love, declares his willingness to 'die by love' and pictures a fellow-lover at his funeral declaring 'Thine was a death accorded with thy life'.

> felix, quem Veneris certamina mutua perdunt!
>   di faciant, leti causa sit ista mei!
> Induat adversis contraria pectora telis
>   miles et aeternum sanguine nomen emat.
> quaerat avarus opes et, quae lassarit arando
>   aequora periuro naufragus ore bibat.
> at mihi contingat Veneris languescere motu,
>   cum moriar, medium solvar et inter opus;
> atque aliquis nostro lacrimans in funere dicat:
>   'Conveniens vitae mors fuit ista tuae!'

Mr. H. S. Meller has suggested a source in an emblematic design, accompanied by a sonnet, in Giolito's edition of Petrarch (Venice, 1544). This shows portraits of Petrarch and Laura on a 'well-wrought urn' which is surmounted by a phoenix. Mr. A. J. Smith, accepting the suggestion, pointed out how wholly Donne had transformed the concepts expressed in the design and the sonnet. See *T.L.S.*, 22 April and 13 May, 1965.

Coleridge said of this poem:

One of my favourite poems. As late as ten years ago, I used to seek and find out grand lines and fine stanzas; but my delight has been far greater since it has consisted more in tracing the leading thought thro'out the whole (*Miscellaneous Criticism*, ed. Raysor, p. 137).

For an account of an eighteenth-century imitation of 'The Canonization', see P. Scholes, *Life of Sir John Hawkins*, 1953, app. 6, pp. 262–3.

l. 1. *love*. The poem is rhymed throughout on this word.

l. 5. 'Follow a career, get a position at Court.'

l. 6. 'Dance attendance on either temporal or spiritual dignitaries.'

ll. 7–8.   *And the Kings reall, or his stamped face*
              Contemplate;

1633 is alone in reading 'Or the Kings' The 'editor' in preparing the copy mistook the sense and thought the clause one of a series of alternatives. But Donne is giving a thumb-nail sketch of a careerist: he embarks on a career, gets himself an office, flatters the great, and rises to the inner circle around the King where most profit is to be found. I have strengthened the comma of *1633* after 'Contemplate' to a semicolon to make clear that the verb governs the preceding nouns.

l. 8. *what you will, approve*: try anything you like.

l. 15. *man*. *1633* follows *C 57* and *Lec* in the less vivid reading 'more'.
the plaguie Bill: the printed list of deaths from plague. They appear to have been first issued in the great plague of 1592–3 and to have appeared weekly during outbreaks. See F. P. Wilson, *The Plague in Shakespeare's London*, 1927.

ll. 19–27. Mr. Josef Lederer ('John Donne and Emblematic Practice', *R.E.S.*, xxii, 1946) justly observes of this stanza 'It looks as if Donne were running quickly through the pages of an emblem book'. He notes the use of the word 'ridle', often another term for 'emblem', and of the word 'mysterious', commenting that 'emblem writers often emphasize the esoteric character of their art'. See also Mario Praz, *Studies in Seventeenth Century Imagery*, 1939 and 1947.

l. 20. *flye*. The comparison of lovers to a butterfly attracted to its death by the flame of a candle derives ultimately from Petrarch. The emblem is very common with the motto 'Brevis et damnosa voluptas'.

l. 21. *Tapers.* This image arises out of the preceding one. I have not come across it as an emblem. The taper that consumes itself in burning is a type of the lover who destroys himself by love. Cf. 'Farewell to Love', ll. 24–25 and note (p. 213).

l. 22. *the' Eagle and the Dove*: emblems of strength and gentleness. Joined, they symbolize the perfection of masculine and feminine qualities; cf. Crashaw's address to St. Teresa, 'By all the Eagle in thee, all the Dove'. See Hadrianus Junius, *Emblemata*, Antwerp, 1565, emblem 39.

ll. 23–25.   *The Phœnix ridle hath more wit*
                           By us, we two being one, are it,
                           So, to one neutrall thing both sexes fit.

I have restored, against Grierson, the full stop of *1633* after 'fit', and emended its full stop after 'it' to a comma. I take l. 25 as an elucidation and expansion of the two preceding lines. The next two lines add the further resemblance of miraculous resurrections.

   hath more wit: makes more sense.

   The Phoenix, with the motto 'Unica semper avis', is a common emblem. There was but one phoenix, sole and self-propagating, which consumed itself in fire and rose again the same from its ashes. The perfect union of the lovers creates a 'neutral thing' neither masculine nor feminine.

ll. 26–27. *prove | Mysterious*: become a mystery, that is, something beyond reason, accepted by faith.

l. 29. *hearse.* Memorial inscriptions were hung on hearses.

l. 30. *legend.* As saints and martyrs of love they have created a 'legend'.

l. 31. *no peece of Chronicle.* Love has no concern with time and so lovers have no history.

l. 32. *sonnets*: love-lyrics.

   roomes. Possibly as Mr. James Reeves suggested, there is a pun on 'stanza', the Italian for 'room'.

l. 39. *that now is rage.* Cf. 'To desire without fruition, is a rage, and to enjoy without desire is a stupidity' (*Sermons*, i. 237).

l. 40. *extract. 1633* is alone in reading 'contract'. This destroys the alchemical metaphor and with it the pun on glasses and makes the verb 'drove' unintelligible. See Textual Introduction, p. lxxxvi.

   The 'soul' of the world is extracted and driven into their eyes as an alchemist makes an extract by sublimation and distillation, driving it through the pipes of the still into the 'glasses', or vessels, in which it is stored. These 'glasses' then become mirrors.

Aire and Angels (p. 75)

MSS.: *Σ* — *L 74, Cy, A 25.*
Miscellanies: *Hd, HK 1.*

This and the following three poems may be regarded as 'Problems of Love' or 'Lectures on Love's Philosophy'. For discussion of interpretations of this poem, see Helen Gardner, *The Business of Criticism*, 1959, pp. 62–75 and A. J. Smith, 'New Bearings in Donne: "Air and Angels" ', *English*, xiii, 1960, reprinted in *Twentieth-Century Views: John Donne*, ed. Helen Gardner, Englewood Cliffs, N.J., 1962.

ll. 1–2. Cf. 'The Good-morrow', ll. 6–7.

l. 3. *in a shapelesse flame*: not a steady but a sudden flaring light. Cf. the old saying, 'By this fire, that's God's angel'.

l. 5. *still*: always.

l. 6. *lovely glorious nothing.* Cf. 'Negative Love' and notes (pp. 177–8).

l. 9. *subtile:* delicate, fastidious.

l. 18. *pinnace*: a light scouting vessel.

l. 22. *Extreme*: extremely.
inhere. Like 'assume' this word has theological connotations. The redeemed 'inhere' in Christ. Love cannot inhere in nothing or in things that however beautiful are still material, but only in love.

l. 23. *Then as an Angell*, &c. Grierson cites Aquinas, *S. T.*, pars, Iᵃ q. li, art. 2: 'Utrum Angeli assumant corpora.' All matter consists of the four elements. Since angels appear and, as suddenly, vanish their bodies cannot be made of earth or water; neither can they be made of fire which burns all it touches or of air which is invisible. They make for themselves bodies of air condensed into cloud: 'Angeli assumunt corpora ex aere, condensando ipsum virtute divina, quantum necesse est ad corporis assumendi formationem.'

l. 24. *not pure as it, yet pure.* Though pure, that is, simple and unmixed, air is still a material element and has not the purity of spirit.

l. 25. *so thy love may be my loves sphaere.* Cf. 'The Ecstasy', l. 52, where souls are equated with Intelligences, ruling bodies as they rule spheres. Throughout the poem the lover is the active, or masculine, principle seeking a proper passive complement. Cf. 'Love's Deity' where Love's proper object is 'to fit actives to passives' and make 'correspondencie'. His love is regarded as soul seeking a body, that is, form seeking matter to inform; and here it appears as an intelligence finding the sphere it can animate and rule.

ll. 26–28. That women's love is less pure than men's is orthodox doctrine. Cf.

the Homily 'Of the State of Matrimony' (*Second Book of Homilies*, 1563) and
Orsino in *Twelfth Night*, II. iv. 96–98:

> Alas, their love may be call'd appetite—
> No motion of the liver, but the palate,—
> That suffer surfeit, cloyment, and revolt.

Even those who take a less low view of women's love than this have to come
to terms with the universal assumption of the superiority of all things
masculine. Philo, the lover, in Leone Ebreo's *Dialogues*, apologetically explains
to Sophia that his love is superior to hers:

> Suffer me to say, O Sophia, that the love of man, who gives, is more perfect than that
> of woman, who receives (p. 181).

A. J. Smith quotes from Sperone Speroni (*Opere*, Venice, 1740, i. 33) a passage
to the same effect.

Franciscus Georgius *Problemata in Sacris Scripturis*, Paris, 1574, asks why men
and women naturally desire each other and replies:

> Nonne (ut Plato inquit) cum alter sit dimidium alterius, uterque appetit dimidium
> sui? . . . Sed cur foemina magis appetit virum quam e converso? Quod innuere videtur
> Arist. dum ait. Materia appetit formam, sicut foemina virum. An, quia vir perfectior
> est: et imperfectum magis appetit perfectum, quam e converso? Propterea materia
> appetit formam, et non forma materiam. An (ut alii opinantur) foemina appetit
> virum, id est esse virum, ut sortiatur meliorem sexum et statum? Est itaque mutuus
> amor inter eos: quamvis ardentior sit in minus perfecto.

In the light of the universal assumption of the superiority of masculine love
Donne's close seems aimed to diminish the distinction between man's love
(which is pure spirit) and woman's (which is the most rarefied of material
things).

Loves Growth (p. 76)

MSS.: *Σ* — *H 40, L 74, HK 2, A 25.*
Miscellanies: *Grey, Hd, HK 1.*

I have rejected *1633* on two occasions (ll. 15 and 23) where Grierson retained its readings. On both occasions the edition has no support except from
S. The variants in ll. 9, 10, 11, and 28 suggest at first sight that there might
be two versions of the poem; but the fact that in ll. 10 and 28 the witness
of Group III is divided makes this doubtful. If the variants are authorial
it is impossible to suggest which is the earlier and which the later version.
I agree with Grierson in retaining the text of *1633* which has the support of
Groups I and II, particularly since this is a poem that Group II does not share
with *L 74*; see Textual Introduction, pp. lxviii–lxx.

For a different treatment of this theme, see Shakespeare, Sonnet cxv, 'Those
lines that I before have writ do lie'.

Title: 1633 has, as usual, taken its title from Group II, though this is one of the
few poems with a title in Group I. The title there and elsewhere is 'Spring'.

l. 1. *pure*: simple and unmixed, therefore not subject to change.

ll. 7–8.   *But if this medicine, love, which cures all sorrow*
                  With more, not onely bee no quintessence,

Cf. Puttenham, *Arte of English Poesy*:

  Not with any medicament of a contrary temper, as the *Galenists* use to cure (*contraria contrariis*) but as the *Paracelsians*, who cure (*similia similibus*) making one dolour to expell another (I. xxiv).

  quintessence. Paracelsus held that every substance contained a quintessence which, extracted from it, contained the force or virtue of the substance purged of all impurities. See Paracelsus, *Archidoxis*, I. iv. 35, cited by Grierson. Paracelsus sometimes speaks as if there were one 'quintessence' giving virtue to all substances, the 'generall balme' of 'A Nocturnal' (l. 6); and sometimes as if each substance had its own quintessence; cf. 'To the Countess of Bedford' (Grierson, i. 190):

                  In every thing there naturally growes
                  A *Balsamum* to keepe it fresh, and new.

Belief in the quintessence justified the use of chemical medicines by the Paracelsians who aimed at stimulating the natural forces to resist disease. Galenists aimed at restoring the natural balance of the humours. See *Letters*, pp. 97–98.

ll. 13–14. *elemented*: made up of elements, mixed.

  sometimes would contemplate, sometimes do. In Mystical Theology the Mixed Life, part active and part contemplative, is the life proper to prelates and was the life led by Christ on earth; see Aquinas, *S.T.*, IIᵃ pars, IIᵃᵉ partis, q. clxxxii, art. 1.

ll. 15–18. *And yet not greater, but more eminent*, &c. I cannot accept Grierson's explanation that l. 18 means that stars are not enlarged by the sun but are made to seem larger. I think 'by the Sunne' means 'near the sun'. Love has risen higher in the heavens by spring and shines the more brilliantly as do stars when near to the sun.

ll. 25–28. As in 'A Lecture upon the Shadow', Donne concludes by rejecting his analogy between the times and seasons of the natural world and the course of love.

Loves Infiniteness (p. 77)

MSS.: *Σ* — *L 74*, Group II, *Cy, O, K*.
Miscellanies: *RP 117 (2)*; Brit. Mus. MS. *Egerton 2230*; Bodleian MS. *Eng. Poet. c 50*; Rosenbach MS. *1083/16*.

  I have rejected *1633* in l. 5 where it has no manuscript support. I have also supplied elision marks in the second person singular of the verbs in ll. 12, 28, and 30.

HK 2, O, P, and *A 25* have variants in the third stanza (ll. 25–26 and 29–30) and on the second occasion *JC* has a variant of their variant. The general credit of these manuscripts is low, and the fact that in l. 32 they disagree in bad readings suggests that the copy that lies behind them was damaged or illegible and their variants in ll. 25–26 and 29–30 are only better efforts at sense than they made in l. 32.

For a setting of what appears to be a modified version or an imitation of this poem, see Appendix B, 'Musical Settings of Donne's Poems'.

Title. The only title found in manuscript is 'Mon Tout' (*A 25*). The title supplied by the editor of *1633* was a good one; but I have accepted Grierson's suggestion that 'Lovers' should be emended to 'Loves'.

l. 5. *All my treasure.* All the manuscripts agree in beginning this line with the emphatic monosyllable 'All'. This is weakened by the 'And' prefixed in *1633* to provide an initial weak syllable. Both the second and third stanzas of the poem open with lines that lack an initial syllable.

A Lecture upon the Shadow (p. 78)

MSS.: *Σ — Cy.*
Miscellanies: *HK 1, La*; Brit. Mus. MS. *Egerton 2230.*

For no reason that I can suggest this poem, though present in both Groups I and II, was not printed in *1633*. It appeared in *1635*. The text there follows closely the text in *L 74*, II, *HK 2*, which differs considerably from the text in *H 40*, I, except in l. 26 where *1635* has an erroneous reading not found in any manuscript. I agree with Grierson in accepting the readings of *1635*, *L 74*, II, except in l. 11 where I adopt a singular noun from *H 40*, I.

l. 11. *care.* 'Cares' (*1635*, *L 74*, II) would mean 'griefs and anxieties'. But this is not what is meant, as reference to ll. 16–17 shows. The disguises and shadows arose from their 'care' to hide their love from others.

l. 17. *come behinde*: come later. 'Behinde' cannot be an adverb of place, implying that the shadows of the first stanza which were 'before' them are now 'behind'; for this would mean the lovers had spent three hours walking steadily in one direction, which is absurd. They have been 'walking here', that is, strolling to and fro, with their shadows sometimes behind them, sometimes in front.

l. 19. *faint . . . decline.* Donne usually employs the subjunctive in conditional clauses.

ll. 25–26. Cf. the close of 'Love's Growth'. As love's year has no winter, so his day has no afternoon.

The Dreame (p. 79)

MSS.: *Σ* — *H 40, D 17, JC, K.*
Miscellanies: *CCC, Grey, HK 1, RP 31, Wel.*

The text in *1633* is strikingly independent of the usual sources of the edition. In ll. 7–8 it reads with Groups I and II and in l. 10 it has a reading elsewhere found only in Group II; but in ll. 14 and 29 it reads with Group III, in l. 20 it has a reading found only outside the main groups and in l. 19 a reading peculiar to itself. My text differs from Grierson's which follows *1633*; see notes to ll. 7–8, 10, 19, and also l. 20 where I agree with Grierson in accepting *1633* against the *consensus* of I, II, and III.

As in 'The Flea' Donne has transformed a stock Renaissance theme, that of the dream in which the lover enjoys what his mistress denies him waking, by treating it dramatically. See Professor Praz, 'Donne's Relation to the Poetry of his Time' (*A Garland for John Donne*, ed. Spencer, 1931), for analogues, and Professor Legouis, *Donne the Craftsman*, 1928, pp. 75–77.

ll. 4–5. Cf. 'Image and Dream', ll. 9–10, and note (p. 182).

ll. 7–8.   *Thou art so true, that thoughts of thee suffice,*
                  To make dreames truth; and fables histories;

To construct the original text the variants in these two lines need to be considered together. The poem is not present in *H 40*, so there is no check on the Group I tradition which reads 'so truth' and 'dreames truth'. Group I is supported by *TCD*; but *L 74* and *TCC* read 'dreames truths'. The Group III manuscripts agree in reading 'so true'; but divide in l. 8, *Lut, S 96* reading 'dreames truth', *Dob* 'dreames true', and *O'F* 'dreames truths'. *HK 2* and its dependants read 'so true' and 'truths'.

In l. 8 it seems clear that the original reading is 'truth' and that 'truths' has arisen independently in *L 74, TCC, O'F, HK 2*, &c., from attraction to the other plurals in the line. This seems more likely than that 'truth' has been caught from the line above since we find it in *Lut, S 96* which read 'true' in l. 7.

In l. 7 the choice is between 'so truth' (I, *L 74*, II) and 'so true' (III, *HK 2*, &c.). In spite of Grierson's defence of 'so truth' as the more difficult reading and his quotation from Aquinas to support the interpretation that Donne is equating the lady with God who is truth itself, I find 'so truth' a very forced expression and the repetition of 'truth . . . truth' unpleasing to the ear. Also, to impute divinity to the lady at this point is to spoil the fine audacious climax by anticipation. I therefore adopt the reading of Group III and regard 'truth' as caught from the line below.

l. 10. *do. 1633* adopted from Group II the reading 'act'. As the poem is common to *L 74* and Group II, readings peculiar to Group II have little authority. 'Act' is less direct than 'do', carrying the suggestion of a performance. For

811835   P

'do', cf. 'Love's Growth', l. 14: 'Love sometimes would contemplate, sometimes do.'

ll. 11–12. Grierson cites two Sermons: 'A sodain *light* brought into a room doth awaken some men; but yet a *noise* does it better' (*Sermons*, iv. 211); and 'A Candle wakes some men, as well as a noyse' (*Sermons*, ix. 366).

l. 14. (*For thou lov'st truth*) *an Angell*. I agree with Grierson in retaining the reading of *1633* which reads here with Group III. Groups I and II read:

> (Thou lov'st truth) but an Angel. . . .

By itself, this is a wittier line, the poet apologizing for having thought her merely an angel. But, taken with the following line which begins with 'But', 'but an Angel' is awkward; and taken with the whole stanza it makes the point too soon and spoils the fine hyperbole of the close. It is possible that the reading arose through loss of the initial 'For', the opening bracket having been carelessly made and appearing to cancel the word, and that 'but' was supplied to fill out the line.

l. 16. *beyond an Angels art*. Only God can know the thoughts of the heart. Grierson cites Aquinas, *S.T.*, Iª pars, q. lvii, art. 4 and a passage from the *Sermons*:

> Let the Schoole dispute infinitely . . . let *Scotus* and his Heard think, That Angels, and separate soules have a naturall power to understand thoughts, though God for his particular glory restraine the exercise of that power in them . . . And let *Aquinas* present his arguments to the contrary, That those spirits have no naturall power to know thoughts; we seek no farther, but that Christ Jesus himselfe thought it argument enough to convince the Scribes and Pharisees, and prove himselfe God, by knowing their thoughts (*Sermons*, x. 82–83). See also *Sermons*, iv. 315–16.

l. 19. *doe. 1633* is alone in reading 'must'. Presumably, as in l. 10 where the corrector of the copy took 'act' from his Group II manuscript, he thought 'do' too unemphatic.

ll. 19–20.   *it could not chuse but bee*
              Prophane, to thinke thee any thing but thee.

I concur with Grierson in accepting the reading of *1633* against the *consensus* of I, II, and III, which read 'Prophaness'. I do not doubt that 'Prophane' is a correction made in the copy for *1633* and do not regard its appearance in manuscripts outside the main groups as argument for its authenticity. I reject 'Prophaness', in spite of its high manuscript authority, because I can find no parallel in Donne's lyric verse for a line with an extra syllable attached to its first foot with no possibility of an elision. 'Prophaness' gives a hopelessly unmetrical line and ruins the splendid run of the stanza up to its climax. I cannot believe that Donne wrote it, and prefer the charge of inconsistency to that of being deaf to the music of Donne's verse.

it could not chuse but bee: it must be. For examples of this obsolete idiom, see *O.E.D.*, 'choose', I.5.b.

Like the Deity she cannot be defined or described: she is only she. Cf. note to 'Negative Love', ll. 10–11 (p. 178), and Donne's ejaculation quoted by Walton: 'Blessed be God that he is God only, and divinely like himself' (*Lives*, p. 84).

l. 25. *pure, and brave*: simple, that is, unmixed, and glorious.

ll. 27–28. Cf. 'As a *Torch* that hath been lighted, and used *before*, is easier lighted then a *new torch*' (*Sermons*, ii. 131); see also *Sermons*, iii. 371.

l. 28. *deal'st*. I regard 'doest' (III) as a misreading of 'deal'st'.

Loves Alchymie (p. 81)

MSS.: All collections.

Miscellanies: *Grey*, *HK 1*; Brit. Mus. MS. *Egerton 2230*; Emmanuel Coll. MS. *1 3 16*; Folger MS. *V a 162*.

The text in the main groups shows great consistency.

Title. Except for *O*, *P*, and *A 25* the manuscripts agree in calling this poem 'Mummy'. The title that the editor of *1633* substituted is a better one and reflects credit on his understanding of the poem.

l. 1. *digg'd loves Myne*. Bacon cites Democritus as saying '*that the truth of nature lieth hid in certain deep mines and caves*', adding that 'if it be true likewise that the alchemists do much inculcate, that Vulcan is a second nature . . . it were good to divide natural philosophy into the mine and the furnace' and to divide natural philosophers into pioneers and smiths, 'some to dig, some to refine and hammer' (*Advancement of Learning*, II. vii. 1). Donne makes love's philosophers into pioneers and alchemists.

l. 7. *chymique*: alchemist.

th'Elixar: the *Elixir Vitae*, or quintessence, a perfectly pure substance able to purge all impurities and so cure all diseases, often identified with the Philosophers' Stone which it was held could transmute base metals to gold.

ll. 8–10. Grierson cites a letter to Goodyer: 'I am now, like an Alchymist, delighted with discoveries by the way, though I attain not mine end' (*Letters*, p. 172). Cf. Bacon: 'The search and stir to make gold hath brought to light a great number of good and fruitful inventions and experiments' (*Advancement of Learning*, I. iv. 11).

l. 12. *a winter-seeming summers night*: a night that is both cold and short.

l. 13. *our day*. Cf. 'Farewell to Love', ll. 24–25 and note (pp. 213–14).

l. 15. *my man*: my servant.

l. 17. 'Endure the soon-past indignity of the role of a Bridegroom.'

l. 19. *marry*. The spelling 'marrowe' (*Dob*, *S 96*, *HK 2*) shows that some copyists took 'marry' as a noun. This gives easier sense since it provides a proper antecedent for 'which': 'the loving fool that swears it is not the body's sweetness but the mind's that he finds to be angelic in her . . . '. But the reference to the 'Bridegroomes play' and the vulgar music of the wedding-day inclines me to take 'marry' as a verb and paraphrase:' the loving fool that swears it is not bodies that marry but minds, and that it is her mind that he finds like an angel in her . . . '.

l. 20. *Angelique.* This may mean that he finds her mind angelic or, more probably, that in angelic fashion his mind finds hers without the help of sense.

l. 22. *that dayes rude hoarse minstralsey.* Cf. *Romeo and Juliet*, IV. v, where Paris and Friar Lawrence come with musicians to fetch the bride. The secrecy of Donne's own marriage spared him the jocularities and festivities he fastidiously derides. Sir Thomas Browne takes a more generous view of vulgar music, perhaps remembering this scornful line (*Religio Medici*, ii. 9).

ll. 23–24.   *at their best*
               Sweetnesse and wit, they'are but Mummy, *possest.*
I follow Grierson in removing a rash of commas in *1633*.

'Wit' at this period normally means 'mind' or 'intelligence' or 'native genius'; but the more modern sense of 'superficial cleverness' seems intended here: 'Don't hope for mind in women; those with the greatest sweetness and apparent cleverness are only Mummy when you have had them.'

Mummy: dead bodies, preserved in bitumen, and thought to have medicinal value. Cf. Sir Thomas Browne, *Urn Burial, c.* 5:

The Ægyptian Mummies, which *Cambyses* or time hath spared, avarice now consumeth. Mummie is become Merchandise, *Mizraim* cures wounds, and *Pharaoh* is sold for balsoms.

The theory behind the medical use of mummy was that the dead body was preserved by the 'natural balsam' and this acted as a restorative to reinforce the vital forces of the patient; cf. *Letters*, 97–98.

The later Physitians say, that when our naturall inborn preservative is corrupted or wasted, and must be restored by a like extracted from other bodies; the chief care is that the Mummy have in it no excelling quality, but an equally digested temper.

The insulting close of the poem may be compared with that of 'A Farewell to Love': 'Although you will find you have gained only a mindless lump of dead flesh, it has some medicinal value.'

Farewell to Love (p. 82)

MSS.: *O'F, S 96, S 962*: omit *Σ*.
Miscellanies: *Hd*.

Of the four manuscripts in which this poem is extant, two (*S 962* and *Hd*) probably took it from print. It was printed in *1635* from *O'F*. There has been much discussion of the text in ll. 27–30, where I reject Grierson's emendation; see note. I have adopted the reading of *S 96* in l. 34; see note.

External evidence for ascribing 'Farewell to Love' to Donne is very weak. Neither *S 96* nor *O'F* is a sound witness to the canon, and in *Hd* the name 'Mr. An: Saintlegr' is written against the title. On internal evidence I have no hesitation in including it. Its rarity in manuscript and the obscurity and harshness of the syntax suggest that it may be a draft and not a finished poem.

l. 1. 'While still inexperienced.'

ll. 7–10. The construction makes 'desires' the subject of 'fall' and 'grow'; but sense demands that it is the 'Things not yet known' that 'fall' and 'grow' as our desires become small or increase in strength.

ll. 11–15. Here again the expression is clumsy. The omission of the article in 'From late faire' is unidiomatic and the sense of 'is not lesse cared for' is not immediately clear. As the child will have licked off the gilt from its fairing and eaten the gingerbread we may assume that 'after three days' it has forgotten, and cares nothing for, the object it clamoured for at the fair.

An article on moulds for gingerbread fairings, contributed to *The Times* (5 October 1957), contains illustrations of standing kings and queens. Its author, Mr. Edward Pinto, tells me he has several such moulds, but he has never seen one of a monarch on a throne. Most of the moulds show legendary kings or queens—nursery-rhyme or playing-card figures—but some may be representations of reigning monarchs.

l. 16. 'Once possessed, the enjoyment of it decays.'

l. 18. 'What before pleased all senses now attracts only one.'

ll. 19–20. Henry Howard writing to Edward Bruce in 1602 (*Secret Correspondence*, ed. Dalrymple, Edinburgh, 1766) refers to 'the rule of the philosopher that *omne animal post coitum triste*'. I have not been able to trace this tag in works by, or attributed to, Aristotle except in a slightly different form:

> *Quare animal post coitum tristatur?* Respondetur, quia actus luxuriae est in se turpis et inmundus, et sic omne animal abhorret talem actum, quia homines cum super hoc cogitant, erubescunt, et tristantur (Aristotle, *Problemata*, 1583, p. 129; Englished in *The Problems of Aristotle*, Edinburgh, 1595).

l. 22. *Cocks and Lyons.* The belief that these animals are exempt from post-coital depression derives from Galen. Both are 'Solares', according to Franciscus Georgius (*Problemata*, Paris, 1574, p. 379), and so presumably have an extra share of the sun's working vigour.

ll. 23–30. There have been extensive and extended discussions of the reading of ll. 29–30. Grierson added a comma after 'be' and emended 'Eager, desires' to 'Eagers desire'. He took the 'other curse of being short' to refer to the shortness of human life which sharpens ('eagers') man's desire to propagate his kind. The objection to this interpretation is that it is not the shortness of life but the fact that he has to die that, according to Aristotle, makes man beget children to satisfy his craving for immortality. The brevity of the pleasure in the act of love is so constant a theme with moralists ('Foeda est in coitu et brevis voluptas, et taedet Veneris statim peractae') that it seems obvious that the two 'curses' both refer to that act: it leaves behind it 'a kinde of sorrowing dulnesse' and what pleasure there is in it is only momentary.

For other suggestions, see Hayward, pp. 766–7, G. Williamson, *M.P.*, 1939, pp. 301–3, and correspondence in *T.L.S.*, May–June 1949.

My own solution is to accept the reading of the edition and manuscripts with the addition of a comma after 'minute' in l. 29. This makes 'and onely for a minute' an expansion of 'short' and 'desires' the object of 'made to be eager'. The comma between 'eager' and 'desires' is a normal seventeenth-century way of showing that 'eager' is to be taken with the verb and not with the following noun. It has been objected against this solution that (*a*) 'and onely for a minute' is an unnecessary repetition of the idea already expressed by 'short'; and (*b*) that what is made eager is the desire to repeat the act rather than the desire to have children.

Repetition is not uncharacteristic of Donne's style; see, for instance, 'The Autumnal', l. 48, where 'journey downe the hill' merely expands 'descend'. The second objection seems to me a quibble. Donne writes in *The First Anniversary* (l. 110) 'Wee kill our selves to propagate our kinde', meaning that we kill ourselves by indulgence in love; so here he takes the act of love as equivalent to the act of procreation and sees the brevity of the pleasure as wise nature's provision to secure the continuance of the race, as the curse of after-sorrow is her provision to ensure that men shall not destroy themselves by excessive indulgence.

For the notion that the sexual act debilitates by depriving man of 'radical moisture' see Aristotle, *De Longitudine et Brevitate Vitae* (466b). That each such act costs a day seems an equivalent to the popular notion that each sigh costs a drop of blood and wastes a minute of life.

l. 31 *Since so*: since it is so.

l. 34. *which had, indammage me*. I have adopted the reading of *S 96* which gives better sense than the pluperfect of *O'F* and *1635*.

l. 40. *worme-seed*: Santonica, Semen sanctum, or Semen contra, an anaphrodisiac; see *Historia generalis plantarum*, Lyons, 1587, i. 941: *semen contra*, 'Quidam tamen exponunt quasi impediens concitationem ac venerem'.

the Taile: the penis.

Twicknam Garden (p. 83)

MSS.: All collections.

Miscellanies: *Grey, Hol, La, RP 117 (2), Wel*; Brit. Mus. MS. *Harleian 3511*; Bodleian MS. *Eng. Poet. c 50*; Camb. Univ. Library MS. *Ee V 23*; Emmanuel Coll. Camb. *1 3 16*; Folger MS. *V a 103*.

I have abandoned *1633* twice. In l. 24 it follows *C 57, Lec* against the other Group I manuscripts, supported by *L 74* and Group II, and I agree with Grierson in rejecting it. In l. 15, where there is a *lacuna* in *H 40* and Group I, I differ from Grierson in preferring the reading of all the remaining manuscripts to that of *1633*. I also disagree with Grierson in retaining the reading of *1633* in l. 17; see note.

This is a highly individual variation on a stock theme going back to Petrarch: the contrast between the beauty of spring and the misery of the lover whose mistress is unkind. For its possible connexion with Lady Bedford, see Appendix C, 'Lady Bedford and Mrs. Herbert'.

Title. In many manuscripts there is no title and *B* has simply 'In a Garden'. But since both Groups II and III have 'Twickenham' (in various spellings) in the title it must be allowed some authority.

l. 1. The amount of inversion of stress in this line is so great as to set up a trisyllabic rhythm:

Blasted with | sighs, and sur|rounded with | teares,

instead of

Blasted | with sighs, | and sur|rounded | with teares.

Cf. the opening line of Donne's sonnet on his wife's death. There is a lack of metrical tact in thus opening a poem with a line that sets up the wrong expectation.

ll. 6–8. The spider 'turns all into excrement and poison'; see Swift's fable of the bee and the spider in *The Battle of the Books*. Manna, the food of the Israelites in the desert, was 'a small round thing, as small as the hoar frost on the ground' and 'the taste of it was like wafers made with honey' (Exod. xvi. 14 and 31). Manna was a type or figure of the Host. Love performs the Eucharistic miracle in reverse by turning the sweetness of things to bitterness.

l. 9. *the serpent.* Among the Seven Deadly Sins Envy is always represented as, or accompanied by, a serpent.

ll. 14–16.
> *But that I may not this disgrace*
> *Indure, nor leave this garden, Love let mee*
> *Some senslesse peece. . . . .*

In *H 40* and Group I these three lines appear as two

> . . . this disgrace endure
> Love let mee some senslesse peece. . . .

All the other manuscripts read the text that I print. Faced with two un-metrical lines, the first of which did not rhyme, the corrector of the copy for *1633* either did not consult his Group II manuscript or thought that he could improve on its reading and filled the gap by 'nor yet leave loving'.

I cannot, in view of other sophistications in *1633*, regard its reading here as having any authority. In addition, the manuscript reading can be shown to be intrinsically superior. The speaker could easily spare himself the disgrace of being mocked by the beauty of the garden by leaving it, which would not entail 'leaving loving'. He prays to become a plant or a stone in order that he may remain in the garden without being conscious of its beauty or his pain.

l. 16. *senslesse*: without a 'soul of sense' which man shares with the animals. Though without reason or sense he will still be able to love: cf. 'A Nocturnal', ll. 33–34:

> yea plants, yea stone detest
> And love.

l. 17. *grow*. I differ from Grierson in retaining the reading of *1633* which follows *C 57* and *Lec* against the other Group I manuscripts and Group II. As a general rule I have abandoned *1633* on such occasions; but here *C 57* and *Lec* have the support of Group III and *HK 2*, &c. 'Groane', the reading of Groups I and II, could have arisen independently from the strong association of mandrakes with groans. But the mandrake was not held to groan when *in situ*; it only groaned when it was torn up; see Browne, *Pseudodoxia Epidemica*, book ii, chap. vi.

l. 19. *christall vyals*. It was believed at this time that the small glass or alabaster vessels found in ancient tombs, probably to hold perfumes, were lachrymatories or tear-bottles in which mourners at funerals caught their tears in order to deposit them as tributes to the dead.

ll. 26–27. Although unlike all other women she is true, she is like them in not being what she seems, for her 'truth' to another is really only cruelty to him.

A Nocturnall upon S. Lucies Day, being the shortest day (p. 84)

MSS.: Group II, *DC*, *Lut*, *O'F*: omit *Σ*.

The proper punctuation of the second stanza is uncertain; see note to ll. 14–18.

For comparison of 'A Nocturnal' with 'Twickenham Garden' and discussion of the probable connexion of both with Lady Bedford, see Appendix C, 'Lady Bedford and Mrs. Herbert'. Grierson suggested that the poem was inspired by a serious illness of the Countess in 1612. Others have wished to connect it with Ann More, either with her illness in 1611 or with her death in 1617.

Title. St. Lucy's Day, 13 December, was popularly regarded as the shortest day, the Winter Solstice, when the sun entered the sign of the Goat (Capricorn). The true solstice by the old Julian Calendar (in use in England until 1752) was 12 December and the actual shortest day varied of course. Attempts to date the poem by finding a year in which 13 December was given in almanacs as the shortest day seem hardly in place.

l. 2. *scarce seaven houres*. To experience a day as short as this one would need to be further north than Donne is ever known to have travelled.

l. 3. *his flasks*: the stars, which were thought to store up light from the sun. Cf. the description of the creation of sun and stars in *Paradise Lost*, vii. 354–69.

l. 6. *the generall balme*: the innate vital preservative of all things, according to Paracelsus.

th'hydroptique earth. The dropsical man, though swollen with water, is afflicted with raging thirst. The sodden earth of midwinter has drunk down the life-giving force of all things.

l. 7. *beds-feet*: the foot of the bed. Cf.

> Likewise when the sicke turneth, wrings and tosseth up and downe often times with starting either in sleepe or waking, and making the beds feet where the head should be, casting himself downe, not knowing what he doth, is an evill signe' (*The Book of the Presages of the divine Hippocrates*, 1597, sig. B1ᵛ).

Life *in extremis* shrinks down into the earth (as the dying man slips down to the foot of the bed), to die and be buried there.

l. 14. *expresse*: squeeze out, or extract, a technical term from alchemy.

ll. 14–18. I follow Grierson in supplying a stop after 'emptinesse', thus making 'from dull privations and leane emptinesse' expansions of 'nothingnesse'. It is just possible, as Grierson suggested, that the last three lines of the stanza should be taken together; the sense then being 'His art produced a quintessence from nothingness. From a state of privation and emptiness he ruined me utterly and I am reborn as the quintessence of all non-existent things.' But it seems more likely that Donne here defines 'ordinary nothingness' as the absence of 'something' (privation or emptiness) to prepare us for the hyperbole of the fourth stanza in which he declares he is the Elixir of the 'first nothing', that absolute non-being which preceded all being.

ll. 21–22.   *I, by loves limbecke, am the grave*
                        Of all, that's nothing.

Cf. Milton's description of the 'wilde Abyss' as

> The Womb of nature and perhaps her Grave.
>
> (*Paradise Lost*, ii. 911.)

ll. 30–34. *Were I a man*, &c. Grierson comments:

> 'If I were a beast, I should prefer some end, some means' refers to the Aristotelian and Schools doctrine of the soul. The soul of man is rational and self-conscious; of beasts perceptive and moving, therefore able to select ends and means; the vegetative soul of plants selects what it can feed on and rejects what it cannot, and so far detests and loves. Even stones, which have no souls, attract and repel (ii. 38).

On stones he cites a sermon preached on Christmas Day 1629:

> We are not sure that stones have not life; stones may have life; neither (to speak humanely) is it unreasonably thought by them, that thought the whole world to be inanimated by one soule, and to be one intire living creature (*Sermons*, ix. 147).

l. 29. *the first nothing*. Donne has a long passage in *Essays in Divinity*, discussing the creation, in which he denies the concept of a Nothing 'before the beginning'; see *Essays*, pp. 27–32.

l. 37. *I am None*: I am no ordinary nothing.

The Dissolution (p. 86)

MSS.: Group II, *DC*, *Lut*, *O'F*, *S 962*: omit *Σ*.

Manuscript tradition links this poem with 'A Nocturnal', as it is linked by theme.

The basic conceit is that since at death the body, abandoned by the unifying soul, resolves itself into the four elements, and since they were so united that each was an element of the other, he has now a double portion of the material elements and these weigh down rather than nourish his soul.

l. 5. *involve*: include.

l. 8. *nourish*. Cf.

> Fire, Water, Ayre and Earthe . . . the first, and the common, and most simple Elementes, and beginners of all things, of which verily, both Plantes, and also all living creatures, are engendered, nourished, and increased (Jones, *Galen's Books of Elements*, 1574, f. 3ᵛ).

l. 12. *securitie*: recklessness. The elements he squandered as her lover are now replenished by the addition of hers.

l. 15. *my fire*: my passion.

l. 18. *breake*: go bankrupt.

l. 22 *earnestly*: ardently.

The Blossome (p. 87)

MSS.: *Σ — H 40*, *L 74*, *HK 2*, *Cy*, *O*, *P*, *K*.
Miscellanies: *Grey*, *Hd*.

I agree with Grierson in rejecting the reading of *1633* on four occasions. In l. 38 it follows *C 57* and *Lec*, and in l. 10 it follows Group I in a minor error; in ll. 23 and 24 it has no manuscript support.

This and the following three poems are linked by manuscript tradition. They occur together in Group I and all four are missing from *H 40*, *L 74*, *HK 2*,

Cy, O, P. In other manuscripts they tend to appear close to each other. For Grierson's suggestion that they were written to Mrs. Herbert, see Appendix C, 'Lady Bedford and Mrs. Herbert'.

Title. The title is found in all manuscripts except *A 25.* The same is true of the following three poems.

l. 12. *a forbidden or forbidding tree.* This is the Petrarchan situation where the mistress who denies is married.

l. 15. *that Sunne:* his mistress.

l. 24. *If then your body goe, what need you' a heart?* Professor Praz notes here 'a new treatment of an old Petrarchan *motif*' and refers to the sonnet 'Mira quel colle, o stanco mio cor vago'.

l. 35. *with men:* in company.

The Primrose (p. 88)

MSS.: *Σ* — *H 40, L 74, HK 2, Cy, O, P, A 25, D 17, JC, K.*
Miscellanies: *Grey, Hd.*

The reading of *1633* has been rejected twice. In l. 26 it follows *C 57* and *Lec* and I agree with Grierson in rejecting it. In l. 17 I differ from Grierson in adopting the reading of the great majority of the manuscripts; see note.

For discussion of the date and occasion of the poem, see Appendix C, 'Lady Bedford and Mrs. Herbert'.

Title. I have kept the title of *1633* which is found in all manuscript copies of the poem and relegated the expansion of it in *1635* to the apparatus. The expansion ('being at Mountgomery Castle, upon the hill, on which it is situate') is too circumstantial not to be given credence; nobody surely would have invented it. At the same time it is a clumsy addition and adds nothing to our understanding of the poem. Aubrey notes of the castle of Montgomery, 'a most romancy seate', that it 'stood upon a high promontory, the north side 30+feete high. From hence is a most delightsome prospect, 4 severall wayes. Southwards, without the castle, is *Prim-rose hill:* vide Donne's Poems, p. 53.' He quotes the first stanza of 'The Primrose', writing against the first line the note 'In the parke' (*Brief Lives,* ed. Clark, 1898, i. 308).

l. 4. *Manna.* This seems a purely visual image. Each drop finds a primrose and glistens there like manna, 'a small round thing, as small as the hoar frost on the ground' (Exod. xvi. 14).

l. 6. *a terrestriall Galaxie.* It has been claimed (C. Coffin, *John Donne and the New Philosophy,* 1937, pp. 152 ff.) that this reference proves the poem to have been written after the publication of Galileo's *Siderius Nuncius* in 1610 which announced the proof by telescope of the theory that the Milky Way consisted of innumerable small stars. Against this it can be objected that the theory was current long before Galileo proved its truth; see *Batman upon Bartholome*, 1582, f. 124ʳ. In view of Donne's known interest in Galileo and the *Sidereus Nuncius*, which he refers to in *Ignatius His Conclave*, I incline to think Coffin was right to see a topical reference here.

l. 8. *a true Love*. Chambers refers to William Browne, *Britannia's Pastorals*, book ii, song 3:

> The *Primrose*, when with sixe leaves gotten grace,
> Maids as a *True-love* in their bosoms place.

There are many examples given in *O.E.D.* of four-petalled flowers being called 'true-loves'.

He is searching for a six or four-petalled flower in a field where he is surrounded by flowers with five petals, which symbolize 'mere women'.

l. 16. *sexe*. See note to 'The Ecstasy', l. 31 (p. 185).

l. 17. *to study'her, not to love*. Grierson retained the reading of *1633*, 'to study her and not to love'. This gives a line with an extra foot. I assume that the corrector of the copy, overlooking the necessary elision in 'study'her', inserted 'and' to make his line smooth at the expense of breaking the metrical pattern.

l. 18. *monsters*: freaks.

ll. 19–20. 'I would rather she were falsified by painting her face than made no true woman by nature.' Cf. *Hamlet*, III. i. 143: 'God hath given you one face, and you make yourself another.'

l. 24. *this mysterious number*. Five was a magical number, the most potent of all magical signs being the pentangle. Donne refers to Pico and Franciscus Georgius, *De Harmonia Mundi*, for speculations on the number five in *Essays in Divinity*, and later says of Sarah, the wife of Abraham,

> From *Sarai's* Name he took a letter, which expressed the number *ten*, and repos'd one, which made but *five*; so that she contributed that five which man wanted before, to shew a mutuall indigence and Supplement (Simpson, *Essays*, pp. 10 and 46).

Cornelius Agrippa (*Of Occult Philosophy*, translated J. F., 1651) says of the number five

> The number five is of no small force, for it consists of the first even, and the first odd, as of a Female, and Male; For an odd number is the Male and the even the Female. . . . Therefore the number five is of no small perfection, or virtue, which proceeds from the mixture of these numbers: It is also the just middle of the universal number, *viz.* ten . . . and therefore it is called by the *Pythagoreans* the number of Wedlock, as also of justice, because it divided the number ten in an even scale (p. 188).

But, alas, in the very next chapter we are told that the number six is 'to be altogether applyed to generation and Marriage'. There is little certainty in mystical mathematics.

l. 25. *Ten is the farthest number.* Cf. '*Ten* cannot be exceeded, but that to express any further Number you must take a part of it again' (Simpson, *Essays*, p. 59).

ll. 25–30. There are two opposed interpretations of Donne's conclusion. Grierson took it to mean:

> Let woman be content to be herself. Since five is half ten, united with man she will be half of a perfect life; or (and the cynical humour breaks out again) if she is not content with that, since five is the first number which includes an even number (2) and an odd (3), it may claim to be the perfect number, and she to be the whole in which we men are included and absorbed. We have no will of our own (ii. 49).

Others, notably Professor Legouis, have pointed out that Donne speaks twice of 'each' woman, but says she may take half 'us men', or may take 'us all', and conclude that the poem ends with justifying feminine promiscuity. For an elaboration of this view, see E. D. Cleveland, *Explicator*, viii. 1, Oct. 1949.

I find this second explanation very forced and have difficulty in accepting that 'five' should stand for a single woman and 'ten' for the entire masculine sex. 'Women' (in the plural) are bidden to be content with the number five; and Donne then makes clear that this is the feminine number, the number of 'each woman'. 'Ten', which is 'the farthest number', must surely then be the masculine number, the number of 'each man'. I find no difficulty in taking 'halfe us men' as idiomatic for 'half of each of us men' and 'women may take us all' as meaning 'woman may take the whole of man'.

Donne is assuming as axiomatic the perfection of the male sex and the imperfection of the female; cf. 'Air and Angels', ll. 26–28 and note (p. 205). Ten is the masculine number because man is complete in himself and needs no addition from woman. Five is the woman's number: to become perfect she needs a man. This is a commonplace; cf. the refrain of the Lincoln's Inn Epithalamium:

> To day put on perfection, and a woman's name,

and Marston, *Antonio's Revenge*, III. iv: 'I have read *Aristotles Problemes*, which saith; that woman receiveth perfection by the man.' Since alone she is only half ten, she must, for her perfection, take five from man. But then Donne rounds on himself. If women are not content with this, since five is, in another way, the sum of the numbers, they can regard themselves as entitled to take the whole of man. This may be understood to taste: either, as Grierson does, that they can absorb man, body and soul, or, more idealistically, that they can in the mathematics of love be regarded as equal though different. In support of the latter interpretation cf. the quotation from Franciscus Georgius in the note to 'Air and Angels' (p. 206) where the Platonic view that men and women seek each other because each is half the other is contrasted with the Aristotelian view that the woman's desire is the stronger because she, being imperfect, is seeking her perfection.

The Relique (p. 89)

MSS.: *Σ* — *H 40, L 74, HK 2, Cy, O, P, K.*
Miscellanies: *Grey, Hd.*

The Group II manuscripts (with *DC*) present a distinct text, reading against all other manuscripts in ll. 9, 14, 17, 21, 25–26, 28, and 29. Except in ll. 21 and 29, *1633* has adopted the readings of Group II. I do not see any intrinsic superiority in either version; but, as this is one of the poems that Group II does not share with *L 74*, if the differences are due to the author's corrections Group II is likely to have the later version; see Textual Introduction, pp. lxviii–lxx. I therefore concur with Grierson in accepting *1633* when it agrees with Group II, but differ from him in l. 20 where *1633* follows Group I in minor error, and in l. 21 where I prefer the Group II reading to that of *1633* and other manuscripts.

For Grierson's attempt to connect this poem with Mrs. Herbert, see Appendix C, 'Lady Bedford and Mrs. Herbert'.

ll. 17–18. *Thou shalt be a Mary Magdalen, and I*
A something else thereby;

Mary Magdalen is always represented in art with long brilliant golden hair. The superstitious will take the 'bracelet of bright hair' as a love-token given by the saint to one of her lovers and the arm-bone as his. 'A something else' is contemptuous. It has been suggested that Donne intended that his bone would be thought to be a bone of Christ and this has been supported by the revival of the hoary *canard* that Luther said that Christ and Mary Magdalen were lovers. But however sunk in 'mis-devotion' an age was it would surely be aware that the grave of Christ contained no relics other than his grave-clothes.

l. 20. *at such times*: when relics are authenticated.

l. 24. *Yet knew not what wee lov'd, nor why.* Cf. 'Negative Love' and note (p. 177).

ll. 25–26. *Difference of sex, &c.* Cf. 'Love's Alchemy', l. 20.

ll. 27–28. *Comming and going, &c.* Grierson cites a sermon on the text 'Kiss the Son lest he be angry', which is largely concerned with innocent and laudable kisses:

It is an imputation laid upon *Nero*, That *Neque adveniens, neque proficiscens*, That whether comming or going he never kissed any: And Christ himselfe imputes it to *Simon*, as a neglect of him, That when he *came into his house*, he did not *kisse* him (*Sermons*, iii. 321).

ll. 29–30. *Our hands ne'r toucht the seales,*
Which nature, injur'd by late law, sets free:

For 'seales', cf. 'Tutelage', l. 29, and 'On his Mistress Going to Bed', l, 32.

'Late law' implies that human laws are of comparatively recent origin. The sentiment and phrasing is from Myrrha's speech in Ovid, a main source of Renaissance naturalism:

> humana malignas
> cura dedit leges, et quod natura remittit,
> invida iura negant. (*Metam.* x. 329–31).

The Funeral (p. 90)

MSS.: *Σ* — *H 40, HK 2, A 25, D 17, JC, K.*
Miscellanies: *Grey, Hd*; St. John's Coll. Camb. MS. *U 26.*

The reading of *1633* has been rejected on five occasions. In l. 6 it has no manuscript support and in l. 17 only accidental support; in ll. 3, 12, and 24 it agrees with *C 57* and *Lec* against the other manuscripts of Group I. Except in l. 3 my text agrees with Grierson's.

For discussion of the relation of this poem to the last, see Appendix C, 'Lady Bedford and Mrs. Herbert'.

ll. 9–11. *For if the sinewie thread,* &c. 'Sinews' could mean either sinews or nerves at this time. Both are instruments by which the brain transmits its commands to the members. Cf.

And when sin hath got a heart in us . . . it will get a *Braine*; a Brain that shall minister all *Sense*, and *Delight* in sin; That's the office of the Brain; A Brain which shall send forth sinews and ligaments, to tye sins together (*Sermons*, i. 192).

Cf. also:

> Another part became the well of sense,
> The tender well-armed feeling braine, from whence,
> Those sinowie strings which do our bodies tie,
> Are raveld out. (*Progress of the Soul*, ll. 501–4.)

ll. 17–24. As her gift may have meant kindness or unkindness, so his desire that it should be buried with him may show subservience or defiance, either ascribing to it the preserving power of the soul, or taking part of her to corruption with him.

DUBIA

Sapho to Philaenis (p. 92)

MSS.: Group II (*A 18, N, TCC, TCD*); *DC*; *Lut, O'F*; *O, P*; *A 25, D 17, JC.*
Miscellanies: *Grey, HK 1*; Brit. Mus. MS. *Add. 10309*

For reasons for questioning Donne's authorship of this poem, in spite of its appearance in the first edition and in the manuscripts of Group II, see Introduction II, 'The Canon and Date of the *Elegies*', p. xlvi.

l. 3. *Verse that drawes Natures workes, from Natures law.* I presume that the reference is to the potency of rhyme in spells.

l. 26. *maist thou be ever.* The reading of *O'F* which I have adopted may be only a patch of the metrically deficient line in Group II and *1633*; but it has some support from the metrically excessive line in *A 25, JC.*

l. 37. *Nor needs perfection.* Cf. the quotations in the note to 'The Primrose', ll. 25–30 (p. 221).

l. 49. *lippe to lippe none denies.* Cf. 'The Relic', ll. 27–28 and note (p. 222).

The Expostulation (p. 94)

MSS.: *L 74; N, TCD* (last 16 lines only); *Dob, Lut, O'F, S 96; Cy, O, P; A 25, B, S.*

Miscellanies: *CCC, EH, Hd, HK 1, RP 31* and *H 40, S 962.*

The text printed in Jonson's *Underwoods*, 1640, differs considerably from that in *1633* and the manuscripts. Except for obvious errors all its readings are given in the apparatus. The poem is printed in Jonson's *Works* (viii. 194–7) and I am much indebted to the commentary on it there (xi. 70–71).

For reasons for questioning Donne's authorship of the poem, in spite of its appearance in the first edition, see Introduction II, 'The Canon and Date of the *Elegies*'. It is suggested there that the author may be Sir Thomas Roe. The reference to 'the Kings dogges' (l. 52) dates the poem after 1603.

l. 8. *smile at your perjuries.* Cf. Ovid, *Ars Amatoria*, i. 631–4:

> Iuppiter ex alto periuria ridet amantum.

l. 10. *writ in water.* Cf. Catullus, lxx. 3–4:

> sed mulier cupido quod dicit amanti
> in vento et rapida scribere oportet aqua.

l. 19. *breake*: go bankrupt.

l. 22. 'He that would wish you true to yourself must desire you false.' Cf. 'Woman's Constancy', ll. 11–13:

> Or, your owne end to Justifie,
> For having purpos'd change, and falsehood; you
> Can have no way but falsehood to be true?

ll. 27–32. The listing of impossibilities (*adunata*) is a well-known device in classical love-poetry; see Propertius, II. xv. 29–36, and Ovid, *Tristia*, viii. 1–10:

> In caput alta suum labentur ab aequore retro
> flumina, conversis solque recurret equis . . .
> Omnia naturae praepostera legibus ibunt,
> parsque suum mundi nulla tenebit iter:

Omnia iam fient fieri quae posse negabant,
  et nihil est de quo non sit habenda fides.
Haec ego vaticinor quia sum deceptus ab illo
  laturum misero quem mihi rebar opem.

ll. 39–42. Classical models for curses are provided by the pseudo-Virgilian 'Dirae' and Ovid's 'Ibis'. For curses by Donne see 'The Bracelet', ll. 91–110, and the lyric 'The Curse'. The curse in 'The Expostulation' does little more than paraphrase Catullus and Ovid; cf.

Non equidem dubito quin primum inimica bonorum
  lingua execta avido sit data vulturio,
effossos oculos voret atro gutture corvus,
  intestina canes, cetera membra lupi.
                              (Catullus, cviii. 3–6.)

Unguibus et rostro tardus trahet ilia vultur,
  et scindent avidi perfida corda canes.
Deque tuo fiet (licet hac sis laude superbus)
  insatiabilibus corpore rixa lupis.
                              (Ovid, *Ibis*, 169–172.)

ll. 59–64. Grierson compares Ovid, *Amores*, III. ii. 1–7:

Non ego nobilium sedeo studiosus equorum;
  cui tamen ipsa faves, vincat ut ille, precor.
ut loquerer tecum veni, tecumque sederem,
  ne tibi non notus, quem facis, esset amor.
tu cursus spectas, ego te; spectemus uterque
  quod iuvat, atque oculos pascat uterque suos.
O, cuicumque faves, felix agitator equorum.

ll. 67–70. Cf. Ovid, *Ars Amatoria*, ii. 13–14:

Nec minor est virtus, quam quaerere, parta tueri:
  Casus inest illic; hoc erit artis opus.

His Parting from Her (p. 96)

MSS.: Full Text (104 ll.): *Lut*, *O'F*, *S 96*; *O*, *P*; *S 962*.
  Short Text (42 ll.): *A 25*, B.
Miscellanies: Full Text H *40**, HK *1*, RP *31*, TCD (*2*), lacking ll. 95–104.
  Short Text: RP *117* (*2*); Bodleian MS. *Malone 16*; Emmanuel Coll. MS. *1 3 16*; Folger MSS.: *V. a 97*; *103, 1*; *125, 1*; *170*; *245*; *262*; *339*; *345*. Shorter Texts in *Sp* (30 ll.) and Brit. Mus. MS. *Add. 30982* (18 ll.).

The full text of this poem was not printed until 1669 when it replaced the short text of forty-two lines that had been printed in 1635. It is puzzling that the compiler of *1635* who took most of his additional poems from *O'F* overlooked the text of this poem there and was content to print the abbreviated version from some other source. The text in *1669* is, like other poems first printed there ('Going to Bed' and 'Love's Progress') a poor one and needs considerable correction from the manuscripts.

The manuscript tradition divides very clearly: *Lut*, *O'F*, *S 96* read consistently together against *H 40**, *RP 31* and *O*, *P*. My text, like Grierson's is based on *1669*, collated with *O'F*, *S 96*, *H 40**, *P*, *B*. I give the readings of *1635* when they differ from those of *1669*. I differ from Grierson on eleven occasions. In ll. 21, 31, 46, 66, 70, and 94 I adopt the reading of both manuscript traditions where Grierson retained the reading of *1669*, and in l. 97 I prefer the reading of *O'F*, *S 96* to that of *H 40**, *P* which *1669* follows. For the readings in ll. 42, 53, 54, and 78 see notes.

For reasons for questioning Donne's authorship of this and the following two Elegies, first printed in the second edition of 1635, see Introduction II, 'The Canon and Date of the *Elegies*'.

l. 31. *glad truth*. The agreement of the manuscripts establishes 'glad' as the true reading. The sense would seem to be: 'whereas my willing fidelity may extinguish thy wrath'.

l. 42. *thy towred husbands eyes*. Grierson accepted the reading of *1669* ('towring') against the 'towred' of the manuscripts and thought that *H 40** and *RP 31* were in error in attaching the participle to 'husband' rather than to 'eyes'. He thought the metaphor was from hawking, having the force of 'threatening'.

I think we must accept 'towred' and that it is more appropriately applied to the husband himself, who watches as from a tower while his 'household spies' set ambushes. The whole passage is couched in military terms which make a hawking metaphor seem unlikely.

ll. 45–52. Cf. *Amores*, I. iv. 15–32, and Donne's Elegy 'Jealousy'.

l. 49. 'Disguised by an air of negligence our deepest concerns.'

l. 53. *thy Art*. It seems likely that 'our' (*1669* and all manuscripts except *H 40** and *RP 31*) has been caught from the lines above. It is surely the secrets of the art of Love that they have proved.

l. 54. *Yea, thy pale colours, inward as thy heart.* The reading of *1669*, 'Yea, thy pale inwards and thy panting heart', which Grierson retained, has no manuscript support. He confessed himself unable to make sense of it and was 'tempted to combine the reading of *1669* and the manuscripts and read'

> Yea, thy pale colours and thy panting heart,

the secrets of love's art being then the signs of love, pallor and a beating heart. But as he rightly pointed out such a solution is untenable as it ignores the presence of 'inwards' or 'inward' in both versions.

Accepting the manuscript reading, I take the line as in apposition to 'secrets' and to be a periphrasis for dissimulation. Love's colours are inconspicuous, making no outward show.

l. 78. The line printed in *1669* and retained by Grierson is hopelessly un-metrical. The line I print has an eleventh syllable rhyming with the preceding line's tenth, a licence common in Elizabethan verse; see note to 'The Bracelet', ll. 59–60 (p. 116).

l. 79. *eare.* Grierson points out that the reading 'yeare' in the editions from 1635–69 is a variant spelling for 'eare'.

l. 97. *Pole*: the pole star, the fixed point of the stellar system.
start: swerve.

Julia (p. 100)

MSS.: *Lut, O'F; B.*
Miscellanies: *HK 1.*

My text differs from Grierson's in l. 28; see note.

l. 6. *opinion*: a favourable estimation of oneself; see *O.E.D.*, 'opinion', 5.c.

ll. 13–14. Grierson refers to Mantuan's fourth eclogue 'De natura mulierum' as earning him Donne's title of 'Scourge of Women' and cites references to Mantuan as a woman-hater from Nashe, *The Anatomy of Absurdity* (*Works*, i. 12), and Greene, *Mamillia* (ed. Grosart), pp. 106–7.

l. 19. Tenarus. Grierson refers to Taenarus in Laconia where there was a cavern belching sulphurous smoke thought to be a passage to Hades; see Ovid, *Metam.* x. 13, and Pausanius, iii. 14. 25.

l. 28. *loathes.* Grierson adopted 'oathes' from *B*: but *B* is a weaker witness than *O'F* and 'loathes' gives easier sense. Her hatreds accuse her since she hates all that is good.

A Tale of a Citizen and his Wife (p. 101)

MSS.: *Dob, Lut, O'F; B.*
Miscellanies: *RP 117 (2).*

My text differs from Grierson's on seven occasions. In ll. 16, 24, 32, 66, and 68 (*bis*) I adopt the reading of the manuscripts where he retained *1635*. In l. 65 I retain *1635*, supported by the manuscripts, where he adopted a reading from *1669*.

A crop of topical references dates this poem in 1609.

l. 6. *I touch no fat sowes grease.* Probably, as Grierson suggests, 'I say nothing libellous as to the way in which this or that rich man acquired his wealth'.

l. 9. ore tenus: sentence by word of mouth.

l. 10. *will redd.* I assume that the agreement of *1635* and *Dob* in reading 'looke redd' is accidental, both taking 'redd' as an adjective and supplying a verb for the sentence.

l. 21. *the Plaguy Bill*: the weekly bill of deaths from the plague, first issued in the great plague of 1592–3. There was a severe outbreak of plague in the winter of 1609–10.

l. 22. *the Custome Farmers*. There was perpetual strife between merchants and the farmers of the customs who having paid dearly for their farm were stiff in exacting dues.

l. 23. *the Virginian plot*: the scheme to plant Virginia. Two expeditions were sent to Virginia in 1609, the first under Sir Thomas Gates, Sir George Somers, and Captain Newport, the second under Lord de la Warr, and there was much speculation in Virginia stock. Early in 1609 Donne was trying to be made Secretary at Virginia (*CSP*, James I, 1609, xliii. 76).

ll. 23–24. *whether Ward*, &c. Ward was a notorious pirate who operated in the Mediterranean from a base at Tunis. Grierson cites a letter from Wotton to Salisbury written 7 March 1608 telling of Ward's attacks on Venetian shipping.

Midland seas. I accept the reading of all the manuscripts in place of Grierson's emendation of 'Iland' (*1635*) to 'Inland'. Either 'Midland' or 'Inland' sea was in use for the Mediterranean.

l. 25. *the Brittaine* Burse. Grierson notes this was built by the Earl of Salisbury on the site of 'an olde long stable' in the Strand on the north side of Durham House and cites Stow, *Chronicles*, 1631:

> And upon Tuesday the tenth of Aprill this yeere, one thousand six hundred and nine, many of the upper shoppes were richly furnished with wares, and the next day after that, the King, Queene, and Prince, the Lady Elizabeth and the Duke of Yorke, with many great Lords, and chiefe Ladies, came thither, and were entertained with pleasant speeches, giftes, and ingenious devices, and then, the king gave it a name, and called it Brittaines Burse (p. 894).

l. 27. *Of new-built* Algate, *and the* More-field *crosses*. Aldgate was taken down in 1606 and rebuilt in 1609. Grierson explains 'More-field crosses' as the new walks made across the old marsh of Moorfield and cites Stow:

> And lastly, whereof there is a more generall, and particular notice taken by all persons resorting and residing in London, the new and pleasant walks on the north side of the city, anciently called More fields, which field (untill the third yeare of King James) was a most noysome and offensive place, being a generall laystall, a rotten morish ground, whereof it tooke first the name (p. 1021).

ll. 42–44. Grierson suggests that these lines echo a Royal Proclamation of 1609:

> ... in this speciall Proclamation his Majestie declared how grievously, the people of this latter age and times are fallen into verball profession, as well of religion, as of all commendable morall vertues, but wanting the actions and deeds of so specious a

profession, and the insatiable and immeasurable itching boldnesse of the spirits, tongues and pens of most men (Stow, *Chronicles*, p. 898).

ll. 47–48.   *The much of Priviledg'd kingsmen, and the store*
             Of fresh protections. . . .

Grierson cites Chamberlain to Carleton, 31 December 1612: 'We have many bankrupts daily, and as many protections, which doth marvellously hinder all manner of commerce.' Either 'kingsmen' or 'kinsmen' would give sense, the one being favourites holding monopolies or privileges from the king, the other being relatives and hangers on who acquired such rights from their great relatives and patrons. 'Protections' are exemption from being sued at law; see note to 'Love's Exchange', ll. 8–14 (p. 168).

l. 65. *found nothing but a Rope.* Cf. *Greek Anthology*, ix. 44: 'A man finding gold left his halter, but the man who had left the gold and did not find it, hanged himself with the halter he found.'

Variety (p. 104)

MSS.: *D 17*, *JC*; *HK 2*.
Miscellanies: *HK 1*; Brit. Mus. MS. *Add 10309* (lacking ll. 24–36 and 71–76); Bodleian MS. *Don. b 9* (lacking ll. 1–52).

The text in *1650* is close to that in *JC* and its copy *D 17*. *A 10* is either degenerate or presents an independent tradition. Since it is impossible with a poem preserved only in a few miscellanies to decide which is the true tradition I give all its readings that are not patently erroneous.

My text differs from Grierson's on eight occasions. A major difference is the omission of a line (24 in his numbering) which makes my line numbers one ahead of his from l. 24; see note to ll. 23–24. In ll. 41 and 72 I adopt the reading of all the manuscripts and in ll. 37 and 49 the reading of the majority. In ll. 50 and 53, where Grierson adopted readings from *A 10*, I retain *1650*. For the readings in ll. 6 and 13, see notes.

For reasons for doubting Donne's authorship of this poem, see Introduction II, 'The Canon and Date of the *Elegies*'. The poem may be compared with the Elegy 'Change' and with 'The Indifferent', 'Love's Usury', and 'Confined Love'. For a general discussion of such poems, see L. I. Bredvold, 'The Naturalism of Donne in relation to some Renaissance Traditions', *J.E.G.P.* xxii, 1923.

l. 6. *what ever else seemes.* The reading of *HK 2* which is here adopted gives a metrical line. *HK 1* has dropped 'ever' and *A 10* would seem to have patched the line in *HK 1* by substituting 'is not so' for 'seemes'. The line in *1650* and *JC* has two extra syllables and looks like a clumsy attempt to expand the defective line of *HK 1*.

l. 13. *bank.* A singular seems more likely to have given rise to the misreading 'bark' than the plural 'banks' of *HK 2*. The passage is an obvious imitation of the close of Donne's Elegy 'Change':

> Waters stincke soone, if in one place they bide,
> And in the vast sea are worse putrifi'd:
> But when they kisse one banke, and leaving this
> Never looke backe, but the next banke doe kisse,
> Then are they purest.

ll. 23–24. *A 10* which has a defective text, omitting ll. 24–36 and 71–76, has supplied a line to rhyme with l. 23. Grierson regarded the line as authentic and printed it as l. 24 between ll. 23 and 24 of *1650*, thus producing a triplet.

l. 27. *agreements*: agreeable qualities.

l. 52. 'And whose origin is much sought after.'

l. 63. 'Adhering to the party of Love in spite of his being out of favour.'

The Token (p. 107)

MSS.: *O'F, S 96; Cy, O, P; B; S 962.*
Miscellanies: *Hd, HK 1.*

For reasons for doubting Donne's authorship of this and the following two poems, see Introduction III, 'The Canon and Date of the *Songs and Sonnets*'.

Self Love (p. 107)

MSS.: *Lut, O'F; D 17, JC.*

Song (p. 108)

MSS.: *Lut, O'F, S 96; O, P; A 25.*
Miscellanies: *HK 2, RP 117 (2).*

The beautiful stanza was printed as the first stanza of Donne's poem 'Break of Day' in *1669* and is found in the same way in *S 96* and *A 25*. As its metre is different and it is spoken by a man and not a woman it cannot be attached to Donne's aubade and it seems unlikely that he wrote it. It was printed in Dowland's *A Pilgrim's Solace* in 1612 as the first stanza of a poem in two stanzas; see Appendix B, 'Musical Settings of Donne's Poems'. It may be by Dowland himself.

APPENDIX A

Verbal Alterations in the Elegies *and* Songs and Sonnets *in the edition of 1635*

THE alterations made in the text of *1635* in poems reprinted from *1633* are given here in tabular form, as in Appendix B to my edition of the *Divine Poems*. With two exceptions ('The Canonization', l. 3, and 'Love's Infiniteness', l. 17) all that are not obvious misprints are to be found in *O'F*. Many are peculiar to *Lut* and *O'F*, but a few are found in *O'F* alone. Since two poems extant in *O'F* but not present in *Lut* appear in *1635*, it is clear that *O'F* was the source of the alterations in the text of poems reprinted from *1633*. The readings of *1635* have therefore no textual value. Only in the titles that it added can it be regarded as substantive.

In the following tables the manuscript collections are listed alphabetically in groups as in the List of Sigla on pp. xcvii–xcix.[1]

ELEGIES

1633	*1635*	MSS. agreeing with *1635*
'The Comparison'		
Title: Elegie.	ELEG. VIII. *The Comparison.*	
13 stones lying	lying stones	All *MSS.*
34 her	thy	*Σ* − *JC*; *S*
37 part	durt	*Σ* − Group II; *Cy*
48 where	when	All *MSS.*
'The Perfume'		
Title: Elegie IV.	ELEG. IV. *The Perfume.*	
7–8 *omitted*	Though . . . Cockatrice	*Σ* − Group I; *DC*; *B*
21 To	And to	Group II, *L 74*; *Lut*, *O'F*, *S96*; *W*; *A 25*, *JC*
40 my	mine	*Σ* − Group I; *Cy*
'Jealousy'		
Title: ELEGIE I.	ELEGIE I. *Iealosie.*	
'Recusancy'		
24 then	there	Group II; *Lut*, *O'F*; *Cy*, *O*, *P*; *A 25*, *JC*

[1] *SP* and *D 17* are omitted, as they are copies of *D* and *JC* respectively, and *K* is omitted as worthless.

1633	1635	MSS. agreeing with 1635
26 or	to	Σ — C 57, Lec
upmost	utmost	Lut, O'F; S
33 the	her	Group II, L 74; Lut, O'F; Cy, O, P
who	which	Lut, O'F
41 bred	breed	Σ — D; DC; W; A 25

'Tutelage'

7 call	know	Dob, Lut, O'F (b.c.)

'Change'

Title: Elegie III.	ELEG. III. Change.	

'The Anagram'

Title: Elegie II.	ELEG. II. The Anagram.	
6 rough	tough	Group III
18 the	that	Group II, L 74, DC; Dob; W; A 25, JC; B, S

'His Picture'

Title: Elegie V.	ELEG. V. His Picture.	
8 stormes, being	horinesse	Lut, O'F; W; JC

'The Autumnal'

Title: Elegie. The Autumnall.	ELEG. IX. The Autumnall.	
1 Summer	Summers	
3 our	your	Σ — Group I; DC
8 they'are	shee's	Σ — DC
10 tolerable	habitable	Group II, L 74; Lut, O'F; HK 2; O, P; A 25
14 for	or	Dob, Lut, O'F; HK 2
27 seasonabliest	seasonablest	Group II, L 74; Dob, Lut, O'F; HK 2; JC; B, S
30 large	old	Lut, O'F; HK 2; S
38 soules	fooles	
44 Ancient	Ancients	Lut, O'F; B, S
Antique	Antiques	Σ — Group I, H 40
47 motion natural	naturall station	C 57, Lec; Dob, Lut, O'F
50 out	on	Σ — DC

SONGS AND SONNETS (I)

'The Message'

No title	The Message.	
11 Which	But	Lut, O'F

1633	*1635*	*MSS.* agreeing with *1635*
'Sweetest love, I do not go'		
6 Must dye at last	At the last must part	*Lut, O'F*
7 To use	Thus to use	*Lut, O'F*
8 Thus	*omitted*	*Lut, O'F*
25 not	no	
32 Thou	That	*Dob, Lut, O'F; B*
'The Bait'		
No title	*The Baite.*	
18 which	with	All *MSS.*
23 sleavesicke	sleavesilke	$\Sigma - Cy, O, P$
'Community'		
No title	*Communitie.*	
3 these	there	$\Sigma - C\ 57, Lec; Cy\ (b.c.)$
'Confined Love'		
No title	*Confined love.*	
12 Beasts	Beast	
'Break of Day'		
6 despight	spight	
18 doth	should	Group II, *L 74; Lut, O'F; HK 2; JC; B*
'The Computation'		
1 the	my	*Dob, Lut, O'F; HK 2; O, P; B, S*
7 divide	deem'd	*Dob, Lut, O'F; B*
'The Expiration'		
9 Oh	Or	Group III; *HK 2; O, P; B, S*
'Witchcraft by a Picture'		
10 feares	all feares	*Lut, O'F*
'The Paradox		
No title	*The Paradox.*	
'The Prohibition'		
5 to mee then that which	to thee then what to me	*Lut, O'F, S 96; Cy; JC*
22 stay	Stage	$\Sigma -$ Group I; *JC*
23 Lest thou	Then lest	*D, H 49; Lut, O'F; Cy; JC*
love and hate	love hate	
mee undoe	mee thou undoe	
24 *To*	*O*	*D, H 49; Lut, O'F; Cy; JC*
Oh	*yet*	*Lut, O'F; Cy*

1633	*1635*	MSS. agreeing with *1635*
'The Curse'		
14–16 In early . . . begot.	Or may he . . . sense.	*Σ* — Group I, *H 40*; *DC*; *Dob*; *B*
'The Indifferent'		
21 and that	*omitted*	*HK 2*, *O*, *P*. Group II, *DC*; Group III; *JC* *omit* that
'Woman's Constancy'		
8 Or	For	*Lut, O'F*
'The Apparition'		
10 will	*omitted*	*Lut, O'F*; *O, P*; *A 25*, *JC*
'Love's Usury'		
5 raigne	range	Group III
6 snatch	match	*Dob, Lut, O'F*
15 let report	let not report	Group III
19 or paine	and paine	*Lut, O'F*
24 loves	love	
'Love's Diet'		
6 endures	indues	*DC*
20 my	her	*DC*
21 that that	if that	*O'F (in margin)*; *Cy, O,* *P*
25 redeem'd	reclaim'd	*Σ* — *C 57*, *Lec*; *DC*
27 sports	sport	All *MSS.*
30 and sleepe	or sleepe	Group III; *Cy, O, P*; *S*
'Love's Deity'		
14 till I love her, that loves	if I love who loves not	*Lut, O'F*
'The Damp'		
24 In that	Naked	*Σ* — Group II, *DC*
'The Legacy'		
7 sent	meant	*Dob. (b.c.)*, *Lut*, *O'F* *(b.c.)*, *S 96*
14 me	*omitted*	Group II, *L 74*, *DC*; Group III; *Cy, O, P*
did	should	Group II, *L 74*; *Lut*, *O'F*; *HK 2*; *Cy, O, P*
23 this	that	Group II, *L 74*; *Lut*, *O'F*; *HK 2*; *Cy, O, P*; *A 25*
'The Broken Heart'		
8 flaske	flash	Group I — *Lec*; Group II, *L 74*; Group III; *HK 2*; *Cy*

		MSS. agreeing with
1633	*1635*	*1635*

'The Will'

| 36 did | do | *Dob, Lut, O'F; S* |

SONGS AND SONNETS (II)

'The Undertaking'

No title	*The undertaking.*	
18 attir'd	*omitted*	*Lut, O'F*

'Image and Dream'

| *Title: Elegie.* | ELEG. X. *The Dreame.* | |

'The Ecstasy'

6 With	By	*Lut, O'F*
9 entergraft	engraft	Group III; *HK 2; A 25, JC; B*
15 their	our	*Lut, O'F; O, P*
25 knowes	knew	*Σ — C 57, D, Lec*
48 soules	soule	
64 makes	make	
76 gone	growne	*Lut, O'F, S 96; O, P*

'A Fever'

| 19 much | more | *Lut, O'F; HK 2; Cy, O, P* |

'A Valediction: of my Name in the Window'

15 tempests	tempest	
36 these	those	*Σ — C 57, Lec; DC; S*
58 pane	Pen	*Lut, O'F; S*
64 this	thus	*O'F; HK 2; S*

'A Valediction: of the Book'

53 there something	their nothing	*Σ — O, P*
55 vent	went	

'The Good-Morrow'

17 better	fitter	*Σ — Group I, H 40; DC; JC*
20 or	both	*Lut, O'F; HK 2; O, P; JC*
21 Love so alike, that none doe slacken, none	Love just alike in all, none of these loves	*Σ — Group I, H 40; DC*

'The Anniversary'

3 they	these	*Lut, O'F*
20 their graves	their grave	

		MSS. agreeing with
1633	*1635*	*1635*

'The Sun Rising'
12 Why shouldst thou | Dost thou not | *Lut, O'F*

'The Canonization'
3 five | true |
30 legends | legend | Σ — Group I, *H 40*; *DC*
35 these | those | Group III; *Cy*

'Love's Growth'
9 paining | vexing | Group III; *Cy, O, P; S*
10 working | active | *Lut, O'F; Cy, O, P; S*
28 the | this | *Lut, O'F; Cy, O, P; S*

'Love's Infiniteness'
11 Thee | It | *Lut, O'F*
17 and | in | *Dob; H K 2; O, P; JC; B, S*
20 is | it | All *MSS.*
21 is | was | Group III—*Dob; H K 2; O, P; A 25*

'The Dream'
7 truth | true | Group III; *H K 2; Cy, O, P; A 25; B, S*

'Twickenham Garden'
4 balmes . . . cure | balme . . . cures | *TCC*; Group III; *H K 2; Cy, O, P; B, S*
15 yet leave loving | leave this garden | Σ — Group I, *H 40*; *DC*
18 my | the | Σ — Group I, *H 40*; *DC; B, S*

'A Nocturnal'
12 every | a very | *Lut, O'F*

'The Dissolution'
10 earthly | earthy | *O'F*
12 ne'r | neere | All *MSS.*

'The Blossom'
10 labours | labourest | Σ — Group I
15 that Sunne | the Sunne | Group III

'The Primrose'
Title: The Primrose. | *The Primrose, being . . . situate.* |
17 and | *omitted* | Σ — *S 96; B*
29 and | since |
30 this | *omitted* | *Lut, O'F*

	1633	1635	MSS. agreeing with 1635

'The Relic'

| 25 | no more wee | we never | Σ − Group II, DC |
| 26 | Then our | No more then | Lut, O'F |

'The Funeral'

| 17 | by me | with me | All MSS. |

DUBIA

'The Expostulation'

Title: Elegie.   ELEG. XVII. *The Expostu-*
                                            lation.

16	sweeter	sweetend	Group III, B, S
24	thought	thoughts	Group III
30	would	will	Group III, Cy, O, P; B, S

Musical Settings of Donne's Poems

THERE has been considerable interest in recent years in the contemporary settings of Donne's poems. In 1958 Professor Vincent Duckles of the University of California, Berkeley, read a paper on the subject to the International Musicological Society at Cologne[1] and in the following year he broadcast a talk with illustrations, based on his paper, in the BBC Third Programme. In 1961 M. Jean Jacquot introduced a collection of poems by Donne, Herbert, and Crashaw as set by their contemporaries.[2] My summary account is based on the lists supplied by Professor Duckles and M. Jacquot and I have had also the advantage of discussion with Dr. F. W. Sternfeld.

Words and music in a song may be related in two opposed ways. A poem may be written to music or music may be written to a poem. In the first case the tune shapes the poem, in the second the musician's art has to match the words. The writing of new words to old tunes, or, to use the technical term, the writing of parodies was an established exercise in the sixteenth century and, according to manuscript tradition, Donne practised it. He also appears, from the second stanza of 'The Triple Fool', to have expected his lyrics to be set to music. With only two possible exceptions, the settings that have survived are art songs, in which 'some man, his art and voyce to show' has set Donne's words.

According to one group of manuscripts (A 18, N, TCC, TCD) three of Donne's lyrics were written to 'certain ayres which were made before'; and another manuscript (DC) adds to these a further three. These six poems are the first six lyrics in this edition: the 'Mandrake' song, 'The Message', 'Sweetest love, I do not goë', 'The Bait', 'Community', and 'Confined Love'. No music survives for the last two; but settings are extant for the first four.

Strictly speaking no setting exists for 'The Bait'; but in William Corkine's *Second Book of Ayres*, 1612, there is a lesson for the lyra-viol with the incipit 'Come live with me, and be my love'. The tune has

---

[1] *Bericht über den siebenten Internationalen Musikwissenschaftlichen Kongress Köln 1958*, Kassel, 1959, pp. 91–93.

[2] *Poèmes de Donne, Herbert et Crashaw mis en musique par leurs contemporains*, Paris, 1961.

something of the quality of a folk-tune and it seems likely that this is the tune to which Marlowe's famous poem was sung and for which probably he wrote it. But with Raleigh's answer and the anonymous poem that follows it in *England's Helicon* and Donne's 'The Bait' we are in the region of literary rather than musical parody. The model is, that is to say, a poem rather than a tune. I give the melody,[1] for the sake of completeness, as a tune to which all the poems with this opening can be sung and which may have been running in Donne's head as he wrote his poem.

The Bait (p. 32)

[Come live with me, and be my love, And we will

some new plea - sures prove of gol - den sands, and

cry- stal brooks, With sil - ken lines, and sil - ver hooks.]

There are two versions of a setting of 'Sweetest love, I do not goe'; a plain version in Tenbury MS. 1018 and an embellished one in British Museum MS. Add. 10337. The tune, in its plain form, which I print below,[2] has some of the characteristics of popular song; but it is unlikely that this is the tune to which Donne wrote his poem. It is more probably a poor setting. The text in the musical version is corrupt; but apart from obvious memorial corruption the sixth line of the second stanza has been shortened from 'But believe that I shall make' (seven syllables and four stresses) to 'Since I doe make' (two stresses) to make this stanza fit the pattern imposed on the first stanza in which the sixth line has been divided after the second stress. But the sixth line of the three subsequent stanzas remains, as in Donne's poem, too long for the corresponding musical phrase. In Donne's poem the first stanza differs from the four that follow in that its sixth and seventh lines have only six syllables (three stresses) whereas in

---

[1] Transcribed by Dr. F. W. Sternfeld, who has fitted Donne's words to Corkine's melody.

[2] Unless otherwise shown the melodies are given from the collection edited by M. Jacquot.

the subsequent stanzas they are both extended to seven syllables (four stresses). It is probable that we have here a setting composed on the first stanza, with the second stanza adapted, and that the performer was expected to make his own modification in the last three stanzas. It is just possible that Donne wrote an initial stanza inspired by this tune and then made a variation which he followed for the rest of the poem.

Sweetest love, I do not goe (p. 31)

(Anonymous: Tenbury MS. 1018)

Of the settings that survive of the 'Mandrake' song and 'The Message' the first is probably, and the second certainly, an art song, written with the text before the composer. That for the 'Mandrake' song (British Museum MS. Egerton 2013) is anonymous: that for 'The Message' (MS. Tenbury 1019) is by Giovanni Coperario. Both are settings for voice and lute and in both only the first stanza of the poem is given. I agree with Professor Duckles in finding Coperario's setting over-rhetorical.

Song (p. 29)

Goe and catch a fal - linge star, gett with child a man-drake roote,

tell me where all past tymes are, or who clefte the Di - vells foote,

teach me to heare Mer-maydes sing-inge, or to keepe off En - vyes sting- inge,

and find what winde serves to ad - vance an hon - est minde.

(Anonymous: British Museum MS. Egerton 2013)

The Message (p. 30)

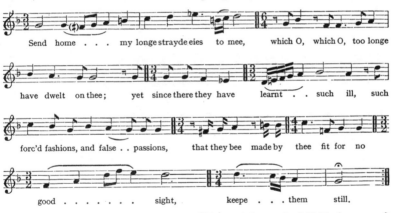

Send home . . . my longe strayde eies to mee, which O, which O, too longe

have dwelt on thee; yet since there they have learnt . . such ill, such

forc'd fashions, and false . . passions, that they bee made by thee fit for no

good . . . . sight, keepe . . . them still.

(Giovanni Coperario: MS Tenbury 1019)

Three more of the *Songs and Sonnets* were set to music in the seventeenth century: 'The Expiration', 'Break of Day', and 'The Apparition.' Two settings survive of 'The Expiration'. It is found in Alphonso
Ferrabosco's *Ayres*, 1609. (This is the first appearance of one of
Donne's poems in print.) There is also an anonymous setting in a
manuscript in the Bodleian (MS. Mus. Sch. 575). Both settings are for
voice and lute. In both the texts are sound, following the version

found in the majority of manuscripts rather than the version in Group II printed in *1633*. Ferrabosco's setting is strikingly beautiful and brings out the musical beauty of this most musical lyric.

The Expiration (p. 36)

(A. Ferrabosco, *Ayres*, 1609)

We ask'd none leave to love, nor . . . . will wee owe   a - ny so

cheap   a death . . .   as say - - ing goe.

(Anonymous: Bodleian MS. Mus. Sch. 575)

'Break of Day' was set by William Corkine and appears in his *Second Book of Ayres*, 1612. It is set for voice and viol. The text has variants from that printed in *1633* and is close to that in the Bridgewater manuscript.

Break of Day (p. 35)

T'is true,   t'is day,   what though it be   and

will you there-fore rise . . . from me?   what will you rise,   what will you

rise   be - cause t'is light? Did we lye downe . . . be-cause twas . . .

night? Love that in spight of dark-nesse brought us heth-er,   in spight of light .

. . should keepe us still to - ge - ther,   in spight of light should keepe us   still to -

- ge-ther, in spight of light should keepe us   still to-ge - - - ther.

(Corkine, *Second Book of Ayres*, 1612)

A setting of 'The Apparition' by William Lawes is extant in the library of Edinburgh University (Music MS. Dc 1 69). It was reported to me by Dr. F. W. Sternfeld who kindly lent me his transcription. The setting is for voice and bass, but unfortunately there is no vocal part for ll. 4–10, 14, and the first part of 15, though the bass is given. Since the melodic line is incomplete, and it would be rash to attempt to complete it, I do not give it here. The setting is, as one would expect from the nature of the poem and the date, declamatory.

All these poems are to be found in the set of *Songs and Sonnets* that I date before 1600. There is an interesting poem, printed by Grierson from *O'F*, which looks like a rewriting of one of the poems in my second set, 'Love's Infiniteness'. This appears, set for voice, lute, and viols, in Dowland's *A Pilgrim's Solace*, 1612. I give the melody and the text[1] here for interest, even though it is not a setting of a poem by Donne.

To ask for all thy love

(Grierson, i. 449)

(Dowland, *A Pilgrim's Solace*, 1612)

To sue for all thy Love, and thy whole hart
were madnesse.
I doe not sue, nor can admitt,
(Fayrest) from you to have all yet;
Who giveth all, hath nothing to impart
But sadnesse.

Hee who receaveth all can have no more;
Then seeing
My love by length of every howre
Gathers new strength, new growth, new power;
You must have dayly new rewards in store
Still beeing.

---

[1] Melody from E. H. Fellowes, *English School of Lutenist Song Writers*; text from *O'F*, punctuation emended.

You cannot every day give mee your hart
For merit;
Yet if you will, when yours doth goe
You shall have still one to bestow,
For you shall mine, when yours doth part
Inherit.

Yet if you please weele find a better way
Then change them,
For so alone (dearest) wee shall
Bee one and one another all;
Let us so joyne our harts, that nothing may
Estrange them.

Of the poems I print under the heading Dubia, the beautiful stanza 'Stay, O sweet, and do not rise' inspired many musicians. It appears as the first stanza of a poem in two stanzas in Dowland's *A Pilgrim's Solace*, Part I, 1612, set for voice and lute. In the same year it appeared alone, set for five voices, in Orlando Gibbons's *Madrigals and Motets of Five Parts*, the text beginning 'Ah, dear heart'. Professor Duckles also lists an anonymous setting in British Museum MS. Add. 29481 and a setting by Henry Lawes in his autograph manuscript, British Museum MS. Loan 35; he notes an anonymous setting with a text beginning 'Lie still, my dear' in British Museum MS. Add. 10337 and another, also anonymous, with the same opening in Bodleian MS. Don. *c* 57. I give here the poem and the setting from Dowland.[1]

Stay, O sweet, and do not rise (p. 108)

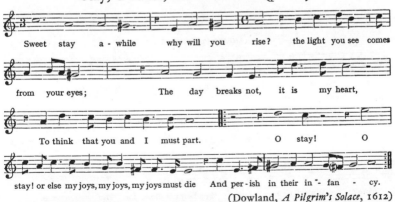

Sweet stay a - while why will you rise? the light you see comes

from your eyes; The day breaks not, it is my heart,

To think that you and I must part. O stay! O

stay! or else my joys, my joys, my joys must die And per-ish in their in - fan - cy.

(Dowland, *A Pilgrim's Solace*, 1612)

[1] Melody and text from E. H. Fellowes, op. cit.

Sweet, stay awhile; why will you rise?
The light you see comes from your eyes;
The day breaks not, it is my heart,
To think that you and I must part.
O stay! or else my joys must die
And perish in their infancy.

Dear, let me die in this fair breast,
Far sweeter than the Phoenix' nest.
Love, raise desire by his sweet charms
Within this circle of thine arms.
And let thy blissful kisses cherish
Mine infant joys that else must perish.

To complete the account of the settings of Donne's poems in the seventeenth century we must add settings for one of the Hymns and also a setting in three parts by Thomas Ford of the first two stanzas of Donne's paraphrase of *Lamentations* (Christ Church MSS. 736–8). Walton tells us that Donne caused the 'Hymn to God the Father' 'to be set to a most grave and solemn tune and to be often sung to the Organ by the Choristers of St. Paul's Church'. This setting has not survived; but there is a setting by John Hilton (died 1657), who was organist of St. Margaret's Westminster, which is preserved in British Museum MS. Egerton 2013, and there is a later one by Pelham Humfrey in *Harmonia Sacra*, 1688.

Hymn to God the Father

(i)

(*Divine Poems*, p. 51)

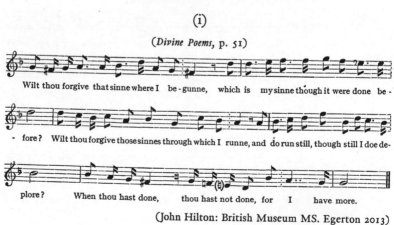

Wilt thou forgive that sinne where I be-gunne, which is my sinne though it were done be-
- fore? Wilt thou forgive those sinnes through which I runne, and do run still, though still I doe de-
plore? When thou hast done, thou hast not done, for I have more.

(John Hilton: British Museum MS. Egerton 2013)

(ii)[1]

Wilt thou for-give that Sin, where I be-gan, which was my Sin, tho'
it were done be-fore? Wilt thou for-give that Sin through which I run, and
do run . . still, tho' still . . I do de-plore? When thou hast done, thou
hast not done, for . . . . I have more:
Wilt thou for-give that Sin, by which I've won o-thers to sin, and made my Sin their
dore? Wilt thou for-give that Sin, which I did shun a Year or two,
. . . yet wal-low'd in a score? When thou hast done, thou hast not done, for . .
. . . . . . I have more. I have a Sin of Fear, that when I've spun my last
Thread, I shall per-ish on the Shore; but swear by thy self that at my
Death, thy Sun shall shine, as he shines now and here-to-
-fore, and hav-ing done that thou hast done, I fear no more.

(Pelham Humfrey, *Harmonia Sacra*, 1688)

[1] There is a modern edition of this setting, edited by Michael Tippett and Walter Berg-
mann, Schott & Co., London, 1947.

APPENDIX C

Lady Bedford and Mrs. Herbert

IN the course of his long introduction on 'The Poetry of Donne', Grierson came to Donne's Verse-Letters to noble ladies and allowed that among the ladies whose virtues Donne celebrated the 'highest place is held by Lady Bedford and Mrs. Herbert'. He paid tribute to the 'dazzling and subtle vein' of the letters to Lady Bedford, noted that those addressed to Mrs. Herbert, notably the letter 'Mad paper stay' and 'The Autumnal', are 'less transcendental in tone but bespeak an even warmer admiration' and added:

> Indeed it is clear to any careful reader that in the poems addressed to both these ladies there is blended with the respectful flattery of the dependant not a little of the tone of warmer feeling permitted to the 'servant' by Troubadour convention. And I suspect that some poems, the tone of which is still more frankly and ardently lover-like, were addressed to Lady Bedford and Mrs. Herbert, though they have come to us without positive indication.

He proceeded to argue from its title that Lady Bedford is the person to whom 'Twickenham Garden' is addressed and that 'A Nocturnal on St. Lucy's Day' was also written to her, 'for Lucy was the Countess's name, and the thought, feeling, and rhythm of the two poems are strikingly similar'. Turning to Donne's friendship with Mrs. Herbert, Grierson spoke of the letter and elegy referred to as 'instinct with affection and tender reverence', noted that Donne sent her 'some of his earliest religious sonnets, with a sonnet on her beautiful name', and added:

> To her also it would seem that at some period in the history of their friendship, the beginning of which is very difficult to date, he wrote songs in the tone of hopeless, impatient passion, of Petrarch writing to Laura, and others which celebrate their mutual affection as a love that rose superior to earthly and physical passion. The clue here is the title prefixed to that strange poem *The Primrose, being at Montgomery Castle upon the hill on which it is situate*.

Grierson had picked up from Gosse the notion that 'The Primrose' was 'a mystical celebration of the beauty, dignity, and intelligence of Magdalen Herbert'. He went on to claim that 'The Blossom' was in 'exactly the same mood' and was 'possibly written in the same place and on the same day, for the poet is preparing to return to London', hesitated, as well he might, to connect 'The Damp' with Mrs. Herbert, but declared that 'all these poems recur so repeatedly together in the manuscripts as to suggest that they have a common origin' and that 'with them go the beautiful poems "The Funeral" and "The Relic". In the former the cruelty of the lady has killed her lover, but in the second the tone changes entirely, the relation between Donne and Mrs. Herbert (note the lines

> Thou shalt be a Mary *Magdalen* and I
> A something else thereby)

has ceased to be Petrarchian and become Platonic.'[1] The argument is that five poems are connected by manuscript tradition, that two of these are connected with Mrs. Herbert, and that, consequently, all five must be, even though one is a generalization on the relations of the sexes, one a Petrarchan poem with a cynical imputation on the lady's virtue, one a rather brutal assault on honour, one devoutly Petrarchan, and the last Platonic.

(i)

Grierson was, I think right, to connect 'Twickenham Garden' and 'The Nocturnal'. Both are seasonal poems: the first is on a stock theme, going back to Petrarch, the contrast between the beauty of spring and the misery of the lover whose mistress is unkind; the second is a midwinter poem, in which the desolation of the season is excelled by the desolation of the lover whose mistress is dead. In both other lovers are appealed to: to come with crystal vials and collect true tears, and to study the lover as one in whom 'love wrought new Alchimie'. In both, for different ends, the conception that 'plants and stones' are able to 'detest and love' is employed. Although 'Twickenham Garden' is metrically less adventurous than 'A Nocturnal', in versification (as opposed to metrical form) the two poems are like echoes of each other in the sombre weighting of their lines and their slow pace. Considered as works of art they stand together; interpreted biographically they are poles apart. The first mourns the 'cruelty' of a mistress whose 'truth' to another kills her lover; the second mourns the death of a mistress with whom her lover had been wholly united.

[1] See Grierson, vol. ii, pp. xx–xxv.

In view of all we know of Donne's relations with the Countess of
Bedford and the tone of his letters to her in prose and in verse, it
seems incredible that either poem should be thought to be concerned
with Donne's actual feelings for his patroness.

The poems may, all the same, very well be connected with her,
although it is not her cruelty or her imagined death that they mourn.
A poem may be written 'for' someone without necessarily being
'about' that person. 'Twickenham Garden' appears without title in
many manuscripts and is headed simply 'In a Garden' in *B*; but the
title we know it by is found in the manuscripts of both Groups II and
III and outside these groups as well, and must be allowed to have
some authority by wide dissemination. I would suggest that the
poem was written for Lady Bedford possibly on a theme she gave
Donne, and perhaps in response to some verses of hers that she may
have shown him in '*Twicknam* garden'.

As well as having been a great patron of poets Lucy Bedford
appears to have tried her hand at writing poetry herself. On one
occasion, it has been suggested, she entered into a kind of competi-
tion with Donne by writing a pious *riposte* to the extravagant Elegy he
wrote on her friend Mrs. Bulstrode in 1609.[1] In a letter to her, unfortunately undated, Donne asks to be given some verses of hers that
she had shown him:

Happiest and worthiest Lady,

I do not remember that ever I have seen a petition in verse, I would not
therefore be singular, nor adde these to your other papers. I have yet adven-
tured so near as to make a petition for verse, it is for those your Ladiship did
me the honour to see in *Twicknam* garden, except you repent your making and
have [*for* having] mended your judgement by thinking worse, that is better,
because juster, of their subject. They must needs be an excellent exercise of
wit, which speake so well of so ill: I humbly beg them of your Ladiship, with
two such promises, as to any other of your compositions were threatnings:
that I will not shew them, and that I will not beleeve them; and nothing
should be so used that comes from your brain or breast. If I should confesse a
fault in the boldnesse of asking them, or make a fault by doing it in a longer
Letter, your Ladiship might use your style and old fashion of the Court towards me, and pay me with a Pardon. . . .[2]

[1] In some manuscripts Donne's Elegy that begins 'Death I recant' is followed immediately by a second Elegy on Mrs. Bulstrode that begins 'Death be not proud, thy hand
gave not this blow', which reads like an answer to the first. Grierson suggested that this
poem, which opens with the opening words of Donne's own defiance of death in the 'Holy
Sonnets', and which is ascribed to 'C. L. of B.' in *H 40* and to 'L. C. of B.' in *RP 31*, was
written by the Countess.   [2] *Letters*, pp. 67–68.

It would seem that these particular verses were verses of compliment to Donne, probably in reply to one of his Verse-Letters asking her favour. It is possible that on other occasions she showed him others of her 'compositions', or that they wrote poems on similar themes or answering each other. The actual subject of 'Twickenham Garden' is so trite and conventional that it might well have been a subject proposed, or a subject on which Lady Bedford and Donne competed. 'A Nocturnal', another of Donne's greatest lyrics, is a companion piece to 'Twickenham Garden' and it is possible that the idea of writing a poem on St. Lucy's Eve was a gesture of compliment to the Countess. If so, the poem far transcends its original conception and has become the most profound expression of the sensation of utter and irremediable loss. The sombre and passionate intensity of both poems, their haunting slow rhythms, may more properly be ascribed to the date at which they were written than to some imagined crisis in Donne's relations with his patron. If they are connected with Lucy Bedford they must have been written after 1607 when Donne was approaching middle age and his verse was developing the intensity of his *Divine Poems*, which is different from the ecstatic intensity of his celebrations of love's mysteries.

(ii)

Donne's friendship with Mrs. Herbert was less tainted with worldly motives than his relationship with the Countess of Bedford, and it grew throughout his life. Its best memorial is the *Sermon of Commemoration* that he preached after her death in 1627.[1] Two of his poems were certainly written to her: the Verse-Letter 'To Mrs M. H.' ('Mad paper stay, and grudge not here to burn') and the sonnet 'Of St. Mary Magdalen'.[2] A third poem, 'The Autumnal', is connected with her by Walton and by some manuscripts. The dates of all three poems are in question and there is uncertainty over the date when Donne's friendship with Mrs. Herbert began, since Walton's account is confused and inconsistent.

Grierson proposed a date of 1604 for the Verse-Letter 'Mad paper stay'; but on no very strong grounds.[3] Dr. Garrod suggested that it was most probably written just before Magdalen Herbert's second marriage, to Sir John Danvers in 1608, and is a fanciful plea by Donne, who has heard rumours of a projected marriage, for a continuance of

---

[1] See *Sermons*, viii. 61–93. For an account of Donne's friendship with Mrs. Herbert, see the introduction to vol. viii (pp. 3–9) and H. W. Garrod, 'Donne and Mrs. Herbert', *R.E.S.*, 1945, xxi. 161–73.   [2] Printed by Walton in the *Life of Herbert*, 1670.
[3] Grierson, ii. 132.

their friendship and a declaration that he will 'love him that shall be lov'd of her'. The dating of the sonnet sent with some 'Hymns' depends on giving the correct date to a prose letter accompanying them, which is dated by Walton 11 July 1607. This date cannot be right as the letter was written on a Sunday and 11 July in 1607 was a Saturday; but the error is most probably in the day, not the month or year. Walton also printed, in an appendix to the *Life of Herbert*, three other letters by Donne to Mrs. Herbert, two of them also dated in July 1607 and the third in August of the same year.

Walton's account of Donne's friendship with Mrs. Herbert occurs in his *Life of Herbert* written in 1670. It is there that he states that 'The Autumnal' was written for her and 'is a Character of the Beauties of her body and mind'. This receives some, if not strong, support from titles in manuscript. *B* has 'An autumnall face: on the Ladie S^r Ed Herbart mothers Ladie Danvers'; and *Lut*, followed by *O'F*, has 'On the Lady Herbert afterwards Danvers'. More impressive than the testimony of these rather unreliable manuscripts is the laconic 'Widdow Her' of *L 74*. Another name is suggested in *S 96* which heads the poem 'Elegie Autumnall on the Ladie Shandoys'; *O* and *P* call the poem simply 'Widdowe' and *S* gives it the general title 'A Paradox of an ould woman'. It will be seen that, apart from *L 74*, the most reliable manuscripts do not connect the poem with any particular person. It is possible that Walton's story, which is riddled with inconsistencies, is only an embroidery on a guess made by some collector of Donne's poems who knew of his friendship with Mrs. Herbert and attached to her a poem that was not written about any particular woman but was a witty variation on an ancient theme. But I think, in view of the title in *L 74*, we should give some credence to Walton and that we may accept that in his praise of an 'autumnal beauty' Donne had Mrs. Herbert in mind.

If we accept this we should also, I think, accept Walton's account of how the poem came to be written. This gives us a date consistent with the poem's manner and style as the date usually proposed (*c.* 1608) is not. Although Walton matriculates Edward Herbert at the wrong college (Queen's, when he was in fact at University College), is unaware that he married while an undergraduate, and makes Mrs. Herbert spend four years at Oxford with her son, substantially he has the story right. Mrs. Herbert, after being left a widow, went to live at Oxford, where Edward Herbert had returned, after the interruption caused to his studies by his father's death, and was there from

1599 to 1601. Walton says that it was while she was at Oxford that Donne 'came accidentally to that place', met her, and on leaving Oxford wrote and left behind the poem. He goes on to say that both he and she were 'then past the meridian of mans life', that their friendship began when Donne was 'about the Fortieth year of his Age', a married man with seven children and that 'when his necessities needed a daily supply' she was 'one of his most bountiful Benefactors'. He then printed the letter dated 11 July 1607 and the sonnet that accompanied it. Walton is making two quite incompatible statements: that Donne's friendship with Mrs. Herbert began with a casual meeting when she was in Oxford around the year 1600 (when Donne was not quite thirty and unmarried) and that this was the occasion of 'The Autumnal'; and that their friendship began when he was a married man with seven children, nearing forty.

Dr. Garrod suggested that Walton had confused Edward Herbert with a relative of the same name who matriculated from Queen's College in 1608 at the same time as Mrs. Herbert's third son, William. He suggested that Mrs. Herbert came to Oxford for this occasion and that Donne, coming there accidentally, met her and on leaving sent her 'The Autumnal'. One difficulty in accepting this suggestion is that the letters that Walton prints from Donne to Mrs. Herbert show them as well acquainted by the middle of 1607 and Walton's anecdote of how 'The Autumnal' came to be written implies that it was on the occasion of Donne's introduction to Magdalen Herbert. Another difficulty is that the style of 'The Autumnal' does not suggest so late a date. Its classical source and classical references, its lack of any elaborately developed conceits, and its strain of paradox relate it to the *Elegies* and the earlier *Songs and Sonnets* and distinguish it from the Verse-Letters to Lady Bedford and the Funeral Elegies of the years 1608 to 1609. It is a very odd poem for Donne to be writing in 1608.[1]

I would suggest that Walton knew very well that Donne's close friendship with Mrs. Herbert began in 1607, when he was a married man of thirty-five and she a woman of forty.[2] The tone of the letters that he prints, and their number (four in the space of four weeks) suggest that they belong to the enthusiastic beginning of a relation-

[1] Drs. Percy and Evelyn Simpson rightly stigmatized as grotesque the attempt to date 'The Autumnal' by seeing a topical reference to its opening lines in Jonson's *The Silent Woman* of 1610.

[2] Walton is notoriously bad at dates and figures. His statement that Donne was near 'the Fortieth year of his Age' and had seven children is, of course, untrue for 1607. For a discussion of Walton's story and correction of some of his errors, see D. Novarr, *The Making of Walton's Lives*, Cornell University Press, 1958, pp. 336–8.

ship rather than to the calm of an established one. It was at this time that Donne most needed and received her bounty. But the very fact that Walton relates the anecdote about 'The Autumnal', in spite of its being so inconsistent with his desire to prove that their close friendship had nothing of youthful heat in it, should make us regard it with respect. There is no reason why he should invent it. The solution that I would propose is that Walton is failing to distinguish between the date when Donne first made the acquaintance of Mrs. Herbert and the date when they became close friends. 'The Autumnal' is a gallant poem of compliment; I cannot agree with Grierson that it shows any particular warmth of feeling. It has been suggested that there was a reason for Donne's visiting Oxford in 1599 when he was Egerton's secretary, for Egerton's stepson, Sir Francis Wooley (who went with Donne on the Islands Voyage and later gave him and his wife shelter), graduated in that year. It may well have been through Wooley that Donne met Edward Herbert and his mother in Oxford.[1] If it was at this time that Donne wrote her a poem of compliment, we can explain why the acquaintance thus begun did not ripen into friendship for some years. In 1601 Mrs. Herbert moved to London; but by the end of that year Donne had married and from then until 1605, when he moved to Mitcham and took a room in the Strand, he was buried in the country. During the Mitcham period, when his circumstances were at their most desperate, he may well have sought out again the rich and charming Mrs. Herbert whom he had met some years before as a young man with a promising future who had delighted her by his wit and his tribute of a poem. He would be doing for himself what Goodyer at about the same time was doing for him with Lady Bedford, trying to find a patroness. In this case he found a lifelong friend.

Grierson's case for connecting five of the *Songs and Sonnets* with Mrs. Herbert rests partly on his statement that these five poems ('The Funeral', 'The Blossom', 'The Primrose', 'The Relic', 'The Damp') occur frequently together in manuscript. This is true, with the qualification that 'The Funeral' is not invariably found with the other four; and it is also true that a manuscript that lacks one will lack others of the group.[2] In one of the Group I manu-

---

[1] This suggestion is made by Mario M. Rossi, *La Vita, le opere, i tempi di Edoardo Herbert di Cherbury*, Florence, 1947, i. 39.

[2] *H 40*, *HK 2*, and *K* lack all five; *L 74* and *Cy* lack all but 'The Funeral'; *HK 1* lacks all but 'The Damp'; *O* and *P* lack all but 'The Funeral' and 'The Damp'. *A 25* has only 'The Blossom' and 'The Relic' and *JC* only 'The Blossom', 'The Relic', and 'The Damp'.

scripts, *H 49*, the collection of lyrics ends with 'The Funeral'; 'The Blossom', 'The Primrose', 'The Relic', and 'The Damp' occur together slightly later. In the other four manuscripts of Group I these four poems have been moved back to form, with 'The Funeral', the last five poems of the collection. This suggests that the last four must have been physically connected in *X*, the exemplar of the Group I manuscripts, either by being copied together on a separate quire or by being fastened together. Their appearance and absence in other manuscripts strongly supports this.[1] But the same would seem to have been true of another group of poems ('The Ecstasy', 'The Undertaking', 'Love's Deity', 'Love's Diet', 'The Will') which immediately precede 'The Funeral' in the Group I manuscripts. These poems, in the same order, appear as the last five poems of the collection of lyrics found in *H 40* and *HK 2*, both of which lack 'The Funeral', 'The Blossom', 'The Primrose', 'The Relic', and 'The Damp'. This group does not show the same coherence elsewhere as do 'The Blossom', 'The Primrose', 'The Relic', and 'The Damp'; but 'Love's Deity', 'Love's Diet', and 'The Will' tend to occur together, and 'The Funeral' very frequently follows 'The Will'. I do not think it is possible to argue, from the deduction that certain poems must have been physically connected in Donne's papers, that they must have been composed at the same time and addressed to the same person.[2]

There remains Grierson's argument for attaching 'The Primrose' and 'The Relic' to Mrs. Herbert. 'The Primrose' is given this short title in all the manuscripts in which it occurs as well as in *1633*; but the second edition of 1635 added to it the words 'being at Mountgomery Castle, upon the hill, on which it is situate'. This addition is too circumstantial to be ignored and cannot be dismissed as an editorial invention. The existence of a '*Prim-rose hill*' southwards of the

---

[1] Group II has all five, but only 'The Damp' and 'The Relic' appear together. In *DC*, *B*, and *Dob* 'The Funeral' follows 'The Will' at some distance from the other four which appear together but in varying orders. In *S* all five appear together, but not in the Group I order. In *Lut* and *O'F* all five appear together, but with 'The Curse' inserted among them, and not in the Group I order.

[2] There is an obvious reason why Donne, or anyone else, sorting the *Songs and Sonnets*, might put 'The Blossom' and 'The Primrose' together: both are poems that take for their symbol a flower. There is an equally obvious reason for bringing 'The Will', 'The Funeral', 'The Relic', and 'The Damp' together: they are all poems which open with the speaker imagining his own death.

It is perhaps worth noting that the last fourteen poems in the Group I manuscripts are (except 'The Undertaking') given titles. (The nine other titled poems in the Group I collection of lyrics appear scattered.) If, as I have suggested elsewhere, the Group I manuscripts represent a collection that Donne himself was making in 1614 but abandoned, perhaps this group of poems, all with titles, was the beginning of an attempt to arrange the lyrics for publication.

castle of Montgomery is attested by Aubrey who quotes the first stanza of this poem, writing against its first line the words 'In the parke', in his jottings on Sir Edward Herbert.[1] It is surely with Sir Edward, rather than with his mother, that a poem associated with Montgomery Castle should be connected. He resided there, on and off, throughout his life and described himself when he entered Gray's Inn in 1613 as 'of castle Montgomery', whereas Mrs. Herbert left Wales, first for Oxford and then for London, after her first husband's death in 1599. 'The Primrose' is, unlike the great majority of the *Songs and Sonnets*, not addressed to any woman, nor has the speaker any particular woman in mind; he is looking for 'a true love'. The poem is undramatic and speculative, divorced from any love-affair real or imagined. I would suggest that its ironic and cynical tone makes it an admirable cooling-card to such high-flown poems of Herbert's as the three called 'Platonick Love'; and that it was for the benefit of the master of Montgomery Castle rather than for that of his mother, that Donne argued in this curiously frigid poem the superiority of a 'mere woman' to those rare 'monsters' who were 'more or less then woman'.

Donne's friendship with Edward Herbert appears to have been one that included a certain amount of poetic rivalry. Jonson reported to Drummond that he wrote his Elegy on Prince Henry in 1612 'to match Sir Ed: Herbert in obscurenesse'. Three years before they had both written Elegies on Mrs. Bulstrode, and in 1610 Donne wrote a long Verse-Letter to Herbert, then abroad at the siege of Juliers, which it has been plausibly suggested, was a reply to Herbert's Satire 'The State progress of Ill', written in France in August 1608.[2] Grierson suggested that 'The Ecstasy' was probably the source of Herbert's best-known poem, 'Ode upon a Question moved, Whether Love should continue for ever?'[3] It is possible that the relation of the two poems is not simply that of imitation by Herbert of a poem by Donne; but that both poems are rival rehandlings of Sidney's dialogue of lovers in a spring setting, 'In a grove most rich of shade'.[4] Herbert's poem, in which the lady speaks first and her lover replies, is much nearer to Sidney's poem (in which Astrophel speaks first and Stella answers him) than is Donne's 'dialogue of one'. This is what we should expect if both

[1] *Brief Lives*, ed. Clark, 1898, i. 308.
[2] See D. A. Keister, 'Donne and Herbert of Cherbury: an Exchange of Verses', *M.L.Q.*, viii, 1947.
[3] See Grierson, ii. 41.
[4] See G. Williamson, 'The Convention of *The Exstasie*', *Seventeenth-Century Contexts*, 1960. This develops a suggestion by Morris W. Croll in his study of Fulke Greville, Philadelphia, 1903.

were writing poems on 'a question moved', setting against Sidney's
Petrarchan lovers, divided and 'passion rent', lovers united by a love
that 'no change can invade'. If Herbert were simply imitating Donne
his poem should be further from Donne's model, Sidney's. 'The
Ecstasy', like 'The Primrose', is exceptional among Donne's poems in
setting a scene, and its narrative form is as unusual as is the purely
argumentative generalization of 'The Primrose'. The two poems have
another point in common, which connects them with Herbert's
intellectual interests. They both use the structure of a flower for
argument. The five-, four-, and six-petalled primroses and the single
and double violet of 'The Ecstasy' are without parallel in other poems.
One of the most entertaining passages in Herbert's autobiography is
his description of his prowess as an amateur physician in which he
attacks 'Chymique or Spagyrique Medicines', declaring that their
effects are 'more happily and safely perform'd by Vegetables' and
adds:

> I conceive it is a fine Study and worthy a gentleman to be a good
> Botanique, that so he may know the nature of all Herbs and Plants . . .; for
> which purpose it will be fit for him to cull out of some good Herball all the
> Icones together with the descriptions of them.[1]

I would not wish to press this suggestion too hard, but am content to
say that there is a strong case for connecting 'The Primrose' with
Herbert and at least a case for connecting 'The Ecstasy' also with
him.

One manuscript, *H 49*, tells us that Donne was on his way to visit
Herbert in Wales when he wrote 'Good-Friday' in 1613. (The poem
itself was, according to another manuscript, *A 25*, sent to Goodyer.)
Dr. Garrod argued that 'The Primrose' could not have been written
on this occasion since in 1613 Herbert's cousin, Philip, was living at
the Castle; but if Herbert was in Wales he would surely have been
staying with his cousin and I do not think, on the principle of Occam's
razor, that we should postulate another visit to Wales than this.
Professor Coffin suggested that 'The Primrose' must be dated after
the publication of Galileo's *Sidereus Nuncius* in 1610, and I accept his
suggestion.[2] I would therefore date 'The Primrose' in the spring of
1613.

As for 'The Relic', I concur with Dr. Garrod in thinking that there

---

[1] *The Life of Edward Lord Herbert of Cherbury Written by Himself*, 1770, pp. 35–36.
[2] See Commentary, pp. 219–220.

is no need to assume that the lady in the poem who gave her lover a 'bracelet of bright hair' was herself called 'Magdalen' because the Bishop and King in a time of 'mis-devotion' will declare this to be a relic of the saint who 'loved much' and who is always depicted in art with brilliant golden hair. The starting-point in both 'The Relic' and 'The Funeral' is the shudder at the thought of a love-token around the arm of a skeleton or of a corpse. What did it mean to the dead man, and what will it mean to those who come upon it? In the one case it was a token of a mystical union of lovers, in the other the token of a lover's servitude. The irony in 'The Relic' lies in the misunderstanding of the token: by the grave-diggers who will think it a device of a 'loving couple', and by the King and the Bishop who will think it a love-token given by the great penitent of Christian tradition in her unregenerate days. Instead, it is a symbol of a love for which no penance need be demanded and which was in itself a miracle. 'The Relic' makes the same equivocal play with the mysteries of religion and the mysteries of love as 'The Canonization'. What experience in life lies behind it I do not see that we can ever know: but I cannot think, from what we know of Donne's relations with Mrs. Herbert,[1] that there is any strong reason for connecting this poem with her.

[1] I hope it is not frivolous to suggest that it is unlikely that Mrs. Herbert's hair was still 'bright' by the time that she and Donne had become close friends.

APPENDIX D

'The Ecstasy'

THE interpretation of 'The Ecstasy' has been so much discussed and disputed that the poem requires more extended treatment than is proper in a commentary. To Coleridge 'The Ecstasy' was the quintessential 'metaphysical poem'; and to Mr. Ezra Pound it is equally, beyond question, a great 'metaphysical poem' in the truest sense. But among scholars there has been flat disagreement over the genuineness of the poem's 'Platonism'; and even among those who regard it as seriously intended, there has been a recurrent note of reserve in their praise of the poem. This appears in what may be taken as the classic statement of the orthodox view of the poem:

This justification of natural love as fullness of joy and life is the deepest thought in Donne's love-poems, far deeper and sincerer than the Platonic conceptions of the affinity and identity of souls with which he plays in some of the verses addressed to Mrs. Herbert. The nearest approach that he makes to anything like a reasoned statement of the thought latent rather than expressed in *The Anniversarie* is in *The Extasie*, a poem which, like the *Nocturnall*, only Donne could have written. Here, with the same intensity of feeling, and in the same abstract, dialectical, erudite strain he emphasizes the interdependence of soul and body.

But, after quoting some lines, Grierson added:

It may be that Donne has not entirely succeeded in what he here attempts. There hangs about the poem just a suspicion of the conventional and unreal Platonism of the seventeenth century. In attempting to state and vindicate the relation of soul and body he falls perhaps inevitably into the appearance, at any rate, of the dualism which he is trying to transcend. He places them over against each other as separate entities and the lower bulks unduly.[1]

Against Ezra Pound's 'Platonism believed' we have to set Grierson's 'Platonism modified and transcended, and yet perhaps not fully believed'.

In 1928 Professor Pierre Legouis put forward an opposite view: that the poem was not a philosophic poem at all but, within a narrative framework, displayed in quasi-dramatic form a very skilful piece of

[1] Grierson, vol. ii, pp. xlvi–xlvii.

seduction. The couple 'have been playing at Platonic love, sincerely enough on the woman's part', and Donne imagines 'how they would pass from it to carnal enjoyment'.¹ This view was strongly countered by many scholars who pointed out that the argument for the body's rights in love was a common topic among Italian and French Neoplatonists and brought supporting passages from Donne's poetry and prose to parallel the supposed argument of the poem as Grierson interpreted it.² A summary of the debate and a detailed interpretation of the poem, can be found in my article 'The Argument about "The Ecstasy" ' (*Elizabethan and Jacobean Studies*, 1959) which this appendix is based on and excerpts from.³

The disputants over the poem's meaning argue from a common ground. Both sides assume that the point of the poem is a justification of physical love, and that it ends with a plea that the lovers, having enjoyed spiritual communion should turn to the enjoyment of physical union. My view is that this is a misreading of the last section of the poem (ll. 49–76) and that the only plea made in these lines is that the lovers' souls should return from their ecstatic communion to reanimate their bodies. They retreat from the 'blessed death of ecstasy' preferring to take up again life in this world, where the soul and body unite to make up man and the spiritual is mediated through the physical. The key phrases are

> But, O alas, so long, so farre
> Our bodies why doe wee forbeare?
>
> To 'our bodies turne wee then,

and

> ... when we'are to bodies gone.

In the context of the poem the obvious sense appears to be 'But, O alas, why do we for so long and to such a degree shun the company of our bodies?', 'Let us return to our bodies', and 'when we are gone back to (our) bodies'. The final, and one must suppose from its

---

¹ *Donne the Craftsman*, Paris, 1928, pp. 68–69.
² See particularly Merritt Y. Hughes, 'The Lineage of "The Exstasie"', *M.L.R.* xxvii, 1932, and 'Kidnapping Donne', *Essays in Criticism*, Berkeley, 1934, pp. 83–89; G. R. Potter, 'Donne's *Extasie*, Contra Legouis', *P.Q.* xv, 1936; and the debate between Professor C. S. Lewis and Mrs. Joan Bennett in *Seventeenth-Century Studies presented to Sir Herbert Grierson*, 1938, pp. 64–104. See also A. J. Smith, 'The Metaphysic of Love', *R.E.S.*, Nov. 1958 (published while my article was in press), which gives extensive examples of love-casuistry from Italian writers to parallel Donne's.
³ For a criticism of my view, see Robert Ellrodt, *Les Poètes Métaphysiques Anglais, Seconde Partie*, Paris, 1960, pp. 401–10. Professor Ellrodt holds with M. Legouis, that 'L'assurance que les mystères de l'amour se lisent dans le corps est . . . un prélude logique à l'invitation faite à un témoin d'observer l'union charnelle'.

position conclusive, reason for such a return of the separated souls is not that it will benefit the lovers themselves, but that only in the body can they manifest love to 'weake men'.[1] I am not attempting to deny that, as a corollary to its main line of thought, the poem implies the value of physical love; but only that this is the poem's main argument. As its title suggests its subject is an ecstasy, a rare experience in which the lovers discover the truth about their love. Having discovered it they choose to return to ordinary life; just as the lovers in 'The Anniversary', though knowing that they may well 'prove' even greater love in heaven, prefer to being 'throughly blest' in heaven the bliss of their union on earth. The last section of the poem asserts the interdependence of soul and body and argues that souls may meet and mingle by other than such extraordinary means as ecstasy. I believe that Donne's starting-point was not the desire to write a philosophic poem but to explore imaginatively the notion of ecstasy as he had met it in his Neoplatonic reading.[2]

'The Ecstasy' is unique among Donne's poems in being a narrative; but by means of the device of the hypothetical listener it turns into a poem in the dramatic present. It stands apart from other poems in the same convention[3] in that its lovers enjoy an ecstatic union so absolute that the dialogue of lovers becomes in this poem a 'dialogue of one', not a persuasion by one lover and a response by the other. The poem falls into three parts. In ll. 1–28 the scene is set, the souls of the lovers go out from their bodies, and the hypothetical listener is introduced. In ll. 29–48 we learn by this device of the imagined bystander what the lovers learned in their wordless communion. In ll. 49–76 the lovers decide that the time has come to reanimate their bodies and proceed to a justification of life in the body in which they believe that the union of souls will subsist.

The setting (ll. 1–4), too brief to include the usual ingredients of a *locus amoenus* (shade, running water, bird-song), is more frankly an

[1] In his 'Platonic' poems Donne's lovers often speak as if they had a kind of mission to the world, to impart a glimmering of 'love's mysteries' to the 'laity' in love. It seems to me impossible that the lovers here should include themselves among 'weake men'. Donne's lovers always assume their superiority to the rest of mankind; and these have just given proof that they are extraordinary. I do not see why M. Ellrodt assumes that the sacred book of the body contains only one text.

[2] Leone Ebreo has a long passage on the semi-death of ecstasy which includes an analysis of the nature of the soul and of its relation to the spirits (pp. 199–207). I have found this book so useful in annotating 'The Ecstasy' and other poems that I am convinced that Donne must have known it well. Many of the ideas are commonplaces and can be found scattered in other writers. It is their collocation in Leone Ebreo that is striking.

[3] Sidney's Eighth Song in *Astrophel and Stella*, Fulke Greville's *Caelica* 75, Herbert of Cherbury's *Ode upon a Question Moved*, and Wither's *Fair Virtue*, sonnet 3.

incitement to love than the setting of other poems in the tradition.
On the other hand, the violet, which to M. Legouis suggested
'languor', and which has erotic associations in classical poetry, is in
Elizabethan literature invariably 'modest', 'pure', and 'the virgin of
the year'. It would seem to be here not for its symbolic significance
but because it is a flower that exists in a single and a double form and
so provides an analogy with the creation of a new soul. The final line
of the first stanza makes clear that this is not to be a poem concerned
with a wooing, as the setting might suggest. The lovers are 'one
anothers best'; each is equally lover and beloved.

The lovers are described as first united by means of the senses: the
lower sense of touch and the higher sense of sight (ll. 5–12). Ficino
has a long passage (*Commentary*, pp. 221–2) on the emission of spirits
by means of beams from two lovers' eyes which Burton quotes:

> *Lycias* he stares on *Phaedrus* face, and *Phaedrus* fastens the balls of his eyes
> upon *Lycias*, and with those sparkling rays sends out his spirits. The beams of
> *Phaedrus* eys are easily mingled with the beams of *Lycias*, and spirits are joyned
> to spirits. This vapour begot in *Phaedrus* heart, enters into *Lycias* bowels: and
> that which is a greater wonder, *Phaedrus* blood is in *Lycias* heart (*Anatomy*,
> part 3, sect. 2, memb. 2, subs. 2).

Castiglione has a similar passage on the 'lively spirits that issue out
of the eyes' (p. 247), and Professor Praz, who cites also Bruno
(*Candelaio*, I. x), has drawn attention to Petrarch's sixty-third
sonnet *in vita*: 'Quando giunge per li occhi al cor profondo'. The
horticultural terms ('entergraft' and 'propagation') point forward to
the analogy with the transplanted violet. It is often suggested that the
words 'as yet' imply a longing for closer physical union and that there
is disappointment in the witticism that 'looking babies' was their
only 'propagation'. In the context the plain sense is surely: 'We were
united so far by the joining of hands and the mingling of our eye-
beams and not yet by the union of souls.' A desire for physical propagation is not a feature of Donne's love-poetry and we should not
take this jest as implying that these lovers are longing to propagate
their kind. It hardly needs pointing out that the language of these first
twelve lines is 'pregnant' with sexual meanings and I do not doubt
that Donne intended thus to suggest that his lovers were young and
ardent and fit for all the offices of love. I do not know why it is always
assumed that so far they have only loved chastely.[1]

---

[1] 'One anothers best' at least implies that there has been no question of one refusing the
other.

By means of the corporal sense of touch and the spiritual sense of sight such an ardent desire for union is generated that the lovers' souls go out from their bodies which, having 'thus' conveyed soul to soul, yield up their forces and rest senseless.[1] The first thing that Donne's lovers learn in the illumination of ecstasy is something that Leone Ebreo's Philo was at great pains to teach Sophia. They learn what is hidden from most lovers, 'what they love': that it was not sexual desire that attracted them to each other but 'perfect love', not born of appetite but of reason.[2] They then see how love has first reconcocted their souls and then united them to create a 'new soule'. This new and 'abler' soul is, unlike all separate and individual souls, gifted with complete self-knowledge. It understands its own essence, or nature, of what it is 'compos'd and made'.[3] And it recognizes its own immortality. The lovers learn that their 'love will continue for ever', having found the answer to the question upon which Lord Herbert wrote his Ode.

The union of their souls is indissoluble because it is the union of perfect with perfect, or like with like. It is only those things that are unequally mixed that are subject to decay or mutability. The force of love has united all the diverse parts of each soul wholly to its own intellectual nature, which is its true essence, and 'new soule' of their union, being wholly intellect, knows itself.[4]

With the revelation that their love is beyond change, the ecstasy of the lovers reaches its climax. Unless they are to pass out of this life altogether they must now return to their bodies. The conclusion of the poem justifies this retreat from ecstasy to normal life (ll. 29–76). It does so by reference to the doctrine of the circle of love. The heart of

---

[1] See ll. 53–56.

[2] Leone Ebreo teaches that there are two kinds of love: 'imperfect' which is engendered by sensual appetite and dies when that is satisfied, and 'perfect' love which itself 'generates desire of the beloved . . . : in fact we first love perfectly and then the strength of that love makes us desire spiritual and bodily union with the beloved.' Sophia asks 'If the love you bear me does not spring from appetite, what is its cause?' and Philo replies: 'Perfect and true love, such as I feel for you, begets desire, and is born of reason. . . . For knowing you to possess virtue, intelligence and beauty, no less admirable than wondrously attractive, my will desired your person, which reason rightly judged in every way noble, excellent and worthy of love. And this, my affection and love, has transformed me into you, begetting in me a desire that you may be fused with me, in order that I, your lover, may form but a single person with you, my beloved, and equal love may make of our two souls one, which may likewise vivify and inform our two bodies. The sensual element in this desire excites a longing for physical union, that the union of bodies may correspond to the unity of spirits wholly compenetrating each other' (pp. 56–57).

[3] Cf. 'Negative Love':

> If any who deciphers best,
> What we know nor, our selves. . . . .

[4] See note to l. 35.

Leone Ebreo's book is that the world as it exists and was created is such a circle. The inferior desires to unite in love with what is superior; but equally the superior desires to unite itself in love with what is inferior. The inferior desires the perfection that it lacks; the superior desires to bestow its own perfection on what lacks it. The final cause of love in each is the desire for perfection, for the union of all the parts of the Universe so that it may perfectly realize the divine Idea of its being, and be itself united to its perfect Source and End. The illustration that Philo gives at some length to show the love that superior bears for inferior is the love of intelligences for the spheres which they move and govern, and Sophia comments: 'I suppose it is for the same reason that the spiritual intelligence of man unites with a body as frail as the human: to execute the divine plan for the coherence and unity of the whole Universe' (p. 189). The same force, love or the desire for union, that has united the lovers' intellectual souls, brings those souls back to their bodies. 'Love is the condition of the existence of the world and all in it'; and intelligent souls would not 'unite with human bodies to make them rational, if love did not constrain them thereto' (p. 191).

The souls of the lovers yearn towards their bodies, which are 'theirs', though not 'they'.[1] They own their debt to them and they find an analogy in the way 'heavens influence' works to support them in the belief that they need not fear that descent into the body will make it impossible for soul to flow into soul. Donne is here referring, I think, to the fundamental Paracelsian doctrine that the influence of the heavenly bodies, whether good or evil, is the 'smell, smoke or sweat' of the stars mixed with the air.[2] It is, like the analogy with violet, an illustrative parallel: 'heavenly bodies cannot act upon man without the material intermediary of air, so we may believe that souls which are in the body can communicate through the body's aid'. The famous lines which follow display the working of the cosmic principle of the circle of love in the microcosm, or little world of man:

> As our blood labours to beget
> Spirits, as like soules as it can,
> Because such fingers need to knit
> That subtile knot, which makes us man:

[1] M. Albert Gérard has pointed out that in ll. 1–28 of the poem the 'principle of identity' to be found in the body, the attitude being 'we are bodies which have souls'; that in ll. 29–48 the souls have so far 'advanced their state' that the position is reversed, 'we are souls which have bodies'; and that in the last section Donne attempts to argue that we exist not as a soul or as a body but as a union of soul and body ('Mannerism and the Scholastic Structure of Donne's "Extasie"', *Publications de l'Université de l'État à Élisabethville*, 1961).

[2] *Paramirum*, I. viii. *Der Bücher und Schrifften*, Basle, 1589–90, i. 15.

So must pure lovers soules descend
T'affections, and to faculties,
That[1] sense may reach and apprehend,
Else a great Prince in prison lies.

The blood strives to become spiritual, to produce the spirits, or powers of the soul, which are necessary to unite the intellectual and corporal in man. Conversely souls must condescend to the affections and faculties of the body in order that man's sense organs may become rational. The mind, as Philo teaches Sophia, 'controls the senses and directs the voluntary movements of men'. 'For this purpose it must issue from within the body to its external parts and to the organs of sense and movement, in order that man may approach the objects of sense in the world around him, and it is then that we are able to think at the same time as we see, hear and speak' (p. 201). If the soul does not thus inform all the activities of the body, it is abandoning its task which is 'rightly to govern the body'. Its duty is to take 'intellectual life and knowledge and the light of God down from the upper world of eternity to the lower world of decay' (pp. 189–90) and thus realize the unity of the Universe. A soul that does not perform this divinely appointed function is like a prince in a prison. The concordance of Donne's poems shows how fond he is of the metaphor of the soul as prince and the body, with its limbs, as his province. If the soul does not thus animate the body in all its parts, it is imprisoned in a carcass instead of reigning in its kingdom. Donne is contrasting the Platonic view of the soul imprisoned in the flesh with the Aristotelian conception of the union of the soul and body in man. A prince is no prince if he does not rule his kingdom and a kingdom without a prince is a chaos. Prince and kingdom need each other and are indeed inconceivable without each other. In the final lines of the poem the lovers find a further justification for life in this world, in the duty to reveal love to men, and declare that, if one of 'love's Divines' has heard their 'dialogue of one', he will not be aware of much difference between their union when 'out of the body' and their union when they have resumed possession of their kingdoms.

[1] For defence of this reading, see note to l. 67.

APPENDIX E

The Marshall Engraving and the Lothian Portrait

WE are fortunate in the number of portraits that have survived of Donne and in the fact that they belong to all periods of his life. We are even more fortunate in their quality. The earliest, which appears facing p. 1 of this edition, is a portrait that was prefixed as frontis-piece to the second edition of Donne's *Poems* in 1635, engraved by William Marshall from a lost original. It shows Donne with fashionable love-locks and ear-ring, dressed in a suit of black with a plain white collar and cuffs, clasping his sword-hilt. The costume is plainly 'costly' but 'not express'd in fancy'. The portrait is dated 'ANNO DNI. 1591. ÆTATIS SUÆ. 18'. It must, therefore, have been painted in the early months of 1591 when Donne was at, or about to enter, Thavies Inn. The Spanish motto 'Antes muerto que mudado' is adapted by a change of gender from a line in the first song in Montemayor's *Diana*. Donne has taken as a boast of his constancy ('Sooner dead than changed') the protestation of a fickle mistress.[1] Laurence Binyon first suggested that the lost original of the engraving was by Hilliard and this suggestion has been generally accepted. Mr. John Bryson, the discoverer of the Lothian portrait, who is collaborating with Mr. John Woodward in a study of the portraits of English poets, asserts that the Marshall engraving 'is certainly based on a lost miniature by Nicholas Hilliard'.[2] Donne's admiration for Hilliard was expressed in his poem 'The Storm' where he declared that

> a hand, or eye
> By *Hilliard* drawne, is worth an history,
> By a worse painter made.

---

[1] Sidney's translation of the relevant verse is

> On sandie banke of late,
> I saw this woman sit,
> Where, 'sooner die then change my state',
> She with her finger writ:
> Thus my beleefe was staid,
> Behold Love's mightie hand
> On things, were by a woman said,
> And written in the sand.

(*Poems*, ed. Ringler, 1962, p. 158.)

[2] *The Times*, 13 Oct. 1959.

The verses under the portrait were supplied by Isaak Walton who, in an addition made in the final version (1675) of his *Life of Donne*, after saying that he had seen 'many Pictures of him, in several habits, and at several ages, and in several postures', refers to this as a picture 'drawn by a curious hand at his age of eighteen; with his sword and what other adornments might then suit with the present fashions of youth, and the giddy gayeties of that age', and adds 'his Motto then was,

How much shall I be chang'd
Before I am chang'd.'

Walton's mistranslation allows him to contrast this youthful portrait with the portrait of the dying Donne, as his verses contrast the love poet with the divine poet.

The Lothian portrait (facing p. 29) was left by Donne to his friend Sir Robert Carr (or Ker), later Earl of Ancrum, and has remained in the possession of the family ever since.[1] At some time in the early eighteenth century it was inscribed in the top left-hand corner 'John Duns', and the picture, which was in poor condition, thus came to be described in inventories of the house as a portrait of Duns Scotus. Inquiries by various scholars as to whether the descendants of Ker still possessed the portrait of John Donne bequeathed to their ancestor were unsuccessful, until Mr. John Bryson asked the right question: not whether the family possessed a portrait of Donne but whether they possessed a portrait corresponding to the descriptions of the painting. Mr. Bryson announced his discovery in an article in *The Times*, 13 October 1959, to which I am here indebted.

In his will Donne bequeathed to his 'honourable and faithful friend Mr. Robert Carr of his Majesty's bed-chamber that picture of mine which is taken in shadows and was made very many years before I was of this profession' (Gosse, ii. 363). In a manuscript preserved among the Hawthornden manuscripts in the National Library of Scotland, William Drummond has made a note that

J. Done gave my L. Ancrum his picture in a melancholie posture w[t] this word about it De Tristitia ista libera nos Domina.[2]

Another of Donne's friends referred to this portrait. R. B. (Richard Baddily) in his *Life of Dr. Thomas Morton*, 1669, tells us that he had

---

[1] The marquessate of Lothian was conferred on the family in 1701.

[2] In David Laing's *Account of the Hawthornden MSS.* (*Arch. Scot.* iv (1847), p. 81) where this note is transcribed the last word of the motto is misread as 'Domine'. The transcription given above was supplied to Mr. Bryson by the Keeper of Manuscripts in the National Library of Scotland. There is no doubt about the 'a' of 'Domina'.

long since seen his (Donne's) Picture in a dear friends chamber of his in
Lincolne's Inne, all envelloped with a darkish shadow, his face and feature
hardly discernable, with this ejaculation and wish written thereon: *Domine
illumina tenebras meas* (pp. 101–2).

The painting is in remarkable contrast to the usual Elizabethan
style of portraiture without shading. It is in strong light and shade.
Donne, a connoisseur of painting, distinguishes it thus as 'taken in
shadows' and R. B. remembers this striking feature. Donne is posed
with folded arms, an unusual pose for a portrait at this period, and
wears a large-brimmed hat with the brim turned back to show his face.
'Folded arms and melancholy hat' are the signs of lovers' melancholy.[1]
This is, as Drummond realized, 'J. Done . . . in a melancholie posture'.
The fact that the hat is not pulled down might be taken as a sign that
Donne is guying the melancholy lover's pose; but no portrait in
which the whole of the upper part of the face was obscured would be
worth commissioning. It is sufficient to establish Donne here as the
melancholy lover, that his arms are folded, and that he wears the
traditional large-brimmed hat that could be pulled down at any
moment to signalize the lover's despondency. The doublet is, like the
doublet of the Marshall engraving, dark but it is adorned with a fine
lace collar. The lawn collar above this is open at the neck, a pleasingly
Byronic touch at first sight. Here it signifies the carelessness of the
unhappy lover.[2] One hand is bare, the other gloved. This too may
have some symbolic meaning. The motto, 'Illumina nostras tenebras
Domina', is a parody of the opening words of the third collect for
Evensong, a more daring adaptation than the alteration and appro-
priation of the fickle lady's protestation in the Marshall engraving.
Mrs. Duncan-Jones has provided me with a parallel here in an
impresa in Camden's *Remains*, 1657 (p. 344): 'His devote mind to his
Lady he devoutly, though not religiously shewed which under Venus

---

[1] Mr. Bryson gives references from William Cornwallis, *Essays*, 1600, where love is
said to bring forth 'Rimes, and Songs full of passion, enough to procure crossed arms, and the
Hat pulled down', from Shakespeare, *Love's Labour's Lost*, 'with your hat penthouse-like o'er
the shop of your eyes, with your arms cross'd on your thin-belly doublet' (III. i. 12–13), and,
from the same play, III. i. 171 and IV. iii. 130–2. He also cites the verse on John Ford,
author of *The Lover's Melancholy* (1629),

> Deep in a dump John Forde was alone got,
> With folded arms and melancholy hat,

and refers to the title-page of Burton's *Anatomy of Melancholy* where 'Inamorato' apppears
with arms folded and a wide-brimmed hat pulled down over his eyes.

[2] Hamlet, whose appearance suggested to Polonius an advanced case of love-melancholy,
appeared to Ophelia with 'his doublet all unbrac'd'. Donne has merely left his collar undone.

in a cloud changed the usuall prayer into SALVA ME DOMINA.'
Drummond remembered rightly that the motto was a religious
petition redirected to a mistress, but misremembered the phrase.
R. B. remembered the phrase but forgot that it had been adapted to
become a lover's petition.[1] We may compare R. B.'s lapse of memory
with Walton's no doubt unconscious mistranslation of Donne's
Spanish motto. Walton read the Spanish in the light of his over-
riding conception of Donne as a great convert: R. B., writing many
years after he had seen the picture, remembered it coloured by his
knowledge of Donne's subsequent career as divine poet and preacher.
The exact date of the portrait cannot be established but Donne's
words that it was 'made very many years before I was of this profession', that is before 1615, the strong resemblance to the Marshall
portrait, and the youthful pose suggest a date in the middle of the
1590's, about the time Donne went on the Cadiz voyage.

The painter of the Lothian portrait has not been identified. Whoever he was, he was a painter of remarkable accomplishment and has
given us what might be claimed to be the most striking portrait we
have of any English poet. We do not know who painted the portrait
of Donne that hangs in the Deanery of St. Paul's. This too is strikingly
effective in suggesting a very interesting and powerful personality.
We must acknowledge that Donne showed remarkable taste and
judgement in his choices of portraitists. To have been painted in
1591 by Hilliard, in 1616 by Isaac Oliver, and to have had one's
effigy carved by Nicholas Stone in 1631 shows remarkable discrimination. Donne had, as is well known, many pictures in his possession
when he died. In bequeathing them he identified them by their place
in the Deanery and their subject, not by the artists who painted them.
But one of those that he left to Sir Robert Carr passed from Carr to
King Charles and from his collection to a permanent home in the
Louvre whose catalogue records that a Titian Madonna and Child
was once 'in the collection of Doctor John Donne'.[2] From an aside in
one of his sermons it would seem that Donne collected pictures for the
best of reasons:

Though Princes, and Judges, and Magistrates be pictures, and Images of
God, though beauty, and riches, and honour, and power, and favour, be, in a
proportion, so too, yet, as I bought not that Merchants picture, because

---

[1] It is, of course, just possible that 'Domine' for 'Domina' is a printer's error and that R. B.
remembered rightly.
[2] See W. Milgate, 'Dr. Donne's Art Gallery', N. and Q., 23 Sept. 1947.

it was his, or for love of him, but because it was a good peece, and of a good Masters hand, and a good house-ornament . . . (*Sermons*, iv. 308).

On the one hand, it may be said that the number of portraits of Donne that we possess is testimony to his egoism and devouring interest in his own personality. On the other, it may be said that it is a testimony to his discriminating interest in the fine arts.

INDEX OF FIRST LINES